WHERE IS GOD?

Where Is God?

An African Theology of Suffering and Smiling

Stan Chu Ilo

Maryknoll, New York 10545

Founded in 1970, Orbis Books endeavors to publish works that enlighten the mind, nourish the spirit, and challenge the conscience. The publishing arm of the Maryknoll Fathers and Brothers, Orbis seeks to explore the global dimensions of the Christian faith and mission, to invite dialogue with diverse cultures and religious traditions, and to serve the cause of reconciliation and peace. The books published reflect the views of their authors and do not represent the official position of the Maryknoll Society. To learn more about Maryknoll and Orbis Books, please visit our website at www.orbisbooks.com.

Copyright © 2025 by Stan Chu Ilo

Published by Orbis Books, Box 302, Maryknoll, NY 10545-0302.

All rights reserved.

No part of this publication may be reproduced or transmitted in any form or by any means, electronic or mechanical, including photocopying, recording, or any information storage or retrieval system, without prior permission in writing from the publisher.

Queries regarding rights and permissions should be addressed to: Orbis Books, P.O. Box 302, Maryknoll, NY 10545-0302.

Manufactured in the United States of America

Library of Congress Cataloging-in-Publication Data

Names: Ilo, Stan Chu author
Title: Where is God? : an African theology of suffering and smiling / Stan Chu Ilo.
Description: Maryknoll, NY : Orbis Books, [2025] | Includes bibliographical references and index. | Summary: "A theological exploration of the meaning of God and the response to suffering from an African perspective"— Provided by publisher.
Identifiers: LCCN 2025005073 (print) | LCCN 2025005074 (ebook) | ISBN 9781626986299 trade paperback | ISBN 9798888660843 epub
Subjects: LCSH: Theology, Doctrinal—Africa | Suffering–Religious aspects—Christianity | Africa—Religion
Classification: LCC BT30.A35 I46 2025 (print) | LCC BT30.A35 (ebook) | DDC 230.096—dc23/eng/20250605
LC record available at https://lccn.loc.gov/2025005073
LC ebook record available at https://lccn.loc.gov/2025005074

To Prof. Virginia Ugoyibo Okwu-Delunzu (1975–2025)

You left so soon,

but the light of love you lit in my heart will burn forever.

Thank you for your friendship, inspiration.

encouragement, and unconditional love.

Contents

Acknowledgments xi
Introduction: Suffering and Smiling 1
    "Don't kill my child. Kill me instead" 4
    Theological Social Autopsy of Suffering and Deaths in Africa 11
    Method: Diversity of Theological Voices and Perspectives
        from Africa and Beyond 17
    Listening to the Past; Paying Attention to the Present 28
    Conclusion 32

1. **Doing African Theology in a Wounded and Broken World** 41
    On Losing Three Family Members in One Year 42
    New Directions in Catholic Theology 49
    New Directions in African Theology 58
    The Context of African Theology 63
    African Theology as Missional Theology 72
    African Theology as an Account of the Lived Faith of
        God's African People 76
    African Theology and the Question of Cultural Identity
        and Agency 82
    Changing Times, Changing Focus for African Theology 86
    Conclusion 95

2. **Can We Really Make Sense of This Suffering in
Africa or Elsewhere?** 99
    Can We Really Make Sense of This Suffering in
        Africa and Elsewhere? 100
    Theological Accounts of Suffering: Five Voices 108
    Conclusion 125

3. **Suffering and Smiling:**
   Doing *Matatu* Theology on the Streets of Africa 127
   Suffering and Smiling:
      Theology on the Streets and at the Bus Stops 130
   Where People Found God: While Searching for Work 137
   Where People Found God: In Bad News 139
   Where People Found God: In the Scriptures 142
   But Who Is God? 145
   Where Is God? The Lessons of *Living in Bondage* 148
   Lessons from Doing *Matatu* Theology at the Peripheries 154
   Conclusion 155

4. **God in Africa:**
   Modernity, Christianity, and Africa's Future 157
   Why a Theological Inquiry about God in Africa? 161
   God in Africa: Creator and Source of Human and
      Cosmic Flourishing. 170
   The God of Our Ancestors 187
   God in Africa: A Western God in an African Robe? 196
   Fighting with Witches and Wizards in Africa:
      The Politics of God and the Crisis of Religion in Africa. 201
   Conclusion: God in Africa, God in the World 212

5. **Freedom, Suffering, and Predestination:**
   Lessons from a Slave Narrative 216
   My Aunt Cried All Night on Her Knees. 218
   The Journey of Freedom for People of African Descent 222
   Freedom: A Short Conceptualization 226
   Olaudah Equiano: The African Enslaved Person Who Told
      His Own Story 228
   Captivity, Condemnation, Suffering, and Divine Providence 230
   Three Lessons 233
   Conclusion 236

Conclusion: Hope in God 242
   Five Claims of This Book 243
   God as an Existential Crisis for People of African Descent in
      Their Search for Hope 249
   Where Is Hope? 255
   The Praxis of Hope 260

Bibliography 265
Index 287

Acknowledgments

This work is the result of conversations and engagement with so many people. The ideas in this book have been tried in many international conferences and in my classrooms. This book project began in 2019 when I received the Allan Richardson Fellowship at the Center for Catholic Studies, Durham University, England. Chapter 4 is an expanded and modified version of the Allan Richardson lecture that I delivered on December 2, 2019, at the Durham University. I thank both Prof. Paul Murray and Prof. Karen Kirby, who invited me for this fellowship and who spent a lot of time with me in conversation on the theme of suffering and theodicy in both Western and African theologies and philosophies. Chapter 5 of this book is the fruit of two public lectures delivered first at the University of San Francisco at a memorial lecture for James Cone and Katie Cannon titled, "Black Theologies of Liberation and Racial Justice." The narrative of Olaudah Equiano analyzed in chapter 4 is in part the fruit of the research on slave narratives for the course I teach on slavery at DePaul University, and the plenary discussion on "Freedom and Eschatological Fulfillment" delivered at the Catholic Theological Society of America (CTSA) convention in Milwaukee, Wisconsin, in 2023. I thank Prof. Lilian Dube for inviting me to the lecture at the University of San Francisco, and I thank Prof. M. Shawn Copeland for the engaging conversation after my lecture on the topic of suffering and lamentation in the black communities of America. Prof. Copeland pointed me in the direction of some of her publications, which make a significant appearance in this book. I also thank Prof. Kristin Heyer, then-President of CTSA, for her kind invitation to the CTSA convention.

Materials for chapter 1 were originally developed for a lecture on "Cultural Diversity, Methods and Tasks of Contemporary African Theology," delivered at a conference on African Theology organized by the University of Notre Dame in Rome in 2018. I am grateful to Prof. Paulinus Odozor for his kind invitation and ongoing friendship and continued conversation on the question of God in Africa which helped me in the work on a section of chapter 4 of this book. Prof. Emmanuel Katongole has been my constant conversation partner on the central topic of this work since 2015 and was generous to read through the section of this book focused on his work on how to find hope in the midst of suffering.

I am grateful to my African brothers and sisters in the Pan-African Catholic Theology and Pastoral Network (PACTPAN), my intellectual family and community of practitioners, with whom I continue to grow in my understanding of African theology and in service to the Church and society in Africa and beyond. I am most grateful to two of my colleagues at the Center for World Catholicism and Intercultural Theology, DePaul University, Prof. Bill Cavanaugh and Prof. Mike Budde, whose friendship and mentorship are invaluable in all that I have been able to accomplish since 2015, including their contributions to this book by reading some parts of the work. My other colleagues at the center, Karen Kraft and Marlon Aquilar, have continued to be sources of inspiration and support in all I do at the Center.

A special thanks are due to Bernard Marrocco, my long-term editor, who put in a lot of effort in editing this work and made extensive suggestions that helped to improve this work. I thank my son in the Lord, Jude Nnamdi Ilo, who accompanied me with the ethnographic study in Nigeria, and Fr. Alex Ojacor and his team, who conducted the ethnographic study in Uganda and Kenya. I thank the following spiritual fathers who have been my friends and companions along the way: Cardinal John Onaiyekan, Cardinal Fridolin Ambongo, Archbishop Fortunatus Nwachukwu, Archbishop Jeff Grobb, Bishop John Okoye, Bishop Matthew Hassan Kukah, Bishop Anthony Borwah, Bishop Hiiboro Kussala, Bishop Sithembele Sipuka, and Bishop Godfery Onah.

This work has benefited from the conversation and friendship of Prof. Ikenna Okafor, Fr. Idara Otu, Sr. Rosemary Nyirumbe, Fr. Barry Eneh, Prof. Susan Abraham, Sr. Leonida Katunge, Sr. Akunna John-Emezi, Sr. Beatrice Iguem, Prof. Leonard Ilechukwu, and Prof. MarySylvia Nwachukwu. I am grateful to the parishioners and staff of the Igbo Catholic Mission of Chicago; St. Mother Guerrin Parish, Elmwood Park, Illinois; and St. Francis Xavier Parish, La Grange, Illinois, for their prayers, faith, friendship, support, and encouragement. I thank Orbis Books for warmly accepting this project and Robert Ellsberg, whose review comments really encouraged me to proceed with this book.

The last person to thank, but by far the greatest, is my mother, HRH Lolo Roseline Akunna Ilo—my favorite and most credible teacher and theologian!!!

Introduction

Suffering and Smiling

The expression "suffering and smiling" was popularized in Nigeria and the rest of Africa by the 1978 song of the late Nigerian Afrobeat star, Fela Aníkúlápó Kuti. Part of the lyrics goes like this:

> This is what happens to we Africans every day
> Now wetin I want tell you now
> Na secret o, na confidential matter …
> Now listen
> As I dey say before
> E dey happen to all of us every day
> We Africans all over the world
> Now listen
> Every day my people dey (are) inside bus (chorus: suffering and smiling!)
> Forty-nine sitting, ninety-nine standing (suffering and smiling!)
> Them go pack themselves in like sardine (suffering and smiling!)
> Them dey faint, them dey wake like cock (suffering and smiling!)
> Them go reach house, water no dey (suffering and smiling!)
> Them go reach bed, power no dey (they sleep in homes without electricity) (suffering and smiling!)
> Them go reach road, go-slow[1] go come (suffering and smiling!)
> Them go reach road, police go slap (suffering and smiling!)
> Them go reach road, army go whip (suffering and smiling!)
> Them go look pocket, money no dey (suffering and smiling!)

---

[1] Go-slow means traffic congestion in Nigerian pidgin English.

> Them go reach work, query ready (suffering and smiling!)
> Every day na the same thing (suffering and smiling!)
> Suffer, suffer for world (amen!)
> Enjoy for Heaven (amen!)
> Christians go dey yab (amen!)
> "In Spiritum Heavinus" (amen!)
> Muslims go dey call (amen!)
> "Allahu Akbar" (amen!) . . .

This song, rendered in Pidgin English by Fela, was a hit in Nigeria. Fela was a social critic who used his songs to confront the social contagions, inequality, and oppressive political structures, systems, and institutions in Nigeria and the rest of Africa. He was particularly critical in this song of the successive brutal military governments in Nigeria of 1975–1993. This song also served as a searing condemnation of the religious leaders in the country, who, according to the song, were tranquilizing the social consciousness of the people with religious platitudes of hope for better days. Fela decries the ubiquity of suffering for ordinary people. This suffering, he sings, follows the majority of people in Africa everywhere they go, namely, in their homes, on the road, and in the overloaded buses where they are squeezed like tinned sardines. The ordinary people, Fela sings, have no food, water, electricity, money, or hope. Furthermore, their situations are worsened by violence, including police brutality and military atrocities. The security forces meant to guarantee the people's safety are themselves agents of violence against the people. They constantly suppress the cries of the poor by beating people down with whips and imposing imprisonment for any attempts at revolt against their oppressors.

In this famous song, Fela further decries the religious messages preached to Christians and Muslims. Such messages, the singer bemoans, encourage the people to bear their sufferings here on earth with patience, in the hope of heaven in the life to come. He reminds the ordinary people that religious leaders—whether in Nigeria, Mecca, Rome, or Lambeth Palace are enjoying a good life. At the same time, the poor faithful are preoccupied with prayers in churches and mosques. Preoccupied with prayers and spiritual activities which, sadly for Fela, have done no good because their fortunes remain unchanged, the people live with the religious sentiment of "suffering and smiling."

The question arises as to whether this typical attitude of "suffering and smiling" is an adequate response to unacceptable social conditions in Africa or if this singer is right in interpreting this attitude as a false and unhelpful quietist submission to an evil and unjust social context. When people say in Nigeria, "I am suffering and smiling," are they using religion as an opiate to cope with the harrowing conditions of life, or are there other layers of meaning present that point to something deeper for theodicy and an ethics of hope? Suffering, in the logic of grace in Christianity, can produce enormous good and character. It can be a way of living through the Paschal Mystery, but it can also lead to utter destruction of people.[2] All kinds of suffering expose the limits of our naked humanity at the deepest level of human vulnerability and fragility, where we often thirst for meaning, escape, a finite horizon, and some transcendence. The political scientist Patrick Chabal asserts that the story of Africa told by Fela is tragic that people often do not comprehend. It is not simply a story of tragedy, but also a demonstration of something beyond suffering: "Africans show great resilience and infinite ingenuity in their struggle to live a decent life. And they do 'smile' a lot, as Fela Kuti used to sing. In recent years, however, they have also suffered grievously from violence, conflict, and illness—the combination of which have had disastrous effects."[3]

I believe that addressing the sources and causes of the suffering of the masses of God's people in Africa by churches and theologians in Africa is central to the survival of religious faith in Africa in the long term. Thus, rather than simply surviving or spiritualizing the disastrous effects of suffering and the anguish of the poor and vulnerable in Africa, theologians in Africa must plunge deep into the contradictions of history in Africa. In plunging deep this way they will unmask, as Desmond Tutu proposes, "the organized oppression and exploitation" of the unfortunate poor in Africa who suffer the misfortune of being "emasculated and treated as less than what they are: human persons created in the image of the Triune God, redeemed by the one Savior Jesus Christ and sanctified by the Holy Paraclete."[4]

---

[2] Fiona Clements and Fiona Tasker, "Living through the Paschal Mystery: Surviving Cancer Narratives Told by Older Roman Catholic Women," *Journal of Religion, Spirituality & Aging* 27, no. 1 (2015): 48–66.

[3] Patrick Chabal, *Africa: The Politics of Suffering and Smiling* (Pietermaritzburg, South Africa: University of Kwazulu-Natal Press, 2009), 170.

[4] Cited in Gustavo Gutiérrez, *On Job: God-Talk and the Suffering of the Innocent*, trans. Matthew J. O'Connell (Maryknoll, NY: Orbis Books, 2009), xv.

What is always at stake is the source of the suffering and the good to be achieved by bearing suffering patiently or resisting it in an agentic movement to transform suffering through a praxis of hope for better days. As W. E. B. Du Bois argues specifically about the suffering of Black people in America because of slavery, lynching, racism, and discrimination, God is always on trial as to whether the suffering of Blacks is the direct result of divine providence, and whether the freedom and liberation that Blacks obtain is a vindication of divine power.[5] The question remains to what extent the suffering in Africa or any other parts of the world is the direct result of a divine positive act or divine retribution. Thus, in situations where suffering is persistent, what does theology say to the victims of history who are bearing the brunt of this suffering? A way out of suffering must be available to seek transformative hope through redemption and liberation. But where does God come in, and where do human agency and the convergence of many structural issues in local, national, and global history and politics come into play in inflicting so much pain and suffering on God's people through structural violence and structures of sin?

"Don't kill my child. Kill me instead"

Nicholas Kristof's reporting and analysis for the *New York Times* of the atrocities happening in Sudan (2024) was titled, "In Sudan, Evil Is Resilient—and So Is Heroism."[6] The title captures what anyone living in Africa or visiting Africa sees so clearly: the existence of suffering and smiling; pain and joy; hope and hopelessness; faith and despair; community and broken social bond; as well as claims about God and of demons in tow. Emmanuel Katongole has captured these contrasting dominant realities through what he calls "churches and coffins in Africa" in these words: "If churches and coffins represent two dominant cultural realities in Africa, they also represent the predicament of a continent suspended between hope and despair. They capture the hope and pain, the

---

[5] M. Shawn Copeland, "Wading through Many Sorrows: Toward a Theology of Suffering in a Womanist Perspective," in *Womanist Theological Ethics: A Reader*, ed. Katie Geneva Cannon, Emilie M. Townes, and Angela D. Sims (Louisville, KY: WJK, 2011), 137n6.

[6] Nicholas Kristof, "In Sudan, Evil Is Resilient—and So Is Heroism" *New York Times*, September 29, 2024. Accessed October 11, 2024.

beauty and tragedy, the dreams and frustrations of a continent that is at once overwhelmingly Christian and at the same time politically, economically, and socially distressed."[7]

Kristof begins his narrative with these words: "Side by side with the worst of humanity, you regularly encounter the best. And so it was that while covering murder, rape and starvation in Sudan, I was awed by a heroic refugee, Naima Adam." The atrocities being committed against Black African ethnic groups in Sudan remain some of the worst crimes against humanity in Africa. These atrocities predate the yet unresolved crimes and continuing suffering of millions of people in Darfur. Kristof captures the ambiguity and even the incomprehensibility of the fact that with so much tragedy and pain, there are people like Naima who reveal a different response to suffering through her refusal to allow that evil to "eat" her. According to Kristof, "When civilization collapses and we humans are tested, some people reveal themselves as sociopaths, but a remarkable number turns out to be saints like Naima." Forty-eight-year-old Naima belongs to one of the Black ethnic groups that have been the target of persecution and extermination by Sudan's Arab leadership. "Four times in the past 20 years, Arab marauders have burned her home in their efforts at ethnic cleansing of non-Arab groups, and the Janjaweed Arab militia murdered her husband nine years ago. After two military factions started a civil war in 2023, one of them—a descendant of the Janjaweed called the Rapid Support Forces, armed and supported by the United Arab Emirates—tried once again to drive Black Africans from Darfur. Naima recounted the same pattern I heard from so many people: The militia surrounded her village, lined up men and boys, then shot them one by one."[8]

"We're going to get rid of this Black trash," Naima quoted the Arab gunmen saying. Then the gunmen went house to house to kill, plunder and rape. Mostly, those they raped were girls and women, she said, but they also raped at least one man. Two men took one of Naima's daughters into a room and closed the door; she suspects they raped the girl, but sexual violence is such a taboo that she never asked her daughter what happened. Rape survivors bear the trauma on their own."[9] To protect her ten-year-old son, Naima carried

---

[7] Emmanuel Katongole, *The Sacrifice of Africa: A Political Theology for Africa* (Grand Rapids, MI: William B. Eerdmans, 2011), 31.
[8] Kristof, "In Sudan, Evil Is Resilient—and So Is Heroism."
[9] Kristof, "In Sudan, Evil Is Resilient—and So Is Heroism."

him on her back, making him small so that he would look like a baby, but the militia men were not deceived. They pulled her son from her back and told her that they would kill him because he was a boy. Naima rushed to them and fought with her bare hands to pull her son from these evil men, begging them not to kill her boy but rather to kill her instead: "Don't kill my child; kill me instead." During the struggle, they clubbed her and shot her twice through the breast and in the leg. However, she would not surrender her boy even as she was bleeding profusely. The men relented and went into the hut of Naima and grabbed her fourteen-year-old niece wanting to rape her. Naima again fought to stop this rape asking the men of the Rapid Support Forces to rape her instead. She also resisted their attempt to rape her and fought back with every sinew in her body until the two men again relented and left her bruised and bleeding, with her son and niece.

Naima's story fits into what Marilyn McCord Adams refers to as "horrendous evil," which moves one to question God's love, but also such evils "devour ... in one swift gulp ... the possibility of positive personal meaning."[10] According to Adams, horrendous evils—like rape, cannibalizing one's offspring, genocide, intimate partner murder, torture among other horrible evils the world has seen—defeat our humanity. They are portraits of our naked humanity. They render meaningless for the most part our human attempt to account for suffering and to justify the existence of a good God in the midst of such horrors as the ones Naima went through.[11] The story of Naima represents the sad reality that the world sees on a regular basis not only in Sudan and South Sudan, but in many parts of Africa that are engulfed in wars, civil unrest, rebel movements, and breakdown of law and order—Somalia, Central African Republic, Southern Cameroun, North-East Nigeria, Congo-Kinshasa, Tigray, and in the African Sahel. Naima's mother was murdered, and her father and her sons were missing at the time Kristof wrote this account. She had fled her home with the surviving family members to "the safety of a refugee camp across the border in Adré, Chad, where one of her adult sons remains hospitalized after brutal torture in Sudan. He suffered a mental breakdown and can't talk about what he endured."[12]

---

[10] Marilyn McCord Adams, *Horrendous Evils and the Goodness of God* (Ithaca, NY: Cornell University Press, 1999), 27. Cited in Karen Kirby, *God, Evil and the Limits of Theology* (London: T&T Clark, 2021), 71–72.

[11] Kirby, *God, Evil and the Limits of Theology*, 72.

[12] Kristof, "In Sudan, Evil Is Resilient—and So Is Heroism."

Naima is recovering from her wounds (at the time this story was written) and spends her time helping orphans and women in the camp as much as she can. But when Kristof asked her if she was seeking revenge against the Sudanese Arabs who caused her so much suffering, she responded with a strong "no" stating, "we are human beings."[13] This was her way of saying that we are all the same people, and we must accept each other, live in peace, and work for human and cosmic flourishing by being the guardians of one another. In the words of Nicholas Kristof, people like Naima teach humanity that there is a different way of living. Particularly in Africa, this is a powerful way of capturing what I have learned from the everyday experiences of my fellow Africans: Africans are daily holding in balance a strong faith in God and hope for a better future amid the complexities of history in Africa that bring so much suffering and pain: "So, yes, Sudan reveals the human capacity for evil, but it's also a reminder of an equally powerful human capacity for strength, resilience and courage. It's thus possible to return from a land aching from famine, massacres and rape and feel honored to be part of the same gallant species as those Sudanese like Naima who emerge from an ultimate test as moral exemplars for us all."[14]

Kristof concludes his riveting but unsettling stories of the horrors going on in Sudan in the story of another woman, Maryam Suleiman, who watched the Rapid Support Forces execute five of her brothers and wanted to rape her. The question that she mustered as an act of resistance to these evil men was, "Are we not humans?"[15] This was similar to the question that flooded my mind and shook me to the marrow when I visited the concentration camps in Europe in 2018 and the Holocaust Memorial, Yad Vashem, in Jerusalem in 2008: Where is our humanity? Where is the God that the perpetrators of these heinous crimes against humanity claim to worship?

Elie Wiesel, in his book *Night*, shares this painful account of the experience of a typical execution in the concentration camp: "The SS seemed more preoccupied, more worried, than usual. To hang a child in front of thousands of onlookers was not a small matter. The head of the camp read the verdict. All eyes were on the child. He was pale, almost calm, but biting his lips as he stood in the shadow of the gallows.... The men died quickly, but

---

[13] Kristof, "In Sudan, Evil Is Resilient—and So Is Heroism."
[14] Kristof, "In Sudan, Evil Is Resilient—and So Is Heroism."
[15] Nicholas Kristof, " 'Are We Not Humans?' My Attempt at Explaining the Murder, Rape and Famine in Sudan," *New York Times*, October 12, 2024.

the death throes of the youth lasted for half an hour. 'Where is merciful God? Where is he?' someone asked behind me. The youth still hung in torment in the noose after a long time lingering between life and death, writhing before our eyes. And we were forced to look at him at close range. He was still alive when I passed him. His tongue was still red, his eyes not yet extinguished. I heard the man call again: 'For God's sake, where is God now?' And I heard a voice in myself answer: 'Where is God? He is hanging there on the gallows.' That night the soup tasted of corpses."[16]

Wiesel makes a distinction between human silence and divine silence. Human silence is often self-destructive, especially if it is the result of apathy, lack of compassion, and the failure to see the other and feel the suffering of another person. This kind of silence is a form of sickness. Divine silence, however, is not inaction on the part of God: "In the Midrash, there is a story that God sheds two tears when a person dies. They fall in the ocean and make a sound that can be heard from one end of the horizon to the other. And in Auschwitz? Where was God in Auschwitz? Were we unable to hear God's tears because we have not wept enough?"[17]

A similar question on the silence of God was posed by Martin Luther King Jr. in his "Eulogies to the Martyred Children." He described the children as "the unoffending, innocent, beautiful victims," whose redemptive suffering should not be passed by in silence. King delivered this eulogy to three little children—Addie Mae Collins (age fourteen), Denise McNair, (age eleven), and Cynthia Diane Wesley (age fourteen)—who were killed in the bombing of Birmingham's Sixteenth Street Baptist Church on September 15, 1963, by white racial terrorists. This heinous hate crime was committed less than three weeks after King's now famous "I Have a Dream" speech, in which he spoke of little Black boys and girls joining hands of friendship in love with little white boys and girls. King's response to this evil and the suffering of the families is captured this way: "At times life is hard, as hard as crucible steel. It has its bleak and painful moments. Like the ever-flowing waters of a river, life has its moments of drought and its moments of flood. Like the ever-changing cycle

---

[16] Elie Wiesel, *Night*, trans. Marion Wiesel. *Night* (New York: Hill and Wang, 2006), 64–65.

[17] Ekkehard Schuster and Reinhold Boschert-Kimmig, eds., *Hope Against Hope: Johann Baptist Metz and Elie Wiesel Speak Out on the Holocaust*, trans. J. Matthew Ashley (New York: Paulist Press, 1999), 97.

of the seasons, life has the soothing warmth of the summers and the piercing chills of its winters. But through it all, God walks with us. Never forget that God is able to lift you from fatigue of despair to the buoyancy of hope and transform dark and desolate valleys into sunlit paths of inner peace."[18]

But for many who suffer in these terrible circumstances the question is: How will God help us? How will God intervene in our long nights and dark days? Might it have been better actually to assert that God was not there in these horrors? Surely, humanity cannot make sense of such horrors as the holocaust or racist hatred and violence, wars, and murders. Rather, theology can simply relate to these evils as instantiations of the mystery of iniquity that are ineradicable and opposed both to God and the essence of what it means to be human. This response seems to me a valid stance to adopt rather than the failed attempts of theodicies like Moltmann's, for example, to reconcile God to the horrors of Auschwitz by identifying God as a companion to the victims when he wrote, "As a companion in suffering God gave comfort where humanly there was nothing to hope for in that hell."[19] Yes, many Christians believe that in the cry of the poor and the oppressed, there is the silent cry of Jesus, who shares in their sufferings and pain, but the question is always how does this logic of grace work in the lives of the sufferer, and how does this translate into changing the status quo?

This book is my attempt to wrestle with these questions and to provide some outline for a theology of suffering and smiling using the stories and daily realities of everyday Africans like Naima. I am particularly concerned in this book with the suffering that emerges from the social context as a result of moral evil and social sins and how the name of God is inserted into all these complexities in Africa. God is ubiquitous in Africa. As Stephen Ellis and Gerrie ter Haar rightly assert, "Religious belief operates at every level of society in Africa. Popular priests and prophets work in areas where the poor live, while the rich may have their own more exclusive spiritual advisors. Some religious leaders minister to both the rich and the poor. In most countries, plural religious allegiance is common at all levels of society so that an individual may be a member of several religious congregations simultaneously and in many parts of the continent, may even practice religious rituals regarded in

---

[18] Cited in James H. Cone, *The Cross and the Lynching Tree* (Maryknoll, NY: Orbis Books, 2013), 88.

[19] Jürgen Moltmann, *History and the Triune God* (London: SCM, 1991), 29.

the West as belonging to different systems of belief, such as Christianity and Islam, or Christianity and 'traditional' religion, or Sufism and reformed Islam, as in Sudan."[20] Arguably, God has no hand in the suffering and misfortune that afflict the poor and vulnerable in Africa. Rather, it is the injustice in the world, neoliberal capitalism with its architecture of violence, the oppressive structures in the nation-states of Africa, and exploitative structures in some false religious practices in Africa that have brought so much suffering, misery, and unfulfillment on the poor and the entire continent. The African condition today is not the result of an act of God. It is not a natural progression of history; rather, it is the result of the sinful agency of those who hold the levers of power in Africa and globally, in politics and religious institutions.

I am concerned in this book with giving voice to the cries of the poor who continue to ask, "Where is God?" I am concerned with voicing the frustration of many silenced poor in Africa who are asking, "Who is this God whose name is always on the lips of African religious and political leaders, but whose precepts are so absent in the social and political lives of the people?" I often wonder why the strong faith Africans have in God has not translated into changing the trajectory of history in Africa or to the conversion of people who hold positions of power and influence in the state and religious institutions in Africa. Associated with the question, "Where is God?" is the other question, "Where is the Human in Africa?" It is a question of theological anthropology: What does it mean to be an African in the Africa of today with the joys and sorrows that define the African predicament? What does it mean to be human in Africa when people are surrounded by a cycle of suffering and frustration in their daily lives, most of which result from failed leadership and unjust structures?

The social condition in Africa is particularly distressing because Africans and the churches and the state in Africa today are in the firm hands of Africans. So Africans must take the primary responsibility for the painful living conditions of Africans, the fragmentation of African communities, churches, and states, and the lack of progress in democratization and building self-sustaining and less dependent churches. As I travel the length and breadth of Africa and see and hear of many atrocities and terrible suffering and pain among my people, especially women and children, I cannot but wonder why

---

[20] Stephen Ellis and Gerrie ter Haar, "Religion and Politics in Sub-Saharan Africa," *Journal of Modern African Studies* 36, no. 2 (1998): 177.

is it that life has become so expendable and disposable on our continent? What makes us human and why are people losing their humanity in many parts of Africa, while the same people have the name of God constantly on their lips? Conscious of the ancestral wisdom I drank to the dregs at the feet of my uncles, aunties, and parents on the primacy of life as an unquantifiable good; believing as I do that life should be prized not priced and that killing anyone is to kill oneself because "I am in and through the other person," I reject as being part of God's plan these social evils in Africa and seek to theologically account for them in this book.

Post-Independence Africa has witnessed so much suffering and pain but has also been animated by so much hope and exuberant faith expressions. Is this hope failing Africa? Is the faith of Africans simply a false coping mechanism as Fela sang in his famous song? Will this faith weaken the agency of the people to become protagonists in their own lives and their capacity to resist the local, national, and international forces that have conspired to turn the continent of Africa into a site of the most heart-wrenching socioeconomic condition in the world with persistent poverty, wars, failed states, failing governments, and dependent religious organizations that rely on external funding for their survival? Will this faith leave a legacy of churches in Africa that are preoccupied with external cultural, social, and ornamental Christianity and a burgeoning population, but empty of prophets capable of creating the institutional, spiritual, and pastoral structures to meet the social, political, economic, and spiritual challenges facing Africa? These questions have been on my mind for over two decades and they inspired me to write this book as the first volume in a series of theological reflections on God (*Where is God in Africa?*), ecclesiology (*Where is the Church in Africa?*), and social concerns in Africa (*Where are God's people in Africa?*).

Theological Social Autopsy of Suffering and Deaths in Africa

The Good Samaritan is employed by Pope Francis in *Fratelli Tutti* to provide a good symbolism and a diagnostic tool for a structural analysis of suffering, especially in the moral domain, to show how wrong choices and the neglect of the poor by the powerful lead to structural violence. It is also a tool for socio-praxis for implementing a theory of change capable of reversing the globalization of indifference through a globalization of solidarity. It also offers us a language for root cause analysis of why people are wounded today, the kinds of wounds they carry, the causes and sources of their wounds, where they can get help, and how the help can be brought to their sites of pain and anguish. Particularly, it can help us focus on two aspects of suffering identified in many works of literature on suffering: causality and functionality.[21] The reason people wish to find the cause(s) of their suffering is so that they can find some motivation to function well by confronting the source(s) of their suffering and finding liberation from it. In the case where another person is suffering or has died, the search for causality is always a desire to prevent further deaths and promote abundant life. Jason McMartin and M. Elizabeth Lewis Hall propose that when faced with suffering of any kind, religious people seek meaning in their suffering and find God's will through suffering. In this search, there is an interaction between causality and functionality, but McMartin and Hall argue that the functional approach is the most important because "functional views of suffering consider the function or role that suffering plays in human life. They allow consideration of *what* God may be doing with one's suffering, without requiring an answer to the question of *why* God allowed the suffering to occur."[22] Causal appraisal of the cause of suffering, McMartin and Hall argue, only leads to focusing on why suffering occurs and God's involvement in the suffering (e.g., by sharing in human suffering, having a hand in it, using suffering as a divine pedagogy, a sign of apocalypse, divine silence, and the suffering of Jesus in inaugurating the kingdom of God and the invitation to take up the Cross).[23] However, none of these approaches furnishes a total horizon. What is essential in the midst of suffering is to find out what God wishes the individual and the community to do in order to function better. As McMartin and Hall put it, the functional approach to suffering is "teleological in nature" and "may direct sufferers toward specific active coping processes."[24] The functional approach moves away from looking

---

[21] Jason McMartin and M. Elizabeth Lewis Hall, "Christian Functional Views of Suffering: A Review and Theoretical Overview," *Mental Health, Religion & Culture* 25, no. 3 (2022): 247–62.

[22] McMartin and Hall, "Christian Functional Views of Suffering," 252.

[23] These are some of the ways through which Christians have understood suffering in the Christian scriptures across the ages, according to Daniel Harrington in *Why Do We Suffer: A Scriptural Approach to the Human Condition* (New York: Rowman and Littlefield, 2000).

[24] McMartin and Hall, "Christian Functional Views of Suffering," 253.

at God as the causative factor for suffering, which may lead a believer to question God's love, justice, grace, power, and divine providence; rather, it focuses on how God journeys with the one who suffers to function fully through meaning-making processes that occur through one's faith, relational resilience found in communities of faith and strong communal bonds, and solidarity. In order to make sense of suffering, the functional approach focuses strongly on successful meaning-making in the midst of suffering that leads to positive outcomes.[25] McMartin and Hall particularly focus on what they call "lived religion" by reviewing the findings of fifty-seven Christians who were diagnosed with cancer, whose responses converged around a common theme that "God can redeem suffering" and that all things work together for the good of those who love God (Romans 8:28).[26]

McMartin and Hall offer us a useful framework similar to the African functional approach to suffering and evil. This is particularly related to the everyday struggle of people who are facing suffering and wishing to make sense of their experience through an appeal to their faith. The search for causal roots of evil within the African worldview is an attempt to help those who are living to address the issues that led to the tragedy or evil that took the lives of people or hampered people from realizing the abundant life that is the goal of human existence. In this dynamic, the movement is not to dig into the past simply out of fear or fantasy, but to move forward and function better by looking back. A good example will suffice here. Among the Achi clan of the Igbo tribe in Eastern Nigeria, there are two kinds of death: a good death (*onwu chi*) and a premature death (*inwu chu*). My father died in his eighty-fourth year. He died as the head of the clan, with six children and twenty-three grandchildren. He died following complications from congestive heart failure. His death was considered a good death because he lived to a fruitful old age, lived a good life, and passed on the torch to the next generation who will continue his legacy. He is regarded as a great ancestor today. His death was a good death (*onwu chi*). Consider the death of my sister at twenty-nine years old or my niece at two years old; these were considered premature deaths (*inwu chu*) because both did not fulfill the purpose of their lives in the understanding of our people. Both deaths interestingly were the result of accidents. In my sister's case, she died from preeclampsia; in my niece's case she died from drowning, both preventable causes.

---

[25] McMartin and Hall, "Christian Functional Views of Suffering," 248.
[26] McMartin and Hall, "Christian Functional Views of Suffering," 254.

At such times, some of the people who came to comfort me said words like: "It is God's will," "God has called your niece; she is now in a better place," "God knows, God has allowed it, we leave everything in God's hands." This Christian interpretation is dialectically opposed to the interpretations of African ancestral tradition that such deaths are *premature death* (*inwu chu*). When I lost my immediate elder sister, Bibiana Okoye (who shared the same birthday with me), through blatant medical carelessness at a government hospital in Nigeria, it was obvious then as it is to me now that I could not accept the narrative that God was responsible for my sister's death. I cannot accept this narrative of a God whose name is used to justify the high rate of maternal mortality in Africa resulting from health inequities, medical malpractice, and glaring and avoidable failures. I cannot also accept the high rate of infant mortality of under-fives in Africa, to give just a few examples. The millions of people who die in Africa every year from preventable and treatable diseases, and the many women who are dying in Africa like my late sister from pregnancy, are all sad realities of where the name of God has been dragged in to fill in the gaps in our broken political and public services. However, faced with these tragedies, diseases, deaths, and losses, belief in God is growing rather than waning. African Christians put all their hopes in God and most people in Africa are holding onto God as the only secure foundation to give them hope beyond present uncertainties and suffering when many events around them are showing signs of weakness and instability.

Inwu chu brings with it so much suffering and anxiety, and even fear, upon the family and community. The village elders in traditional society will visit the oracle to find out the cause of these accidental and early deaths and the rituals to be performed to appease the gods. Family members will pray a lot and question the ancestors through all forms of rituals and spiritual communication to find out the cause. In many cases, they will review the social and cultural contexts of the person who died, and his or her relationships (family, friends, social, and spiritual networks): Did he or she have some enemies? Did he or she commit some heinous crimes? Did he or she owe money? These questions are all asked with a view to addressing the past in order to remove the negative forces and spirits from the past so that the living can function well and the conditions for human and cosmic flourishing can be restored. These practices have been abandoned today in my clan because the majority of our people have embraced Christianity, but the uncertainties that surround such deaths have not gone from African societies with the embrace of the Christian faith. As I explain later in this work, when these deaths occurred in my family, many of my extended family members sought for some explanatory cause in order to protect the living from meeting with the same fate. This is because in this worldview every bad death has a spiritual cause, and in finding the spiritual cause one could also discover other associated causes that conspired to end the life of the young.

What I have just described here is called *ofia ajuju* (literal meaning: searching in the forest for causative factors) in my community. It describes an evolving area in sociology and forensic science that is called social autopsy. Social autopsy is a field of study that holds that "by studying death we gain capacity to understand life as well as to protect it."[27] How would we read the story of the Good Samaritan if we did a social autopsy of the reason why many people like the wounded man in the story were being murdered along the highway from Jericho to Jerusalem? How would we understand the suffering in Africa today if we did a social autopsy of the *excess deaths* or *stupid deaths* or *deaths of misfortune* occurring in Africa today?

It is because of the need to answer these questions that I pay attention in this book to the social construction of suffering in Africa today. In other words, what are the religious and political systems that manufacture deaths in Africa? I also wish to do a theological social autopsy by raising the questions as to why we have so many people dying needlessly on our continent. Theological social autopsy simply proposes that by exploring the reasons and circumstances that led to people's deaths, we can interpret better the conditions of those who are living within the same milieu with a view to offering the living helpful pathways to live abundant life as willed by God. Through theological social autopsy, especially of the poor, we honor the memory of the dead by righteously denouncing the convergence of social injustice and structural violence that led to their deaths and fighting to secure the living from similar circumstances so that they do not die needlessly like their ancestors.

It is our Christian duty to bury the dead and celebrate their memories. But theological social autopsy particularly in Africa should challenge us to make sure that we do not bury the dead as well as bury the contradictions of history that continue to kill so many people in Africa. Theologians and church leaders should no longer simply offer thanksgiving masses to God for

---

[27] Eric Klinenberg, "Denaturalizing Disaster: A Social Autopsy of the 1995 Chicago Heat Wave," *Theory and Society* 28, no. 2 (1999): 246.

saving those who have escaped these contradictions of wars, natural disasters, violence, outbreak of infectious diseases, and failed governments. The name of God—that God has called them home to heaven—cannot simply be used to fill every hole in the social ecosystem and moralize or sermonize to people who are dying without fulfilling their mission on earth as understood in African culture. Indeed, for the most part it is not God that called them home, but often "hunger called them home," "HIV/AIDS called them home," "malaria called them home," "violence and wars called them home," "bad economies killed them," "failed government killed them." African theologians and church leaders cannot simply associate the name of God with every evil that emerges from the contradictions of history in Africa. Rather, theologians and church leaders in Africa must accompany God's people in their struggle to live again, by confronting the social context that has persisted in Africa and that continues to kill people and bury the dreams of the young in Africa and destroy God's plan for our continent.

In doing this theological social autopsy through this book, I tell the painful stories of the deaths in my own family while pointing at the deaths occurring in many hot spots in Africa as a result of religious persecution, xenophobia, racism, ethnocentrism, failed and corrupt governments, religious manipulation, and global health inequity. At the same time, I pay attention to the sources of solace and how religious faith operates in the lives of people as they struggle with their pain through the "flight or fight" approach of acceptance, rejection, transformation, and hope. Through the ethnography we carried out, I identify the sources of resilience and hope in the faith of Africans and how to translate this faith into a theological God-talk and praxis of hope and transformation.

My goal is to offer some preliminary thoughts of an African theology that arises from this ambiguity of suffering and smiling that can accompany our people and be a source of action through pastoral and social transformational approaches to being Church. Here, we attempt to begin a conversation on thinking and talking rightly about God and the theology of the Cross from an African perspective. Related to this shift is also a different approach for accompanying those whose pain-filled lives and reality are in dire need of grace, divine presence, healing, and hope at the deepest level of their human vulnerability. I collected these stories in Nigeria, Kenya, and Uganda on how African Christians talk about God, and the implications of this belief and religious outlook for the fate and future of Africa. The question "Where is God in all this?" is one that I have heard in the pains and pathos of many people in Africa, especially during my humanitarian work in six African countries with the Canadian Samaritans for Africa between 2006 and 2018. I heard these questions from mothers in South Sudan, where people of my age have not known peace in their whole life. I heard these questions from mothers in Northern Uganda who have lost all their children and their husbands to floods, wars, and internecine conflicts. I also heard these cries through the research project on human trafficking and modern-day slavery, undertaken by the Pan-African Catholic Theology and Pastoral Network (PACTPAN)—in this project, girls who have been raped or violated or trafficked like Naima share their stories and are given healing, comfort, and hope in the Tamar homes run by our volunteers. Are these not also the cries of many poor people in other parts of the world outside Africa in their distress and despair about the injustice in the world, the cry of the poor, the cry of the earth, the betrayals in our churches, in our families, and in our politics? Why do many people in Africa see their suffering as a punishment from God or an attack from demonic forces? How can the poor be freed from thoughts and actions that portray God as being in a perpetual fight with the devil, and with negative spirits and witches? How could religious faith in Africa be freed from instrumentalizing God as the one who will heal Africa and fix all the broken aspects of the social context in Africa, without people becoming protagonists through the agency of their faith in building a future that offers them the eschatological fruits of God's kingdom in their present history?

Method: Diversity of Theological Voices and Perspectives from Africa and Beyond

Laurenti Magesa has rightly observed that for many African theologians today, there is an increasing awareness that one cannot describe the experience of the *numinous* in African Christianity, or develop a God-talk, or understand the African perception of reality, morality, spirituality, and so on without being immersed in the symbols, arts, images, signs, and worldview that make up the African universe.[28] But does the diversity of symbols among diverse African cultures and tribes point to a common philosophical and religious outlook?

---

[28] Laurenti Magesa, *African Religion: The Moral Traditions of Abundant Life* (Maryknoll, NY: Orbis Books, 2002), 30.

This is a very contested debate, which I have addressed elsewhere. However, it is worth noting that the argument that African religion should be rendered as singular goes back to J. V. Taylor's conclusion in his *The Primal Vision: Christian Presence amid African Religion* (1963)[29] that there is a remarkable number of common features as well as basic ideas about religion throughout Sub-Saharan Africa. Many Africanists still hold on to this position not only with regard to African Traditional Religions (ATRs) but with regard to African history and identity. Douglas E. Thomas presents such a generalizing tendency when he writes: "We can begin by admitting that there is in the Black world a certain unity of conception of a spiritual character. But it is a unity in a great diversity of forms."[30] Bolaji Idowu, in agreement with Taylor, notes that concerning beliefs in Africa, the phenomenology of religion in Africa might lead one to think of a multiplicity of systems of beliefs and practices loosely held together by factors of common localities and languages. However, through careful examination and actual observation and comparative studies one will notice

> a common Africanness about the total culture and religious beliefs and practices of Africa. This common factor may be due either to the fact of diffusion or to the fact that most Africans share common origins with regard to race and customs and religious practices. In certain cases, one could trace specific cultural or religious elements which are common over wide areas which lie proximate to one another; and often, there are elements which jump over whole territories to re-appear in several other scattered areas on the continent. With regard to God, there is a common thread.[31]

Idowu's argument is that the real cohesive factor in religion is God and because there is an identical concept of God in all African ethnic groups and religious systems, we can only speak of African Religion in the singular.

---

[29] J. V. Taylor, *The Primal Vision: Christian Presence amid African Religion* (Nairobi, Kenya: Acton Press Edition, 2005), 27.

[30] See Douglas E. Thomas, *African Traditional Religion in the Modern World* (Jefferson, NC: McFarland, 2005), 21.

[31] E. Bolaji Idowu, *African Traditional Religion: A Definition* (London: SCM Press Limited, 1973), 103.

Idowu's conclusion that all African peoples have a belief in a Supreme God has been called to question.[32]

E. E. Evans-Pritchard argues, for instance, that having a theistic belief, as is common among all ATRs, does not necessarily mean that each of them has a monotheistic faith. While there are marked similarities between the theistic beliefs of the Acholi, the Luo, and the Nuer in East Africa, the theistic belief of the Nuer embraces a polytheism that is similar to that of the Dinka of Southern Sudan, and different from those of the Luo and Acholi. As Evans-Pritchard states:

> A theistic religion need not be either monotheistic or polytheistic. It may be both. It is a question of the level, or situation, of thought rather than of exclusive types of thought. On one level, Nuer religion may be regarded as monotheistic, at another level as polytheistic, and it can also be regarded at other levels as totemistic or fetishistic. These conceptions of spiritual activity are not incompatible. They are rather different ways of thinking of the numinous at different levels of experience.[33]

However, the arguments for a common religious belief among Africans have gained traction. It was defended in the Vatican document, *Meeting African Religions*, which argues that ritual manifestations in African Traditional Religions are apparently different but that they are based on the same religious beliefs and proceed from a common mental structure: "At the heart of all the traditional religions, we find similar structures and aspirations so that despite the variations of beliefs and rites, we can realize that we are dealing with homogenous forms and we can affirm a certain African Religious unity."[34]

It is important to state that acknowledging a common religious tradition in Africa is not an attempt by me to homogenize African religion as was done

---

[32] I take up this argument in chapter 4, where I deal with the question of how the African God is like and unlike the European God. Ter Haar deals with this question, though it is very limited by the lack of ethnographic data. See Gerrie ter Haar, *How God Became African: African Spirituality and Western Secular Thought* (Philadelphia: University of Pennsylvania Press, 2009).

[33] Edward Evans-Pritchard, *Nuer Religion* (NY: Oxford University Press, 1974), 316.

[34] *Meeting African Religion* (1969), 27.

by the missionaries or as many African theologians do following the missionary method of lumping everything together about African religions and cultures. I am interested in giving value to the representations of the African religious system in its diversity. I do not reject some commonalities in African religious experience and expression. But it must be admitted that the assertion of a common religious outlook in Africa, like the contestations about ethnicity in Africa today, is more the result of history and politics than any ontological constitution of sameness. This idea of sameness also emerged through the ferment of cultural nationalism, which resulted from uncritical postcolonial assumptions by Africans of African homogeneity or an idyllic common African past. Rosalind Shaw highlights the limitations: "Where other African cultural writings sought to affirm African 'otherness' from the West as a positive feature, 'theological' cultural nationalism developed instead as an ideology of sameness: sameness in relation to western Christian forms and sameness in relation to an asserted African homogeneity."[35] The horizon of faith in Africa is not fixed, nor is African Christianity a single reality. Any assumption of cultural and religious homogeneity in Africa is misleading.[36] Just as Africa is geographically immense, culturally diverse, and religiously and politically complex, so is

---

[35] Rosalind Shaw, "The Invention of 'African Traditional Religion,'" *Religion* 20, no. 4 (October 1990): 347.

[36] Jared Diamond proposes that beyond the ethnic diversity of Africa, the continent also comprises European and Asian races with populations numbering several millions who have settled and intermarried with African native tribes. The populations of the African countries of South Africa, Zimbabwe, Namibia, Angola, Mozambique, Madagascar, and Ethiopia are a rich mix of African, Caucasian, Asian, and Indian races. There is also a significant Arab and Arab African population in the Maghreb region of Africa, as well as in Madagascar, Sudan, Somalia, and parts of Chad and Nigeria. The racial and cultural diversity of Africa is more elaborate than that of Europe and Asia according to Jared Diamond, who writes: "Even before the arrival of the White colonialists, Africa already harbored not just Blacks but five of the world's six major divisions of humanity and three of them are confined as natives to Africa. One quarter of the world's languages are spoken in Africa.... Africa's diverse peoples resulted from diverse geography and its long prehistory. Africa is the only continent to extend from the northern to the southern temperate zone, while also encompassing some of the world's driest deserts, largest tropical rain forests, and highest equatorial mountains. Humans have lived in Africa far longer than anywhere else." See Jared Diamond, *Guns, Germs, and Steel: The Fate of Human Societies* (New York: W. W. Norton, 1999), 377.

African Christianity. An African theology cannot be constructed without attention to the cultural and faith traditions, whose meaning lives on in the diverse religious beliefs and practices of African Christians. The inductive cultural hermeneutical method in African theology, which gives me tools to pay attention to particular stories and phenomena, does not scrap theory or metaphysical systems as vestiges of the past or the West. On the contrary, these systems can be appropriated only when the social context is taken seriously, as well as when one grasps the intricate web of meanings, beliefs, complex social relations within African Christian history, beliefs, communal ethics, and practices. Gleaning this web of relationships in the lives of individuals or communities becomes necessary, through a mix of multidisciplinary approaches that use sociocultural anthropology, philosophical hermeneutical phenomenology, scriptural exegesis, and traditional methods for theology. This requires engaging these cultural forces on their terms as sources for theology and for faith.

This approach often generates concern from African and Western theologians who prefer a strict or mainstream method in systematic theology. The then Cardinal Joseph Ratzinger (later Pope Benedict XVI) expressed reservation at the Catholicity of African theologies flourishing in the 1970s with the emergence of the Ecumenical Association of African Theologians. He expressed anxiety that Catholic unity might be sacrificed in favor of more restricted cultural communities.[37] African theologies are not isolationist and closed off to the wider Christian gospel or without relevance to world Christianity. Made-in-Africa theologies are also Catholic theologies because they have universal relevance for understanding and receiving the Gospel message.

The African theologian today is confronted with new questions that cannot fit into the traditional questions posed in Western theology, nor can they be interpreted through purely Western epistemological frames or methods. African theologians, for the most part, are practicing "rolling theologies." This is because they go with the flow. In many instances, African theologians are confronting new problems and challenges from the social context of Africa every day that need response. In this regard, specialization is often a luxury that most of us cannot afford. Disciplinary boundaries and canons disappear in the face of severe and complex issues facing the faithful that require the art

---

[37] For Cardinal Ratzinger's argument, see Jean-Marc Ela, *My Faith as an African*, trans. John Pairman Brown and Susan Perry (Maryknoll, NY: Orbis Books, 1990), 181.

of unlayering and peeling off complex iterative aporias. The boundaries are shifting at a frightening pace in Africa, and the features and dimensions of religious faith and practice are fluid. We are confronted ineluctably with the perennial tensions between theologians who seek to mediate truths following a product-based model of transmission of the faith, and those who see their role as performative participation in mediated truths.[38] In the first approach, the theologian seeks to maintain orthodoxy through a faithful preservation of the deposit of the faith, based on a normative understanding of truth, faith, and history.[39] In the second, critical appropriation of truth claims is done, along with critical engagement with history to expand the role of theology within the social context in dialogue with other disciplines, other faiths, and the world of politics. In this regard, Jean-Marc Ela opines:

> Disciplinary procedures could paralyze the theological reflection that is striving now to establish the coherence of dogmas within the context of African culture and society. Indispensable, above all, in Africa is a climate that will allow us to design a style for living our faith in the midst of our current contradictions and hidden dependencies.[40]

---

[38] William Shea conceives this role of mediated theology as defining the subjectivity of the theologian: "The theological self, then, is not an abstract, 'academic' self—unless, God forbid, that is the only self of whom one can speak! The theological self can only be a self in relation to and in various degrees of participation in traditions of witness. The self who speaks theologically is the self who lives and dies, suffers and rejoices, hopes and fears, does good and avoids evil—and all this always in one or another community of witness. This is the accessible self, the self to be mediated in fundamental reflection, even if one grants that the self cannot be wholly mediated." See William M. Shea, "The Subjectivity of the Theologian," *The Thomist* 45, no. 2 (1981): 206.

[39] R. Daniel Shaw sees this as a static and product-oriented approach (source-message-receptor approach, or SMR), which is unhelpful as a missional method because it does not engage the cultures or the receptors on their own terms. See R. Daniel Shaw, "Beyond Contextualization: Toward a Twenty-First Century Model for Enabling Mission," in *International Bulletin of Missionary Research* 34, no. 4 (October 2010): 209.

[40] Ela, *My Faith as an African*, 181.

In this book, I maintain a rigorous theological method that is intentionally phenomenological, as will become evident to the reader. I take seriously here the actual faith of Africans and their living conditions. I am interested in how these two interact and manifest themselves through cultural knowledge, artifacts, behaviors, and concrete symbols informed by the Gospel—in daily personal, social, and ecclesial human and cosmic encounters. The judgments we make about these interactions and the movement of history form an essential task of theology in Africa today. This is because of the dynamic nature of religious narratives today vis-à-vis the sources and canons for validation of revelation and the Christian tradition. It applies in Christian life, and the larger context of the social life of Africans in local, national, regional, and continental settings, and the diaspora. This book combines theological accounts with personal and pastoral concerns.

I privilege the narrative structure of the Christian scripture as a template for writing theology as an African, as will be demonstrated in chapters 1, 3, and 4. Because I am a Christian theologian and pastor, the primary phenomenological source of theology for me is the Word of God. I encounter this Word in the revelation of God in Christ; in the communities of faith and life to which I belong; in the *suffering and smiling* of my brothers and sisters, especially the poor, the marginalized, and those who inhabit the existential peripheries; and in my joys and sorrows as an African living the ambiguities of history as a Black man. I also hear God's Word in the teachings and traditions of the Church and in the liturgical assembly, and I draw from all these sources when writing theology. This revelation in history is the good news of life, love, mercy, truth, and light. It is illumined by the truth which the Holy Spirit helps to bring into the mind of all poor creatures, including this poor and limited creature called Stan Chu Ilo.

These diverse encounters specify for me the logic or illogic, the path and pattern for seeing all things in history, especially human cultures and societies and their associated patterns as divine revelation because they reveal the footprints of God, even in small ways. These encounters even with the minutest of creatures bear the small imprints and seeds of the Incarnation. The Spirit of God reveals to individual believers and faith communities in Africa and the world the presence of God in different and hidden ways in the *suffering and smiling* of God's people in Africa, and in the exponential growth in the Christian population in the continent. My theology, preaching, advocacy, and life as a theologian, priest, and everyday African cannot simply be a re-presentation of pre-packaged answers.

Many African historians argue that to understand African history of any kind, one must study oral traditions in Africa. To understand oral tradition, one must understand in depth the African language of discourse, especially the art of storytelling. African ethnic groups are storytelling societies rather than logocentric (word-centered) ones. In such a world, life is a portrait cast in stories about interactions between a moral and spiritual universe and the everyday practices of people. Stories bring together connections of shared participation and mutual interaction between nature and spirit, humans and nonhumans, God and humanity, the living and the dead, and animals and humans.[41] Obiechina describes the Igbo of Eastern Nigeria:

> The Igbo have always remembered that they have a tree and their storytellers have always reminded them of the need to tend it. For them, stories are important because they are anchored in memory. For them, the story is eternal, it belongs in time but it has a timeless quality, its power to instruct, to remind, to renew, and to direct is not circumscribed by time. So that in their travels and through all vicissitudes of flux and change, they carry with them a memory instructed by their stories.[42]

The persistence of stories in African culture is anchored in memory. A community remembers because memory in African traditional society is the storehouse of the worldview of the people. It is the repository of the great stories and great deeds of people in their cultural and religious history. Memory furnishes interpretive keys for understanding time and space. It is also a key to understanding the past, as well as the present and the future. Whether one is speaking about cyclical time, temporal time, or genealogies, the stream of consciousness embedded in history can be understood in African ontology and in African Christian narrative only through entering into this memory bank. This storehouse is also mediated through the lives of members of the community of faith.

The importance of oral tradition or the so-called memorial culture as a source of valid history has been challenged by the "hard school of history,"

---

[41] See Emmanuel Obiechina, *Nchetaka: The Story, Memory and Continuity in Igbo Culture*, Ahajioku Lecture 1994 (Owerri, Nigeria: Ministry of Information and Social Development, 1994), 26.

[42] Obiechina, *Nchetaka*, 47.

which argues that "proper history must be reconstructed from written documentary sources of sufficient vintage and, therefore sufficient distance, from the events it is concerned with."[43] This challenge can be met by entering into the story of the past, using the conveyor belts of memory with humility and reverence. Further, every tool possible can be deployed to show that the African past—religious, political, economic, social, and spiritual—is not "one long night of savagery from which the first Europeans acting on God's behalf delivered them."[44]

Theological ethnography is applied in this book in collecting and reporting the stories of the actual faith of the people. As a result, this book emerged from a process of attentive listening, in-depth digging, and following the movement of the Spirit in African Christianity with patience and hope to see with my people the new roads God opens to them in the complexity and suffering of their daily existence. The phenomenological approach to religion operates on many principles, the most fundamental being the principle of *epoche*: the suspension of preconceived judgment about the phenomenon, so letting it speak for itself.[45] Writing the history of God's mission in Africa, as seen through the actual and lived faith of Africans and the mission of ecclesial communities in Africa, is like stepping on holy ground in a nonjudgmental way. The stories from the field of faith are sacred. They are the living testimonies of people's daily choices, led by the Holy Spirit through their belief in the God of the Lord Jesus Christ and the God of our African ancestors. While they illumine the heart of the African Christian religion, they also show the limitations of that narrative and faith experience, which are in constant need of translation, conversion, and transition to better orient the course of history in Africa to conform to the reign of God. This book is thus a nonjudgmental account of what I have seen and heard in Africa in solidarity with my brothers and sisters in Africa and all suffering people throughout the world.

---

[43] G. N. Uzoigwe, "A Half Century of Historical Writing in Africa, 1950–2000," in *Emergent Themes and Methods in African Studies: Essays in Honor of Adiele E. Afigbo*, ed. Toyin Falola and Adam Paddock (Trenton, NJ: African World Press, 2009), 112.

[44] Chinua Achebe, *Hopes and Impediments: Selected Essays* (New York: Anchor, 1990), 45.

[45] For a clear expression of this view, see Mariasusai Dhavamony, "Religion II: Phenomenology," in *Dictionary of Fundamental Theology*, ed. René Latourelle and Rino Fisichella (New York: Crossroad, 1994), 833.

Writing this kind of spiritual portrait can be compared to what Clifford Geertz and others propose as an attempt to find understanding within understanding, to see religious symbols through the eyes of the religious adherents, to step outside one's narrow cultural backgrounds and experience the inconceivable prospect of God's great deeds in the lives of people, and to have a nose for the *sensus fidei fidelium*. To understand the conjunctures of these factors in this regard is to grasp the inner meaning of the religious phenomena under investigation. It is to enter the inner world of a religious symbol, to grasp the inner Word revealed in history and to appreciate, in general, the hidden cultural grammar and the interior of a religious phenomenon.[46] In hearing and responding to the reality of *suffering and smiling* in Africa, I will not simply appeal to traditional answers provided through theodicy. Still, I shall pay attention to diverse answers and approaches from the lived faith of our people. We shall listen to the voices of the African ancestors to draw some lessons from how they responded to suffering and evil especially in the moral and social spheres. We shall also draw from the evidence of scripture as foundational but reinterpret the scripture where possible through an African lens.

The approach taken here of paying attention to particular settings, stories, and context means that I do not use one single method for doing theology in Africa, but rather I embrace multiple methods and an interdisciplinary approach. African theologians and pastors must go beyond a single narrative of African religiosity in its history, forms, and expressions. An example could help demonstrate my point. A 2015 workshop was organized by the Symposium of Episcopal Conferences of Africa and Madagascar (SECAM) to articulate Africa's position ahead of that year's Vatican Synod on the Family. During the workshop, Cardinal Robert Sarah insisted that Africans should speak at the Synod with a single, clear, and credible voice. The eventual Synod brought out all the divisive doctrinal and moral fault lines in contemporary Catholicism.[47] Sarah's desire for the Catholic Church to be a strong and unshakable bastion

---

[46] Clifford Geertz, *Local Knowledge: Further Essays in Interpretative Anthropology*, 3rd ed. (New York: Basic Books, 2003), 5.

[47] Catholic Information Service for Africa, "Ghana: Speak with One Voice, Cardinal Sarah Tells African Bishops," *Cisa News Africa*, June 12, 2015, http://cisanewsafrica.com/ghana-speak-with-one-voice-cardinal-sarah-tells-african-bishops-on-synod/.

of truth in a changing ecclesial, cultural, and historical landscape has drawn both admiration and criticism in Africa.[48] For example, his book with Pope Benedict *From the Depths of Our Hearts: Priesthood, Celibacy and the Crisis of the Catholic Church*[49] was received with mixed reactions, as have some of his other writings and interviews.

My approach in this book is more nuanced. I demonstrate commonalties in African experience and history, but I pay greater attention to particularities. Africa has more than one voice, but I need to qualify this at this preliminary stage.[50] The new voices in Africa are as various as the cultures, traditions, and social contexts in Africa. These voices need to be listened to in order to hear the voice of God, who continues to reveal new truths to the Church. Speaking about myself, I sometimes feel inadequate in talking or writing about many aspects of African cultures, religions, and theologies, or indeed of African Catholicism. This invites me to listen more to our people, to be present more to them, and to understand them as they understand themselves. In humility, I accompany my fellow African Christians at their level of meaning. What does it mean for me to be called an expert in African theology or African studies when I have barely scratched the richness and beauty of Africa? This is why I have spent more time within the last fifteen years doing ethnographic study than armchair speculation.

Africa's rich harvest of faith and exciting social realities cannot be understood through a single theological method. We need diverse approaches to doing theology in Africa. Each approach can bring something unique to our experimental dance with God, and our ceaseless search for the intelligibility of who we are, what we believe, and how our actions and stories are adding together in bringing us closer to or farther from the eschatological fruits of God's reign in our personal and group history. Thinking through whose interests are served in the contestations that characterize our world, churches, and social spaces could help us find our way back to God's original dream

---

[48] Lucie Sarr, "The Image Cardinal Sarah Cuts in Africa," *La Croix International*, February 1, 2020, https://international.la-croix.com/fr/afrique/the-image-cardinal-robert-sarah-cuts-in-africa.

[49] Pope Benedict XVI and Robert Cardinal Sarah, *From the Depths of Our Hearts: Priesthood, Celibacy and the Crisis of the Catholic Church*, trans. Michael J. Miller. (San Francisco: Ignatius, 2020).

[50] This will be more fully developed in chapters 1, 3, and 4 of this work.

for us. This can also help us see how the Christian faith and theological discourse—formal and informal, systematic and pastoral—can show the footprints of God in the suffering of God's people. This will help us confront those signs and realities that are sinful, while working courageously and prophetically in changing them so that the light of Christ will shine brighter in our lives, churches, and wider society.

Listening to the Past; Paying Attention to the Present

Today's World Christianity teaches us that, unlike in the past when Christianity identified itself with cultural, political, and economic privilege, domination and influence, today the mission of God calls us to move away from earthly dominion and powers and principalities that threaten to empty the gospel of its liberating, healing, and saving truth when faithfully received with a humble heart. It also calls for exploring the rich possibilities of developing a humble and expansive theological engagement, which can birth intercultural and theological border-crossings in the beauty, diversity, and cultural pluralism of World Christianity and interfaith dialogue of life with all God's people.

World Christianity and diversity in the world today challenge theologians to a more comprehensive and diffuse narrative, leveraging multiple voices on where God is at work in the church and in history, beyond the dominant, restrictive Western account. This is particularly important in telling the story of African Christian expansion, because as Andrew Walls writes, "African Christian history is ... distorted by attempts to make it an appendage of a 'general' church history, which is really a form of European clan history."[51] Writing African Christian history through biographies and spiritual portraits of everyday Christians or focusing on the men and women of our continent who left legacies of faith as African ancestors challenges the universalizing dominance of historical canons that often have marginalized the voices of minorities; it also challenges the essentialized sociological form of institutional Catholicism, for instance, which often hampers the flourishing of the charisms of individuals, the growth of local churches, and cultures in diverse contexts of faith and life. It calls for an open-structured empirical

---

[51] Andrew Walls, "Eusebius Tries Again," in *Enlarging the Story: Perspectives on Writing World Christian History*, ed. Wilbert Shenk (Maryknoll, NY: Orbis Books, 2002), 11.

approach that privileges the narrative of living-faith-in-action of ordinary everyday Christians at the multiple frontiers of proclamation, witnessing, martyrdom, worship, and service.

In this regard, one cannot claim that there is an original Christianity, by which other forms will be judged or an archetypical church-form that generates other churches by rote without attention to cultural mediation and appropriation led by the surprising creativity and genuine newness of the Spirit of the Living God. Nor can one claim that there is a traditional language of Christianity or give preference to any particular historical form in which Christianity has appeared as an ideal model that must be retained, reformed, restored, and replicated everywhere. Attempts to absolutize particular cultural mediations of the faith are either cultural romanticism or cultural idolatry, both of which threaten the ever-renewing impulse of the Gospel to speak from within and beyond human culture. In addition, one cannot insist on a transcendental ecclesiology or an ecclesiological archetype which has to be replicated root, stock, and branches from Rome to the margins.

Writing African theology as the stories of the lived faith of God's people amid suffering and smiling demonstrates that there are reforms and fundamental changes taking place in the way the Gospel is being received and lived outside the West, beyond institutional privileges and power, particularly by the least of the brethren. The power of God is shown in paying attention to the stories of many unsung heroes of the Christian mission in Africa. This approach is an attempt at detraditionalizing the writing of Christian history in Africa. Allan Anderson, for instance, has called African Pentecostalism a new reformation.[52] Some of these new revelations of different ways of believing and witnessing to the Gospel are taking place in the lived lives of everyday African Christians without receiving much attention because they are happening at the margins—the new frontiers of faith. Some of the signs of reform identified by Lamin Sanneh include: the ecumenical, cross-cultural, and inter-cultural nature of Christian expansion in many societies in the Global South; the variety and diversity of its expressions; the structural and anti-structural nature of the changes taking place in organization, worship, and social engagements; the familiar and non-familiar manifestations of spiritual experiences among new Christians in these areas; the wide spectrum

---

[52] Allan Anderson, *An Introduction to Pentecostalism: Global Charismatic Christianity* (Cambridge: Cambridge University Press, 2004), 104.

of theological views and ecclesiastical traditions represented; the diffuse and inclusive nature and style of authority and leadership; and the process of acute indigenization that fosters liturgical renewal; the production of religious art, music, hymns, songs, and prayers—all of which have given Christianity in the non-Western world a stunningly diverse and changing profile.[53] These cultural processes and the "modern-day Indigenous formative process" in the Global South, Sanneh argues, may not fit into established canons of orthodoxy or canon law in the institutional narrative of Catholicism. As a result, they are not accounted for as reforms within the old historiography of Christianity, or in Church history, which is still dominant globally. Lamin Sanneh invites scholars to "break out of their preoccupation with the European heartland and its structures of power, and look to the frontier, scarce in institutional assets but with a teeming diversity that attests to the religion's genius for fostering a spirit of unity along with a variety of styles and idioms."[54]

When this shift in thinking and writing of African Christian history occurs, African theologies emerge as the anti-structural and unofficial renewal of the church, as in the Christian witness, spirituality, and ethics of the great movements in Christian history, such as the rise of monasticism in Egypt; new religious movements in Africa; the exponential rise in vocations to the priesthood and religious life; healing ministries and growth in charismatic and Pentecostal Christianity, among others.[55] While the Church needs institutional structures to ritualize practices of any kind in the church, the history of our church and of society have proven again and again that institutional authorization or approval is driven mainly by the protection of institutional privilege and power. This is why a central impulse of reform today from the margins concerns how the movement of the Spirit in history could proceed in the direction of the eschatological fulfillment of the mission of God enabled by these institutions, and not predicated on institutional predilections that may not always correspond with the overall goal of the reign of God. It is also the reason why it is important to write African theology from an ancestral perspective to excavate rich oral narratives and eyewitness accounts of the great

---

[53] Lamin Sanneh, *Disciples of All Nations: Pillars of World Christianity* (Oxford: Oxford University Press, 2008), xix.

[54] Sanneh, *Disciples of all Nations: Pillars of World Christianity*, 55.

[55] Lamin Sanneh, *Disciples of All Nations: Pillars of World Christianity*, 55.

deeds of God in Africa, and the mission of God in African Christian history that may be forgotten in African Church history.[56]

The task of theology is accountability—what the writer of Luke-Acts calls an "ordered account" of what has happened after careful consideration of the facts.[57] The great deeds of God show what is moving forward in particular history and in group history. This justifies the now largely accepted conclusion that every theology is contextual, because it grows out of a particular history, and pays attention to the social change that emerges from that culture as well as the daily struggle of the people for survival and their search for God.[58] Theology assumes an important place in the life of the people because it is a cultural instrument of humans for giving account of the faith. Doing theology is a grace-filled moment through which the theologian and the community of faith seek to understand the place and principle of faith, in the daily choices of people of faith as they work in bringing about the reign of God. Theology is the history of God's deeds—past, present, and yet to come. The theologian is one who has a nose to perceive the fragrance of God in all things, and motivation to follow the stories of God's mighty deeds by following the daily stories of people—the living and the living-dead. The results demonstrate the rationality of faith, and the concreteness of "hope that does not disappoint" (Romans 5:5). The African theologian, in particular, is one who constantly demonstrates how the Word of God takes concrete forms in individual lives, and how the diverse experiences of individuals and communities lead to or away from God, through a fulsome embrace of God's mission in history and our active participation in this mission for the realization in small ways of the eschatological fruits of God's reign.

Theology is valid only when it locates in these stories the portrait of how God's people are bringing about God's reign in history through their daily

---

[56] Michele Miller Sigg, "*The Dictionary of African Christian Biography* and the Story of Ethiopian Christianity," *International Bulletin of Missionary Research* 39, no. 4 (October 1, 2004): 206.

[57] "Many people have set out to write accounts about the events that have been fulfilled among us. They used the eyewitness reports circulating among us from the early disciples. Having carefully investigated everything from the beginning, I also have decided to write a careful account for you, most honorable Theophilus, so you can be certain of the truth of everything you were taught" (Luke 1:1–4).

[58] Stephen Bevans, *Models of Contextual Theology* (Maryknoll, NY: Orbis Books, 2001), 1, 10.

lives. African theology is a narration that does not cease to grow. Even in being set in any fixed form through text, it exudes fuller dimensions beyond the text because it is born out of a living, dynamic environment. The theologian was traditionally regarded as the master of the sacred pages. If this definition is still valid, African theologians must become masters and mistresses of the sacred steps of God in the biblical texts, the traditions, the lives of the saints, the life of faith and worship, as well as in the lives of our African ancestors. They are to follow the stories of the footprints of God in God's great and small deeds in the lives and contexts of everyday witnesses of faith who are standing strong against the harsh winds of history as models of life and faith; we encounter these witnesses of faith as modern prophets and heroes of faith.

Conclusion

Christianity in Africa is alive and active. It exudes immense diversity, creativity, and freshness. This can only be called a modern-day miracle. Allan Anderson has referred to this growth as the African Reformation.[59] However, African theologians cannot be triumphant about the momentum of Christian expansion in Africa, nor embrace every restorationist Christian project in Africa. African Christianity is not one thing; it is a rich and diverse evolving movement, with many narratives and many streams of God's immense action in history. However, many complex and convoluted challenges face African Christianity. All can be understood by paying attention to the doctrine of God in Africa, a quest which unfortunately has not interested many African theologians. Today this should become a central discussion in Africa, especially on Christology and pneumatology, concerning the work of God in history through the mediation of the church, ministers in the church, nature, and material objects. This is an urgent theological task because of the rise in African Pentecostalism, African Evangelicals, African Catholic Charismatic movements, healing ministries, the growing phenomenon of witch-doctor priests, healing priests in some of the mainline churches in Africa, white garment churches, new chiliastic religious movements, and apocalyptic groups.

These groups and religious actors are bringing into Africa different and often bewildering narratives of God, including the prosperity Gospel,

---

[59] Allan Anderson, *African Reformation: African Initiated Christianity in the 20th Century* (Trenton, NJ: Africa World Press, 2001).

doomsday predictions, claims of miracles, conversion narratives, as well as a mixture of different accounts of God in both the Bible and in African Traditional Religions (ATRs). African faithful migrate from one zone of meaning and belief to another without seeing any disjuncture or contradiction. Indeed, a new word is being used to describe some of the modern-day African preachers—"pastorpreneurs." This reflects their uncanny ability to combine entrepreneurship and religious zealotry.[60] Perhaps, understanding the God narratives may unleash the huge potential of faith in Africa. Understanding the God narratives may also deconstruct some of the pathologies of power, the politics *of you chop I chop* (that being in any position of power is a right to enrich oneself and one's reference group, friends, and loyalists), and the structural violence that have endured in Africa because of these God narratives. It could also bring about the transformation of Africa and bring about prophetic religious faith and conversion at different levels of consciousness. It could also help promote the kind of faith that does good works beyond the fantasy of enthusiastic faith or the constant use of God's name in vain, in the transactional role that religion is playing in some African sociopolitical, economic, and expanding religious terrains.

The chapters contained in this volume were written between 2019 and 2024 during the time of COVID-19. They constitute an integral development of my thought on the task of a theology of suffering and smiling in Africa, on one hand, and the irreplaceable role of African theodicy in the World Church, on the other. This book is the most personal of my writings—partly autobiographical and partly prosopographical (telling the story of my people). I write of my faith as an African believer in the Gospel of the Lord Jesus Christ and someone for whom this Gospel means so much that I am willing to defend it with my life. I have written this book also as conversations with the daily struggles of my people and my own search for a Gospel-driven narrative on which I can build my faith and hope that history is moving toward fulfillment or some realization for my people of the fruits of the eschatological reign

---

[60] See, for instance, Jacob T. Hundu and Joseph Azembeh, "Pastorpreneurship: A Critical Analysis of Proliferation of Churches in Nigeria," *SBS Jos J Religious Studies Humanities* 1 (2018): 43; see also Mark Alan Charles Jennings, "Great Risk for the Kingdom: Pentecostal-Charismatic Growth Churches, Pastorpreneurs, and Neoliberalism," in *Religion and Theology: Breakthroughs in Research and Practice* (Hershey, PA: IGI Global, 2020), 160–72.

of God. I have written this book in dialogue with the works of many other theologians and social scientists who have reflected on human suffering as well as on the African predicament and the contradictions of history that have held Africa and the people of African descent in a chokehold of history for too long. I engage particularly with the writings of many Black scholars who write specifically on the changing faces of Christianity in Africa, white supremacy, racism, Christian nationalism, suffering, hope, faith, community, and the fate and future of God's people in Africa.

Some of the materials in this book have been shared in public lectures and in my classroom lectures, particularly in the research courses and seminars—"African Christian Theology" and "World Christianity in Intercultural and Interreligious Perspectives"—that I facilitate occasionally at the Catholic Theological Union in Chicago. By 2023, as I went through these chapters, it became clear to me that they form a fairly consistent, coherent, and cumulative development of a single thought, reflecting my love for the continent of Africa, for my Church, and for the world. These chapters together form the kernel of what I consider important foundational and methodological issues in thinking through theodicy in the face of some of the complex and challenging realities that we see as a people of faith in these complex times in Africa: How can one make sense of history for those who continue to suffer, and for a people who are struggling to live again by holding strongly to their religious faith in God, who saves, heals, and liberates all people from bondage, sin, suffering, and oppression?

I have written this work as my humble attempt to interrogate the Christian faith and the intelligibility of that faith, and its spiritual, moral, social, and cultural relevance in bringing our people and society closer to the will of God. This book is also a conscious effort to demonstrate how to integrate the Christian faith as African Christians in our lives and social context. Particularly, I explore how this faith acts credibly and effectively in determining the quality and relevance of the witness of local faith communities, in their collaborative and ceaseless effort to bring to birth the kind of society we all long for in Africa.

Finally, there are two important distinctions that I wish to make for readers of this book. The first is the *need to reject Afro-pessimism*. Theology must give hope to the people because the Lord Jesus is the principle of hope. This must be hope on something concrete, and hope that is anchored in the lived faith and agency of the people as the means through which God's grace works for the realization of God's will in history. Many Africans are losing hope about the possibility of social transformation in Africa. I am often shocked by how some Africans talk about ourselves, our history, and our institutions. Afro-pessimism has its roots in white supremacy and racism. This is the false notion that Africans are inferior to white people, that their institutions are backward, and that their postcolonial attempts at building a new Africa have failed because nothing good can come from these lands. Our theological construction should move away from narratives of contamination, to showing how God's footprints among our people open for us narratives of redemption.

Theologies in Africa must show the light by identifying what is working in our communities, across the many sites of hope in Africa. As an example, I have studied how Nigeria defeated Ebola, and how the poorest country in Africa, Liberia, defeated that epidemic in less than a year. I think of the effort and sacrifice of Africans during the COVID-19 pandemic, and the successful effort of the African Catholic Church to organize fourteen successive weeks of online conversations on all the themes of the synod on synodality in 2024. I think of the great works of African women in our villages, how they are uniting in micro-credit unions to roll back the destructive hand of poverty. These are but a few among many other examples. I think of the giant sacrifice of many ordinary Africans—laity, priests, teachers, frontline workers, and church leaders—who are changing lives in many hidden parts of Africa, outside the limelight. However, rejecting despair and pessimism does not mean masking the challenging social context of Africa.

There is the need to distinguish between Afro-pessimism and *critical Afro-centric realism*. Afro-pessimism says that things will not get better in Africa, thus making what is historical in Africa—poverty, failed states, and religious pathologies—a cultural problem (that is, that these problems are co-natural to African being and identity). This book is a project on critical Afro-centric realism. This is set against an unrealistic romantic optimism about Africa, which claims that things will get better, without taking the time to do the work of looking at our history and the stultifying epistemic handcuffs, economic dwarfism, and political albatrosses that weaken critical, creative, and transformative thinking and education in Africa. This new approach says that we must critically engage our institutions, systems, structures, and cultural traditions—whether they are sacred or secular, whether they are Western or non-Western—and ask a simple question: Is a particular institution generating the knowledge, transformative ethics, and praxis which can bring human and cultural flourishing in these rich lands? The time has come for Africans to embrace religious, political, and educational systems not because of reception from missionaries or colonialists, but because we think they work for us. And we think we are actively playing a part in reforming them, refining them, or totally changing them, and building new institutions and systems. This is a collective project that is not simply the product of the "ivory towers." Social change is a process not a product. Hope is a daily praxis not an empty expectation of divine intervention.

This book's overarching theme is how African Christians can think rightly about God so that we can act rightly in our religious beliefs and practices in courageously addressing the social suffering in Africa. We are concerned in this book with what the practice of faith means, and how theology can lead to the practice of religious faith as action and missional praxis of social transformation through proclaiming and living the Gospel as hope for God's people in Africa. This latter theme of religious faith as action and as acting is the differentiation that Atalia Omer makes between *knowing religion* and *doing religion*. In knowing religion, there is an embrace of faith as something that is wedded to one's being and one's relationship with everything, once God is placed at the center of life. Everything then revolves around this experience of God, and the attitudes, ethics, spirituality, morality, and worship flow from this intimate relationship with God, and with all things because of God. However, merely "doing" religion is only the functional or instrumental deployment of religion to serve ends that do not give glory to God or honor God. Such pursuits make God and religious beliefs and practices as means to an end, having nothing to do with God. When this is the case, particularly in religious groups, the purpose is not for the leaders to develop deeper knowledge of God, of the things of God, or of the traditions. Instead, religion serves simply to advance the organization's goals, and those of the leaders and their allies. As Omer notes, "This is what is meant by *doing* religion. Within the neoliberal framework, this emphasis on *doing* denotes a horizontalization of religious virtuosity, which also entails reducing traditions to sound bites."[61]

Demonstrating the intelligibility and rationality of Christian religious beliefs and practices in Africa could be achieved by bringing together knowing

---

[61] Atalia Omer, *Decolonizing Religion and Peacebuilding* (Oxford: Oxford University Press, 2023), 124.

God and applying this knowledge to responding to the daily challenges and opportunities of life in Africa in an authentic, credible, faithful, and fruitful way. I invite you to pay attention to the precarity of life in Africa today and the suffering and hopes of God's people. Theologies in Africa should emerge from these complexities and return the fruits of theological reflection to help the people of God to find hope and courage in meeting the challenges of daily life. I challenge my readers to focus on the lived lives of God's people in Africa, and the *sensus fidei* mediated through how everyday Christians are thinking about God, perhaps in part outside of the formal structures and rituals of the Church.

For theologians and churches (particularly mainline churches) to contribute to a better future for Africa, and capture the imagination of today's evolving African societies, they must contribute to reversing the unacceptable history which Africa has lived for centuries. They must pay attention to this lived and actual faith of suffering and smiling. The Church in Africa and its theologians and leaders must go beyond mouthing the mantra that the faith is growing in Africa. They must focus on broken links between theology and life, between official teaching and the actual faith of the people. An African Christian faith unliberated from some of its entanglements with slavery, racism, colonialism, violence, oppression, neoliberal capitalism, negation of African history, religiocultural identity, and agency will become over time simply another social and cultural option among the bazaar of options now on display in modern Africa. There is real risk in offering little toward the necessary pilgrimage of God's people in Africa to the exit door of inherited Western repetitive traditional Christian rituals and practices that leave many African Christians constantly searching for more outside the formal structures of the Church.

Following this introduction, this book has six chapters and a concluding section. Chapter 1 addresses the task of African theology and my proposals for how to do this kind of theology. But I argue that African theology is not simply a localized theology that deals with the African context. Rather, African theology also has something to say to the World Church about how to deal with contradictions and polarization in the world and in the Church; how to deal with suffering and pain and how to find solace through community and religious faith, and how to find God in history. Chapter 2 explores some contemporary theological voices and magisterial teaching on suffering and uses the parable of the Good Samaritan as a critical hermeneutical framework for analyzing how social structures and injustice in society manufacture unbearable suffering for so many people in the world. I particularly propose how lament and outcry against injustice and suffering can be translated into protests, pragmatic solidarity, and collective consciousness and action to repair the world. In chapter 3 I present an ethnographic study carried out in Nigeria, Kenya, and Uganda, and a critical theological analysis of some Nollywood movies and how they construct God and human attempts in Africa to escape from suffering and poverty. This is my attempt to take seriously some of the "popular theodicy," or *matatu theology* or the theology done through *radio trottoir*.[62] This is the theology done on buses and street corners, of what people mean when they talk about God in Africa, where they find God, and how they hold in tension the contradictions of history that they live with at the existential peripheries of life. I also analyze some of the popular representations of God and survival in some African films. Chapter 4 addresses how the images of God are changing in Africa because of the contestations for meaning presaged by modernity; I also look at how to reframe these images in a way that helps the faith and witnessing of individuals and churches in Africa bear fruits of abundant life. Particularly, the chapter delves into the world of witches and wizards in African politics and how these are evidence of the crisis of religion and of the state in Africa. The argument is made for how to think rightly of God, in order that people can think rightly about themselves and their world and how to change it to conform to God's will. Chapter 5 analyzes one of the most famous slave narratives—Olaudah Equiano's—and its portrayal of God, suffering, divine providence, and hope. I enunciate some issues with theology as applied to the suffering and racism endured by people of African descent, especially in the United States. I answer the question whether there is a meeting point between African theodicy and a Black theology of the Cross. Finally, the concluding section takes up the questions of hope amid suffering, and of eschatology and divine providence while restating the five main claims of this book.

---

[62] *Radio Trattoir* or roadside radio were in post-independence Africa the place where people gathered to listen to the latest national and international news and to debate about them in the light of their faith and political leanings. It reflected the enduring value of oral culture in Africa and the oral proclamation of the Gospel. See Stephen Ellis, "Tuning in to Pavement Radio," *African Affairs* 88, no. 352 (1989): 321–30.

Any theology that does not offer hope to God's people is empty. A theology that does not help believers make sense of history in holding to God as the beginning and the end of all things is misleading. My definition of a theologian is the one who points to God's presence and absence in all things. A theologian makes a case for a God-centered universe in which the human is not thrown into a wilderness but sent on a ceaseless but complex and sometimes uncertain pilgrimage in which God is present in many ways and accompanying the human through multiple agencies, the most decisive being the presence of Jesus Christ and our African ancestors. We are called to travel with all people and all things in the name of God and in doing so we participate in the dance of life that is bigger than each of us, and together we realize the cosmic *Ubuntu* and shalom for the flourishing of all creation. Because this human and cosmic flourishing is often affected by human suffering, this book makes a case for a theology that engages human suffering with courage and hope. It is possible for Africans and indeed all people of faith to laugh at life with the eyes of faith as people open themselves to God's boundless grace. Ultimately, our Christian faith opens us to the infinite horizon of God, which is capable of helping the believer bring the ambiguities of history and unjust suffering to the foot of the Cross, where the perpetual cycle of unending, unmerited, and avoidable suffering meets its limits.

1

Doing African Theology in a Wounded and Broken World

> Theology that matters will be theology where the Christians are; and it looks as if the bulk of Christians are going to be in Africa, and Latin America and in certain parts of Asia. If these churches—the world's big and growing churches—do not produce theology, springing from reflection on the word of God and in tune with the real minds of their leaders and the real lives of their members, to that extent they are unlikely to produce disciples. And in addition, it may well mean that there will be no theology in the world worth talking about. For, from the standpoint of history, it is doubtful whether any theology is worth talking about that does not have some noticeable effect in the lives and minds of a significant number of people.
>
> —Andrew F. Walls[1]

My own personal experience of pain and suffering is what stimulated my theological search for how to make sense of suffering. But I am also immersed daily in the joys and sorrows of God's people in my pastoral and humanitarian work in Africa, North America, and Europe. In the words of

---

[1] Andrew F. Walls, "Towards Understanding Africa's Place in Christian History," in *Religion in a Pluralistic Society: Essays Presented to Professor C. Baëta*, ed. John S. Pobee (Leiden: Brill, 1976), 182–83.

the final document of the Synod on Synodality, our eyes are daily opened "to the suffering of those around us and the tragedies of history—the faces of war-stricken terrorized children, weeping mothers, the shattered dreams of so many young people, refugees who face terrible journeys, the victims of climate change and social justice."[2] These narratives are the sources for theological reflection in Africa and in today's wounded and hurting world. I also demonstrate in this chapter the new directions in Catholic theology and how African theology fits into this new design in making intelligible the meaning of faith in God and offering the people of God practices for transformation and some wisdom for pastoral accompaniment. The chapter makes a case for an African theology that is also addressed to the world Church as a gift on the integrative power of faith, the strength and coping strategies that come from communal resilience, and the expansive possibility that can be found in theology when theologians and church leaders embrace a hermeneutic of humility in a depolarizing discourse as they hear and do God's will by paying attention to the peripheries. The chapter particularly elucidates the three directions of theology in the Catholic Church today developed as a response to the renewed call for missionary conversion and a focus on the synodal missionary face of the Church.

On Losing Three Family Members in One Year

Writing the story of African Christian religion requires developing the right kind of tools and navigational maps. So too does accounting for the context, content, process, and dynamic and differentiated levels of consciousness that are embedded in these stories. These new maps must have an extensive and expansive outlay of a hermeneutic of multiplicity, and one of humility. The African theologian, by paying attention to the narratives of everyday Christians, begins from what is going on in the daily realities of African Christians, which imposes some limitations and opens new horizons to one's scientific study. Furthermore, the theologian humbly listens to what God is saying through the daily expressions of faith in Africa, in all its variegated and complex manifestations. Writing this story is an effort at a spiritual biography written as a religiocultural portrait of a people, all the while accounting for the total picture beyond a restrictive or judgmental account arrived at through

---

[2] Synod on Synodality, *Final Document* (October 26, 2024), no. 2.

aprioristic generalization. Without this humble attitude and open framework, one loses the essence and depth of meaning that can be achieved through a patient and engaged cultural tracing of the inner Word as incarnated in the actual faith of people and how this faith is driving the movement of history and Christian expansion in Africa through a renewed expression of faith in God and the Gospel message.

Three significant personal experiences and encounters, among many others, have been shaping my thinking since 2007 on this new way of studying Christian expansion in Africa and the meaning of faith in the God of the Lord Jesus Christ in the social context of suffering and smiling in Africa.

The first took place in July of 2007, when I was studying at the Maryknoll Institute for African Studies at the then Tangaza College in Nairobi. I had conducted field research under the guidance of the late Professor Laurenti Magesa. My study required spending at least eighteen hours every week in the field collecting ethnographic data on my selected topic, which was on ancestral beliefs and practices in African Christian religion. I was interested in researching the retention of ancestral worldviews in African Christianity, and how this is manifested in the structures of meaning and symbols in Christian beliefs and practices. I was also interested on how mythical consciousness in African Traditional Religions (ATRs) and cultures has shaped the predominance of communion with ancestors in the human world. I also wanted to understand how this ancestral worldview strongly shapes the cultural knowledge of Africans. Particularly in this regard, I desired to know how those Africans who have accepted Christianity frame their beliefs about suffering and pain and the unseen spiritual forces and presence of the ancestors, which work together in either producing abundant life today and guaranteeing a better future for tomorrow, or in producing curses and tragedies for their progeny.

I met one Christian healer in the Lang'ata area just a little outside the barracks near Uhuru Park in Nairobi. What struck me was my own response to her invitation to pray for me after interviewing her. I bowed spontaneously when she asked me to do so to receive her prayers and blessings, and she prayed over me for some time. She said three prayers for me, which I remember vividly: that the ancestors should protect me from all witchcraft and sorcery; that they should protect me from suffering any evil or sudden death so that I can live to a glorious old age and see my great-grandchildren; and that the ancestors should shield me against the wicked forces of this world and men and women who may harm me. At the end, she offered me a water of blessing which I declined to drink because I was not comfortable drinking from an unknown source. I was unsure what she felt about my refusal, but she did not show any bitterness, nor did she withdraw her blessings. However, I felt good inside after the prayer.

Later at night as I lay down to sleep and did my usual self-reflective debriefing, I thought to myself: You are a Catholic priest and you just bowed to receive blessing from this elderly woman who was not ordained by a bishop, whose theology was not deep, and whose claims from the interview at least at this preliminary stage for me lacked scientific proof? Then there was the other surprise that beyond all my theological systems I was inwardly grateful at an existential level for the themes of her prayers and at being blessed by an elderly woman, as is traditional in my Igbo culture. Some of her prayer points for me were valid concerns of mine, which I may not have thematized in my own faith journey and personal peregrinations. I was asking myself quietly whether I really believed in witchcraft and in ancestral communion, and whether I am convinced that my enemies could harm me or bewitch me and even cast spells on me without the help of prayers and protective spiritual armor from faith healers like this woman. Did I bow to receive her blessing because she was an elder who wanted to wish me well through her blessing, or because I thought she had an extraordinary power that could be an aid to me in my life's journey?

This inner questioning was life-shattering and traumatic for me, but it also posed to me a theological and sociocultural challenge: This is the reality of your history and the reality of many Africans like you, including those like you who are well-educated and well-immersed in postmodern thoughts and systems. Therefore, if this is my own reality and the reality of my people, I must seek to understand the hidden cultural grammar behind these symbols, prayers, blessings, and worldviews to determine if this is a text of revelation pointing to where God is at work in the pathos and fears of African Christians. More important, it also reveals to me how my fellow Africans are reading their history in the light of God's mission in Africa. I wondered to myself amid this new realization: How can I enter this story? How can I see myself and my people in this story? What does this story reveal to me about myself and my people, and their construction of meaning and the choices they are making in bringing about the realization of God's mission in Africa? Do narratives like these make sense? Are they believable? What are the canons for establishing the value of these stories?

The second experience was in 2013. I was crossing the Busia border from Uganda to Kenya by bus. Everyone in the bus had to cross the border by foot while the customs and police officers did their normal security check of the bus and the baggage of the passengers. This will normally take an hour or more. As we waited for our bus to be cleared, having passed through immigration, I was quite hungry and decided to buy some bananas and cashew nuts. I bought a bunch of bananas and started to eat and was suddenly surrounded by about eight small boys whose ages I will put to be under twelve. These boys were begging for alms from passersby. They approached me begging that I share my bananas with them because they had not eaten all day. These were street boys, whose home was most likely here in the open space of the border, under the elements. It was about 2:00 p.m. I bought the entire offering of bananas at the table there and shared with them. I wished them well, and then boarded the bus to continue my journey. I had one banana left, which I ate inside the bus and threw the peel away through the window. Much to my pain, these young boys ran after the banana peel to scrape whatever remained there worth eating!

It was a scene which will always remain with me as a point of reference and a source of sorrow, but also a challenge: What does religious faith mean for many young Africans who, like these little boys, are suffering along the borders and highways of life? Of what relevance will the theology I write be to these little boys, their parents, churches, and religious and political leaders? When I shared the bananas with the boys, they had thanked me saying that they knew God would bring them some help that day. The question for me then as well as now is: What is this experience of God that these young boys expressed to me in their condition? How could this God have sent me to share bananas with them when they should be living in well-functioning societies with good food, good education, a good home, and all that makes life beautiful, fulfilling, and joyful? How can the theology that I write emerge from the dumps of history, from the experience of poverty and powerlessness of many poor Africans, and be a source of light and hope? What theological method can account for the story of these boys and the society in which they are growing up, which has robbed them of their childhood and a future while giving them a wretched existence in their present life? How can I articulate the Christian religion in Africa in such a way that one can find in it hope, agency for the self, group transcendence for the poor, and a praxis for transformation for these young boys and many like them who are growing up in Africa today? How can one see in the stories of these boys the narrative of God's revelation of the realization of the reign of God in the mission that churches in Africa must carry to the men and women, and the young and old people, who are living in poverty and those on the margins in Africa?

My third narratives are two experiences of death that touched me personally.

On the weekend of the Second Sunday of Easter in 2014, in a remote parish near my home in Enugu State, Nigeria, seven pre-teens who were altar servers went to clean the sanctuary of the church and decorate the altar for Mass. As they were working, the walls of the building collapsed and killed five of them instantly. A friend of mine was the pastor of the church. This was an incalculable tragedy in many ways. There were many unanswered questions: Why did the walls collapse exactly at the time when the kids were there serving God? Why was the wall not reinforced? Who designed the wall? Who should be held responsible? The responses were varied in the community. Some claimed that this was the attack of the devil and that there should be an exorcism to kill the spirit of the devil. For some, the kids were martyrs because they had died in the house of the Lord serving the good Lord. Because they died as martyrs, they will be carried into the bosom of the Most High God and enjoy the heritage of God (which is our ultimate goal in life), or "to make heaven" as is commonly expressed in Nigeria. There were one or two dissenting voices that some accounting should be done for the inexcusable loss of the lives of five little ones whose voices, talents, and creative spirits and souls will no longer grow to enrich the world. But these voices were muted. Again, the question arises for me: What is the goal of life here on earth and what kind of theology can help people live with the daily tragedies of life? How can one theologically account for preventable deaths in Africa—through poor construction of homes and churches, diseases, wars, terrorist attacks, preventable accidents, poor healthcare systems, poor nutrition, etc.—and the Christian narratives used to account for them? What kind of theology can be discovered through stories like these in the light of the reign of God and Christian narratives of the afterlife and God's will in all these?

The other death that is still a pain in my soul is that of my stepsister Eugenia, who had a narrow mitral valve in her heart. She had earlier been taken to Israel as a young girl of eleven, through the help of the Nigerian government, for open-heart surgery to correct the problem. At the age of twenty-three, there was a need to put a stent to open up the valve, since there had been some blockage. I showed her medical report to a cardiologist at St. Michael's

Hospital in Toronto, who told me that her problem was a minor one, and could be corrected through a simple two-hour surgery. We began the process of getting the necessary papers to have her treated in Canada, but which at the end of the day was unsuccessful. Meanwhile, everyone in the family intensified their prayers for her to survive, to obtain a visa from the Canadian consulate in Nigeria, and for God's intervention. There were many in my extended family who visited many "prayer houses" and many prophets seeking healing, but somewhere in the world there was a simple procedure that could have saved her life. However, the main point of the story is that a few months before her death, Eugenia stopped taking her medications. She was simply tired of taking too many medications, and in her deep faith she trusted God to heal her. But she had a stroke and died. Was it that God did not listen to our prayers, or that what we were praying for was not the kind of thing God is interested in responding to? Within four months of her death, I lost two cousins from the same Ilo-Maduakor family. Between October and December 2013, we had buried three young girls in the same compound, all under thirty years of age. These were considered premature death (*inwu chu*) in the family.

The family elders and the wise men and women of the village went to work to consult the oracles from both our clan and other surrounding clans, at least to get a second opinion. All the oracles came down with the judgment that there was a great-great aunt (*ada*) from the family who was angry because she was not given a proper burial when she died. The oracle warned that this great-great aunt will continue to take (kill) the young girls of the family unless certain burial rituals and ancestral rites were performed for her. The oracle's verdict was accepted without any protestations by most members of my extended family, excluding my immediate family and one or two others in the extended family. But the full funeral and ancestral rituals were conducted, with many in the village in attendance. My village in Nigeria is 98 percent Christian, but for most of them there was nothing wrong in celebrating this ritual to avert further tragedies in the family, even if it meant seeking the help of the oracles. As many said in the village, *akataghi nka n'uka* (this kind of solution must be found outside the church, or this is beyond the answers which Christianity offers). Many people in the family wanted to do this ritual because they felt that there was nothing wrong in celebrating a late ancestor if that would bring resolution to the problems which they were facing.

In conversation with the family elders, I could see their anguish and pain. It is not often in our traditional society you see elderly men crying from the depths of their hearts. However, I found my family elders in tears, in fear, and devastated by the deaths in the family. I too was heartbroken and cried for many nights because these were some of the closest members of my family, whom I loved deeply and with whom I had a special connection, especially Eugenia and Chinyere. I was also worried about the deaths and how they all happened at the same time within a space of three months. Again, the question came ringing in my head: As a theologian, how can I tell my family story and anguish? Why did the family not consult me—an ordained Catholic priest—before consulting the oracle? Was my priestly power judged beforehand as incapable of providing the answers to these limit situations battering my extended family? How can I account for some members of my extended family combining traditional ancestral rituals and the Catholic ritual of praying for the dead without any sense of contradiction or syncretism? One of my uncles, longing to make sure that all the angles were covered, offered a Mass for all the deceased members of the family, including all our ancestors. How can one understand what is going on in the history of people who straddle these two worlds most of the time, without any sense of ambivalence or ambiguity as they do so? Should not the text of their story be the narrative for the study of Christian religion in Africa today? How is the mission of God for the redemption of all and the final consummation we hope for incarnated in these stories?

These stories, though personal to me, are typical everyday stories in Africa. The ethnographic study by the Pew Research Center from 2010 points to the need for more scientific investigation on African religiocultural worldviews. However, large numbers of Africans who are deeply committed to practicing Christianity or Islam believe in witchcraft, evil spirits, sacrifices to ancestors, traditional religious healers, reincarnation, and other elements of African religions.[3] The African religiocultural worldview continues to occupy the interests of many scholars today because it is central to Africa's appropriation of Christianity. My stories are the kinds of stories priests, pastors, and healers are dealing with every day in their churches in Africa. They are shaping Christian consciousness, and Christian narratives, and Christian daily praxis in Africa. These stories are also sources of despair and hope, and of fear and faith, for many Africans who embrace the Christian faith and place their hope that this faith will provide answers to their problems and sufferings. They are the

---

[3] See Pew Research Center, "Tolerance and Tension: Islam and Christianity in Sub-Saharan Africa," April 15, 2010, section "Executive Summary."

stories that are creating conflicts in families and clans. They also are bringing people together and elevating communal living and ecclesial life to a new level of awareness and consciousness of where people are searching for God in their personal and group history. These should be the indispensable texts for doing theology in Africa today. Any scientific study of African Christian religion must place these stories at the center of theological reflection and pastoral accompaniment.

New Directions in Catholic Theology

The apostolic constitution *Veritatis Gaudium* on ecclesiastical universities, promulgated January 20, 2018, offers lessons on the role of Catholic theology in a reforming and renewing world Church.[4] It also serves as the theoretical and conceptual framework for my analysis of my personal experience of family tragedies, and the views and perspectives that I gained from talking to my fellow Africans on the streets of some of the major cities of Nigeria, Kenya, and Uganda, and in the villages. What is the type of theology that can meet these challenges and opportunities? Pope Francis's wisdom here is a helpful starting point:

> Against this vast horizon now opening before us, what must be the fundamental criteria for a renewal and revival of the contribution of ecclesiastical studies to a Church of missionary outreach? ... This then is a good occasion to promote with thoughtful and prophetic determination the renewal of ecclesiastical studies at every level, as part of a new phase of the Church's mission, marked by witness to the joy born of encountering Jesus and proclaiming the Gospel, that I set before the whole people of God as a program in *Evangelii Gaudium*.[5]

This missionary engagement with the Gospel and the witness of faith of God's people is the starting point for the three directions of theology I identify in Catholic Church today.

---

[4] Francis, *Veritatis Gaudium*, apostolic constitution, December 17, 2017, https://www.vatican.va/content/francesco/en/apost_constitutions/documents/papa-francesco_costituzione-ap_20171208_veritatis-gaudium.html. All the papal documents mentioned in the notes can be found at vatican.va.

[5] Francis, *Veritatis Gaudium*, sec. 4, 1 of foreword.

The first direction is through a theological aesthetics that emerges through a culture of encounter. In *Veritatis Gaudium*, Pope Francis writes that theology should be done as "a culture, we might say, of encounter between all the authentic and vital cultures, thanks to a reciprocal exchange of the gifts of each in the luminous space opened up by God's love for all God's creatures."[6] The message of Pope Francis is on how to create a global fraternity built on the culture of encounter.

Ubuntu is an African ethic of community that affirms that a person is only a person through other persons. *Ubuntu* begins with a recognition that we are all related in a bond of love and community. *Ubuntu* is a spirituality of encounter that moves everyone to see in the other person a shared implication in each other's life and future. Only in encountering each other, and in affirming the subjectivity of the other with respect and reverence, can we create conditions for human and cosmic flourishing.

I see such a striking resonance between the "culture of encounter" of Francis and African *Ubuntu*. I propose that the culture of encounter is Pope Francis's *Ubuntu* for global fraternity and solidarity. The culture of encounter is the pope's proposal for building relationships as the basis for solidarity among humans, and between humans and nature. The emphasis on relationship by Francis is an important theological aesthetic for reconceptualizing the intersubjective ethics of recognition and action today.

As an *Ubuntu* model for building the global community, in *Fratelli Tutti* Pope Francis applies the culture of encounter as a way of seeing the other (a revelatory moment) as well as a way of being-with the other (existential ethics) in the world—each of us is fully a person when we are part of a people.[7] This invites people to move away from a single narrative of culture and identity[8] to a more expansive embrace of the connections between all things—humans, God, and nature.[9] The culture of encounter is a social ethic that is capable of shattering the walls constructed by socially and historically designed narrow structures, systems, and institutional practices that have built walls and

---

[6] Francis, *Veritatis Gaudium*, sec. 4b of foreword.

[7] Francis, *Fratelli Tutti*, encyclical letter, October 3, 2020, https://www.vatican.va/content/francesco/en/encyclicals/documents/papa-francesco_20201003_enciclica-fratelli-tutti.html, sec. 182.

[8] Francis, *Fratelli Tutti*, sec. 12.

[9] Francis, *Fratelli Tutti*, secs. 34, 66, 50.

social hierarchies between peoples, cultures, and religions.[10] The culture of encounter inspires a new ethical vision and momentum that can move people to transcend themselves. They can die to the enslavement to self, race, nation, and other forms of identities, and enter into the ever-expansive encounter with otherness and a deeper dialogue with the other.[11]

In embracing this way of seeing and being-in-the-world, people receive the inconceivable prospects of discovering the beauty of otherness, and an ingress into a new world and a new Gospel every new day, in every new moment of encounter. This movement of the heart, head, and will motivates people to search for new solutions and approaches to repairing the world. They can, for instance, seek new ways to reweave the bonds of love that have been broken by violence, ideological battles, structural violence, injustice, and destructive economies of scale that often discard the vulnerable and the poor.[12]

The culture of encounter is trinitarian. This is because in the Trinity the three persons encounter each other in a mutual embrace and in-dwelling, and the three persons love, affirm, and respect, and participate in intimate social friendship.[13] The culture of encounter is also a summons for a perichoretic insertion of each of us into the world of nature and into the lives of all of us. This insertion offers humanity the possibility of a cosmic dance in which everyone is participating in everyone's joys and sorrows. In this way, as Pope Francis said in his inaugural homily, we can become the guardians of one another and of nature.[14]

When Francis writes that "everything is, as it were, a caress of God,"[15] one sees the key to understanding the structure of the theological aesthetic of the culture of encounter. This is particularly evident in the pope's constant

---

[10] Francis, *Fratelli Tutti*, sec. 195.

[11] Francis, *Fratelli Tutti*, sec. 111.

[12] Francis, *Fratelli Tutti*, secs. 18–20.

[13] Francis, *Fratelli Tutti*, sec. 85.

[14] Francis, "Homily of Pope Francis," Mass, imposition of the pallium and bestowal of the fisherman's ring for the beginning of the Petrine Ministry of the Bishop of Rome, March 19, 2013, https://www.vatican.va/content/francesco/en/homilies/2013/documents/papa-francesco_20130319_omelia-inizio-pontificato.html.

[15] Francis, *Laudato Si'*, encyclical letter, May 24, 2015, https://www.vatican.va/content/francesco/en/encyclicals/documents/papa-francesco_20150524_enciclica-laudato-si.html, sec. 84.

insistence that people need to be in touch with reality in its concreteness as a beginning of a deeper encounter with God;[16] we need to meet each other at the deepest level;[17] we need to come in direct contact with the context and history of people; and we need to have our boots on the rough ground where the poor are suffering.

This principle of intersubjectivity begins from within the hearts of all persons, as an inner grace and interior logic of love. From this interior desire arises a movement in which the human person seeks the connection with the other, in what the African ancestors captured as *Ubuntu*, the wisdom that says that the recognition of the other makes me human, or rather that in affirming the humanity of the other, I affirm my own humanity.

Pope Francis often uses phrases like "gaze upon," "openness of heart," "spiritual encounter," "the art of listening," "contemplation with wonder,"[18] and the "gaze of Christ."[19] Francis invites people to this culture of encounter so they can appreciate the different forms of beauty in their lives, in the lives of others, and in the world of nature. The culture of encounter opens a sense of mystery, which moves people to appreciate beauty even in the complexities of life, and in the brokenness of the pains in the lives of so many people suffering in the world today. Through an encounter with nature and with our fellow human beings from every and any part of the world, one can grasp a deeper level of truth in the sublimity of being and the beauty of all things.

Sadly, rather than encounter the other as a gift, the modern world often puts a tag on, distorts, and objectifies the other. As Pope Francis bemoans, modern society "seeks to domesticate the mystery"—God, nature, people, and others.[20] In this kind of culture, there is a loss of beauty, and, instead, there is the instrumentalization of the other. People are no longer encountering the other as a gift. Everything is seen through a transactional exchange of products

---

[16] Francis, *Evangelii Gaudium*, apostolic exhortation, November 24, 2013, https://www.vatican.va/content/francesco/en/apost_exhortations/documents/papa-francesco_esortazione-ap_20131124_evangelii-gaudium.html, sec. 167.

[17] Francis, *Fratelli Tutti*, sec. 216.

[18] Francis, *Evangelii Gaudium*, sec. 170–71; Francis, *Laudato Si'*, sec. 238.

[19] Francis, *Laudato Si'*, sec. 96.

[20] Francis, *Gaudete et Exsultate*, apostolic exhortation, March 19, 2018, https://www.vatican.va/content/francesco/en/apost_exhortations/documents/papa-francesco_esortazione-ap_20180319_gaudete-et-exsultate.html, sec. 40.

and profits among faceless people, as consumers and functional mechanisms of process and systems of power, idols, and domination. However, there is another dynamic of encounter that opens our eyes to see our own naked humanity reflected in every instance of human precarity and vulnerability. The culture of encounter affords a good way for doing theology because it brings the theologian into the rough ground of lived faith and suffering of others. The theologian is forced to learn new languages, develop new ways of perception, and deepen one's view about who God is, and what it means to be human.

Pope Francis makes this culture of encounter more concrete by calling for an epistemological and methodological re-thinking in theological reflection, and for concrete encounters within the contexts of people at the frontiers in these words:

> Theological reflection is therefore called to a turning point, to a paradigm shift, to a "courageous cultural revolution" (Encyclical Letter *Laudato si'*, 114) that commits it, first and foremost, to be a fundamentally contextual theology, capable of reading and interpreting the Gospel in the conditions in which men and women daily live, in different geographical, social and cultural environments, and having as its archetype the Incarnation of the eternal Logos, its entering into the culture, worldview, and religious tradition of a people.[21]

This shift in method invites people to recognize the footprints of God in the rough ground of daily life and in personal and group history, especially in unfamiliar sites, and sites of suffering and pain. All people of faith are invited by Pope Francis to immerse themselves in concrete life contexts and become aware of, and be intimately in touch with, what is going on within them, and what is going on around them.

This invites theologians, for instance, to move away from a disembodied theology that grows from an uncritical quest for and defense of institutional claims and practices. Such a quest comes from efforts to preserve and protect an idealized sociological form of the *ekklesia* and its embodiment of an idealized notion of truth and culture. The shift being proposed here moves theological reflection away from the normativity of the Church's historically

---

[21] Francis, *Ad Theologiam Promovendam*, sec. 4.

conditioned Eurocentric traditions of thought, structures, beliefs, and ecclesial practices. It locates the heart of the Church not in Rome but at the frontiers. The heart of the truth of God, and of humans and the cosmos, is not received by the theologian or Christian teacher simply by memorizing and reproducing catechetical tracts and magisterial documents. Nor does it come from relying supinely on what Pope Francis refers to as "'tactical' attitude" that uses extrinsic approach to meeting the changing contexts of people's lives.[22] On the contrary, a theology of the streets and of the bush paths is one that must intentionally develop deep connection, attention, and recognition of God's footprints in the lived religious experience of the people of God. This requires intimate communication with people and an openness to the surprises of the Holy Spirit in the dumps of history and in diverse cultural processes.

Regarding the second direction in Catholic theology, Pope Francis has changed the spirit of doing theology in the Catholic academy through a greater freedom of the spirit. This has been promoted through his insistence that theology must be carried out in a synodal and communal way, and not simply by what the theologians gather from books, through what Francis calls "desktop theology."[23] In his speech to the Italian Theological Association, Pope Francis speaks of theology as "a free and responsible reflection"; theologians must be part of the missionary and pastoral work of the Church with sensitivity to a changed world and in "creative fidelity." In his address, the pope speaks of Catholic theology as being driven by "the perennial novelty of the Gospel," and in dialogue with the world and as a communal encounter which must be done together.[24] In this regard, *Veritatis Gaudium* encourages greater cooperation among theologians and institutions, to "cultivate" and build "suitable channels of co-operation" and bridges to deepen, diversify, and bring Catholic theology up to date. This new impulse can meet the challenges of social change, cultural pluralism, and pastoral care and accompaniment.[25]

---

[22] Francis, *Ad Theologiam Promovendam*, sec. 2.

[23] Francis, *Ad Theologiam Promovendam*, sec. 3.

[24] Francis, "Address of His Holiness Pope Francis to the Italian Theological Association," December 29, 2017, https://www.vatican.va/content/francesco/en/speeches/2017/december/documents/papa-francesco_20171229_associazione-teologica-italiana.html.

[25] Francis, *Veritatis Gaudium*, sec. 4d.

This stance invites Catholic theologians to courageous and creative reflection born of love. The insistence on doing theology not only on bended knees, but also as vocation to charity needs to be highlighted. Love of God, the Church, and the truth—on behalf of God's people, especially those who are hurting, suffering, poor, and are forgotten—should drive all theological studies, teaching, writing, and proclamation. This commitment to charity for all things is because they are from God, and through them we return all things to God. Otherwise, theology becomes an empty intellectual exercise without connection to the central movement of God's Spirit to fill the earth with divine favor through love.

In the recent past and even in our times, the fear of error in defending the Church's position was the beginning of wisdom for theologians. Pope Francis speaks differently about where wisdom is to be found, and how wisdom can be found:

> Jesus did this with his own disciples: he did not keep them under his wing like a hen with her chicks. He sent them out! We cannot keep ourselves shut up in parishes, in our communities, in our parish or diocesan institutions, when so many people are waiting for the Gospel! To go out as ones sent. It is not enough simply to open the door in welcome because they come, but we must go out through that door to seek and meet the people![26]

Commitment to freedom in research, and application of tools of sociocultural studies through ethnography, for instance, can lead to the production of new knowledge. *Ad Theologiam Promovendam* encourages this strongly when it invites theologians to expand the range of their knowledge to other disciplines and other sciences, including these two ways. First, through embracing theology as a web of relationships. The relational dimension of theology orients the theologian and theology from self-referentiality and a closed narrative, which might make theological formulations irrelevant and meaningless to the people of God, and the fruits of theology useless for pastoral ministry. Second, the web of relationship in doing theology invites theologians to carry

---

[26] Francis, "Homily of Pope Francis," XXVIII World Youth Day, July 27, 2013, https://www.vatican.va/content/francesco/en/homilies/2013/documents/papa-francesco_20130727_gmg-omelia-rio-clero.html.

out their task in dialogue with other sciences, as masters such as Augustine and Thomas did. What is being proposed here is an approach of transdisciplinarity, interdisciplinarity, and a new understanding of multidisciplinarity. According to Pope Francis, transdisciplinarity is

> "the placement and fermentation of all knowledge within the space of Light and Life offered by the Wisdom that emanates from God's Revelation" (Apostolic Constitution *Veritatis gaudium,* Proemio, 4c). Hence the arduous task for theology to be able to make use of new categories elaborated by other knowledge, in order to penetrate and communicate the truths of faith and transmit the teaching of Jesus in today's languages, with originality and critical awareness.[27]

Theologians need to work in an interdisciplinary manner and produce new knowledge beyond regurgitating what other people wrote or simply doing literature reviews. The tools for our research should not be taken only from theological studies. They can arise in dialogue with other sciences. We can gain insights that can help us embrace the entire reality of our people with openness of spirit and with courageous searching for new pathways for transformation. This is what Pope Francis means when he challenges Catholic theologians to produce transformative theologies which will come about not by

> applying rules or repeating what was done in the past, since the same solutions are not valid in all circumstances and what was useful in one context may not prove so in another. The discernment of spirits liberates us from rigidity, which has no place before the perennial "today" of the risen Lord. The Spirit alone can penetrate what is obscure and hidden in every situation, and grasp its every nuance, so that the newness of the Gospel can emerge in another light.[28]

This new spirit of freedom has made possible greater dialogue in the Catholic academy and between Catholic scholars and their colleagues from other faiths and non-faith traditions. At the beginning of the Synod on the Family in 2014, Pope Francis was quoted as saying, "Open and fraternal debate makes

---

[27] Francis, *Ad Theologiam Promovendam,* sec. 6.
[28] Francis, *Gaudete et Exsultate,* sec. 173.

theological and pastoral thought grow.... That doesn't frighten me. What's more, I look for it."[29] In an address to the Synod participants, Francis said, "You need to say all that you feel with parrhesia"—boldly, candidly and without fear—"and at the same time, you should listen with humility and accept with an open heart what your brothers say."[30] He invites all to be open-minded, because "we cannot dialogue with people if we already know all the answers to their problems."[31]

Since the publication of the decree *Pastor Aeternus* of the First Vatican Council in 1870, Catholic theology has been constructed along Scholastic metaphysical principles. In attempts to rightly guard the tradition from the harsh winds of secular culture, the Church has often become adversarial toward culture and history, and too self-confident and uncritical of its own enunciations. The new approach to Catholic theology moves away from a narrow understanding of Catholic intellectual tradition that is old, predictable, dry, manualistic, and lacking in dynamism. The kind of theology that emerges from creative freedom, according to Pope Francis, "helps all Christians to announce and to demonstrate, above all, the saving face of God, the merciful God, especially in the presence of some unprecedented challenges that involve humanity today: such as the ecological crisis; the development of neurosciences and techniques that may modify man; growing social inequalities or the migrations of entire peoples; both theoretical and practical relativism."[32]

For the third direction, Catholic theology should be at the frontier, that is, immersed in pastoral life as the laboratory of theology. Ad Theologiam

---

[29] Ferruccio de Bortoli, "Benedetto XVI non è una statua Partecipa alla vita della Chiesa," *Corriere della Sera*, March 5, 2014, https://www.corriere.it/cronache/14_marzo_04/vi-racconto-mio-primo-anno-papa-90f8a1c4-a3eb-11e3-b352-9ec6f8a-34ecc.shtml.

[30] Francis, "Greeting of Pope Francis to the Synod Fathers during the First General Congregation of the Third Extraordinary General Assembly of the Synod of Bishops," October 6, 2014, https://www.vatican.va/content/francesco/en/speeches/2014/october/documents/papa-francesco_20141006_padri-sinodali.html.

[31] Joshua J. McElwee, "Bishops Deliberate Whether One Rule Applies to All Divorced People after 'Amoris Laetitia,'" *National Catholic Reporter*, October 6, 2017, https://www.ncronline.org/news/bishops-deliberate-whether-one-rule-applies-all-divorced-people-after-amoris-laetitia.

[32] Francis, "Address of His Holiness Pope Francis to the Italian Theological Association."

Promovendam asserts strongly that theology must have "a pastoral stamp," so that the teaching of the faith and the beliefs, practices, and doctrines of the Church are brought down to solving the problems of people, satisfying their hunger for God, and embracing the ultimate moral demand for the transformation of the earth so that God's will may be done on earth as it is done in heaven.[33] All Catholic theologies must have a missionary and pastoral orientation.

Pope Francis proposes that theologians can develop reflective practices that "pour oil and wine onto the wounds of humanity"[34] because there is so much suffering in a post-COVID-19 world. Elsewhere, he gives this definition of theology: "Theology is an expression of a Church which is a 'field hospital' which lives her mission of salvation and healing in the world."[35] He rejects any form of reflection which is comfortable with settled answers, or afraid to meet headlong the big questions and new complexities of our times. In a speech cited earlier, he points out that theology should be done by "people immersed in the broadest theological community possible, of which they feel they are truly part, connected by bonds of solidarity and also of authentic friendship." These communal bonds attained through immersion in the concrete life situations of people will refer not simply to the Magisterium, Francis continues, but to "a sense of the reality of faith that belongs to all the people of God, even those who do not have particular intellectual means to express it, and who ask to be intercepted and listened to."[36]

New Directions in African Theology

African theologians and indeed all theologies must seek new answers to the new contexts and questions which the faith of God's people present to us today. Concurrently, we must appreciate the different tributaries of the vast

---

[33] Francis, *Ad Theologiam Promovendam*, sec. 8.

[34] Francis, *Ad Theologiam Promovendam*, sec. 3.

[35] Francis, "Letter of His Holiness Pope Francis to the Grand Chancellor of the 'Pontificia Universidad Católica Argentina' for the 100th Anniversary of the Founding of the Faculty of Theology," https://www.vatican.va/content/francesco/en/letters/2015/documents/papa-francesco_20150303_lettera-universita-cattolica-argentina.html.

[36] Francis, "Address of His Holiness Pope Francis to the Italian Theological Association."

ocean of God's mission, meeting in love, hope, and faith. This is the earth in which the Church exists. Every theology must be practical, which means that every theology must move from analysis or synthesis to practice and performance. A perennial challenge for Catholicism is that some Catholic theologies are often criticized for being impractical, remote, and abstract. Catholic theologies have always been a source of guidance and illumination for God's people. In our times, theological productions are no longer as decisive as they were in former times as valuable guides. This is not because the Magisterium necessarily ignores theological productions—though this is often the case—but rather because theologians are often not with the people of God, and many Christians do not see their portraits in some of the theologies that are being produced today, which are often driven by some of the contested issues in today's world rather than an encounter with the Word of God and the worlds of people.

In the past, theological enterprise was often proposed as a service to the Magisterium. Without the Magisterium, theologies are only good for the library, for the most part. But more can be done in the use of theological wisdom for magisterial action. On this, Pope Francis makes two important and revolutionary statements. First, theology is at the service of the whole people of God and not just the Magisterium. The Magisterium, along with theology, is presented as one of the many ways in which the Holy Spirit enriches the people of God. Both theology and the Magisterium are placed on the same level with the *sensus fidei fidelium* and charism of the prophets of the Church, and all are placed not above each other, or above the people of God, but as being on the same path of discernment, purification, and reform to meet the needs of the whole people of God. Elsewhere, Pope Francis states that those who are involved in ecclesiastical studies

> are called to be a sort of providential cultural laboratory in which the Church carries out the performative interpretation of the reality brought about by the Christ event and nourished by the gifts of wisdom and knowledge by which the Holy Spirit enriches the people of God in manifold ways—from the *sensus fidei fidelium* to the magisterium of bishops, and from the charism of the prophets to that of the doctors and theologians.[37]

---

[37] Francis, *Veritatis Gaudium*, sec. 3.

Theology is not a second-order act that happens outside of ecclesial life, and outside the context of faith and life. Theology is a means for action and thought,[38] which must simultaneously accompany social and cultural processes as the faith crosses spiritual and cultural frontiers. Pope Francis calls this new pathway for theology "a radical paradigm shift" and a "bold cultural revolution," because it forces theology not to be content with explication of the intelligibility of doctrines and dogmas. It must engage with the daily realities of people by showing the light and leaven of Christ in pastoral approaches that meet new situations with new ideas,[39] but it is also capable of seeing new events of revelation in history.[40]

Theology is being challenged to speak with courage, wisdom, and insight in the face of pressing social and moral complexities. This is quite different from the recent past, with the specter of theologians being branded as "dissenters," and a gulf created between these so-called dissenters and the faithful theologians. The Catholic academy became fragmented, and the Magisterium itself was in perpetual war with those theologians and cultural movements that did not fit into the presumed idyllic and predictable path that Providence opened for the Church. Many Catholic theologians who wanted a more transformational and creative theology receded into their own small worlds in theological retrenchment. Many others simply became the intellectual "rottweiler" in defending the official teaching and theologies of the Magisterium, which simply rejected or reacted to social issues with old answers to new problems.

Particularly in Africa, theologians must pay attention to the living and breathing faith of God's people in Africa, and their hopes, tears, and dreams. Theologians must listen to and respond to the cries of the poor and all those on the margins, and the painful wounds of creation and humanity. This openness is capable of inspiring diverse and creative theological productions. African theologians will be able to recognize, interpret, and engage the new revelations of the footprints of God in some of the inconvenient and uncommon sites

---

[38] Francis, *Veritatis Gaudium*, sec. 5.

[39] Francis, *Veritatis Gaudium*, sec. 3.

[40] Bridget Agnes Downing, "Karl Rahner's Pastoral Theology: A Study of Its Implications for the Christian in the Modern World" (PhD diss., Fordham University, 1986), *ETD Collection for Fordham University*, AAI862854, https://research.library.fordham.edu/dissertations/AAI8628541.

of human and cosmic alienation and suffering in Africa, and the rest of the world, especially since the time of the pandemic.

All theologies, like every experience of faith, must bring about a new reality and deeper understanding of the mysteries of faith. Authentic theologizing must end in a changed, healed, redeemed, converted, and transformed situation, and with a faith that is different from that of former times. Theological reflection grounded in the Word of life must follow the path of the Lord's ministry in bringing a genuine newness to the understanding and transformative living-out of the faith. The Gospel always brings a great reversal in the history of those who make an assent of faith, by bringing down the mighty, raising the lowly, and preferring the foolish and the weak to the wise and the strong. Theologies must help people to see how their present reality and past history are combining in the consummation of all things. This is to be concrete, with advance saving signs and irruption of the eschatological fruits of God's reign.

Theologians working with the people and in the Church are painters who can bring in different hues, both old and new, in differing contexts. Their art can show how humanity and the cosmos would look when God's will is enacted on earth as it is in heaven.

The task of the theologian is to show the footprints of God amid the earthly pilgrimages of God's people. A theologian is thus a follower of the footprints of God in history. He or she reads these footprints through attention to how God's will is revealed in the joys and sorrows of the people, and in their hopes and despairs. To do this, the theologian must have his or her feet on the ground. The theologian must be with God's people and hear their *sensus fidei* in their joys and sorrows, tears and lamentations, and hopes and dreams. The theologian must tell the stories of the daily realities of God's people, using these as the locus of enunciation. The theologian mediates these realities not only from individual accounts, but also through the communal events of meaning, memory, pathos, pain, and hope that emerge from the heart of the local communities of faith and the World Church. In a sense, the theologian points to God's presence in all things, and God's absence in those things which do not reveal or reflect God's will.

To do theology well, the theologian must be a faith-filled friend of God, with a nose for the fragrance of the divine in the stories of people's encounters with God, with nature, and with fellow humans as seen through the economy of grace. What this means concretely is that the theologian must be able to see and name God wherever God is found, interpret earthly realities in the light of divine revelation, and show the absence of God in those places where evil reigns. Theology is to be carried out through a vision of faith, and a faith immersed in history. However, the theologian who is able to see God's footprints in history must be constantly in touch with God by being immersed in the Word of God, and so having a deep relationship with God. The theologian must be grounded in the traditions and teachings of the Church and of his or her local contexts and cultures, so that his or her mind is shaped by an authentic embrace of the faith of the Church, our Mother, and of the truths of the Gospel. In the changing circumstances of life today, the task of the African theologian becomes even more urgent and cogent. She or he is called to make intelligible and visible God's presence in the often confusing and complex movement of the Spirit in history. He or she must prophetically denounce the absence of God, especially where God's name has been dragged as a cudgel or a prop or a defensive fortress to justify or legitimize human distortions of cultures, religions, or social life.

The task of the African theologian today is not easy, nor a populist undertaking. Authentic theology is not often popular or mainstream on first appearance, as was evident in the works of Augustine and Thomas Aquinas. The theologian must be patient and embrace his or her task as a thankless sacrifice, particularly in the short run. Sometimes, the theologian might offer reflections that strengthen the community in belief and morals; but sometimes theology might rouse the faithful from slumber or challenge their assumptions. At other times it might "talk back to" or "talk up to" power, all of which might bring about suspicion, affirmation, or neutral response.[41] However, when one recognizes that theology is dealing with faith and the things of God, especially through anthropological and historical perspective, then one must be open to accepting that theologies will be marked by human temporality, limitations, and finality. Revelation is always received in weak and fragile human and historical vessels. Our human sight is often limited, which is why theology must be done on bended knees, and with broken hearts. We need openness to listen not only to ourselves, but to others who do not agree with us, to those who do not believe what we believe within our own faith traditions, to those

---

[41] Linda Tuhiwai Smith, *Decolonizing Methodologies: Research and Indigenous Peoples*, 2nd ed. (London: Zed, 2012), 226.

outside our faith traditions, and to people who have no faith at all. Theology should meet the people where they are. Theologians of the African continent must pay attention to our people's context as their locus of enunciation.

The Context of African Theology

Three particular realities strike any scholar or student of African theology, whether the person is a beginner or a veteran in the field.

The first reality is that as with all branches of learning in the African academy, theology is carried on in conversation with, or in relation to, or as a response or reaction to, or under the inspiration of, voices and traditions outside Africa. Niche issues mainly from contexts outside Africa seem to dominate African Christian academy these days, such as same-sex marriage, clerical sexual abuse, and women's rights. I am not saying that Africa should not be part of global conversations, nor am I proposing that the churches of Africa and the faithful are unaffected by these issues. However, these issues are largely framed by African theologians and Church leaders in the binaries of liberal and progressive camps. This is done without engaging the ideological and cultural presuppositions at the roots of this discourse in the West, and the culture of silence about some of these issues in Africa. Often these issues drown African voices and distract the African Church's pastoral agents and theologians from confronting these and other issues facing everyday Africans with clear-sightedness, contextuality, transparency, and courage.

It is disappointing that most of the issues facing African peoples today are often ignored by theologians of Africa, or simply scratched on the surface. African theologians and Church leaders often use the "cultural wars" in Europe and America as a template for either "guarding Africa" from being contaminated by these supposedly negative forces, or reinforcing traditional doctrinal teachings and liturgies to "fortify" Africa against succumbing to these externalities. This leads to a universalization of the concern about the effect of the contested moral issues, as if they manifest themselves in the same way in Africa as they do in the West. The way these issues are formulated, problematized, and discussed globally and locally do not help the conversations needed in Africa. This is true for Western theological issues and instructions from the Vatican's dicasteries for education, evangelization, and doctrine of the faith (for example the document, *Fiducia Supplicans*). The problems and challenges are understood and presented in a context far removed from the experience of many African Christians. As a result, in addressing the contested moral issues in today's Church—which often divide African theologians, Church leaders, and laity between the liberal and conservative camps—the immediate problems are missed that face our people, their faith, and their social conditions. If African theologians must engage in these theological battles, and if they must be consumed by them, it should be because they arise from the context of African Christians and not as a reaction to what is happening elsewhere while neglecting what is happening on our continent.

Eric Hobsbawm concludes in his book, *The Age of Extremes*, that what happens in Africa is only an empty mimicry of what has really significantly happened elsewhere.[42] In a similar vein, Adrian Hastings claims that African theology has amounted to an attempt to interpret African religious tradition within the structures of Western theological thought.[43] Ogbu Kalu presents both scholars' views of African theology as emerging from a racist superiority mindset which privileges Western epistemological priority as mainstream learning and the acme of intellectual orthodoxy.[44] However, a sociological analysis of the theological terrain in the African academy at the time of Hastings going back to the 1950s and up to our time shows that most of our theologies in Africa are the result of conversations started outside Africa, or of directives or permission given from Rome. One example is *Des prêtres noirs s'interrogent*, which was written by priests studying in Europe.[45] Most of African theologies—

---

[42] Eric Hobsbawm, quoted in Ogbu Kalu, *Power, Poverty and Prayer: The Challenges of Poverty and Pluralism in African Christianity, 1960–1996* (Trenton, NJ: Africa World Press, 2006), xvi.

[43] Adrian Hastings, *African Christianity: An Essay in Interpretation* (London: Geoffrey Chapman, 1976). See also Bénézet Bujo's account of the debate in the 1960s in East Africa over the universality of truth advanced by Belgian theologian and philosopher Alfred Vanneste, who had proposed that African theologians should show how African thought and symbols within religion, philosophy, and theology can fit into universal notions of objective truth: Bénézet Bujo, "Introduction to the Tshibangu-Vanneste Debate," in *African Theology: The Contribution of the Pioneers*, ed. Bénézet Bujo and Juvenal Ilunga, vol. 1 (Nairobi: Paulines Publications Africa, 2003), 180–82.

[44] Ogbu Kalu, *Power, Poverty and Prayer: The Challenges of Poverty and Pluralism in African Christianity, 1960–1996* (Trenton, NJ: Africa World, 2006), xvi.

[45] Léonard Santedi Kinkupu, Gérard Bissainthe, and Meinrad Hebga, *Des prêtres noirs s'interrogent: Cinquante ans après* (Paris: Karthala, 2006).

particularly doctoral works—are still written under the influence or direction of Western theologians and philosophers at European and North American universities. These are often defined by such traditions that have provenance in the West, particularly regarding method and the art or craft of doing theology. Some of the important voices and schools prominent in African theological works include neo-Scholasticism, transcendental Thomism, phenomenology (especially Maurice Blondel, Edmund Husserl, and Karl Rahner), Bernard Lonergan, John Henry Newman, Paul Tillich, Clifford Geertz, Wolfhart Pannenberg, Stanley Hauerwas, Karl Barth, and Jacques Dupuis. While expertise in the works of these giants is important and useful, it is necessary that African theologians recognize the limits of such methods and approaches.

I study the Christian religion in Africa as a many-layered tapestry of how African history and the so-called African predicament have been shaped by the kind of intellectual traditions struggling for freedom from captivity to Northern epistemological hegemony. This hegemony involves three aspects, among many others. First is the *mainstreaming of ideas and forms of thinking and acting* through occidental thought and thinkers, particularly Greek philosophy. This has shaped the Western Christian thought, practice, and theodicy that we as Africans have embraced, which came with the arrival of Western Christianity in Africa, along with the notions of modernity. Second is the *dualism of thought carried on through this form of knowing*, which always presents reality in oppositional form—black and white, liberal and conservative, heaven and hell, saints and sinners, good and evil, traditionalist and progressive, realist and idealist. Third is the *false search for unity of human knowledge*, which goes back to Plato's attempt to find the origin of all knowledge in the demiurge. Thus, the attempt to see all things as united and all knowledge as one (the perennial default to the universals has been the greatest obstacle to finding and appreciating new forms of knowing), suppressed thoughts and worldviews, new epistemologies, local knowledge, and the needed quest to stretch human knowing and thinking to roads less traveled. Whenever one hears of mainstream ideas, standard practices, educational models, research methods, a distinctive Catholic identity, and unchanging truths, among others, we must realize that these are not disinterested claims. A confluence of cultural and historical factors as well as power dynamics affects the claims people make. Although it is important for us as African Christians to embrace the truths of the Christian faith, it is also important for us to make those truths our own. We must bring our own truths and reality into dialogue with these truth claims. We can then claim ownership of them as something that is birthed and rooted in Africa as a type of truth that has an analogical relationship with the truths of faith as held within the common traits of our Christian family.

Knowledge is power, and those who hold the keys of knowledge hold the keys to the future. The source of wisdom is God, who through God's Son and in many other varied ways has made it possible for truth to be known by us created human beings. However, the battle for the truth and the right faith and right conduct has continued in a polarized church today. Particularly in the Church, this battle has often made it impossible for a deeper encounter with God because contextual cultural appropriation of some moral or doctrinal truths is sometimes presented in an absolute way. We have identified in the introduction the many instances where cultures outside of Africa, like the Western missionaries, imposed their own versions of a Western God or truth or ecclesiology on Africa. This is not simply something that happened in the past; it is something still happening today through the curricula and accreditation of courses in ecclesiastical studies in Africa. The sad thing is that this time it is Africa's own theologians, scholars, Church leaders, and everyday faithful who want a restorationist Church and a synchronic theology and unitary pastoral practice in Africa. African Christians are imposing on themselves an alienating image, practice, and intellectual and ecclesial tradition, which for the most part remain exotic and discombobulating. However, we as Africans must note that if we are thinking other people's thoughts, parroting other people's funds of knowledge, and believing through other people's ways of believing, we will be enslaved spiritually along the historical trajectory defined by other people. We are consuming other people's ways of constructing meaning and enacting praxis and theology, and we will remain with only imitation and inauthenticity.

I do not reject the benefits of Western thought or any thought from other sources outside of Africa. I am drawing attention to knowledge being the domain of power. Those who hold higher power often use their fund of knowledge to control how and what historically dominated peoples and minorities think about themselves, God, and human and cultural development, and how they live, act, and work. Africans cannot understand their present situation without paying attention to the dialectic of knowledge consumption and knowledge production, and how the surplus of the former leads to the deficit of the latter. This has consequences in the Church in Africa and wider African society. We need to reject the thinking in some quarters in African studies, politics, and religions that postcolonial studies and decolonization are passé because Africans and Blacks throughout the world can now move on to the future by constructing the praxis for their future since they have their destinies in their own hands. This is one of the generalized deceptive notions and assumptions which must be rejected because, as Linda Smith argues:

> Research is one of the ways in which the underlying code of imperialism and colonialism is both regulated and realized. It is regulated through the formal rules of individual scholarly disciplines and scientific paradigms, and the institutions that support them. It is realized in the myriad of representations and ideological constructions of the Other in scholarly and "popular" works, and in the principles, which help to select and recontextualize those constructions in such things as the media, official histories, and school curriculum.[46]

Nothing is fundamentally wrong with borrowing from or using the conceptual framework or method from a different zone of meaning and applying it to another context. We live in an intercultural world, and there is no limitation as to how cultures, values, systems, practices, and worldviews are permeating each other from one part of the world to another. However, methods are often defined by worldviews and conceptual frameworks. They also give birth to theoretical structures and are like road maps that lead to looking for certain kinds of data, and certain interests, and to a kind of conclusion that may not have been reached with a different map. As African theologians, we cannot deny that such borrowings affect our theories and concepts, the nature of the data we seek, our analyses of those data, and our conclusions. Ultimately, they affect the kind of theologies we do, the kinds of tasks we pursue through our theology, and the kinds of pastoral recommendations we establish.

This tension between what we received, and what we need to generate or discover from our own contexts, is important. If African theologians are to embrace the theological education, research, and knowledge production needed to bring to birth a vital Church in Africa and a faith that enables good works by our faithful, it is necessary to identify clearly our point of entry, the stories that we are to follow, and the theological battles and projects that we need to engage. If African theologians have not become influential

---

[46] Smith, *Decolonizing Methodologies*, 8.

in shaping the agenda of the Church in Africa and its pastoral priorities and practices, it is because most of our theologies are made in the West, are of the West, and are for the West. We need a made-in-Africa theology for African peoples in the continent and in the diaspora. When I interact with Western theologians and students of theology in Europe or North America, I am surprised that they know more about what I have written or the works of Emmanuel Katongole, Bénézet Bujo, Charles Nyamiti, John Mbiti, Mercy Amba Oduyoye, Elochukwu Uzukwu, Paulinus Odozor, and Teresa Okure than African theologians and students in Africa.

We must therefore raise questions about our locus of enunciation. Whose voices am I representing in my theology? What is the ground on which I am standing? We may not agree on the answers to these questions, but I aver that the viewpoint of the theologian in Africa is characterized by a theological metaxy of the in-between. This means the complex of being caught up between holding in balance an idealized notion of an unmediated and ahistorical Catholic culture, Catholic ecclesiology, or Catholic theology, and a fidelity to the real and concrete questions emerging from the field of faith in Africa, that is, the actual faith of our people. Added to this are the external limitations imposed on our theological sight of the footprints of God in our religious, cultural, and social history. Seeing the infinite horizons of God in an expanded field of view allows us to comprehend the richness and diversity of our religious and cultural contexts, amid our social conditions. An appreciation of cultural diversity and cultural hermeneutics helps address these limitations.

It is urgent and important to interrogate the theological methods employed in doing theology in Africa, and their adequacy for engaging the hidden cultural grammar that is driving the momentum of Christian expansion in Africa. African theology needs to constantly evolve new navigational equipment for charting the complex contours of the ever-emerging pathways—pastoral, cultural, economic, etc.—of religious and ecclesial life in our land. The tools that are presently used for theological and ecclesiastical studies in Africa are no longer adequate for meeting the changing and complex problems and opportunities facing the faith and the wider society, particularly in addressing the social contagion of suffering that characterizes the so-called African predicament. But in seeking and developing these new tools, African theologians must guard against narrowness of mind, which limits theological reflection to one method or approach. Africa's vast and exciting Christian life cannot be contained in a single theological method, hence the need to embrace a hermeneutic of multiplicity and be open to receiving insights and resources for theology from other disciplines and faith traditions.

The third reality for those doing theology in Africa is that at this time in African Christian history, what is needed is more an analytic theology than a synthetic one. African theologians need to analyze, interpret, and understand what is moving forward in history in Africa, to make sense of it before judging how to bring these realities together. This will require focusing on how the Christian religion can play an important role in following this story and shepherding and accompanying this momentum toward the realization of the eschatological fruits of God's kingdom.

Today's African theology is too preoccupied with a synthetic theological search, and the search for a unitary method. This occurs in four ways: (1) an attempt to bring together theological traditions and sometimes incommensurate worldviews without paying attention to how dominant Northern epistemological privilege has framed African tradition; (2) a failure to distinguish between traditions in African Christianity and African cultures and tradition, or treating the categories one employs from other zones of meaning as if they have the same meaning in that context (e.g., Western culture) when employed in African theology, or in the African pastoral context; (3) a failure to be sufficiently self-critical, thus idealizing all things African and failing to acknowledge our own entanglements with the systems and institutions that oppress our people, even within the churches because of the privileged position of many African theologians in the scheme of things; (4) an uncritical assumption of the purity or homogeneity of these theological traditions, or treating them as revelations and thus making African reality and meanings which one discovers subservient to exotic manualist theological methods.

African Christians inherited a theology in Africa that was born in the early twentieth-century battle between integralist and *ressourcement* theologians in the heat of ultramontanism. This was characterized at the time by the rejection of cultural and theological pluralism by the pre–Vatican II Church. The structure of the theological academy in Africa from its origin was constructed to foreclose theological diversity. It was constructed without taking into consideration the findings of historical sociology about the contextual nature of knowledge or the dominant colonial narratives of the so-called natives, which is also present in Christendom's denigration of the non-Western cultural "other." It was also carried on through the enforcement of Thomism as a transcultural theological project for the Catholic Church, and an ahistorical Catholic ecclesiology especially prevalent from the Council of Trent to the Second Vatican Council. This continued in the post–Vatican II Church through many policies, programs, and magisterial teachings.[47]

African theologians need to analyze more and synthesize less. Such synthesis, which should be treated with suspicion in Africa theology, is the attempt to assume a homological meaning to every term in theology in Africa—God, human nature, African culture, African religion, and so on. Further, this synthesis involves a constant effort to answer every question with pre-packaged answers, and especially answers from manualist or baroque theological traditions; and it employs only answers to problems of some other people in some other place, and developed elsewhere. As well, this synthesis leads to the rejection of theological and pastoral pluralism in our parishes, dioceses, and seminaries, even in matters as simple as the menu for the day, or in complex questions about inculturation of the Gospel and the Church, or the curriculum in the African Catholic academy, or the structure of authority.

When I speak of an analytic approach, I am not simply translating analytic philosophy into theology. I mean immersing oneself into the stories from

---

[47] See Joseph Ratzinger, "Christ, Faith and the Challenge of Cultures," Address to the Presidents of the Asian Bishops' Conference (Hong Kong, March 2–5 1993), https://www.vatican.va/roman_curia/congregations/cfaith/incontri/rc_con_cfaith_19930303_hong-kong-ratzinger_en.htmlm sec. 2: "Whoever joins the Church must be aware that he is entering a cultural subject with its own historically developed and multi-tiered inter-culturality. One cannot become a Christian apart from a certain exodus, a break from one's previous life in all its aspects. Faith is not a private way to God; it leads into the People of God and its history. God bound himself to a history which is now also his and one which we cannot cast off. Christ remains man in eternity, he conserves his body in eternity." See also John Paul II, *Fides et Ratio*, encyclical letter, September 14, 1998, https://www.vatican.va/content/john-paul-ii/en/encyclicals/documents/hf_jp-ii_enc_14091998_fides-et-ratio.html, sec. 72: "In engaging great cultures for the first time, the Church cannot abandon what she has gained from her inculturation in the world of Greco-Latin thought. To reject this heritage would be to deny the providential plan of God who guides his Church down the paths of time and history. This criterion is valid for the Church in every age, even for the Church of the future, who will judge herself enriched by all that comes from today's engagement with Eastern cultures and will find in this inheritance fresh cues for fruitful dialogue with the cultures which will emerge as humanity moves into the future."

the daily experience of faith and culture in Africa today. These stories are the data to be analyzed, interpreted, and understood. These stories contain many layers of reality, which need to be excavated and reverenced, as will be discussed in chapters 2, 3, and 4. These stories contain many traditions—biblical, missionary, colonial, racial, ethnic, wars, of hopes, and of dreams, among others—which cry for our attention. Some of these stories are hidden, distorted, and forgotten, and need to be dissected so as to see how they work with or against the flourishing of individuals, communities, churches, and nations, as well as to how they are helping or hurting the resilience needed for people to move from one level of life to another. Following the stories of our people in their richness and diversity requires me as an African theologian to tell that story in the light of salvation history toward the realization of the fruits of the eschatological reign of God. I must show how these stories work together in moving our people closer or farther away from human and cosmic flourishing—abundant life in Christ. This invites the African theologian to greater historical consciousness and to the decolonization of the lingering coloniality of theological imagination in Africa.

Another important argument here is that historical and critical cultural consciousness must be the tool through which we read the Christian traditions in African theology. This is not the endorsement of a homogenizing identity politics, but rather an invitation to a more sophisticated understanding of who we are as Africans, how who-we-are is constantly changing, and how we are affected by the forces of global and local histories. Being aware of these changes without hiding behind a narrow wall of self and group affirmation or some sort of Leibnizian monad (without doors and windows in other worlds of experience) means making a conscious attempt to understand the developing meaning in the stories of faith and life. This invites theologians of Africa to critical and imaginative work. In doing this they demonstrate, as Lonergan proposes, why the message of the Gospel preached more than two thousand years ago by the poor man of Galilee can still be relevant to the context of Africa today and into the future. The stories of God's great deeds in Africa can become a new expression of the Acts of the Apostles, which can help illuminate and expand the range of meaning about the same faith once received by the saints.[48] Such a transition can help the African theologian, for

---

[48] Joseph Putti, *Theology as Hermeneutics: Paul Ricoeur's Theory of Text Interpretation and Method in Theology* (San Francisco: International Scholars, 1994), 54.

instance, to move from one universe of discourse to another, from one stage or level of human culture to another, and from universalist and synthetic thinking to a more focused and direct engagement with the experiences of our people.[49]

African Theology as Missional Theology

What then do I mean by African theology?[50] African theology is understood here as a critical and creative reflection on faith and history and its meaning, implications, and relevance to the deepest hunger and concerns of Africans in their belief in God revealed in the different phases of African history, past and present. African theologies are diverse narratives that emerge from different parts of Africa and beyond. They focus on seeing and naming the footprints of God in the African soil; they reflect critically on the persistence of suffering in African history vis-à-vis the resilient faith and hope of Africans on the possibility of a better future. Every attempt that is made to reflect on the Christian faith in Africa that shows the presence or absence of God in the history and context of our people in their struggle for life and their resistance to the forces of evil and death that harm human and cosmic flourishing is an effort at doing African theology. Such an account pays particular attention to the stories of the people and their daily encounters with the Lord Jesus as the source of abundant life and their embrace of the Gospel message, and how these encounters driven by their faith in God are shaping the cultures and context of Africans and the societies in which they live.

Viewed in this light, African theology is a critical mirror through which the people of God can see their own faces, their faith journey, and their future. It is also in the same dynamic a mirror that refracts to Africans the many faces of God as revealed through God's Son and in the faces of our African ancestors and in the faces of the poor of the land. Because of this location and rootedness in history—past, present, and future—African theologies are decolonizing theologies and rooted in liberation historiography. It is a

---

[49] Putti, *Theology as Hermeneutics*, 97.

[50] When I use the term "African theology" in the singular I am referring to the sum of cognate theological activities (formal, informal, vernacular, folk, academic, etc.) that are African in content and nature, and with specific African interest and concerns. When I use "African theologies" in the plural I am referring to the manifestations of these theological activities in specific and particular contexts, discourses, and performances.

memorial theology that must be constructed from the tombs of our ancestors and the ashes of our mothers which in a unique way watered the path for us through their blood and struggles. African theology today, in this light, must be constructed and reconstructed every day through attention to the footprints of God in the complex, challenging, exciting, and new pathways of history in Africa. It must be an account of how God is present in our midst, attentive to our joys and sorrows, hopes and dreams, and actively working in our history through the agency of faith and the daily efforts of Africans in doing something new and life-giving to reverse the broken and fragmented history of our people. Because the experience of God's people today and since the Western intrusion into the African space has been saturated with neuralgic narratives of suffering and smiling, African theology is constructed today as a theology of suffering and smiling. If theology is a reflection on the mission of God in history and locating God in history, suffering and smiling describe the location of God's mission and presence in Africa today. The narratives of the mission of God in the suffering and smiling of Africans today constitute the task of doing theology in Africa.

In the light of the foregoing, I argue that African theologies are African missional theologies. This is because at this time in African Christian history, theological reflections in Africa deal with the proclamation of the Gospel and the formation of Christian identity as the Christian faith crosses different cultural and social frontiers. The theology of mission, as Stephen Bevans argues, has for the most part concentrated on "the historical developments of the church or how missionaries should proceed in their boundary-crossing work, not on the missionary nature of the church itself."[51] In this sense, emphasis was placed on history, anthropology, and the social sciences, while the identity of the church and the theology of church developed separately. The missionary nature of the Church in Africa is often understood in the sense of what the missionaries accomplished in Africa. Often everyday African Christians speak of the Church in Africa as a post-missionary Church. But as Bevans rightly points out, the mission is about "healing, liberation, and wholeness that emerges fully as individuals and communities live in relation to Jesus Christ and his gospel."[52] It is about how the Spirit is moving the faithful to cross boundaries and to transform lives and the world through the Gospel and the love of God.

---

[51] Stephen B. Bevans, *Community of Missionary Disciples: The Continuing Creation of the Church* (Maryknoll, NY: Orbis Books, 2024), 6.

[52] Bevans, *Community of Missionary Disciples*, 6.

In this regard, the mission of God in African history, how the Gospel is being received and translated into the suffering and smiles of people in Africa and how to discern God's presence and absence in the church and the witnesses of those who profess the faith in Africa becomes decisive for theology. Nothing is fully and definitively fixed in the formation of Christian consciousness in Africa. Thus, the shape, texture, identity, and structures that emerge because of the presence of Christian communities in Africa continue to evolve in conversation with the experience of joys and sorrows among God's people in Africa. African theologies are dealing with the question of the presence of God in African human and cultural history, and the place and fate of Africans in their growing encounters with God through the strong growth in African Christianity. Africans are doing theology from the margins, and at the edge of reality. This requires an expanded view of where God is at work in society, and the relevance of this human-divine dialogue in the exercise of human freedom. A cooperative response is required at the cultural level for the realization of the mission of God in African and world history.

Theological projects in Africa thus must deal with many realities and issues specific to Africa. These might appear irrelevant to other cultural contexts. Such issues include interfaith dialogue, ancestral traditions and curses, funeral rites, the meaning of family life, social and political activism, healing, the search for prosperity to escape from poverty, equity and diversity, ethnic identity issues, national politics, poverty eradication, gender rights, and the rights of minorities. These point to where faith and culture intersect in the daily experience of the people who flock to churches in Africa. At the heart of any theological method in Africa will be how history unfolds, how African history has moved to this point, the place of faith in reversing the painful history of Africa, and conforming Africa to God's plan of abundant life understood as human and cosmic flourishing.

This kind of theology faces four tasks among many others: (1) the challenge of showing within particular and universal history, past and present history through biblical and cultural analysis the presence, texture, and characteristics of the kingdom of God, which the Lord Jesus came to establish on earth; (2) how to locate particular and universal contexts of faith and non-faith within this understanding of the kingdom of God. Thus, African theology will be critical, constructive and creative. Critically, it shows the sins and evils, and the limitations of cultures that are anti-God's kingdom in societies. It also brings a prophetic judgment on social and political systems within any society; creatively, it will show how the transformative grace of God can operate in human societies and in human hearts to remove these evils; and constructively transform cultures and individuals from within, so that societies and individuals will rise to their dignity and play a decisive part in the emergence of God's kingdom. (3) It is concerned with what goes on in the lives of individuals who have embraced the faith as well as those who are outside the faith community who are still within the compass of divine love and divine purposes. Transformational praxis is concerned with both the mission of God and the human response to this divine initiative. God's love and initiative invite us to come out from exile into the light of divine love for transformation. Thus, such a theology will be concerned with the condition of the human in the face of the irruption of the divine. (4) It will be concerned with steps toward bringing about change and conversion in the community through the attunement of hearts and cultures to the divine purpose revealed in the words and deeds of Christ, and that of the early Christian communities, as well as the sterling witnesses of the Christian faith in persons and cultures across the centuries. The realization of the divine initiatives can only come about through the cooperation of human beings and cultures, which in the light of the Incarnation are already being made ready by the Holy Spirit to make this response.

From the foregoing, it is obvious that there is no African missional theology today that will *not first* show how the Gospel has become Good News indeed to Africans in their present challenging social context of *suffering and smiling*. Second, African missional theology today will not fit into any apodictic theological system. It will be a different theology because the Christian mission field in Africa offers a unique challenge, and African Christianity and cultures are in many cases misunderstood, unexplored and unknown. Third, African theologians who integrate a historical and decolonial approach to their theologies will achieve better success in pastoral appropriation because their theologies will be drawn from, be informed by, and lead back to the living condition of the people and their dynamic Christian consciousness. Fourth, a missional theology will undertake cultural hermeneutics as an important approach to seeing what God is doing in Africa. This way, it will help to give an account of the often fragmented and rudimentary narrative of African history, cultures, and traditions and engage them on their own terms. Missional cultural hermeneutics is concerned with how the reign of God is emerging in the lived religious faith of Africans and in their faith communities; and how the fruits of the reign of God are being reaped in Africa in the exponential growth of the Christian population in Africa. It is also concerned with making concrete Gospel-driven proposals for the transformation of Africa.

The role of theology in Africa is conceived in this sense as accountability in terms of how a regenerative ethics of communion, participation, mutuality, and friendship has become active and dynamic as a missionary thrust in the different settings of the Church and in the public square. Theologians of Africa must answer the question: How has Africa used the gifts of the Christian faith to bring about in Africa and beyond signs of the kingdom of God? Accountability here will also relate essentially to the fundamentals of the Christian message (the Trinity, the identity of the Church and Christian identity, revelation and the sources of revelation, the sacramental economy, human nature and destiny, and morality). It will also be concerned with how the dynamic nature of African religious consciousness is appropriating these core elements for the enrichment of the witness of African Christians to the Gospel in the concrete lives of their societies amid the diversity of a global Christianity. Fifth, African mission theology will be an open structure embracing in its articulation those diverse faith experiences (visions, pneumatic experiences, witchcraft, sorcery, ancestral curse, etc.) which might seem strange to non-Africans, but which are decisive for the faith of many Africans. Indeed, it must be admitted that the search for the data for doing theology in Africa will demand an expanded understanding of the meaning of revelation. The search will also deal with the mediation of the divine amid the challenging social context in which African Christianity is practiced today.[53]

African Theology as an Account of the Lived Faith of God's African People

My theological proposal of leaning on the lived faith, context, and practices of ordinary Christians in Africa is inspired by two important developments in theology that I embrace, namely, lived theology and intercultural hermeneutics, both of which help to show the footprints of God in the lived religious experience of God's people.

---

[53] See Mabiala Justin-Robert Kenzo, "Thinking Otherwise about Africa: Postcolonialism, Postmodernism, and the Future of African Theology," *Exchange* 31 (2002): 323–41.

According to Charles Marsh, lived theology begins with asking some fundamental questions:

> How might theological writing, research, and teaching be expanded or reimagined so as to engage lived experience with maximum care and precision? How might the discipline of theology, in its method, style, and pedagogy, appear anew if narrated accounts of faith-formed lives were appropriated as essential building blocks of theological knowledge?[54]

Lived theology is not simply the construction of a scattered patchwork of the social reality of people informed by their faith commitments. It is rather a method and style of theology that proposes that in order to explain who God is or where to find God with unflinching honesty, one must "tell the truth about lived faith."[55] Lived theology shows that "the pattern and practices of social existence" are portraits of faithful Christian living that offer the pathway for understanding the intelligibility of faith in theological discourse. It is a way of showing that the narratives of a "lived life" (cf. Jürgen Moltmann)[56] of the Christian is also God-talk, because it reveals the footprints of God in how the human and the divine interact in the unfolding of history.[57]

What Marsh calls the "particularities of experience," and which furnish the data for lived faith, is what Karl Rahner refers to as "actual faith." Rahner first drew attention to this problem in Catholic systematic theology when he observed that there is often a gap between what the Church officially believes and what everyday Christians believe. The ever-present subjective condition for assent to the official faith may not fully embrace the official faith. According

---

[54] Charles Marsh, "Introduction: Lived Theology: Method, Style, and Pedagogy," in *Lived Theology: New Perspectives on Method, Style, and Pedagogy*, ed. Charles Marsh, Peter Slade, and Sarah Azaransky (Oxford: Oxford University Press, 2017), 6.

[55] Knut Tveitereid, "Lived Theology and Theology in the Lived," in *The Wiley Blackwell Companion to Theology and Qualitative Research*, 1st ed., ed. Peter Ward and Knut Tveitereid (New York: John Wiley & Sons, 2022), 69.

[56] Jürgen Moltmann, *The Spirit of Life: A Universal Affirmation*, trans. Margaret Kohl (Minneapolis, MN: Fortress, 2001), 183.

[57] Charles Marsh, Peter Slade, and Sarah Azaransky, eds., *Lived Theology: New Perspectives on Method, Style, and Pedagogy* (Oxford: Oxford University Press, 2017), 10–11.

to Rahner, "If we consider the material content of the faith, nobody can deny that there exists a considerable difference between that which is explicitly and officially taught as part of the content of the faith and that which the average Christian in the Church knows about the faith and believes. Most Christians believe explicitly much less than what is explicitly present in the doctrine of the Magisterium."[58]

The actual faith of the people may not always be congruent with the official faith; as well, the official faith might many times be at variance with the actual faith, or not fully intelligible to the faithful. I am not sure how many of the faithful in my village can give you a treatise on the Trinity or on *theotokos*, but they do believe in the Trinity and have images and symbols that they might use of to make this explicit in their beliefs and practices. This is the site of actual faith or lived faith and creates a challenge in many cases in terms of the normativity of what is presented in official teaching and the actuality of what the people believe and live. This is particularly true in missionary-founded churches in Africa, where this gulf between what the churches teach and profess and what the ordinary people in the pews believe and live is sometimes based on the differentiation in terms of the language, worldview, concepts, and categories used to communicate this teaching. Thus, one observes that the official faith and doctrinal issues in churches in Africa may not be as normative as the primordial reception identified in the actual faith of African Christians. Knut Tveitereid emphasizes that lived theology searches for meaning in the "experience and expression" of people's everyday faith. Accordingly, "finding meaning, negotiating meaning, creating meaning are at the very heart of lived theologizing. I see lived theology as the attempt to make everyday life theologically meaningful—or to flip the phrase—to make theology meaningful in everyday life."[59]

African theologies, by focusing on the lived experience of Africans of suffering and smiling, seek to find the presence or absence of God in the actual faith of the people. The actual faith might not fit into the canon of orthodoxy of the received faith, but it fully displays how African Christians are

---

[58] Karl Rahner, "Karl Rahner: What the Church Officially Teaches and What the People Actually Believe—1981," in *Readings in Church Authority: Gifts and Challenges for Contemporary Catholicism*, ed. Gerard Manion, Richard Gaillardetz, Jan Kerkhofs, and Kenneth Wilson (Aldershot, England: Ashgate, 2003), 305.

[59] Tveitereid, "Lived Theology and Theology in the Lived," 70.

making meaning through their faith expressions and finding meaning through their faith experiences. This needed commitment to immersion in the lived experiences of our people in a nonjudgmental way involves a greater dedication to history in African theology. I emphasize this dimension of listening to the story of our people in the concrete questions of the poor, the uneducated, women, the laity. So also of the struggling clerics and religious, and of the corrupt or wounded politicians. So also of our young people, who are fleeing from our continent, or whose only community is the virtual universe that offers them a false sense of communal bond and hope.[60]

Henry Okullu sees need to expand the range of theological sources in Africa:

> When we are looking for African theology we should go first to the fields, to the village church, to Christian homes to listen to those spontaneously uttered prayers before people go to bed. We should go to the schools, to the frontiers where traditional religions meet with Christianity. We must listen to the throbbing drumbeats and the clapping of hands accompanying the impromptu singing in the independent churches. Everywhere in Africa things are happening. Christians are talking, singing, preaching, writing, arguing, discussing. Can it be that this is an empty show? It is impossible. This then is African theology.[61]

Actual faith among African Christians manifests itself in many ways: in their deep affinity to God, in church devotions, in social action, in shared ecumenical prayers, and in a solidarity with one another, which they may not fully articulate in any adequate or academic theological language. Actual faith in African Christianity and particularly in Catholicism is much more than instances of popular piety like Marian devotions, novenas, spiritual sodalities, Charismatic prayer meetings, healing sessions, exorcisms, and perpetual adoration, among others. The actual faith in African Catholicism refers to a

---

[60] See Albert Nolan, *Hope in an Age of Despair*, ed. Stan Muyebe (Maryknoll, NY: Orbis Books, 2010), 19.

[61] Henry Okullu quoted in Tinyinko Maluleke, "The Rediscovery of the Agency of Africans: An Emerging Paradigm of Post–Cold War and Post-Apartheid Black and African Theology," *Journal of Theology for Southern Africa* 108 (November 2000): 411–12.

cultural grammar of assent of most African Catholics—their worldviews, their map of the universe, and their understanding of the presence of God in the person of the Lord Jesus Christ in every aspect of life, and of the ever-abiding presence and power of the Holy Spirit.

While actual faith in Africa shares a family trait with Catholicism outside Africa, there is also much in common with other expressions of Christianity and religiosity in Africa. This kind of African Christian religious experience abhors denominationalism. This actual faith has its own internal plausibility structures and logic, and is alive and constantly evolving beyond the restrictive sacramental systems and defined boundaries of what is spiritual or profane, or what is orthodox or syncretistic outside the normative canon of a particular denomination.

African theologians must concentrate on drawing out the values in this actual faith as the people seek to find meaning in their daily lives, rather than dismiss them as the evidence of a Christian faith that has not been fully received and not fully lived, or a faith that is syncretistic or fetishistic. African theologians must dig more deeply into the reasons for this apparent contrast between actual faith and official faith, as well as the observed lack of coherence between faith and life. Our theologians also must embrace with courage and honesty the challenges and opportunities which people's actual faith experiences offer in the task of finding valid theological principles that may be present even in these complex situations.

The second important development in theology that I embrace is intercultural hermeneutics, which offers valuable tools for developing an African theological articulation of faith and life. If lived theology shifts the gaze of theologians from systems and canons to Christian witnessing in daily lives, intercultural hermeneutics invites theologians to history. Many African theologians have noted the importance of history and historical forces in the shaping of Christian and cultural identities in Africa today. Mercy Amba Oduyoye, for instance, argues: "We cannot expect those who cannot tell their story, who do not know where they come from, to hear God's call to his future. We cannot expect a people 'without a history' to respond as responsible human beings living in Africa. If their story is the same as the story of those who live in Europe and America, then they can only echo Euro-American responses."[62]

---

[62] Mercy Amba Oduyoye, *Hearing and Knowing: Theological Reflections on Christianity in Africa* (Maryknoll, NY: Orbis Books, 1993), 54.

Intercultural hermeneutics seeks to make sense of how Christian witnessing offers different narrative identities in diverse contexts. It focuses on the diverse and complementary cultural mediation through which the Christian faith is received and celebrated in the World Church. It also offers a road map for seeing how these canons and doctrines and the logic of believing and acting relate and diverge from one another, as the Christian faith crosses cultural and spiritual frontiers in the search for some common ideals of Christian and ecclesial tradition.

As Henning Wrogemann argues, theology today can no longer take "particular cultural and contextual profiles" for granted, or presume that particular or historically conditioned theological and ecclesial traditions embody the full story of God's revelation in history. He offers possible pathways for intercultural exchanges as one way of promoting the kind of dialogue which can bring about the needed humility to "counteract and revise the absolutizing of one's own understanding."[63] In addition, he proposes that in telling the stories of the Christian mission across different cultural and spiritual frontiers, one must expand the narrow search for the manifestations of God in formal ecclesial structures, rational theorems, polyphonic singing, and written texts, among others, which contribute only a limited intercultural understanding. Rather, one must look at the "highly complex ensemble of symbols, a particular sign of language of faith," which must go beyond European Christian traditions to unfamiliar expressions of faith in Latin America, Oceania, Africa, or Asia, which can help expand the range of options and perspectives in the World Church. Intercultural African theology grows from intercultural hermeneutics because this is a recognition that in the cultural pluralism of World Christianity, and in the diverse Christian tradition in Africa today we all are learning interculturally and interdenominationally from one another. This attitude validates the goal and method of receptive ecumenism. Its wisdom is that African theologians cannot engage in dialogue with only a narrow denominational version of what ecumenism means, or a normative rendition of the goal of the ecumenical work.

Furthermore, dialogue should not be limited to "certain forms of Christian essence" associated with denominations, or even with the World Council of Churches.[64] In the era of World Christianity, one must pay

---

[63] Henning Wrogemann, *Intercultural Theology*, trans. Karl E. Böhmer, vol. 1, *Intercultural Hermeneutics* (Downers Grove, IL: IVP Academic, 2016), 18–19.

[64] See Wrogemann, *Intercultural Theology*, 19–20.

attention to how diverse cultural subjects interpret their lived faith in the Lord Jesus Christ in their Christian beliefs and practices, and the moral and social practices which flow from them. Meaning has become more intercultural than monolithic, and the family traits of the Christian community can no longer be restricted to certain privileged historical accounts without attention to the voices and experiences of the historically marginalized in the Global South, or marginalized groups in our faith communities. It is particularly important how African theologians go about telling the stories of the painful divides in our churches, the tears of our people, and how we socialize ourselves and future generations into the stories of other Christian churches and peoples of other faiths. This is the needed quest for finding common values that will guide our collective existence.[65]

African Theology and the Question of Cultural Identity and Agency

The debate about the origin and nature of African theology is now passé. In 1967 John Mbiti wrote: "The church in Africa is a church without theology, without theologians and without theological concerns."[66] Mbiti's conclusion then pointed to a fundamental concern that gained currency in the middle of the twentieth century, namely, the lack of critical and systematic reflection on the gospel experience by Africans in the light of African history, cultures, and traditional belief systems and the social context.[67] Fifty-eight years after Mbiti's assertion, in this era of world Christianity, theological production by Africans and non-Africans on African Christian experience has been so profuse and varied.[68] Many theologies have emerged in Africa today with

---

[65] Walter Kasper, for instance, shows the limitations and challenges for dialogue with Pentecostals because they lack a developed ecclesiology, and have an aggressive and proselytizing attitude toward Catholics in many parts of the Global South. See Walter Kasper, *That They May All Be One: The Call to Unity Today* (New York: Burns and Oates, 2004), 25.

[66] John S. Mbiti, "Some African Concepts of Christology," quoted in David Busch, "Missionary Theology in Africa," *Journal of Theology for Southern Africa*, no. 49 D (1984): 19.

[67] Diane Stinton, "Africa, East and West," in *An Introduction to Third World Theologies*, ed. John Parratt (Cambridge: Cambridge University Press, 2004), 107.

[68] See, for instance, a detailed study of the rich development of African theologies

diverse inspirations and multiple expressions—inculturation, abundant life, family of God, liberation, ecology, reconstruction, public theology, political theology, and transformational praxis, among others. African theologies in their formal and nonformal expressions have risen from the encounter of African peoples with the Gospel message in the African context.

Most of the theological projects in Africa beginning from the 1950s into the twenty-first century revolve around the question of culture and identity. The first attempt to articulate an African Indigenous theology in 1956 reflected this concern. In 1956, some priests from Africa and the Diaspora studying in France published the epochal work, *Des pretres noirs s'interrogent* (*Black Priests question themselves*),[69] in which they called for an indigenized church in Africa. Some of the questions they asked in the book were: How may the message of the Gospel culturally nurtured in Europe and North America be able to inform and reshape African culture? How can it do so without turning African Christians into Europeans and Americans and thus alienating them from themselves and their world? How can African culture become the basis for enriching Africans through the Christian faith and the means for expressing and living the faith? How can it do this without destroying the identity of the church as a carrier of the Gospel of the Lord Jesus Christ?[70]

Andrew Walls, reflecting on Kwame Bediako's theology of identity and African culture, captures this concern for identity and cultural affirmation very well with regard to the Greek influence on early Christian thought, and the influence that Africa's cultural past and history made to the development of African theology when he writes,

> The twentieth-century question was the possibility of being both Christian and African. We are made by our past; it is our past that creates our identity and shows us who we are. We cannot abandon

---

in Elias Kifon Bongmba, ed., *The Routledge Handbook of African Theology* (London: Routledge, 2020); see also Stan Chu Ilo, ed., *Handbook of African Catholicism* (Maryknoll, NY: Orbis Books, 2022).

[69] So strong was the rejection of this work that it has never been translated into English or any Indigenous African language, nor is it in the libraries of major seminaries and theologates in Africa today. I only knew about this work as a graduate student of theology studying in Canada.

[70] Cf. Léonard Santedi Kinkupu, ed., *Des pretres noirs s'interrogent: Cinquante ans apres* (Paris: Presence Africaine, 2006).

or suppress our past or substitute something else instead, nor can our past be left as it is, untouched by Christ. Our past, like our present, has to be converted, turned toward Christ. The second-century quest was the conversion, not the suppression or replacement, of Hellenistic culture, and in that case, conversion had led to cultural renewal. Today's quest is the conversion of African culture, and perhaps thereby its renewal.[71]

Laurenti Magesa agrees with this concern of theology in Africa when he identifies the theological quest in the churches of Africa as that of "reinvention of tradition," a "consideration and reconsideration of as many aspects of the organism that is the church as possible,"[72] and a conscious attempt to hold in balance the diverse streams of thought-systems—Western and African, for instance—that are often not at home with each other.[73]

By the end of Vatican II, serious questions were being asked by African Christians about African identity and African liberation, because the beginning of the Second Vatican Council in 1962 coincided with the granting of independence to most African countries. As Peter Phan rightly argues, not only in Africa but also in Asia, "the massive and dehumanizing material poverty and oppression bolstered by economic and political structures" and the "destructive legacy of Western colonialism" and the "insidious and manifold forms of neocolonialist capitalism, with its Western models of economic development," have always confronted theologians in the Global South.[74] The Negritude movement in most of French Africa, the United States, and the Caribbean, for instance, gave stimulus to the need for an African Church and an African liberation theology that could generate Christian praxis for

---

[71] Andrew Walls, "Kwame Bediako and Christian Scholarship in Africa," *International Bulletin of Missionary Research* 32, no. 4 (2008): 189.

[72] Laurenti Magesa, "Epilogue: Dreaming about the Future of the Church in Africa," in *Handbook of African Catholicism*, ed. Stan Chu Ilo (Maryknoll, NY: Orbis Books, 2022), 717.

[73] Laurenti Magesa, *African Religion: The Moral Traditions of Abundant Life* (Maryknoll, NY: Orbis Books, 1997), 7.

[74] Peter Phan, "Doing Theology in World Christianities: Old Tasks, New Ways," in *Relocating World Christianity: Interdisciplinary Studies in Universal and Local Expressions of the Christian Faith*, ed. Joel Cabrita, David Maxwell, Emma Wild-Wood (Leiden: Brill, 2017), 119.

the reversal of the burden of history and self-flagellation by Africans, white supremacy, and racism suffered by people of African descent. Within Africa, many independent churches (AICs) grew in East Africa, West Africa, and Southern Africa to challenge the Western traditional orthodoxies of the mainline churches and enact different counternarratives of Christian beliefs, belonging, and behaving for Africa and of Africans.

That the Bible was translated into over 238 African languages by the middle of the twentieth century also gave Africans access to the Word of God in Christ with its impetus for critical self and group examination and transformation in the light of Christ.[75] The African "bible women" contributed to the evangelization of Africa by Africans using the Word of God.[76] Lamin Sanneh, for instance, argues that the translation of the Bible into the vernacular in Africa was an important factor in the exponential growth in Christian population in Africa. This growth, in the postcolonial period, outpaced the slow growth in the missionary phase. In addition, the liberative narratives found in the Bible, once translated into African languages, provided a phenomenological foundation and practical tools for cultural renewal in Africa. In addition, biblical translation in Africa watered the cultural soil for the flourishing of the charisms, the search for abundant life, and theological creativity. It also strengthened the spiritual agencies of Africans, Christian witness, evangelization, and prophetic resistance to imperialism and unacceptable social conditions in Africa, because, as Lamin Sanneh writes, "Bible translation inscribes into the cultural imagination a narrative and wisdom tradition that enhances oral and ethnic affinity with biblical stories of creation, covenant, captivity, wilderness, suffering, restoration, hope, and abundance."[77]

What is obvious today is that one can no longer question whether there are African theologies and African theologians. Rather, the main question now is how these theologies are contributing to the fruitfulness, mission, and relevance of Christianity to human, cultural, spiritual, economic, and integral development of Africans. What is contested today is the extent to

---

[75] See Brian Stanley, *A World History: Christianity in the Twentieth Century* (Princeton, NJ: Princeton University Press, 2018), 60–61, 77.

[76] See Deborah Gaitskell, "Hot Meetings and Hard Kraals: African Bible Women in Transvaal Methodism, 1924–1960," *Journal of Religion in Africa* 30, no. 3 (2000): 277–309. See also Dana Robert, "World Christianity as a Women's Movement," *International Bulletin of Missionary Research* 30, no. 4 (October 2006): 180–88.

[77] Lamin Sanneh, *Whose Religion is Christianity? The Gospel beyond the West* (Grand Rapids, MI: Eerdmans, 2003), 111.

which African theologies and the Gospel message are contributing to shaping the integral mission of the church and society in Africa in the teaching, saving, liberating, and healing priorities and practices of the Lord Jesus. In other words, what kind of African societies have emerged as a result of the presence of these theologies and the agency of African Christians whose population and religious communities are growing exponentially by the day?

Changing Times, Changing Focus for African Theology

The disconnect between theological productions by African theologians and the shaping of the identity, nature, and direction of the church in Africa is a painful reminder of the gap between theologies in Africa, pastoral ministries, and the actual faith of the people. This makes it more urgent for the emergence in Africa of a theology of church that is also a theology of the people, a theology with the people, and a theology for the people of God. As Francesco Asti proposes, theologies are important because they emerge from within the community of faith and serve the community of faith. If the Church is the people of God, then theology must necessarily emerge through a healthy insertion in the life of the people of God who constitute the Church. Theology must then be sustained in a profitable way through this relation with the people of God, because "the communal experience and the gaze towards the future" reflect the proper character of a people growing as pilgrims and journeying together with faces focused on God.[78] The gift of faith and the life of grace conferred by baptism brings about a familial union among all of God's people. African theology of the people is capable of identifying, deepening, and ritualizing this bond of love in the family of God through identifying the theological anthropological foundation for this bond, and the pastoral and practical implications of this union. This way, African theology can provide resources for healing the fragmentation in today's churches and societies in Africa and offer grounds and inspiration for reconciliation, healing of memory, communal cohesion, light and life for God's people in Africa.

For African theologies to play an important role in the church today and in the wider societies of Africa, I propose that it must change its gaze. First,

---

[78] Francesco Asti, *Per una theologica del popolo di Dio: Principio unitario, forme, paradigme e prospettive* (Rome: Libreria Editrice Vaticana, 2022), 154–55.

we must turn to the sick and dying on our continent. In a post-pandemic Africa and the world, in the face of climate change and environmental degradation, the health and flourishing of God's people in Africa in a healthy environment must become an essential starting point of theology and a central concern of churches.[79] There are so many people who are dying on our continent. The Christian response to these deaths cannot simply be reduced to the ethics of death and dying or the ethics of care and disease prevention. Nor can it be about conducting elaborate Christian burials or the explosion of healing ministries and miracle centers in many African settings. African theologians must take seriously these questions: What is sickening our people? Can we see in the faces of our siblings who are constantly afflicted by diseases the face of the poor man of Galilee? What does it mean to say to people who live in clinical deserts that God is love and that we have a God "that healeth thee"? Why are so many of our people dying needlessly in Africa because of the double burden of infectious and non-infectious diseases that are preventable and treatable? What are the wider determinants of health that churches and governments are failing to address in terms of culture, failed governments, weak social and economic structures and systems, worldviews, and shocking poverty in the midst of so much wealth in Africa? Why are our governments and churches in Africa preoccupied with building big structures and gigantic churches rather than committing significant resources for the development of primary healthcare and mobile clinics?

Unless African Christians develop a theology of abundant life and the churches work with African national leaders to protect and improve the health, life and well-being of Africans, theology and church in Africa will continue to be empty of the force and grace-filled promise of the Gospel of abundant life for God's people (John 10:10). African theology must focus on an unequivocal rejection of the culture of death—the diseases killing our people, the breakdown in relationships in our churches and wider societies, the disease of corruption and mistrust destroying our social life—while courageously addressing the social, commercial, and religious determinants of health. Ultimately, the concern of everyone should be how to make the settings of people, especially the poor, the sites for the enactment of the Gospel of abundant life—a central impetus of African moral tradition and communal

---

[79] See Stan Chu Ilo, ed., *Wealth, Health, and Hope in African Christian Religion: The Search for Abundant Life* (Lanham, MD: Lexington Books, 2018), 73–76.

praxis for individual and communal effort at creating conditions for human and cosmic flourishing.

Second, *we must turn to the existential peripheries*—the market women, the roadside vendors, the people who inhabit the suburbs, the rural dwellers, refugees, prisoners, internally displaced peoples in Africa, and the millions of our people who are poor, without a voice and in the throes of suffering and pain. According to Tinyiko Maluleke,

> In these contexts, where the private versus the public binary has long since collapsed, where the rich eat the poor and the poor eat the poor, Black, feminist, and African theologians must seek the face of God. And this must be done in dialogue and in contestation with the many churches of the squatter camps. Some of these churches experiment with violent patriarchies, nihilistic survival tactics, spiritualities of humiliation, miracle making, and violence. Black, feminist, and African theologies are done in the midst of people who are daily dancing in *the glory of monsters*.[80]

Theology and the church in Africa must develop a perspective that is shaped by the experiences and voices from the margins.[81] The peripheries have always been the staging ground for a new irruption of God's power and revelation, and the surprising wisdom of the Holy Spirit. In these margins, we can clearly see the wounded and bleeding face of the Son of God. But these margins are also in Africa the places where we can clearly see both the complexity and contradictions of life in Africa, as well as the transcending force of communal action and solidarity nourished in the African *ubuntu* spirit. The margins offer us in the slums and ghettos, the IDP camps, women's rural self-help communities, and small Christian communities an evangelical and

---

[80] Tinyiko Maluleke, "Why I Am Not a Public Theologian," *Ecumenical Review* 73, no. 2 (April 2021): 307–8.

[81] Jean-Marc Ela writes of a theology that addresses the misery of the peasants in Africa, and a theology that develops the scientific tool to look at our societies without blushes or making excuses so that we can courageously confront the root causes of the suffering in our continent and the local and global factors that are creating so much misery in the land. Jean-Marc Ela, *Afrique: L'Irruption des pauvres: Société contre ingérence, pouvoir et argent* (Paris: L'Harmattan, 1994), 44.

prophetic way of living that often counters the prevailing idols of power and domination in politics and religious institutions, and the divisions in many African societies along the lines of ethnicity, social class, political affiliation, and religious loyalties in Africa.

Yves Congar's wisdom is very helpful here in articulating a theological principle of the revelatory impulses that can be found at the peripheries. Congar argues that the peripheries are sites where one can see "something that is searching and striving for expression." Thus, a spiritual organism like the church is more likely to grow and develop by paying attention to those sites and elements searching for expression, waiting to be born. He shows that in the history of the Catholic Church the most influential religious movements and religious communities have always developed from the margins and not "created by the central power. All such initiatives come from the periphery."[82] African theology must now pay greater attention to the peripheries where these sites and signs of the expressions of the footprint of God are waiting to be explored. These sites often grow in resistance to oppression and failures in government and in the churches. They emerge from the strong faith of the everyday Africans who are searching for God. The majority of these Africans continue to hold on to their faith in God as the only firm anchor that can never let them down when other things around them, sometimes including the churches, often show signs of weakness, instability, and compromises with powers and principalities.

Third, *we must turn to the women in Africa and their art of living and resisting the forces of death.*[83] African women of faith particularly provide us a model of existence through their poetic enactment of a new kind of reversal of history. Faced with many cultural, political, and religious barriers, African women of faith continue to live in generative hope for themselves and for their families and communities. African women are overcoming the obstacles that limit their opportunities and spaces for applying their boundless assets and primary energies. These obstacles have battered and bruised them in the face of life-sapping conditions sustained and legitimated through some entrenched patriarchal practices in our society and in our churches. The perspectives of

---

[82] Yves Congar, *True and False Reform in the Church*, trans. Paul Philibert (Collegeville, MN: Liturgical Press, 2011), 240.

[83] See Mercy Amba Oduyoye and Musimbi Kanyaro, eds., *The Will to Arise: Women, Tradition, and the Church in Africa* (Maryknoll, NY: Orbis Books, 1997).

theology and church in Africa shaped by a womanist narrative can show us the possibility of living and acting toward one another, and resisting the negative forces of history in Africa, in a way that gives birth to new practices of reversal and alternate sites of hope in the midst of conflicts, contestations, and unacceptable living conditions.

Recent scholarship in the social sciences calls attention to a shift away from the epistemologies of the North and methodological canons regnant in the social sciences, and theological and religious studies. Instead, greater attention is being given to "people's everyday practices."[84] Scholars writing about communities that have suffered from injustice and oppression show that the text of one's life can be understood only within these larger contexts and pre-texts of the individual. Henry Louis Gates argues it is only by telling their own stories and the stories of their own heroes and heroines that many people who are on the margins can reclaim a sense of dignity, healing, and a restoration of history. In addition, new epistemic grounds can be created for retrieving a fuller account of their own history. Gates proposes a narrative ethic: "I write myself, therefore I am."[85] Emmanuel Obiechina notes that beginning in the late nineteenth century, missionaries were the main agents for collecting and recording in writing African oral traditions—folktales, fables, myths, proverbs, riddles, songs, and historical fragments.[86] The missionary efforts and documentation lack recognition of the participation of Africans themselves in adapting African languages to Western scripts, and in the translation of biblical and religious education books into vernaculars.[87]

Most of these endeavors were not community experiences, nor were they aimed at writing an African Christian history focusing on the contributions of Africans as missionaries to fellow Africans. As Ogbu Kalu argues, the history that came out of this was limited and biased: "Missionary ideology tended

---

[84] See Michel de Certeau, "Railway Navigation and Incarceration," trans. Steven Rendall, in *The City Cultures Reader*, 2nd ed., ed. Malcolm Miles, Tim Hall, and Iain Borden (London: Routledge, 2004), 266.

[85] Henry Louis Gates, Jr., quoted in Angela Dillard, *Guess Who's Coming to Dinner Now? Multicultural Conservatism in America* (New York: New York University Press, 2001), 100.

[86] Emmanuel N. Obiechina, *Language and Theme: Essays in African Literature* (Washington, DC: Howard University Press), 9.

[87] Obiechina, *Language and Theme*, 9.

to share the scientific racism of the nineteenth century. Thus, missionary historiography is often hagiographic, triumphalist, and disdainful of indigenous non-European cultures. As Peter Foster put it, a premium was put upon distortion and degradation of receiving cultures."[88] Another sad aspect of this kind of history is the absence of the voices of women, as Obiechina renders it, in the telling of stories: "Women and children sit still and say nothing."[89] He might be speaking from a limited African tribal context, because as Mary Modupe Kolawole has shown with historical evidence in Central Sudan, the role of grandmothers in storytelling is so dominant that grandmothers, *habboba*, constitute a distinctive cultural institution. If oral tradition in some settings demonized women using proverbs, folktales, and legends, African women themselves are beginning to tell their own stories.[90]

This effort by African women theologians to tell their own stories has given us some powerful narratives of African women founders of churches, such as Paolina Dlamini (1858–1942), Abiodun Akinsowan (1907–1994), Christina Nku (1894–1980). Many women led the East African revival Balokole movement. And there were faith-based women-led groups to the Christian mission in Africa. These women among many others all contributed to the success of the modern Christian mission in the continent.[91] Musa W. Dube's essay "'God Never Opened the Bible to Me': Women Church Leaders in Botswana" presents a very convincing account of why the story of Christianity should be told through a womanist's perspective.

Most important, basing her research on ethnographic studies and the writings of important African theologians like Mercy Amba Oduyoye and Isabel Phiri, Musa Dube demonstrates the important role of African women in shaping the past and current history and shape of Christianity in Africa.

---

[88] Ogbu U. Kalu, "Introduction: The Shape and Flow of African Church Historiography," in *African Christianity: An African Story*, ed. Ogbu Kalu (Trenton, NJ: African World Press, 2007), 14.

[89] Obiechina, *Language and Theme*, 14.

[90] Mary E. Modupe Kolawole, "Women's Oral Genres," in *African Literature: An Anthology of Criticism and Theory*, ed. Tejumola Olaniyan and Ato Quayson (Malden, MA: Blackwell, 2007), 95.

[91] Leanne Dzubinski and Anneke Stasson, *Women in the Mission of the Church: Their Opportunities and Obstacles throughout Christian History* (Grand Rapids, MI: Baker, 2021), 191–97.

Among many other illuminating points she makes, her account shows that women "have always found ways that subvert the structural exclusion that marginalizes them from power in the society. They have found ways to create and operate in another space, outside the boundaries and by the margins of both written history and culture."[92] Postcolonial and post–Vatican II young African theologians like me continue even today to search for the roots of present African Christian history beyond the normative reading of the accounts of Western missionary activities in Africa and their successful or limited outcomes. It is important that we search not only in the predominant male account that dominates African Church history, but rather that we search sources about women's contributions to the Church in Africa that exists "outside the boundaries of written history in church and in general."[93]

Finally, *we must turn our gaze to the continuing devastation of Africa's lands and the despoliation of its resources by external and internal actors*, the fragmentation of the nation-states in Africa, the fragmentation of churches and religious groups on the continent. Africa is a rich continent, but the sad reality is that the wealth of Africa has not benefited Africans. There are two forms of extraction going on in Africa. First, is the foreign extraction that began with the slave trade and continues today in the extraction of Africa's raw material resources and minerals by foreign conglomerates and industries. The second is the raping of African resources by African officeholders through the extractive leadership in the resource-rich African countries of Nigeria, DRC, Sudan, South Sudan, CAR, Cameroun, Kenya, Zimbabwe, South Africa, and many others.

Sadly, African economies are commodity-based, and most African countries export raw materials rather than industrialized products. So their economies are dependent on commodity prices, which go up and down based on global economic trends, again driven by the destructive and unforgiving logic of neoliberal capitalism. And this global economy is built not to protect the interests of Africa or that of the poor throughout the world. That is why Pope Francis says that the global economy is one that kills (*Evangelii Gaudium*, 53). A country like Nigeria exports its unrefined oil and imports refined oil

---

[92] Musa W. Dube, "'God Never Opened the Bible to Me': Women Church Leaders in Botswana," *Studies in World Christianity and Interreligious Relations* 48 (2014): 318.

[93] Dube, "'God Never Opened the Bible to Me,'" 318.

products. So Africa's economy is susceptible to commodity prices in the global market. We might blame the foreign companies for the extraction and extroversion of Africa's resources, which have impoverished most of our people, but we Africans need to start taking responsibility for these problems. There is so much greed on our continent, and it runs deep and across the board from the top to the bottom. However, the people running the African states, and their religious accomplices and cheerleaders, should take the greatest blame for this client-patron relation of exchange that has created so much poverty, suffering, and pain for God's people in Africa.

The state in Africa has suffered from "state capture," a term coined by the World Bank in 2000 to refer to a situation in post-Communist Soviet Union and countries in Latin America who were dominated by a few powerful elites who corruptly used "overwhelming political muscle to protect and project their economic interests" in the state.[94] This term gained currency in South Africa because a few families and a few thin top layers of the political and religious elites are swimming on top of a sea of wealth, while most Africans are drowning in a sea of poverty. This situation is destroying the lives of Africans. It is creating more poverty, and it is the main driver of social unrest, violence, and war; it is also the reason why political competition for offices in our continent has become so destructive and why those in power along with their client base and reference groups do not easily give up power. We have so many old sit-tight rulers in Africa who do not wish to give up on their stranglehold on their people and who are milking their countries dry. When you steal the wealth of a people, and transfer the profits to foreign countries, as is the case in Africa, the people suffer from lack of the basic necessities of life, including vital services like health and social safety networks. Unhappily, the vast majority of people live unfulfilled lives. The role of theology and the church in Africa is to build and rebuild the frayed social bonds of love; to suture the torn cultural, ecclesial, and political networks in order to hold our societies and people together, and fashion them into cohesive units that work together for the realization of abundant life for God's people. The struggle for survival in Africa and the historical burden of the past have led to mistrust and lack of cohesion in many settings.

Attempts to develop institutional cultures, ritualizing practices, and consolidating some patterns of responses and problem-solving models in

---

[94] See John Crabtree and Francisco Durand, *Peru, Elite Power and Political Capture* (London: Zed Books, 2017), 1–2.

Africa are often lacking. It looks like every day we Africans are starting again; dreams and hopes are born but are often far from being realized; and everyone who comes to power in government or in the church wants to start afresh. There are unfortunately no stable institutional structures being developed as conveyor belts for the movement of our collective goods from one generation to another. Even in the theological academy, it is also the case that many young theologians are not studying theological productions from their ancestors, but rather wish to innovate while neglecting the theological mileage that has been covered and the theological and intellectual bridges that have already been built through which they can connect with the rich theological productions in Africa of the last sixty years.

Ultimately, African theologies ground hope beyond suffering for today and for the future in the continent on Ubuntu and ecological ethics. This is becoming an urgent theological and missional undertaking because of the destructive effects of climate change in Africa today and in the world at large. No theology will make sense today without being linked to climate change and the suffering of Mother Earth.

The African concept of *Ubuntu* has been proposed as an ethics of communal solidarity and stewardship for human and cosmic flourishing and a model for doing theologies that matter to the people in Africa. *Ubuntu* is an ideal, or a vision for a new creation capable of inspiring people to make daily choices to heal the earth. It is also an ethical framework around which theologians can build some principles and practices of solidarity with our fragile earth and the fragile, vulnerable and suffering peoples of the earth who are on the margins of life. Pope Francis invites the world to embrace the spirit of *ubuntu* as expressed in the message of the Bishops of South Africa which he cites in *Laudato Si'*: "Everyone's talents and involvement are needed to redress the damage caused by human abuse of God's creation" (*LS* 14).

Ubuntu is a very poetic notion that invites us into a different space of life in the abundance that God provides. This abundant life is possible for all of God's creatures. We can realize this fullness of life for all of God's people and creatures in our times amid the pain and anguish today in the face of climate change that is creating many dry lands and desert. We all are wounded by the violence, wars, shocking poverty, and human suffering around us; and the tension among and within nations, creating rivers of blood and rivers of tears for many people who are suffering in many painful sites in our world today. In the face of all these tragedies around us that are sadly the results of the abuse of human freedom, the prophetic message of hope sounds so clearly to us: God is coming to do a new thing among us. But how can God do this? I think the church today can mediate the saving, healing, liberating, and teaching mission of the Lord by locating itself in many sites of suffering in the world today where the battle goes on between life and death: sick people and sick populations; sick earth and sick relationships; the poor, neglected, and exploited who inhabit the existential peripheries and those who like the rich fool possess barns overflowing with riches and luxury. It is only when by locating theologies in Africa and elsewhere on these sites can today's theologians participate fruitfully in laying the building blocks for a transformed creation and a transformed and transforming Church.

This transformed creation emerges when the actions of individuals and groups proceed from the intention to advance the highest good of the community. This is most important for those whom the Lord has given so much wealth, opportunities, and privileges. The Lord challenges us to translate our faith into daily action and in choosing those sound socio-ethical choices that emerge from a desire to give of ourselves and our treasures in a selfless manner. This requires courageous effort and sacrifice; a dying to self and a dynamic movement away from the idolization of any temporal reality (for example the idols of the self, of the market, of cultures, nations, races, wealth, and economic orthodoxies, and the rigid attachment to business practices that are driven only by profit without consideration of human good and that of the earth). African eco-theology invites people then to turn toward God and to one another as siblings in a spirit of reverence, care, recognition, and solidarity. I believe that it is in turning toward one another, and to creation in all its wonder, richness and varieties, that we can find the face of God, and our way to our common future in a peaceful and healthy world held in an unbreakable bond of love, destiny, and awe.

Conclusion

This chapter explored the theoretical and practical issues in the construction of an African theology that grapples with an interpretation of belief in God vis-à-vis the challenging social conditions in Africa. The chapter is also a self-reflective exercise, driven by my search for a personal condition and subjective verity for my belief in the God revealed in the person of Jesus Christ. In doing this, I invite other African theologians to enter dialogue with the claims made here through an encounter with their own personal belief in God as Africans. This subjective justification of belief is for me the first step toward authenticity for any theological or methodological standpoint one might propose. It is so easy for any theologian to mouth the appropriateness of different philosophies, theologies, or theories of religious studies for interpreting and understanding African Christian religion. There are many such books, and more will be written. What is most difficult is to write a theology that is a self-portrait of one's faith, and to make oneself vulnerable before the mystery of God and one's own search for the intelligibility, credibility, and relevance of faith.

The African Christian academy has always been subject to having to prove itself as valid, by first showing itself to be grounded in some Western thought or system or theological method. This was how most African theologians were trained, especially in the mainline Christian traditions. This is understandable, because what has until recently been the African understanding of Christianity in Africa has been shaped by what has taken place in the West. Comparative study and creative appropriation of influential Western scholars and voices then became for many African scholars the most valid path for scholarly recognition and even for a job in the Catholic academy or recognition by Rome. Therefore, to speak of Catholic theology through a different language of discourse, or from a different epistemological or methodological standpoint is still considered too difficult or risky an undertaking because it is like bringing water out from a rock.

But it is a challenge and a task worth embracing. However, to do this faithfully and credibly, one must first be at home with the African world to be able to speak of it with confidence and authenticity. But most current African scholars like me are second- and third-generation Christians who were born in post-independence Africa and the post–Vatican II African Church. Most of us were raised as Christians without any direct experience of the world of ATRs and African thought, and no appreciation of their limitations and strengths. We often lack the cultural knowledge to speak confidently about our religious heritage, because it is strange to us. It is worse for the millennials, for whom such matters appear to belong more to a cultural archive than being a matter for serious intellectual engagement. Second, one has to adopt an approach that is faithful to the religious history of Africans by finding a good way to harvest "the story." Third, one must find a suitable language to write the cultural portrait that one gains from the stories of the people from the field. In my own case, the language employed is English, which has its own limitations. As with any foreign language, one struggles in the translation into a foreign language of any meaning that is embedded in cultural symbols, cultural knowledge, cultural artifacts, cultural behavior, and cultural memory. Fourth, one needs to find a way of initiating an open conversation between one's findings and the other conversations going on about Africa outside Africa. In addition, there is the need to find related conversation partners among African theologians who are open to transformative discourse outside the well-charted and mainstream scholarly terrains or dogmatic fortresses in some parts of Africa. One also must find a way to engage with the dialogue between faith and culture, and between faith and Indigenous or local knowledge in World Christianity. Related questions arise about the intentionality and direction of modernity, and how retrieval of African stories could engage the strands within a contested and often divisive discourse on modernity.

My approach to doing African theology surely will come under criticism because of its rejection of the idea that theology is simply the explication of what faith has already received. Or its insistence on lived faith, actual faith, and suffering and smiling as the starting point of theology. It might make some uncomfortable with its historical approach that embraces the Christian community as always in the making. African believers in their limited cultural mediation and their exuberant faith life embody the footprints of God and a portrait of the mission of God in particular contexts. Theology is not simply something that happens after faith; theology is lived faith. The rationality of faith is not a reality that theologians manufacture randomly; it is something that has to be discovered by each theologian in his or her own personal questions, as well as in the stories of faith of the people and communities of faith to which the theologian belongs.

Theology is grounded, normed, contextualized, embodied, and embedded in the narratives of faith. Faith is a dynamic and integrative process, which by its very nature demands a conscious selection and rejection of values, beliefs, and practices. This is based on one's discernment of the ultimate goal and mission of life in one's relationship with God, and with all things in the light of God. Because faith is performative and grounded in one's centering of the ultimate value in dynamic patterns of believing, choosing, and living, faith is inherently cultural in nature and open to transformation and transition. Believing is by its very nature both theological and cultural at the same time. One cannot account for faith theologically without at the same time accounting for faith from the perspective of sociocultural historical understanding. Both go together.

This does not in any way reduce faith's grounding from the point of view of Christian religion as a revealed truth. Its revelatory source does not come from outside as a sudden irruption of the divine into the human. Revelation is found within human and cosmic history, which at its very source and center is sacral. This does not dilute the value of faith as a gift from God, which is beyond the social construction of experience. Rather, it shows clearly that faith is a gift that is embodied within history and embedded in specific culturally defined frameworks of meaning and available to the theologian who accompanies the people in their suffering and smiling, and who is attentive to their own subjective and ultimate concerns.

2

Can We Really Make Sense of This Suffering in Africa or Elsewhere?

> Promoting theology in the future cannot be limited to abstractly re-proposing formulas and schemes of the past. Called to prophetically interpret the present and glimpse new itineraries for the future in the light of Revelation, theology will have to confront profound cultural transformations, aware that: "What we are living through is not simply an era of change, but a change of epoch" (Address to the Roman Curia, Dec. 21, 2013)
>
> —Pope Francis[1]

In this chapter, I wish to develop the hermeneutics of suffering through the teachings of Pope John Paul II and Pope Francis. I will particularly develop this account through a reinterpretation of the Parable of the Good Samaritan as a narrative of suffering, solidarity, and unresolved social evil. I will then use the voices of five contemporary scholars to tell a story of the many faces of suffering, lamentation, hope, resistance, and protest in the world today, especially for people of African descent. These five voices have been my conversation partners for quite some time. The first voice is that of Emmanuel Katongole in his work *Born from Lament: The Theology and Politics of Hope*

---

[1] Francis, *Ad Theologiam Promovendam*, apostolic letter, November 1, 2023, https://www.vatican.va/content/francesco/it/motu_proprio/documents/20231101-motu-proprio-ad-theologiam-promovendam.html, sec. 1.

in Africa, in which he demonstrates what hope looks like in Africa for people who are caught in the cycle of suffering. The second set of voices are those of liberation theologians and feminist theologians, particularly the voices of James Cone, in *The Cross and the Lynching Tree*; M. Shawn Copeland in *Knowing Christ Crucified: The Witness of African American Religious Experience*; Gustavo Gutiérrez, *On Job: God-Talk and the Suffering of the Innocent*; Jon Sobrino in *Where Is God: Earthquake, Terrorism, Barbarity, and Hope*; and finally the voice of Karen Kilby in *God, Evil and the Limits of Theology*, and her ethnographic project on suffering and the Christian life.

Can We Really Make Sense of this Suffering in Africa and Elsewhere?

The human being is thrown into a world with its laws and rhythms, a world that the human person can manipulate but cannot topple. This is why we go through the cycle of years; we grow old, fall sick, recover, bounce back, and one day die. What belongs to time and space and the cycle of birth and death in the natural realm is always open to grace—the life of God given to us in Christ that stretches our limited human horizon into the infinite horizon of God. To the extent to which these relationships and the natural cycle work together in advancing the individual and collective realization of the good of order, and the ultimate purpose of the moral demand, to that extent is the possibility of one experiencing either pain or joy, solace, or abandonment. However, the ubiquity of pain seems to be the daily reality of living in a complex and broken world.

Theodicy seeks to make sense of human suffering by identifying the goodness of God amid suffering and evil. Finding the presence of a good God when faced with human pain (physical and emotional injuries, for example, betrayal, and a feeling of emptiness in the face of evil, etc.) and justifying religious belief through or rather despite human suffering is a continuing quest for all humans. This attempt to make sense of suffering is particularly challenging when we are confronted with the suffering of the innocent.[2] The movement of the human heart for meaning amid suffering is not merely a theological quest to be pursued with intellectual rigor. It is above all, for many

---

[2] Robin Ryan, *God and the Mystery of Human Suffering: A Theological Conversation across the Ages* (New York: Paulist Press, 2011), 5.

Christians, an existential search in which we all are implicated. In this search, there emerges the question: On whom do we lean when we face pain?—the self, God, the community, the church, friends, family, or others? Where can we find solace in the face of the suffering and pain that come our way at one time or another? In responding to human suffering, Robin Ryan's wisdom for theologians is a good principle on how to develop any theology of suffering vis-à-vis a theology of hope:

> Theologies can point people toward God; they can also drive people away from God. Nowhere is that more limpidly clear than in situations of suffering. We may have heard delivered in funeral homilies or at the bedside of a sick person pious nostrums that we found alienating, even oppressive. When, for example, one hears a preacher say that a child has died because 'God wanted another angel in heaven', the image of God that is implied is that of a celestial kidnapper. Such an image has little to do with the God revealed in the Hebrew and Christian scriptures.[3]

At this preliminary stage, a proper understanding of suffering is necessary, going beyond blaming God for human suffering or simply soliciting divine intervention to save or liberate us from suffering or evacuate us or rescue us from a painful sickness, natural disaster, accident, outbreak of infectious disease, or war.

The theological framework for talking about suffering in this book is that of the Good Samaritan. I hope to put this parable in conversation with the theology of suffering and smiling that I posit as a paradigm of reversal of the unacceptable suffering in Africa. The Good Samaritan analogy was used both by Pope John Paul II in his 1984 Apostolic Letter, *On the Christian Meaning of Human Suffering, Salvifici Doloris*, and Pope Francis in chapter 2 of his 2020 encyclical on fraternity and social friendship, *Fratelli Tutti*. This parable answers the question of how to understand and respond to human suffering. The analogy of the Good Samaritan also serves as a particularly useful image for categorizing the humanitarian interventions responding to the cry of the poor in Africa, which often makes heroes of so many people—both Africans and celebrity humanitarians mainly from Europe and North America—who

---

[3] Ryan, *God and the Mystery of Human Suffering*, 5.

have gained global acclaim for helping "save" the lives of people in situations of distress in Africa.

But the question that the parable did not answer and that both popes refer to but did not develop further is the larger social context of suffering, for example: Who were the robbers who attacked the man on the highway from Jerusalem to Jericho? What if the road was secure and people moved freely without being attacked and robbed? Why did this particular man get attacked, since, obviously, he wasn't the only person who moved along that road on this day? If the robbers were still marauding along the highway (that is, if the factors that create wars, epidemics, and social contagions remain in Africa), chances are that the wounded man will be attacked again on his way back home through this same dangerous road after his recovery at the inn. These questions might not relate to the intended message of the parable, but they arise from the application of the parable to human suffering in Africa, for instance, and the need to do a root-cause analysis of the social conditions. We must seriously interrogate the causes of so much social suffering in Africa vis-à-vis the future of society and why this social condition continues to create heroes from the wreckages of wars, disasters, epidemics, and other painful realities that sadly define the social condition in Africa.

John Paul II gives a definition or description of suffering this way,

> Christianity proclaims the essential *good of existence* and the good of that which exists, acknowledges the goodness of the Creator and proclaims the good of creatures. Man suffers on account of evil, which is a certain lack, limitation, or distortion of good. We could say that man suffers *because of a good* in which he does not share, from which in a certain sense, he is cut off, or of which he has deprived himself. He particularly suffers when he ought—in the normal order of things—to have a share in this good and does not have it. Thus, in the Christian view, the reality of suffering is explained through evil, which always, in some way, refers to a good.[4]

Suffering is not identified as an objective reality, but rather is a subjective experience that comes upon someone when the person experiences evil—the absence of some good desired. As Erhard S. Gerstenberger puts it,

---

[4] Pope John Paul II, *Salvifici Doloris*, no. 7.

Any suffering even if it is imaginary, is in a mysterious way my personal affair. Even under the most favorable circumstances, I cannot simply put aside pains, fears, or uncertainties the way one puts hat and coat in the closet. Whatever troubles, hampers, embitters me, whatever threatens to cripple me in body or spirit, belongs, in spite of all counter-measures, to me myself. The pain, and in a certain sense this holds true also for all its causes, and for evil itself, is something alien, fearsome, from which I would like to escape.[5]

The source of suffering is not God, even though, in most circumstances, the reality of suffering of any kind challenges the faith of the believer that God is still in control. John Paul II dismisses the theory of retribution by teaching that suffering is not simply to be understood as the consequence of moral failing; rather, suffering emerges in our daily experience as a result of the negation of some good. Even a just man like Job suffered as presented in the scripture, not because of his moral failing.

The meaning of human suffering and the resolution of human suffering must be sought, according to John Paul II, in the suffering of God. The Lord Jesus throws "the light of salvation" (no. 15) on the "temporal and historical" dimensions of suffering by striking the root of suffering in the evil that wars against creation and definitively by the mystery of the Incarnation and the Paschal Mystery. John Paul II was careful to note that the death of the Son of God was not the just punishment of God on the Son in order to take away the sin of the world. This point is reiterated by Joseph Ratzinger when he raised the question whether "it is not an unworthy concept of God to imagine for oneself a God who demands the slaughter of his son to pacify his wrath."[6] The Cross, he continues, is "a mirror held up to man in which he sees himself unadorned"; and where God identifies Godself with the human person into the abyss of sin and suffering while revealing at the same time "the inexhaustible abyss of the divine love. The cross is thus truly the center of revelation, a revelation that does not reveal any previously unknown principles but reveals to us ourselves, by revealing us before God and God in our midst."[7]

---

[5] Erhard Gerstenberger and Wolfgang Schrage, *Suffering: Biblical Encounters Series*, trans. John Steely (Nashville, TN: Parthenon Press, 1980), 12.

[6] Joseph Ratzinger, *Introduction to Christianity*, trans. J. R. Foster (New York: Herder and Herder, 1970), 222.

[7] Ratzinger, *Introduction to Christianity*, 233.

In embracing suffering, the Son of God puts on full display an exemplarity of what happens when one person conquers greed, selfishness, and pride and gives of himself or herself wholly in love for the sake of others:

> Human suffering has reached its culmination in the Passion of Christ. At the same time, it has entered into a completely new dimension and a new order: *it has been linked to love,* to that love of which Christ spoke to Nicodemus, to that love which creates good, drawing it out by means of suffering, just as the supreme good of the Redemption of the world was drawn from the Cross of Christ, and from that Cross constantly takes its beginning. The Cross of Christ has become a source from which flow rivers of living water. (no. 18).

Christians are invited to follow the Lord in his self-giving love and in taking the Cross and following the Lord and joining "in Christ's redemptive work and a possibility of sharing more deeply in his self-sacrificial love. In this love the believer also participates in Christ's victory over sin and death, i.e., eternal life."[8]

John Paul II notes that modern society more than the previous era has created the factors for a "concentration" of greater experience of suffering through natural disasters, epidemics, pandemics, catastrophes, upheavals, and various social scourges: "one thinks, for example, of a bad harvest and connected with it—or with various other causes—the scourge of famine, and wars." War and conflicts and the scourge of nuclear war, he writes, have led to what he calls *"an incomparable accumulation of sufferings,* even to the possible self-destruction of humanity" (*Salvifici Doloris* 8–9). Thus, the world of suffering experienced by each person has been worsened by the rapid changes in the world. It seems then that rather than reducing human suffering, modern inventions, modern states, and modern economies are manufacturing more suffering, pain, alienation, and unjust structures for people, especially the weak and the poor. Suffering, according to Pope John Paul II, could be moral (when one experiences the pain of the soul) or physical (when the body is hurting) or psychological, that is, "the dimension of pain which accompanies both moral and physical suffering" (*Salvifici Doloris,* 5).

---

[8] John McDermott, "Suffering," in *Dictionary of Fundamental Theology,* ed. René Latourelle and Rino Fisichella (New York: Crossroad, 2000), 1016.

In *Salvifici Doloris* 28, John Paul II proposes the Good Samaritan as the model of "one who brings help in suffering," and a representative of "every individual who is sensitive to the sufferings of others," and one who can give himself or herself wholly for the good of the other. In looking at the example of the Good Samaritan, John Paul II invites people to see how suffering, which empties the human of joy and peace, becomes an opportunity to "unleash love in the human person." He proposes that the world of human suffering can only be transformed and defeated by the "world of human love," which stirs the human heart into action in the face of the suffering of another through human solidarity. The emergence of this kind of solidarity should become, he reasoned, "one of the essential elements of moral culture and universal human civilization" (no. 29).

A similar message of solidarity and hope born from social friendship and solidarity is found in Pope Francis's *Fratelli Tutti* (FT). Pope Francis interprets the origin of suffering in chapter 2 as the rupture in relationship (no. 57). The rebuilding of our social bond as humans can only emerge when we move from isolation to make "contact with human suffering" (no. 68). Francis, like Pope John Paul II, recognizes in the Good Samaritan the summons to the best of the human spirit, which is love that can "restore dignity to the suffering" (no. 71) in order to build a better society. But responding to the wounded of this world will require a prophetic critique of prevailing social hierarchies, destructive economies of scale, the dismantling of structures of manipulation, lies, hypocrisy (75), indifference, racism, and violent nationalism (no. 86). All these social evils create, sustain, and mask the wounds and suffering inflicted on the poor and the vulnerable and those on the underside of history. There is here, though not explicitly stated, an attempt to question the prevailing social conditions—local and global—that create structural violence and senseless suffering in the world through violence, war, discrimination, and politics of domination and extroversion. Saviorism is rejected even though vaguely, but it gives an opening to the development of a new approach to address the suffering emerging from the social context that goes beyond bandaging wounds to stopping people from being wounded by confronting the structures of sin, evil, and injustice.

In the document *Rescuing Fraternity Together*, the Pontifical Academy for Life challenges Church scholars and particularly theologians to focus on "the hermeneutic interpretation of the human condition that was adopted by Jesus through his practice of dialogue with the sacred which lies at the root of all human experiences (birth and death, resentment and forgiveness, poverty and wealth, power and sickness)."[9] In focusing on the human condition, one is offered an inconceivable prospect of seeing the footprints of God in the encounter that takes place when we break down the walls between us as humans, through human proximity in a truly incarnational moment that is always open to grace and transformation.

The image of the Good Samaritan in the Gospel of Luke and the stories of the Canaanite woman, Zacchaeus, and the Centurion are examples that help shape our ecclesial practice and theological reflection because it is through these little moments that the Gospel opens for us the narrative of how the ordinary moments of everyday life are suffused with the glow of the divine and lead one to encounter grace and the sacred as moments of transformation along the road of life. The Good Samaritan shows us "the 'little people's dimension of revelation . . . the 'original picture' that delineates the evidence and testimony of the Church in the human condition we all share."[10] The Good Samaritan is presented as one who gave his time to the wounded man. He stopped, he approached the man, and he cared for him. When confronted with a man who was suffering, he saw in this man, a family member "deserving of his time and attention" (FT, 63). The Good Samaritan goes beyond dry as dust abstract moralizing (FT, 68) to embracing a socio-ethical praxis that is crystallized by love that is translated into action. The Good Samaritan thus teaches us that "we cannot be indifferent to suffering" (FT, 68).

The fundamental question that strikes me in Francis's re-reading of the response of the Good Samaritan is: *What did the Good Samaritan see in this man that the other characters in the story did not see?* This is a key to capturing something that is often lost in our world today—the capacity to see by encountering the suffering of others—to step into the shoes of the other so as to become his or her traveling companion. Indeed, the inability to see the suffering around us and the insensitivity in the world today to human suffering, particularly in Africa, is like the blindness that the Lord condemned in some of his listeners who failed to perceive, hear, and be touched (Mark 8:18; Isaiah 6: 9–10). But there is also a flip side to this blindness worth pointing out to African church leaders and politicians some of whom see so much suffering among their people and turn away. The most painful reality in Africa today for

---

[9] Pontifical Academy for Life, *Rescuing Fraternity Together* (Rome: Libreria Editrice Vaticana, 2021), 17.

[10] Pontifical Academy for Life, *Rescuing Fraternity Together*, 19.

the poor and the downtrodden masses of our people is that their suffering and pain are ignored, and their deaths mean nothing to some of the powerful men and women who sit in state offices and cathedrals. Judith Butler writes of so many victims of violence who are nongrievable victims because society has framed them as expendable. When people are framed in this way, there is no reciprocal recognition that *every life should be prized not priced*; the poor, like the wounded man on the road in this parable, are passed over in silence and left to die. Thus, rather than seeing in people like the wounded and suffering our "shared condition of precariousness," the world today, Butler proposes, has framed people through "a specific exploitation of targeted populations, of lives that are not quite lives, cast as 'destructible' and 'ungrievable.'" The lives of populations such as these, Butler continues, are "lose-able" or forfeited and left to the vagaries of violence, famine, poverty, wars, and pandemics, "when such lives are lost, they are not grievable, since, in the twisted logic that rationalizes their death, the loss of such populations is deemed necessary to protect the lives of the 'living.'"[11]

Pope Francis makes a distinction between those who "care for someone who is hurting and those who pass by; those who bend down to help and those who look the other way and hurry off" (FT, 70). The key to social engagement is the ability for Butler's "reciprocal recognition" proposition; to see clearly the painful reality of those who suffer. This seeing is a diagnostic moment, particularly because the Christian is called always to see like Jesus, to read the signs of the times and the pains of others through a vision that is informed by faith, morality, and a spirituality of love, compassion, and justice. It is a "seeing" or contemplation that is always moving from reflection to action. Francis here appropriates the see-judge-act already proposed in *Mater et Magistra* by John XXIII in 1961 when he wrote, "There are three stages which should normally be followed in the reduction of social principles into practice. First, one reviews the concrete situation; secondly, one forms a judgment on it in the light of these same principles; thirdly, one decides what in the circumstances can and should be done to implement these principles. These are the three stages that are usually expressed in the three terms: look, judge, act" (236).

We can translate the parable of the Good Samaritan into a missional praxis. First, by seeing in each person the face of Christ—*the diagnostic moment*; second by designing this missional praxis through daily practices that translate every aspect of the Church's mission and every act of Christian

---

[11] Judith Butler, *Frames of War: When Is Life Grievable?* (London: Verso, 2016), 31.

witnessing into practical choices for "universal love"—*the kenotic moment*; third by developing the practices and priorities that bring us closer to the concrete experiences of people's daily lives so that the church and Christians can become healing hands of the wounds of people and the world—*the pragmatic moment*. Finally, mission brings transformation, healing, new life, new hope, and new experience of God's love in all those whom we encounter in their suffering—*the transformative moment*. The images of the Inn (the Church as a place of healing); the animal (the means through which the Good Samaritan brought the wounded man to the inn); the interruption of the journey and stepping down to be with the man are all examples of the attitudes required for a renewal of the Church's mission, social engagement, and Christian witnessing to the poor of this world.

It is important to challenge the systems, structures, and institutions that bring so much suffering to people and to balance our commitment to charity and healing of the wounded with a prophetic engagement on social justice issues, policy intervention, systemic changes, in church teaching, in our politics, and leadership. In this task, it is urgent to identify who the robbers are whose violence has robbed the dignity of God's people, and who are the invisible hands who run the iniquitous economies of scale and the corrupt officeholders in Africa who rob their countries of resources. Who are the robbers who have left millions of Africans wounded and dying in the streets, in hospitals, on the perilous sands across the Sahara, and drowning in the Mediterranean and the Atlantic as they try to escape from Africa, where many young Africans are suffocating in a seemingly permanent chokehold of history?

Theological Accounts of Suffering: Five Voices

Emmanuel Katongole

Emmanuel Katongole has produced three books that chart a new path for doing theology in Africa.[12] The central concern of his works is to demonstrate that there is a different logic that is taking place in many alternate and

---

[12] Emmanuel Katongole, *The Sacrifice of Africa: A Political Theology for Africa* (Grand Rapids, MI: Eerdmans, 2011); Emmanuel Katongole, *Born from Lament: The Theology and Politics of Hope in Africa* (Grand Rapids, MI: Eerdmans, 2017); Emmanuel Katongole, *Who Are My People? Love, Violence, and Christianity in Sub-Saharan Africa* (South Bend, IN: University of Notre Dame Press, 2022).

sometimes hidden corners in Africa that tell a different story from the predominant narratives of wars, poverty, ethnic, ecological, and religious violence. This logic is found in the counterwitness of individuals, groups, communities, and networks that are sites for reimagining Africa and thinking and living differently. But to discover the message mediated by these lives, one must step into these sites of reimagination and hear the daily stories of people, and allow us to become part of these stories because "who we are, and who we are capable of becoming, depends very much on the stories we tell, the stories we listen to, and the stories we live."[13]

By telling the stories of people who said to the darkness "we beg to differ," Katongole masterfully helps us retell the stories of contamination that characterize the nation-state and society in Africa, through the redemptive stories of people who have lived differently. Through their heroic acts of resistance, they break the cycle of violence, hate, the politics of extroversion and extraction and provide a site for reimagining the future through a logic of love. The stories that Katongole brings through what he calls the method of *theological portraiture* offer a different account of social ethics and the Church's call to live from memory through lament to a new creation.[14] These stories do even more. When placed side by side with the stories of Africans killing themselves and other atrocities that break the human spirit and create despondency, these redemptive stories of the logic of love can heal, save, restore, liberate, and embody the concrete performative reversal of evil and stupid deaths with the illogic and foolishness of self-sacrificing love. The churches in Africa, as well as the state (Katongole calls the state in Africa successor institutions to the colonial state),[15] often fail to offer a paradigm of a social imagination that serves as a demonstration model of an alternate world different from the cycle of violence and suffering that afflict the continent. The crisis of modernity in Africa can better be understood by paying attention to how politics functions in Africa as well as how religion is associated with politics in creating the dysfunction that defines the African predicament. However, the individuals whose stories are translated in Katongole's works are demonstration models of a social imaginary and provide a credible witness of what faith does when it is translated into concrete acts of resistance as a portrait of love.

---

[13] Katongole, *The Sacrifice of Africa*, 2.
[14] Katongole, *Who Are My People?* 173.
[15] Katongole, *Who Are My People?* 172.

In doing theology this way, Katongole is doing what Pope Francis called theologians to do, as we demonstrated in chapter 1—doing theology as spiritual biography and writing theology as spiritual portraits of God's people. The stories of these individuals provide a site for imagining and reinventing the future in Africa; their stories demonstrate what that future will look like and that such a future can emerge because the conditions for that possibility are validated through these lives. According to Katongole, the lives of the individuals he presents in his books—Maggy Barankitse, Angelina Atyam, Rosemary Nyirumbe, Paride Taban, and others—are audacious markers of a new possibility of hope because they are marked by some common threads, "their willingness to say No to hatred, violence, or tribalism and their Yes to a future of love, peaceful coexistence, and forgiveness."[16]

Katongole does not minimize the gravity of the African condition. He identifies correctly that the nation-states of Africa are the fruits of the lies of modernity.[17] He also shows the reluctance of churches to take seriously the evangelical task of daring to create new stories through a politics of hope to reinvent the future away from the founding narratives of modern African states or narratives of violence of tribe, religion, ecology, and politics. In *Born from Lament*, he begins to give an account of suffering and an African theodicy that emerges from paying attention to the sites and portraits of laments in Africa. He does not simply take readers into the darkness, tragedy, and pain of many people in Africa particularly in the Congo; rather, he asks the fundamental question: What does hope look like for Africans for whom daily life has become a fight with God? What are the concrete, practical, and actual demonstrations of the death and resurrection of the Lord in Africa that can offer a portrait of hope in Africa?[18] According to Katongole,

> In the midst of suffering, hope takes the form of arguing and wrestling with God. If we understand it as lament, such arguing and wrestling is not merely a sentiment, not merely a cry of pain. It is a way of mourning, of protesting to, appealing to, and engaging God—and a way of acting in the midst of ruins. Lament is what sustains and carries forth Christian agency in the midst of suffering.[19]

---

[16] Katongole, *The Sacrifice of Africa*, 193.
[17] Katongole, *The Sacrifice of Africa*, 20.
[18] Katongole, *Born from Lament*, 20.
[19] Katongole, *Born from Lament*, xvi.

Katongole's *Born from Lament* in its intention to demonstrate the politics of hope focused attention on some of the activists in his previous works in addition to new ones whose witness demonstrates the possibility of hope in the context of Africa's cultural, political, and economic history.[20] The strength of his argument is that these activists demonstrate a way of mourning, crying, and lamenting what was lost, but also that "far from passively acquiescing to suffering, lament is an active engagement with the world of suffering."[21] Lament in this work gives a sad portrait of the human condition in Africa and offers us a hopeful portrait of how to find God in the midst of suffering. In the face of suffering, Katongole demonstrates that lament rises to God from the sufferer as a complaint to God who has not delivered on God's promise to liberate, save, or heal. The sufferer who is fighting with God is not magically extracted from a terrible condition or from evil simply because the person is lamenting to God. This is because lamenting to God does not mean that God will save the person who is suffering according to the person's expectations or prayer, nor does it resolve human finality and the incomprehensibility of evil and pain.[22] Why then does God seem to be silent in the face of the suffering and pain of God's people in Africa?

It is obvious from Katongole's account that these activists found God in the brokenness of history—wars, violence, poverty, and atrocities—in God's own vulnerability, in a crucified God, who in many circumstances of pain and evil often seems to be absent, distant, and powerless. In an important paragraph in *Who Are My People?* Katongole makes what I consider his most poignant submission on suffering and redemption in Africa, namely that all the activists who found hope were faced with two forms of sufferings—which I characterize as positive and redemptive, on one hand, and negative and destructive, on the other hand. There is, on one hand, the terrible suffering, pains, poverty, wounds, and brokenness that emerge from "the burden of Africa's history" and that continue to present Africa with excessive deaths and despair. This is negative and destructive suffering and must be accounted for by all Africans and the people of faith in a prophetic and evangelical way. There is, on the other hand, another kind of suffering that is positive and redemptive. It is the positive and redemptive suffering that confronts negative and destructive suffering through the embodiment in people's lives of

---

[20] Katongole, *Born from Lament*, 260.
[21] Katongole, *Born from Lament*, 261.
[22] Katongole, *Born from Lament*, 111.

another form of witnessing, which is suffering from "the violence of love." This redemptive and positive suffering is testified to in the stories of the activists who demonstrate to the world in their heroic way something beyond logic that they have discovered in the self-sacrificing love of God: "Embracing the 'mystery' of suffering is what liberates them and allows them to invent new communities and practices through which they seek to heal, restore, and renew God's love for the other victims of violence."[23]

Katongole's "protest theism: lament, calling God to account, as one of the forms that faith takes in contexts of suffering" is helpful, according to Linn Tonstad, because it helps us see the effect of vulnerability-talk in potentiating acts of solidarity among humans.[24] Lament also in the same dynamic reveals to the sufferer a God who stands in solidarity with suffering humanity. It is thus a turning toward God who is already, as the person who suffers discovers in the act of faith, turning toward the person who suffers.[25] While Katongole offers an attractive portrait of what hope looks like in modern Africa through the narratives emerging from these marginal sites, it does not offer a strong prophetic denunciation of the social condition from which these activists emerged and how the acts of these activists can change the root causes of suffering. As we demonstrated in the analysis of the Good Samaritan, if the robbers along the highway from Jerusalem to Jericho are still marauding along that highway; if the highway continues to be dangerous, chances are that the wounded man going home from the inn of recovery might be attacked again and even inflicted with mortal injuries. Katongole's activists are like the good Samaritans of Africa showing in their own wounds and that of their brothers and sisters that there is healing and hope through "the violence of love."

However, the naming of these sites as portraits of hope may inadvertently serve to excuse the failed institutions and structures that generate the convergence of factors that create so much suffering in many parts of Africa. Could there emerge from such a social analysis an African theology of hope that shows what hope looks like through the collective effort to bring about prophetic religious institutions and well-functioning and inclusive political institutions in Africa? Could this theology of hope become a portrait of what God's dream for Africa looks like, involving the collaboration of an inclusive

---

[23] Katongole, *Who Are My People?* 174.

[24] Linn Tonstad, "On Vulnerability," in *Suffering and the Christian Life*, ed. Karen Kilby and Rachel Davies (London: Bloomsbury, 2019), 183.

[25] Katongole, *Born from Lament*, 161.

state (as opposed to an extractive and centralized state) with a prophetic and poor church (as opposed to a church hosting a bazaar of spiritual claims and endless devotions that often offer false promises to salve the wounds of a bleeding people through the Gospel of prosperity, healing ministries, and delivering people from ancestral curses)? Katongole's emphasis on stories as a theological compass for finding God amid suffering is helpful; particularly helpful is his insertion of the Cross in the transformation of Africa's suffering from the violence of politics, ethnicity, ecology, and others through the violence of love as "an odd logic" that offers hope, healing, and other concrete possibilities of a new creation in Africa.[26]

Katongole's works serve as a good hermeneutical framework for engaging the stories of the people whose voices we listen to in the next chapter. These voices are not activists but everyday Africans on the streets of Uganda, Kenya, and Nigeria. But a more fundamental concern for this chapter that builds on Katongole's but also departs from it is the question of God. The resolution of the suffering of Africans or the African predicament is not settled once and for all through a demonstration of hope in a few activists or in their lamentation. There is the need to enter deeper into this darkness, not with a sense of despair but to excavate and critically analyze what lies hidden in African history and perhaps tell the stories of this pain from the ongoing lives of the everyday Africans. There is the need to literally "descend into hell" with the *anawim* and the crucified people of God in Africa and accompany them by touching their deep pains and wounds rather than using a quick attempt at resolution. In defense of Katongole's approach one might say the same of the Gospel writers who offered the story of the risen Lord as victory over suffering and death, and yet we continue to suffer and to die. But this is where faith and humility meet with patience as we shall demonstrate, and where hope is freedom in embracing human finality, and the limits of theology and human attempt to justify a good God in the face of evil and suffering.

James Cone and M. Shawn Copeland: Black Theology of Protest

James Cone demonstrates a similar complexity on how to find hope amid the suffering of African Americans in the face of violence, lynching, white supremacist terrorism, and hate. These horrible acts against Black bodies

---

[26] Katongole, *Who Are My People?* 174.

created "so much suffering and a deep religious paradox" for Black women, for instance, who began to question the existence of a good God. Suffering like "destructive violence" led to "a spiritual anguish" for many Blacks and connected them with "the spiritual wrestling of the prophets of Job and the psalmist" as they asked God the question: "How long?"[27] Such spirituals like "Wrestling Jacob" and "We Are Climbing Jacob's Ladder" were songs for the individual and collective resistance to suffering and injustice.[28] Cone was not satisfied with pointing to the triumph over suffering through some victories gained. Rather, his work is actually a clarion call to enter deeper into the struggle to liberate the people from oppressive structures. This contrast between struggling to overcome the structures of suffering and evil in African American theology is in sharp contrast with the movement in African theological scholarship where the emphasis is to see the Cross as a symbol of victory and triumph. Both traditions look toward hope. The African American tradition focuses on hope as an ongoing battle that involves small victories and constant reverses from what has been gained. The African theological tradition focuses on hope as already realized in some of the success stories. Whereas African American Christians look at the Cross from ideological and prophetic perspectives in terms of power differentials, idolatry critique, the structural and systemic nature of oppression and injustice, racism, domination, and the need for resistance, coalition, protest, and fighting for redemption, African Christians generally have a triumphalist notion of the Cross (victory, conquest, healing, exorcism, accession to power, prosperity, etc.).

Comparing these two diverse perspectives is a good starting point for further historical, cultural and theological inquiries. Both perspectives are rooted in the complicated histories of Black people in Africa and in North America, the Caribbean, and other parts of the world. Africans have a long past that was hope-filled when they celebrate the memories of their ancestors and the often idyllic mythical portrayals of a peaceful and prosperous past before slavery and the catastrophic Western invasion into African space. So, hope for many Africans has a concrete face in the anamnestic embodiment of a past that they can talk of, dream about, re-create, and ritualize. But

---

[27] James Cone, *The Cross and the Lynching Tree* (Maryknoll, NY: Orbis Books, 2011), 123.

[28] Cone, *The Cross and the Lynching Tree*, 24.

for African Americans the past, like the present, is a world that wishes to void them of their humanity, and the memory of the past is a ghostly and neuralgic destruction that fills people today with a sense that freedom is often elusive and that hope is not a realized eschatology but an ongoing fight with the system. Both perspectives are unified, however, in the common entanglement of Blacks throughout the world with the complicated history of slavery, racism, and white supremacy, and the unfortunate complicity of Christianity in telling the story of the Cross and of eschatology in ways that give the poor imaginary hopes, but no definite change in the trajectory of their history.

This sharp contrast is brought out effectively in M. Shawn Copeland's book, *Knowing Christ Crucified*, where she makes a case for lament that begins with a confession of sin for the complicity of the church and all agencies in the iniquitous acts of violence against Blacks (slavery, lynching, racism, violence against the Black bodies). The confession of sin, she proposes, should also be a movement of conversion, soul-searching, and seeking for new ways of acting and being part of the struggle to defeat evil by placing the promise of hope in the horizon of concrete time and circumstances. In its orientation toward eschatological hope, lament and mourning are manifestations of hope, as Katongole argues. But then there is the important component of African American theological reasoning on lament that Copeland brings out here that is not present in Katongole's and other African theologians of hope. First, lamenting is also a way of naming and denouncing evil and injustice; it is a form of protest not against God (protest theism) or a denial of God (protest atheism), but a protest against unjust structures and an embrace of a hope "that neither forgets nor fails to remember." Second, lament "grieves publicly and creates 'spaces of recognition and catharsis' that prophetically and courageously make a case for 'the reparations of justice.'" Third, lament equips the oppressed and all men and women committed to accompanying the wounded and hurting and the victims of history for the work of justice. By embodying the stories of those who suffer from avoidable social evils, lamenting with and for them is a form of solidarity and bonding together to resist "the calculus of power" that continues to impoverish the weak, oppress the poor, and abuse the innocent. In the words of Bradford Hinze quoted by Copeland, "Laments serve as a furnace that releases base ingredients of pity and anger, retribution and remorse" to repair the world by rejecting the factors and forces that "produce deadly toxins" in the world, and equips us to acts of solidarity, compassion, love-in-action through the struggle to live again for those who are condemned to die.[29]

To conclude, Katongole offers us the narratives of those who have apparently triumphed through suffering to hope, and now become models or best practices of hope. However, the traditions of African American theology offer us the stark reality that many of our brothers and sisters are still hanging on the Cross, and we should not forget the past. In this regard, the theological social autopsy of these deaths must involve grieving these tragic and violent losses of lives, memorializing our collective losses, and committing to ongoing battle to stop the bleeding by addressing the root causes of the problems. Thus, the question remains valid and urgent: What does hope look like for the street boys of Kampala, for the little kids roaming and panhandling on the national borders in Africa? As we will show in the work of Karen Kilby, it is not always useful to justify God's existence through inserting God into the suffering of people as an answer to their suffering or a solution to their liberation from evil. The suffering of people does not simply go away because they have found the "crucified God" in their pain and tragedy. The circumstances that conspire to inflict suffering on so many people in Africa are neither natural nor are they divine. Thus, there is the constant desire of African Christians to find solutions to deal with the consequences of these circumstances. Or, alternatively, there is the valid desire that God might help "destroy" the systems that are creating these sinful social conditions. It is that aspect of resistance, fighting (not with God) but with the systems of oppression and structures of sin, that liberation theology offers.

Liberation Theology

It is the aspect of resisting, protesting, struggling, and fighting with the structures that I found very energizing in liberation theology, particularly in Gustavo Gutiérrez's commentary on Job and Jon Sobrino's *Where Is God?* This tradition of protest theology is markedly absent in African theology. It is not possible to span the entire gamut of these two voices. However, I wish to highlight three developments in the theology of suffering and evil in these two works that I find helpful in analyzing my encounters with my fellow

---

[29] M. Shawn Copeland, *Knowing Christ Crucified: The Witness of African American Religious Experience* (Maryknoll, NY: Orbis Books, 2018), 101–2.

Africans on the streets of some African cities in their suffering and believing, suffering and smiling, suffering and struggling. In a very illuminating line in *The God of Life* Gustavo Gutiérrez writes, "The clouds visible on the horizon should not dismay believers. They should be able to think correctly of God."[30] It is important that theologians speak correctly of God. It is most important in the face of suffering that the victims of history are not led astray and their situation tranquilized, as Fela sang, through false images of God or through the impoverishment of the self. It is important not to have false imaginations of elusive hope while confronting the reality of the oppression of the poor and the assault on people's cultures. Gutiérrez notes that even in his last moment on the Cross, Jesus spoke correctly of God.[31] In his cry from the Cross, the Son of God who was publicly crucified on the crossroads uttered a word of protest, a *cantus firmus* (Bonhoeffer), to "which all the voices of those who suffer unjustly are joined."[32] The insertion of God into the world of human suffering comes in the form of crucified love as "a communion in suffering and in hope, in abandonment of loneliness and in trusting self-surrender in death as in life."[33]

However, I argue that the insertion of created human beings in the world of suffering is not the result of a divine positive act, but the result of evil and specifically moral evil in the social ecosystem of injustice and wickedness. This is why Gutiérrez proposes that taking up the Cross and following Jesus is not a sleepwalking on the painful roads of life, but rather "a watchful solidarity" and "commitment to the alleviation of human suffering, and especially to the removal of its causes as far as possible."[34] In order to do this, believers and theologians who accompany those who walk through the bitter valley of avoidable suffering are invited to take upon themselves the burden of the Lord by taking up the burden of the poor and their suffering. They must engage with the historical factors and conditions that generate the suffering in the world, and be present with the poor.[35] There is the need

---

[30] Gustavo Gutiérrez, *The God of Life* (Maryknoll, NY: Orbis Books, 1991), 16.

[31] Gustavo Gutiérrez, *On Job: God-Talk and the Suffering of the Innocent*, trans. Matthew J. O'Connell (Maryknoll, NY: Orbis Books, 1987), 101.

[32] Gutiérrez, *On Job*, 102.

[33] Gutiérrez, *On Job*, 100.

[34] Gutiérrez, *On Job*, 101.

[35] Gutiérrez, *On Job*, 101.

to find, as Gutiérrez rightly recommends, the right tools for analyzing this shocking suffering of the poor and "the requisite historical effectiveness" and compare the stories we hear in these sites of pain and faces of anguish with the Word of God vis-à-vis the healing, saving, and liberating promises of the Lord. Just like in Latin America, it is not yet *uhuru* for Africa. There are many of our brothers and sisters who are disappearing every day in our countries, drowning in the Mediterranean, victims of modern-day slavery and human trafficking. Millions of God's people in Africa are dying from preventable and treatable diseases. Many of our young people are fleeing from Africa; and women are still being marginalized and denied their rights; and many of our people are exiles and immigrants and being subjected to racism, inhumanities, and insults in North America and Europe. So, with Gutiérrez I agree that we are still at war with the forces of darkness in our continent and in the world. We are still at war with different idols in our societies and in our churches, who, like the destructive *Moloch*, are killing our children and devastating our lands. Thus, we as Africans are not in the *post-this or post-that* in Africa that is past; rather, we must deal with these problems now; we must deal with them not as "past but, unfortunately, as a cruel present and a dark tunnel with no apparent end."[36]

The warning of Gutiérrez against what he calls "sclerotic theology" is still valid today against all quick attempts to justify suffering through some false theologies of the Crucified God, false theologies that imprison people in idolatry (blaming God for evil, blaming human sin for evil, and soliciting endlessly for divine intervention without our human exercise of our graced agentic freedom)[37] because they do not bring the sufferer into contact with the gratuitous embrace of the God of love.[38] What Gutiérrez proposes here is reiterated by Jon Sobrino in his third theodical approach to suffering in his *Where Is God?* in which he proposes that theodicy is not an attempt to make God look good. Indeed, justification of God's goodness or love is not the goal here, but rather how we are touched and affected by suffering and what our faith invites us to do in the face of human suffering. There are three responses that theology and believers should embrace in the face

---

[36] Gutiérrez, *On Job*, 102.

[37] See, for instance, Juan Luis Segundo, *Our Idea of God*, trans. John Drury (Maryknoll, NY: Orbis Books, 1974), 43.

[38] Gutiérrez, *The God of Life*.

of suffering in what Sobrino calls "praxic theology."[39] First *is indignation at human suffering* (what human beings have done or what God has failed to do), which I interpret as protesting and denouncing avoidable suffering that is brought upon the poor through structural violence and the structures of sin. Second, is *the "utopian moment of hope,"* which is the firm conviction of faith that God has the power to nurture hope and praxis ("turning history upside down"—Ellacuría) in people to fight the good fight against evil. Third, *the honesty* we as people of faith, love, and hope must embrace to courageously commit ourselves to making a difference. It is a graced moment that we can make a change through the practice of justice and kindness by taking responsibility for the suffering in the world and working together and walking humbly in compassionate ways to repair the world. But ultimately, the stance here is of protest and being always immersed in the situation and accompanying everyone as we go.[40] How can we then speak of God in the suffering of God's people in unjust social conditions?

Gutiérrez's analysis of the suffering of Job makes the affirmation that God is a God of life and therefore is not the source of evil and suffering. Thus, in order to speak about God in any circumstances, especially in the midst of suffering, "we must first establish ourselves on the terrain of spirituality and practice; only subsequently is it possible to formulate discourse on God in an authentic and respectful way."[41] One must first experience suffering or share in the suffering of others in contemplation and silence before one can actually speak of God and of the reality that is revealed through the suffering of people. The voice of silence and/or of symbols are ways through which we can speak of God in the suffering and context of life. This is because in the face of the tragedy that surrounds modern societies, and particularly the suffering of the innocent poor, it is tempting to write theologies, proclaim homilies, and present hope that might be offered innocently to help people make sense of their suffering. Gutiérrez invites theologians and pastoral agents to enter deeper into the *mysterium iniquitatis* of suffering, injustice, violence, and economic exploitation that force so many people to ask how God's love is revealed in their misfortune and what words theology is using "in telling

---

[39] Jon Sobrino, *Where Is God? Earthquake, Terrorism, Barbarity, and Hope*, trans. Margaret Wilde (Maryknoll, NY: Orbis Books, 2004), 143.
[40] Sobrino, *Where Is God?*
[41] Gutiérrez, *On Job*, xiii.

those who are not even regarded as persons that they are the daughters and sons of God?"[42]

What Gutiérrez proposes here is quite deep and convincing: "The primary response to the suffering of the poor is clearly an active solidarity that includes accompaniment of the people and struggle against the causes of suffering."[43] There are many possibilities of talking about God in the midst of suffering, as Jon Sobrino proposes; one of the most valid is to talk of God using the language of the poor and victims of history.[44] This will require being present with and in the setting with the poor as an eyewitness.[45] Theology, in this sense, is a second order, but the first moment is the encounter that begins with descending into "the world of everyday suffering, of consuming anguish, of ever-burning hope" in the lived reality of the victims of history.[46] But theology is also both prophetic and transformative. As a prophetic mission, theology draws people closer both to the mystery of God and that of suffering. As in the case of Job, theology cannot deny or minimize the suffering of people but rather should amplify their lament and draw the attention of the human audience and the divine auditor (in this case God) into the depths of the pain of victims.

Within this prophetic accompaniment of those who suffer is the possibility of transformation and grace. In this dynamic theology journeys with the victims, as in the case of Job, to an openness to the grace, solidarity, and gratuitousness of God and relationship with others who suffer in the common fight to eliminate the causes of suffering and its consequences. For Gutiérrez, only in this dynamism can justice be established "within the framework of God's gratuitousness. Only in this perspective of the latter is it possible to understand God's predilection for the poor."[47] Ultimately, when we place suffering side by side with the God of life, what becomes evident is our human fragility, finality, and contingency vis-à-vis God's eternal desire to love.

---

[42] Gutiérrez, *On Job*, xv.

[43] Ryan, *God and the Mystery of Human Suffering*, 252.

[44] Sobrino, *Where Is God?*

[45] Stan Chu Ilo, *A Poor and Merciful Church: The Illuminative Ecclesiology of Pope Francis* (Maryknoll, NY: Orbis Books, 2018), 137, 168.

[46] Gustavo Gutiérrez, "Theological Language: Fullness in Silence," in *The Density of the Present: Selected Writings* (Maryknoll, NY: Orbis Books, 1999), 188.

[47] Gutiérrez, *The God of Life*, 162.

Whereas God's desire to love cannot be defeated by created realities, even by our human freedom, we as humans cannot grasp this fully even through the light of reason nor can created freedom realize fully God's definite intention through the assent of faith. But we can lean on God and on each other in the act of love and solidarity. In many contexts of injustice and structures of oppression, leaning on each other and on God is an act of protest and resistance, and a praxis of hope. Ultimately, God's will of abundant life for humans is God's final word spoken from the Cross; it is stronger than anything and remains in history as a mystery to be encountered and lived again and again.[48] In order to lean on God and on each other we need a huge dose of humility, as Karen Kilby proposes.

Karen Kilby

Karen Kilby offers a very sophisticated approach to suffering and evil that might on the surface appear radical but is an invitation to a different way of believing and living. Kilby invites theologians and pastoral agents to humility when trying to make sense of suffering, because a quick attempt to give meaning to suffering either in one's life or in the life of another does not often result in sound theology. For example, the attempt in the premodern world to give an account of suffering as the disruption in the ordered completion of things as willed and determined by God led to the justification of God's existence by finding a way of extricating the name and presence of God from the commotion and destructive forces of evil. In the modern world, driven by the Enlightenment, God is dismissed, on the one hand, and replaced, on the other hand, by different idols. However, the justification of belief and the existence of a good God amid evil remains in the modern era as a constant because human precarity and finitude is not resolved simply by the dismissal of the divine or the assertion of human freedom. However, the insertion of God into the picture through the claim to God's permissive will or the presence of God in the suffering either to conquer it by grace or through the salvific work of the Son of God, and other related theodical justifications of a good God amid evil, minimizes the destructive range of evil in the world. Kilby argues, for instance, that the common approach to theodicy that claims that God is suffering with the person who suffers or that the Son of God knows

---

[48] Gutiérrez, *On Job*, 66.

what it means to suffer and thus identifies with all human suffering through the Incarnation does not satisfy the human quest to make sense of suffering. This is true, she argues, because inflicting so much suffering on one's child is not made less heinous because the parent also claims to have inflicted the same suffering on herself.

What Kilby is proposing is that humans and theologians must admit their limits in the face of evil and human suffering. They must constantly seek to address the problem of suffering because it is proper to human beings and theologians and spiritual masters to pursue such inquiries. However, she argues that "why" questions about "where is God?" in the face of evil are valid, the answers given are not always valid and often complicate the problems further. According to her: "Is God powerful and good if we suffer either moral or natural evil?" These questions are "legitimate," but they are also "utterly unanswerable."[49] She argues further:

> Christians believe God is working salvation and trust that ultimately God will bring good out of all conceivable evils, but this does not make these evils good, nor render their presence explicable, nor allow us to understand how they can take place in the good creation of a loving and faithful God. Sometimes of course we can already see, and must look for, good coming out of evil—suffering can bring growth, sin is an occasion to turn back to God's forgiveness with trust, dependence and gratitude. But we cannot turn these things into explanations, in part because suffering can also, through no fault of the sufferer, bring about degradation and corruption, and sin can build on itself and perpetuate itself. When we see good coming from evil, we can see this as the beginning of the hoped-for work of God, but not the beginning of any kind of explanation.[50]

Kilby invites us to move away from quickly rushing to explain evil. However, she says that neither should such questions for the explanation of God's presence in the face of horrendous evil in the lives of individuals or in the world be dismissed. Not offering solutions or inadequate answers to the

---

[49] Karen Kilby, *God, Evil and the Limits of Theology* (London: T&T Clark, 2021), 81.

[50] Kilby, *God, Evil and the Limits of Theology*, 81.

problem of suffering does not mean inaction or spiritual capitulation or theological retrenchment; it is an invitation to enter the realm of mystery. Evil is a mystery but of a different kind from the mystery of God.[51] To understand the implication of this assertion by Kilby and her call for some theological dissonance in the face of evil, the distinction that Gabriel Marcel makes between a problem and a mystery is useful.[52] A problem relates to something that you cannot figure out immediately because you do not understand the issue, but most likely through the application of your human intellect, research, and inquiry you will get some information that can help you to understand the issue. Problems are like puzzles that can be figured out with some patience and effort. Mystery, on the other hand, is "something in which I myself am involved."[53] It is something I live; something that actually I cannot make go away but something that I must learn to live and grow with to find strength and hope by entering deeper into it. Most often we wish that suffering will go away, that an act of injustice done to us should simply disappear, or that God will destroy those who bring so much harm upon us. But often the situation remains the same for some time or might change for the better or even lead to the destruction of life; hence the need to find a way of living with, resisting, and coping with the mystery of suffering and evil.

Fiona Clements and Fiona Tasker in their research on older Roman Catholic women cancer survivors found that the more the women embraced their condition as a mystery—something beyond their control—they found an inner strength to endure the suffering and found a purpose in life. These women did not simply submit to the inevitability of their deaths; there was some dynamism about their attitude rather than passive acceptance. It was observed that in embracing the mystery of the sickness through their faith in the Paschal mystery they found an inner disposition and freedom that took the "responsibility for their recovery, or for their death, out of their own hands." The acceptance of this mystery became for them not a threat to annihilation, but a source of calmness that came from the certainty of faith in embracing human finality with a disposition that suffering and death are "transitional

---

[51] Kilby, *God, Evil and the Limits of Theology*, 83.

[52] Gabriel Marcel, *Being and Having* (New York: Harper Torchbooks, 1965), 117.

[53] Marcel, *Being and Having*, 117. Cited in Stephen Bevans, *Community of Missionary Disciples: The Continuing Creation of the Church* (Maryknoll, NY: Orbis Books, 2024), 159.

stages in the on-going process of redemption, an idea encapsulated by the Paschal Mystery, where death is situated between suffering and resurrection."[54]

There are three important aspects of Kilby's arguments that are helpful in designing the questions for our encounter with African Christians in the bus stops. The first is the framework of "suffering and struggling." Kilby's claim that suffering is not good and thus "suffering and loss are not part of God, or grounded in God's being, or desired by God"[55] is validated by the fact that the people we encountered on the bus stops were not comfortable with the conditions of life in their countries. They did not see their suffering as part of the plan of God or sharing in the passion of Christ. Rather, they were fighting and struggling to overcome their suffering while adopting different coping and survival techniques and experimenting with different religious options in search of solutions. Any identification of their suffering to the passion was with an eye on the victory of the Resurrection.

The second is the aspect of suffering and believing. Kilby offers us a way of understanding kenosis, human vulnerability and fragility, through her interpretations of the responses of La Retraite Sisters. In the face of suffering, the believer is called to bear witness not to the triumph of the human spirit, but to the triumph of grace. There is always an aperture that opens in the darkest pit of suffering for the believer to testify to the work of God and grow toward the goodness of God. The third point is similar to Katongole's interpretation of his encounters with some heroes of faith who bore witness in the midst of the genocide in Rwanda. Bearing witness amid suffering is the result of battling with God and is characterized by anger, pain, complaint, and lament similar to Job's and Jeremiah's experiences. Bearing witness is also sometimes reflected in our own anger toward ourselves and to others when we sense our own inability to fix the situation that is causing suffering or to prevent avoidable suffering.[56]

Finally, suffering exposes human vulnerability and limitations. Some cultures deny or suppress the reality of suffering, loss, and evil. However,

---

[54] Fiona Clements and Fiona Tasker, "Living through the Paschal Mystery: Surviving Cancer Narratives Told by Older Roman Catholic Women," *Journal of Religion, Spirituality & Aging* 27, no. 1 (2015): 61.

[55] Karen Kilby, "The Seductions of Kenosis," in *Suffering and the Christian Life*, ed. Karen Kilby and Rachel Davies (London: T&T Clark, 2021), 162.

[56] Kilby, "The Seductions of Kenosis," 169.

admitting human finitude is liberating but not a capitulation to the inexorable forces of history—whether for good or ill. Rather, it opens the believer to the work of the Spirit and the encounter with grace in the darkness and amid "diminishment, woundedness and brokenness."[57] We have here a critical framework that must be placed on the theological dashboard in contemplating the face of the Lord Jesus in the wounded and bleeding faces of our suffering brothers and sisters. There is the need for some restraint, as Kilby proposes, instead of rushing in to fix the problem of evil and human suffering. Many theological systems and some Christian proclamation in the past and in today's Africa are offering solutions to suffering that require a more critical analysis to determine their relevance for making sense of the complexities of life in Africa. There is the need to journey with God's people and to gain a more sophisticated understanding of the African condition today and the suffering that Africans are enduring. There is also the need to embrace a certain incompleteness in the search for interpretative frames to suffering, as Kilby has suggested, because "we have to remember to keep a place in our theological systems, or our theological reflections, for hope in that which goes absolutely beyond anything these systems can offer or grasp, hope in the eventual triumph of love over suffering, joy over loss."[58] This takes the believer always back to the source of life, God, and our human finitude, which is not a boundary for God's operation. This finitude is also an invitation not to give up hope. In the stories and movies that I analyze in the next chapter, we meet some Africans in their daily struggles to live without giving up on life and hope trusting in God, whom Pope Francis spoke of in these words: "The God who created the universe out of nothing can also intervene in this world and overcome every form of evil. Injustice is not inevitable. A spirituality which forgets God as all-powerful and Creator is not acceptable."[59]

Conclusion

Christianity is not simply about belief, it is also about how Christians live—believing, belonging, and behaving. Ultimately, what is at stake is the nature of love that believers are invited to embrace, as exemplified in the

---

[57] Kilby, "The Seductions of Kenosis," 174.
[58] Kilby, "The Seductions of Kenosis," 174.
[59] Pope Francis, *Laudato Si'*, 75.

Good Samaritan, and the nature of what they worship, as exemplified in their religious beliefs and commitments. It is also about what kind of power people seek, and what kinds of power prevent or threaten people's existence and flourishing in Africa and bring so much suffering and pain. Suffering brings the human creature face to face with human finitude, but it also reveals the painful reality of human choices and the social evil that emerge with the abuse of human freedom by those who have power in how they exercise that power for the common good or against the common good. The concern of this chapter is on the social consequences of the abuse of power in societies and how such abuses manufacture avoidable suffering for so many poor people who inhabit the existential peripheries of life. I have argued that theologians and preachers cannot use the name of God to justify such avoidable sufferings produced through the abuse of human freedom by the powerful against the weak in places like Africa or against Blacks in the United States or peoples in the Global South by the corporations and institutions in the Global North. A theology of reversal of history moves from lament to condemnation, from condemnation to solidarity, and from solidarity to protest and active social engagement and even martyrdom in the struggle to disrupt the convergence of destructive factors that are harming the poor so that power can be equally redistributed to build new conditions for human and cosmic flourishing. Whatever is opposed to human and cosmic flourishing is opposed to life and love and thus opposed to the God of life and love. Authentic religion must align itself with God's creation and through the gratuitous power of love that gives life to creation and thus honors God. As John Macquarrie puts it, "It is a question of love versus power, and that fundamental opposition underlies every conflict between true religion and false, God and the idols. To what does our heart finally cling? What is truly our god? Security and power, or love with all its vulnerability?"[60]

---

[60] John Macquarrie, *The Humility of God* (London: SCM, 1978), 33.

3

Suffering and Smiling

Doing Matatu *Theology on the Streets of Africa**

> Listening to our brothers and sisters at the existential peripheries was the most transformative experience for me as both a priest and theologian. I learned more from these encounters than all my studies in the seminaries and in the theology faculties. Following the wisdom of the Lord Jesus and Pope Francis, I learned that the best method to accompany so many of our siblings who are often forgotten, judged, condemned, and abandoned is to step into their shoes with reverence and respect, and listen to them to hear the voice of God speaking to me in a most eloquent and convincing way.
>
> —Stan Chu Ilo

---

* On "*matatu* theology" see Rodrigo Mejia, "'*Matatu* Theology': My Experience as a Hekima Pioneer Living in St. Joseph the Worker Parish, Kangemi," *Hekima Review*, no. 68 (May 2024), particularly 173–74, where Bishop Mejia describes *Matatu* theology as a theology that shifts the epistemological framework from what the theologian thinks to the questions emerging from the ordinary people. This shift occurs by having "the smell of the sheep" through closeness to the people such that the theology is about "what is the question" of the people rather than what is the answer and teaching that I have to offer them as a theologian. These questions trigger a corresponding quest in the theologian to pay attention to the kinds of discussion, proclamations, and disputations that one could hear in packed buses (called *matatu*) in Kenya or at bus stops, on street corners, and in many existential peripheries of life.

One of the most valid approaches to doing theology is to be with the people and to follow their stories so that theological writing becomes a story written from an environment of faith in which the characters in the plot see themselves and the face of God in the theology that is written or spoken. Paying attention to the environment of narration is so vital. Doing theology from the stories of God's people involves every effort at explaining and interpreting events in the past and connecting the past to the present within the environment in which the people are living, suffering, and smiling. This approach is traditionally captured in the Twi word, *Sankofa*, literally meaning "go back and get it," but which signifies that in following people's present life, one must pay attention to the past to understand the present. One cannot judge people without understanding their history and context, nor should one make theological proposals and offer solutions to addressing one problem or another without seeing the total picture through the context of the people.

In this light, the theologian must enter the history of people and the context in which they live. The success of such immersion in people's narratives, according to Paul Ricoeur, "depends on our ability to follow a story."[1] But following a story is not simply chronology, where one recounts a person's life from birth to death in sequence; rather,

> the activity of narrating does not consist simply in adding episodes to one another; it also constructs meaningful totalities out of scattered events. This aspect of the art of narrating is reflected on the side of following a story, in the attempt to 'grasp together' successive events. The art of narrating, as well as the corresponding art of following a story, therefore require that we are able to extract a configuration from a succession.[2]

Following a story involves a succession of activities and immersion in the world and ecclesial and social contexts of people's lives. To write a spiritual portrait in this light is analogous to bringing together layers of meaning; to reflect, as Ricoeur proposes, on events with the aim of "encompassing them in successive totalities."[3] What this means in writing African theology through

---

[1] Paul Ricoeur, *Hermeneutics and the Human Sciences*, ed. and trans. John B. Thompson (Cambridge: Cambridge University Press, 1981), 278.

[2] Ricoeur, *Hermeneutics and the Human Sciences*, 278.

[3] Ricoeur, *Hermeneutics and the Human Sciences*, 279.

the lived faith of Africans, to use the words of Walter Benjamin, involves "a lot of digging beyond the surface." This might involve going through community sources (the context), the worldview and social facts (the pre-text), and returning to the same matter, "to scatter it as one scatters earth, to turn it over as one turns over soil. For the 'the matter itself' is no more than the strata which yield their long-sought secrets only to the most meticulous investigation."[4] This attitude of "digging beyond the surface," and "following closely" was the hermeneutical framework that informed my encounter with my brothers and sisters whose stories shape the content of this chapter.

I lived in Lagos in Western Nigeria between 2000 and 2002 and had daily encounters and conversations with many young men who hung around churches and offices and major streets looking for menial jobs or for aid. These young men are called *alayes*, or "area boys." Whenever I greeted them with "How are you?" they often responded simply with the words: "Suffering and smiling." It is their way of saying to themselves and their conversation partners that life is difficult, but they are not giving up on life. Variants of this expression occur in many Nigerian and African local parlances.[5] In the Igbo language, people often say in response to the question, "How are you?": *amachie uwa george* (literally, we are just happy to cover our body with a wrapper). In local pidgin in many parts of Nigeria people say, in response to the pidgin "how body" (meaning "how are you?"), *body dey inside cloth* (my body is covered by my cloth). This means, "Well, things might not be moving well, but I still have a cloth over my body."

These responses capture the contradictions of history but also point to practical theodicy—everyday people on the streets of major African cities are suffering, but they are saying "even though we are surrounded by suffering,

---

[4] Walter Benjamin, "Excavation and Memory," in *Selected Writings*, vol. 2: *1927–1934*, trans. Rodney Livingstone and others, ed. Michael W. Jennings, Howard Eiland, and Gary Smith (Cambridge, MA: Belknap Press of Harvard University Press, 1999), 576.

[5] This attitude of holding in a healthy tension, suffering, and smiling is also found among African Americans. According to Shawn Copeland, "Suffering squeezes a delicious ironic spirit and tough laughter. Consider the Gullah (woman's) proverb: 'Ah done been in sorrow's kitchen and ah licked de pots clean.'" See M. Shawn Copeland, "Wading through Many Sorrows: Toward a Theology of Suffering in a Womanist Perspective," in *Womanist Theological Ethics: A Reader*, ed. Katie Geneva Cannon, Emilie M. Townes, and Angela D. Sims (Louisville, KY: WJK, 2011), 136.

we will not give up hope." The people believe in God and a better future, even though they face heart-wrenching social precarity and pain. This led me to conduct this research to understand how my fellow Africans who are facing a lot of painful social conditions express their faith and hope in God. What is driving their religious faith and their never-say-die attitude in the face of very challenging social conditions? In the second part, I will analyze what I learned from my fellow Africans through interviews conducted on the streets of Kampala, Uganda, and Lagos, Nigeria and on buses in Nairobi. This kind of immersing oneself in the lives and narratives of those who inhabit the existential peripheries of life is what has come to be identified in East Africa as *matatu* theology (learning about God and interpreting religious faith through the messages of preachers on buses and bus stops, and through stepping into the messy world of people who are suffering). This chapter is my attempt to do what Pope Francis's *Veritatis Gaudium* proposes: that theology should be done as spiritual biography.[6]

Suffering and Smiling:
Theology on the Streets and at the Bus Stops

One of the most significant findings from my conversations with African Christians on bus stops in Kampala, Uganda, in 2017 and 2022 is that most of them defined suffering as avoidable and blamed their suffering on the government. The thirty-four people I interviewed were under twenty-five years of age and were asked to describe the suffering they faced in their lives. Only one person spoke that he suffered from an ailment. The thirty-three others did not speak of their sickness even though from the interview I knew that seven had some chronic sickness. In Nairobi, I interviewed thirty participants. Fourteen did not finish high school and were hawkers along the streets. Twenty-six were Catholics and four were Anglicans. Twenty two were female and eight were male. Six of the women between the ages of eighteen and twenty-four years were not married, fourteen of those between the ages of twenty-six and forty-five years were married, and two were single. All the men between the ages of twenty-four and forty were married.

---

[6] Stan Chu Ilo, "Reform from the Margins: Pope Francis and the Renewal of Catholic Theology," in *All the Ends of the Earth: Challenge and Celebration of Global Catholicism*, ed. Jane E. Linahan and Cyril Orji (Maryknoll, NY: Orbis Books, 2020), 161–62.

Twenty-one of the respondents said that they faced some challenges of war, tribal conflict, natural disaster, epidemic, and poverty. Eight said they had not faced these challenges. Of those who faced the challenges, twenty had hope for the future. One respondent despaired, but the rest were hopeful for a better future despite the challenges they faced. Most of them cited the example of Jesus Christ who faced challenges as well but "one day he was glorified by sitting on the right hand of the Father" as one respondent emphasized. They too hoped that one day they would overcome and defeat those challenges. Twenty-nine of the thirty respondents in Nairobi, like the people I encountered on the streets of Kampala, spoke of their suffering in the four categories slightly edited below:

Socioeconomic Suffering (Kampala, Uganda)

- There are many people still homeless in Kampala; they are suffering along the streets.
- I think being sick brings suffering especially if you have a killer disease, especially HIV/AIDS or Ebola.
- High levels of poverty characterized by lack of money in both cash and kind.
- Too much unemployment, especially of the youths, and coming from a poor family that cannot afford the necessities of life.
- Increasing crime rates characterized by murder, rape, and defilement, and homosexuality which is seriously spreading in East Africa.
- There are too many people (overpopulation) in many of our areas amidst little/no food, insufficient water, housing, and other basic necessities of life.
- Pollution and environmental damages which could also have an effect on people's health.
- Some rich people and political authorities destroy nature because they build big homes or for their businesses, and it creates suffering and pain for those who used to work in the farms that were converted to houses.
- There is a growing lack of trust in financial institutions of the society. Much of the stress is on profit maximization, not on serving society. Many individuals have lost their money in such institutions.

- The poor and the rich in our society alike continue to struggle with prejudice, suspicion and distrust based on how many achievements one has. There is still a huge gap between the poor and rich as regards socialization.
- Affirmative action efforts continue to draw criticism in our society. Little appreciation is shown for those who give much for the good of society.

Political Pain and Suffering in Uganda and Kenya

- Democratic progress has been rolled back in our country (Uganda). Some politically vocal individuals die mysteriously amidst insincere and hardly reliable/credible postmortem reports.
- Scandals have tarnished many politicians and the very systems they operate in. Many of these scandals are moral and financial. Corruption has become a daily bread and a normal practice and easily escaped by only sleeping a few days in prison.
- Dirty politics have polarized our society.
- There is an increasing general lack of faith in current "democratic" government because of the way politics proceeds in the country.
- Unemployment.
- Poor attitudes towards life.
- Some people are homeless, and others only have indecent housing facilities.
- Lack of enough food.
- Delayed salaries of government workers.
- Loneliness and single parenthood.
- Social discrimination and exclusion.
- Disappointments with plans leading to attainment of dreams, like refusal of visa entries to leave for greener pastures abroad.
- Lack of hope for the future.
- Tribalism, favoritism, and gender imbalances in sharing the national cake of employment opportunities.
- Depression manifested by sadness, fatigue, feelings of being worthless, or hopeless, agitation, restlessness and irritability, suicidal thoughts, and having problems with sleeping.
- Feeling of guilt (guilty conscience) for not being able to support our parents after they have trained you in school because you have no job.

- Domestic violence.
- Thoughtless words and actions of friends who turn their back on you because you are poor and jobless can cause extreme pain and sadness.

Immigration and Public Health Failings as Source of Pain and Sorrow

- The increasing influx of people (legal and illegal) and refugees too are leading to resentment and clashes. We have many refugees in Uganda and Kenya, and it is a source of suffering and anxiety. This has increased the crime rate in our area. There are so many people whose origin are unknown in Uganda and Kenya (some are from Sudan, South Sudan, Congo, Somalia and Ethiopia).
- The government continues to struggle with providing basic services but is failing to provide the needs of many people in our area. There are too many people who are hungry and unemployed, and they suffer. Joblessness and not having money brings so much suffering.
- Total or partial deprivation of basic human needs, including food, safe drinking water, sanitation facilities, health, shelter, education, and information.
- Lack of income and productive resources to ensure sustainable livelihoods.
- Hunger and malnutrition.
- Ill health amidst no medication.
- Limited or lack of access to education and other basic services.
- Increased morbidity and mortality from illness.
- Homelessness and inadequate housing.
- Unsafe environment, social discrimination, and exclusion.
- Many disabled people (like the blind, crippled, mentally impaired, and the chronically sick).
- Inability to decently bury dead friends and relatives due to lack of resources and land.
- Inability to send children to school.
- Lacking able-bodied members who can fend for families or society amidst crises.
- Presence of many children in child labor instead of in school.
- Many single parents with many children to care for.

- The readiness to accept demeaning work or low status work with any available pay.
- Having no food security.
- Total dependence on common property resources.
- General decay in infrastructure.

What I learned from this sampling of opinions of young Africans is that they do not blame God for their suffering, but rather blame the system of government in their countries. They also do not think that God should be solving these problems, since they clearly see the convergence of factors in the way their countries are run as the cause of the problems that they face. Thus, one can say that for these young people their suffering is avoidable, and once the causes of the suffering are removed, things will improve. Hope for these young Africans is not through any divine intervention but on improving the situation in Africa in both the states and religious institutions.

In analyzing the data from Nigeria, there is a similar convergence in how African Christians interpret the suffering they face—their suffering has a name, and it is failed leadership in the state and in religious institutions. There are three categories under which I have grouped these insights focusing on the narratives from the streets of Nigeria, which tell stories similar to the stories of my conversation partners on the streets of Kampala and Kenya.

First is *suffering and smiling*. Most of the young people I encountered suffer because of poor living conditions and the absence of the necessities of life, but they are hopeful for a better future. In Kampala, particularly, thirty of the thirty-four young people spoke of their beliefs that the Catholic Church in Uganda is better suited to affect the lives of the people. They point to the most successful bank in the country, Centenary Bank, run by the Catholic Church, as a good example of a well-functioning business. The same logic they proposed could be applied to other aspects of life like agriculture, education, and health to address the suffering and pain of people.

Second is *suffering and struggling*. Persistent poverty and increasing desperation generate much anger and frustration among Africans, especially the young. However, many people claim that Africa is not poor, though impoverished by the external and internal actors and the ravages of African history. The structural nature of poverty in Africa is one that I and many people have addressed in many publications, but for the African who has no food, shelter, healthcare, or hope, what does our structural analysis bring to them?[7] Do the poor in Africa even have time to read the books of African theologians? How can the hungry, the forsaken, and the abandoned read theological books or listen to our homilies? How can these young Africans find hope in our solemn liturgies and processions and devotions?

Amid these questions, a new sense of urgency and a new commitment has arisen among many young Africans. They see the present historical exigencies in Africa as a kairotic moment for the second liberation of Africa. This was demonstrated in the youth-led "end SARS" movement in Nigeria in 2020, and the youth-led end-tax-reform revolt in 2024 in Kenya, to mention but a few.

Third is *suffering and believing*. Many Africans find their Christian faith as the unshakable ground for working hard, hoping for a better future, challenging oppressive structures, and finding inspiration for social activism and acts of solidarity, all to reverse the course of history in Africa. The Christian faith in many instances has become the strongest agency for the gradual and steady emergence of all forms of social capital in Africa. These include women's cooperative groups, capacity-building among the marginalized, political activism to challenge the corruption in some African countries, and all kinds of biblically grounded prophetic witnessing against injustice, exploitation, and manipulation of the poor through ethnic, social, and cultural cleavages. We posed these questions to people:

1. Suffering and smiling: Why are you hopeful for a better future amid the challenges you face today?
2. Suffering and struggling: Can you share with me a personal experience of God's intervention in your life?
3. Suffering and believing: How do you find God in your suffering, and who is God for you?

---

[7] See, for instance, Stan Chu Ilo, "Ebola and the Ravages of History in Paul Farmer: A Catholic Theological Ethical Response to Global Health Inequity in Africa," *Journal of Moral Theology* 4, CTEWC Book Series 4 (February 19, 2023): 271–98; Stan Chu Ilo and Gabriel T. Wankar, "Church and Development in African Catholicism," in *Handbook of African Catholicism*, ed. Stan Chu Ilo (Maryknoll, NY: Orbis Books, 2022), 340–66; Stan Chu Ilo and Idara Otu, "Theology of Development," in *The Routledge Handbook of African Theology*, ed. Elias Bongmba (New York: Routledge, 2020), 220–42.

The analysis that follows is a brief thematic presentation of the ethnographic data collected among thirty Christians across denominational lines in Nigeria. My goal is to present a portrait of an African theodicy from the views of my brothers and sisters, a *sensus fidei fidelium*. These brothers and sisters see God differently, beyond what the theological and doctrinal texts say. The result is a different kind of Gospel. African theologians and pastors should read this type of Gospel as often as possible. My conversation partners believe in God and look up to God to liberate, heal, and save them in the challenging social context of Nigeria. We specifically targeted Christians struggling to survive; people who despite the difficulties faced in present-day Nigeria still hold on to God as the One who will not fail them, even when most things around them are showing signs of decay and instability. This portrait offers a window into the lived faith of God's people in Nigeria.

We have also analyzed some Nigerian movies to assess the popular characterization of God, suffering, and coping in art. As it is said, art mimics life. The final section of this chapter uses the first Nigerian movie "blockbuster," *Living in Bondage*, to demonstrate key issues for theology, pastoral leadership, and the Church in Africa. These are the search for abundant life, integral salvation, and integral development in our continent, and why the solutions being given to this search are worsening the precarity of people.

Research Demographics	
Research sites	Lagos, Ebonyi, Kaduna, Enugu, Nasarawa
Time frame	March–July 2022
Population and Sampling	
Number of respondents	30
Gender	Male (18) and Female (12)
Age distributions	18–30 =17, 31–50 = 8, 51–85 = 5

Where People Found God: While Searching for Work

The discussion we conducted on the streets shows that religious faith is a powerful source of strength and hope for people in Nigeria. God is found in every aspect of people's lives, and God narratives pervade everything people do and their outlook in life. This pervasiveness is not limited by age or sex but is present at every stage of people's lives and in all circumstances. It is empowering as a source of hope in most of our respondents, particularly in moments of uncertainties. Also noticeable is that God is not an object of critical inquiry for most people. Nor did I hear any self-critical reflection on the claims about God. Nor did the respondents question the veracity or verifiability of the things they attribute to the agency of God or divine intervention.

This is significant in the analysis, because here one could grasp easily a different kind of theodicy at work. Theodicy is an attempt to justify the existence of God and the presence of a good God in the face of human suffering and pain. If God is a good God, why does God allow evil and unmerited suffering for God's people? Why does God allow a beautiful country like Nigeria and a beautiful continent like Africa to be so abused through extractive leadership and destructive global exploitation and other factors that conspire to bring about the African predicament?

Through the faith of these respondents, one grasps quickly and directly the construction of God's existence through a direct lived experience of suffering and smiling. The stance of these Christians is not simply a quiescent submission to negative forces of entropy that create the architecture of violence and structural injustice, but rather a form of resistance against these forces. These Christians are not saying they accept the condition or the failings of their governments and their religious leaders, or that they will acquiesce to these unacceptable conditions. Rather, they are saying to the forces of darkness: "You are oppressing us, but we will not allow your oppression to take away the smile on our faces and our hope." The face of a smiling victim of oppression is cruciform, for it says to the darkness, "I will not be defeated by you, and you will not have the last words." It is in this sense that these voices are grains of theological wisdom that should be thematized as foundations of African theodicy.

Miss A.A. is twenty-seven and a graduate who has resorted to shoemaking due to the lack of employment in Nigeria. She calls herself a strong believer in God and professes that she has no other source of hope than God for her survival of the hardships in Nigeria. She admits that God is her only hope for the future. She contends that she finds God through her daily reading of the Bible, and it is from the Bible that she finds inspiration and strength in handling the challenges and difficulties she faces in Nigeria. She also points to her being taught from childhood that nothing good comes easily, but with faith in God and hard work, she would overcome every obstacle. She says that her Christian faith invites her to put her trust in God always, and never to depend on anyone else.

Where did she find God in a very concrete way in her life? In 2014, A.A. gained admission to university, but the excitement was cut short when her father suddenly went down with a strange sickness, which claimed all the money she had saved. Hence there was no money to pay for either the acceptance fee or school fees. A.A., determined not to defer her admission, sought financial assistance from friends and family members, but to no avail. According to her, God intervened in that situation when she approached a man in her church who had donated in support of an ongoing church project. The financial assistance she received from the man enabled her to make the payments for the acceptance and school fees. She disclosed that her sick father got well with the restoration of his financial fortunes. Miss A.A. found God in the concreteness of her complex life situation, particularly in the loss of income, loss of money, loss of hope, and loss of support. God is thus found, in the logic of A.A., in moments when all hope is lost and when most things appear to be failing around us.

God is also found when people seem to have lost their way in life because of the uncertainty in the country. Kendo, age thirty, graduated with a degree in dentistry in Eastern Nigeria, but searched in vain for years without work. We met Kendo at a petrol station where he was selling fuel. His faith in God is the only way he has been able to find meaning in this setback that led him to seek for a job at a petrol station, through which he is able to put food on the table. He believes that hope should be sustained, and that everybody in Nigeria, particularly young people, should stand up for their future. He emphasizes that without hard work, faith is futile, which is why he decided to work in a petrol station to save some money. This would enable him to seek a visa to travel overseas in search of a greener pasture. This respondent was confident that there would be "light at the end of the tunnel," and insists that hard times should not define anyone. Kendo, who lost his parents early in life, shared an experience of God that made a lasting impression on him, through which he imbibes the "I still believe" attitude. As an orphan he was a street vendor and never really imagined that he would be able to attend school. Through the help of relatives and friends, he was able to go to school, because of God's intervention in his life. Thus, he reasons, the same God who saw a poor orphan through to get a dental degree will one day help the same orphan to find a well-paid job.

The same attitude of faith in a God who is the answer to all problems is what we found in our conversation with Mr. IIgw. Aged thirty, a graduate and tricycle operator commonly known as *Keke*. He could not find a job after graduation, but he claimed that God has helped him to find a means of survival through being a tricycle operator. Where did he find God? Through prayer, and in his daily life. He affirms that he sees God's hands in his challenges almost every day. He shared a story of how he had no money and no job after graduating from the university, though he desperately needed something to support himself and his family. God brought someone who assisted him to purchase a tricycle.

"With my determination and faith in God, I am certain to go into a better business compared to what I have now." This was how the twenty-seven-year-old roadside trader Mrs. Feco describes her experience of God. She works as a roadside seller of roasted plantains and yams. Despite her current financial difficulties, she truly believes that God will bless her business and open doors to better times soon. Feco sees God's hands in her life and business situations. According to her, most times she would roast plantains and yams, but customers didn't come, and hence she would be upset because of lost income. However, whenever she found herself in this kind of situation, she would cry out to God, spontaneously asking God to send customers to her. She professes that God has always responded to her prayers by sending customers to buy food from her. For her, customers buying whatever quantity of yams she roasts each day is God's intervention. She opines that through prayers, she works with fellow Christians to bring about change and socioeconomic empowerment in her society. Feco attests to the importance of patience and trust in God for any true believer.

Where People Found God: In Bad News

"Bad news" here is simply things not working according to plan because of internal or external factors. It could result in loss of work, loss of life, sickness—especially terminal or chronic illnesses—or breakups, or injuries.

Sixty-five-year-old Mr. Denco, who is a carpenter, recalls how he had suffered a lot. He became an orphan before his twelfth birthday. Much later in life, he was involved in a motor accident, which resulted in the amputation of his left leg and rendered him partially disabled. Surviving this road mishap marked a turning point in his life, as he was convinced that God had a purpose for his life by saving him from such a horrific incident. Today he is fully engaged in charitable evangelism. By trusting God and leaning on God's help, he no longer sees his disability as an impediment to pursuing a better future. Rather, because of the experience of miracles in his life, he has learned to trust God more and more each day, knowing that God will provide for all his needs.

Faith in God backed by love can make a Christian unstoppable in the face of the unspeakable suffering in present-day Nigeria. So, says Mr. Gabby, seventy-nine, who is a furniture maker and an evangelist in Afikpo, Ebonyi state, in Eastern Nigeria. Mr. Gabby reveals that God's love has enkindled his faith in a better future. He admits that his motivation to work hard and to encourage others comes from God. He admits that things are critical in Nigeria, and that people are struggling to survive. This respondent, who was critically ill in March 2022, recounts the miracle he experienced in his life, and how God intervened in his health through people of goodwill who expressed much love and solidarity. Against this backdrop, Mr. Gabby believes that Christian love could be a veritable weapon to surmount times of trial in Nigeria. Working together with other Christians for economic empowerment is possible through hard work and love, especially in northern Nigeria where Christians are being attacked in churches, at their farms, and in their homes. He urges Christians to remain steadfast and undaunted in their faith in God, and hope for a better future.

It is folly not to learn a skill in contemporary Nigeria, stresses twenty-one-year-old Kemi, who recently completed her secondary school education. Without funds or support to proceed to university, Kemi decided to move to Lagos with her aunt, to learn how to plait hair and save money to further her education. She makes known that her faith in God and desire not only to return to school but to support her family motivate her to work hard for a better future. She employs the slogan "survival of the fittest" to describe the present situation in Nigeria, where everybody is struggling to survive. In her case, she accepts God's help, and she has been able to learn some skills and save a significant amount of money. Where does Kemi find God? She shares a story of how she was accused of having stolen money from her madam (that is, her boss) and was threatened to be fired if she failed to provide the missing money. She pleaded innocence, but the madam would not believe her. She turned toward God, asking for vindication. She professes that God intervened in that situation, when her madam's daughter admitted that she removed the missing money. To this end, her madam apologized to Kemi, and promoted her to a better position. Kemi emphasizes the need for Christians in Nigeria, particularly young people, to keep helping one another while striving for a better future.

Challenges, suffering, hardship, and trials should not define a Christian, according to twenty-two-year-old A.K. Instead, courage and faith in God should be expressed in the face of human suffering. A.K. is a computer operator who told me that he grew up without the ability to read and write. However, he trusted that God would grant him the understanding he desired as a student. According to the respondent, God granted his request. He became a better student with improved ability to read and write. Having completed his secondary education, but without sufficient funds to further his education, A.K. decided to work in a cyber café to raise money for his undergraduate studies. Through God's intervention he became a computer whiz without ever going to the university. "Things are very hard now in Nigeria, but I have faith that God will bless my effort, and I will achieve my dream of going to university. 'I know I will make it.'"

Consider the experience of a blind preacher woman. "My purpose in life is to preach the Gospel, encouraging people to remain good Christians, and never grow weary despite the hardship and suffering in Nigeria," asserts Pastor G.B. She is forty-five years old and a mobile pastor and worshipper at the Path of Truth Gospel Church International. She makes known how her faith in God became the source of strength and motivation, after recovering from an illness that claimed her sight. The respondent acknowledges that she is suffering—like most Nigerians—because of bad governance. Nonetheless, she is smiling because she is confident the future will be better, because God holds the future in God's mighty hand. Pastor G.B. discloses how she dedicated her life to spreading the Good News after God miraculously healed her from a critical health condition. Being a blind preacher woman, Pastor G.B. depends solely on the help she receives from people on the buses and at the bus stops where she preaches the Gospel. She uses her preaching the Word of God as an instrument to bring about positive change and encouragement in the lives of Christians struggling to make ends meet. God uses her ministry, which depends on people's generosity to provide for her. She does not have any congregation, and depends solely on God who usually supplies her needs through the people to whom God sends her each day on the buses and at the bus stops.

"My faith in God helps me so much in overcoming challenges and difficulties I encounter in my life. I am suffering but still smiling," says E.P., nineteen, a student and a sales representative. She notes that things are really hard in Nigeria, and that life had become even more difficult as university workers had been on strike for over five months at the time of the interview. The respondent discloses how she decided to become a saleswoman in a mini-market, so as not to remain idle until the end of the strike. "If you stay idle, hunger will kill you," she says. As a student, she needs to work and save money, so as to supplement whatever she receives from her parents, who are also poor. The respondent is resolute and hopeful for a better future, and sees the strike by university lecturers as an opportunity to learn a new skill and make some money. She relates an incident from 2019, when she lost her school fees and was helpless. According to her, God touched the hearts of her friends, who contributed to help her pay her school fees. E.P. believes she can work with other Christians for improved human conditions in Nigeria by helping those in need, and praying for everybody.

Where People Found God: In the Scriptures

The Bible is an important source for religious faith for many African Christians. In his study of the rise of the independent churches and Pentecostalism in Africa, David Barrett points out that one cannot overestimate the important contribution of Bible reading to the expansion of Christianity in Africa.[8] Kenneth Enang, in his study of independent religious movements in Nigeria, agrees with Barrett's comprehensive study, noting that the Bible "colors the vision and practices" of African Christians. Enang, however, draws attention to what he calls "crude biblicism" among the new churches, because they often do not have a sophisticated understanding of the biblical text.[9] The

---

[8] David Barrett, *Schism and Renewal in Africa: An Analysis of Six Thousand Contemporary Movements* (Nairobi: Oxford University Press, 1968), 127.

[9] Kenneth Enang, *The Nigerian Catholics and the Independent Churches: A Call to Authentic Faith* (Nairobi: Paulines Publications Africa, 2013), 139–40.

concern for me in this section is how the Christians we encountered on the streets use passages from the Bible to make sense of their daily struggles. How do they relate the message of the Scripture to their lived faith and experience of "suffering and smiling"? This section gives accounts of how people found God through reading the Bible in the face of the avoidable human suffering ravaging Nigerian society.

Forty-seven-year-old Mr. C., a civil servant and pastor, relates how he aligns his life to the promises of God irrespective of the struggles and difficulties of the present time. He asserts that people in the past faced even greater challenges and never lost their faith in God; hence he believes the same God will not forsake him in the face of the suffering and struggles of life. The respondent stresses that "suffering and smiling" is an integral part of human life and the Christian experience. He is a follower of Christ, and his faith aids him in making sense of life as a Christian, and of the need to depend solely on God while making a conscious effort to better his life and the lives of others. Regarding an instance of God's intervention in an extremely difficult situation, he narrates how God turned things around for him during his undergraduate studies. In the second year of his studies, he did not have money to continue his education. He almost gave up and was ready to withdraw from school. He says the spirit of God reminded him to employ his knowledge in the field of generator repair, and payment for that work would generate funds for his fees. Mr C. was taken to Lagos by his uncle, who promised to register him for the General Certificate Examination (G.C.E) and ended up sending him to learn how to repair generators. During the time he was struggling to pay his school fees, he realized that learning how to repair generators was a blessing in disguise. He found many clients interested in his services, through which he raised money and continued his education, and graduated. His name appeared on the merit list for the National Youth Service Corps (NYSC), although his age should have disqualified him. Mr. C. sees all these events as the hands of God in action, and affirms he is working together with people of the same faith to bring about economic empowerment and improve the social conditions in his society. With other Christians from different denominatons he established Destiny Changers Enterprise, a self-help charity to help the less privileged.

Eighteen-year-old O.E. was asked to explain how her Christian faith gives her hope, and allows her to be smiling while she is suffering. She is a point-of-sale (POS) operator at the BRT bus stop in Igando, Lagos. She says her faith in God as a believer motivates her to work hard in the face of the many difficulties in Nigeria and gives her hope for a better future. She contends that only faith and hard work are needed to survive in present-day Nigeria, despite enormous suffering, hardship, hunger, insecurity, and limited or no access to social amenities. When asked to share a personal experience of where she has found God in her life, O.E relates a challenge she faced as a house-keeper in 2019. Her uncle took her in and promised to help her register for the final exams administered by the West African Examination Council (WAEC). Her aspiration was to further her education at university level, desiring to study mass communication. Unfortunately, she faced unexpected disappointment when her uncle was unable to fulfill his promise, due to a downturn in his business. O.E., for her part, was confident that God would provide the funds for her to register for the examination. She consulted with her pastor, who decided to make the payment for her. Though she has yet to gain admission to the university, O.E. contends her ability to register and sit for the WAEC are certainly God's intervention. She has faith that someday she will realize her dream of graduating. O.E. recounts the importance of prayer in her discovery of the footprints of God in her life.

In Nigeria today, people face enormous economic hardship. Miss Och, a thirty-seven-year-old secondary-school teacher, affirms that God exists, and will see Nigerians through present difficulties. She explains that her faith in God has helped her make sense of her struggles, especially in reading the Bible. She cites 1 Peter 5:6–7, wherein Christians are exhorted to cast all their burdens onto God and that God would save them from their trials. The respondent criticizes the government for being the major cause of the present awful situation in Nigeria. She states that her faith in God gives her hope for a better future, as she trusts that God is the giver of life and every good gift, and not the government. Miss Och says God intervened in her life in many instances, but to a great extent during her undergraduate studies. One of her professors wanted to exploit her sexually, so that she might gain higher grades. She declined, and the professor vowed to fail her in his unit. However, Miss Och would not give in to the threats. Instead, she prayed, asking God to intervene in her case as she did not want to spend extra years in the university if the professor failed her. She says that God hearkened to her prayers, and that when the results were released, to her greatest amazement she scored a high grade in the unit taught by the professor whose sexual overtures she had declined.

Responding from both existential and biblical points of view, Miss A.Ak., thirty-five and a roadside grocery seller in Abuja, insists that nothing good comes easily. She recalls the fathers of faith in the Bible, such as Abraham, Joseph, and David. Despite their faith in God, they faced numerous challenges but overcame these and emerged victorious at the end. Thus, her belief in a better future rests on the potency of the Word of God, and the promises of God in Scripture that "in me [Jesus Christ] you will find peace, and, in the world, you will have tribulation, but be of good cheer, I have conquered the world" (John 16:33). Her perception of the present hardship in Nigeria is that it is a stepping-stone to a better future. She says her faith in God has equipped her with willpower, courage, and perseverance. She has the firm belief that she is well able to overcome any difficulty in life. She adds, "No doubt, the current economic meltdown in Nigeria contributed hugely to the challenges I face today. However, I have continued working hard and believing in a better future." Although she views the current Nigerian condition as damaging to human relationships, and finds that everyone seems suspicious of the other, she prays together with fellow Christians for good governance in Nigeria.

But Who Is God?

Most of our respondents were not interested in defining who God is. They were more concerned with pointing to where God is found in their lives and how God works in their favor. It seems a clear definition of God is more a concern for theologians and pastors than for the people who did theology with me on the streets and bush paths of Nigeria or the preachers in buses who did theology in bus stops (*matatu* theologians). My interlocutors had direct apprehension of God's presence in their lives, rather than a clear idea of God's identity, essence, or inner trinitarian relations.

For instance, when Mr. SoIg, thirty-two, was asked about who God is, this automobile electrician points out there is no hope for those who do not believe in God. In his words, "When I wake up in the morning, I say my morning prayers, commend my day unto the hands of the Lord, ask God to prosper my business and protect me from harm.... Sometimes, I fast, and go for thanksgiving in the church for the gift of life." According to SoIg, with prayers, faith, and hard work, God will secure SoIg's future, and of all those who do not doubt God's existence. SoIg notes the mortality rate of COVID-19, and says that Africans were praying to God, while people elsewhere put their trust in vaccines. God answered the prayers of Africans and saved them from having a high number of victims, unlike in Europe and North America.

M.G., a single mother of one daughter, says that God manifested Godself to her through people who helped her at the lowest point of her life. She tells how God intervened in a difficult situation when she became pregnant as a first-year university student. She describes how she slipped into depression due to rejection from her parents, friends, and worse still, her boyfriend, who was responsible for her pregnancy. "I contemplated taking my own life, having dropped out of school," she says. A turning point came when she told of her ordeal to a man she had met through a church activity. The man had compassion for her condition, rented a room for her, took care of her until delivery, and also gave her a job. The respondent trusted that the man was God-sent. For M.G., God is simply to be found in good persons, like the man who helped her without abusing or exploiting her vulnerability as a pregnant first-year university student.

Mr. R.A., seventy, recalls the suffering he went through during the Nigeria-Biafra war between 1967 and 1970. He believes his survival during the civil war was the greatest intervention of God in his life, along with other people who witnessed the war. For him, God was made manifest for the starving Biafrans through the international charities that brought food, aid, and medical supplies to save some of the lives of millions of people of Eastern Nigeria, especially the children who were suffering from kwashiorkor.

"The hardship in Nigeria is overwhelming, but 'God *dey shaa*,' and he is my only hope," laments E.F., a twenty-four-year-old barber in Afikpo, Ebonyi state. E.F. is convinced the future will be better due to his faith in God, and because he is working hard and staying focused. According to E.F., he is "suffering and smiling" because, "Things are really tough, and especially here there is no light, I have to buy fuel every day to provide services to my customers, and tax collectors still come to my shop to collect money from me, but I am looking up to God for better days ahead." He says hardship and lack of employment opportunities can push people into stealing and money rituals, and young girls into prostitution, but "God will definitely rescue this country one day."

Trust in divine providence was expressed by L.D., twenty-five. She is a bar attendant in a hotel who was out of school because of the teachers' strike. She finds God in this sad situation and is hopeful that "things go better." She adds,

"No matter what happens, I am keeping hope alive. I will keep pushing once there is life and God." She helps her fellow students secure menial jobs in hotels and supermarkets, which is how she contributes to economic empowerment in her locality. In this way, she "pours into others as God pours into me."

Faith and hope can help someone smile amid suffering and pain, asserts Mr. L.N. He is a prospective graduate student at UNN (University of Nigeria, Nsukka), who is working as a POS operator in Enugu due to the 2022 strike of the ASUU (Academic Staff Union of Universities). He notes his Christian faith as a Catholic teaches him that in every situation, one ought to give glory to God, and that God is the source of help and comfort in the face of all difficult situations. L.N. says his faith enables him to see the positive aspects of all situations, and to capitalize on these for his growth and development. Regarding the relationship between work and prayer, he not only trusts in God, but he also works hard for a better future. "It is ridiculous to just hope for a better future without working toward it," he insists. His faith teaches him to work hard, and to engage in active labor to make life better for himself and for people around him.

The situation in Nigeria is frightening, but one can only trust in God and work hard for a better future, affirms O.P., a thirty-three-year-old phone technician in Enugu. O.P. says his faith in God and as a Christian gives him hope for a better future, since God is aware of everything happening in Nigeria and how people are suffering. O.P. believes his faith has helped him survive difficult times, particularly since having graduated from university but with no good job: "It is hard and sad at the same time, when your people sacrifice to train you in school, but you stay forever without a job upon graduation. I am hopeful that I will get a better job, and I am working towards that."

Many of the respondents speak of God. Miss G.E., twenty-nine, describes God as "the one who will not let us down in our suffering and struggles in this land." U.G., twenty-five, speaks of God as "the only Savior who will free us from this extreme difficulty of daily struggle and battle for survival," and the one who will make their dreams of escaping from Nigeria possible. God is also the one who will make their daily effort bear fruit, as sixty-six-year-old Mrs. I. T. puts it:

> After my retirement from the civil service, I have been farming and trading in the Eke market, and by the special grace of God, people have been patronizing me. Some days I would come to the market

and customers won't be willing to buy anything because there is no money, and I return home with the goods and come the next day. It is tough, but I have no option other than to keep working hard and believing for a better future.

Some of our young respondents—including U.G., and Mrs. I.O., thirty-four—express their frustration with the social context in Nigeria. They blame the rise in crime as the failure of governance, as well as the lack of opportunities for young people. As Mrs. I.O. puts it, the suffering in Nigeria is not because Nigerians are lazy, but because of the unjust and unworkable structures in the country that make it difficult for hard-working people to "make it in life" without cutting corners. She believes that only God can bring about a moral revolution in Nigeria, so that things can improve in this generation. According to her:

> When you look around, you will discover that everybody is working hard to meet up with family responsibilities, and God has been helping us. Business is very slow due to hardship and economic decay. I am looking up to God and trusting that this country will elect a good leader who will govern the country well so that people would stop suffering.

She prophesied that God would not abandon Nigerians in their struggles, and compares the present situation to that of the COVID-19 pandemic. People thought that COVID-19 would wipe away the African population, but God helped Africans survive, so for Mrs. I.O. "God is our survival." She believes in the capacity of Nigerians to survive crises because of their resilience, while acknowledging God's intervention in the lives of all believers so that they can survive in Nigeria.

Where Is God? The Lessons of *Living in Bondage*

According to Jonathan Haynes, "The 1992 Igbo language film, *Living in Bondage*, inaugurated the video boom. It also established the first great Nollywood thematic complex—'get rich quick'—and its signature genre, the money ritual film, in which human sacrifice magically produces wealth."[10] "Nollywood" refers to the Nigerian movie industry, the influence of which extends to Africa and Hollywood.

The film *Living in Bondage* tells the story of Andy, who wants to change his fortune from a poor miserable existence to becoming a rich man.[11] He is so obsessed with making money that he fails to appreciate his greatest asset, the gift of his wife, Merit.[12] His understanding of the circumstances surrounding his poverty-stricken existence is captured at the beginning of the movie when he says, "What have I done to deserve this miserable existence?" He questions God, asking, "Why, God, did you bring me into this world to suffer? Am I bewitched or is this my destiny?" These questions posed by Andy to himself are like the questions many of our respondents posed to themselves as they "suffer and smile," "suffer and struggle," and "suffer and hope." Andy's wife comes in to comfort him, telling him not to think of his life as wasted, or that someone was after him. She also warns him that if only he knew what many people turn to to make money—like scamming people, money-doubling, murders, theft—he would stop having negative thoughts about his own condition.[13]

Andy is a religious man and never thought he would soil his hands by an effort to be rich. The biting economic conditions and his desire for prosperity to be like his friends push him to follow the counsel of those friends who want to show him how to make money through any means. One friend, Paulo, advises him that "money is the emperor of the world and he who does not have it is as good as dead." This friend promises to show him how to make money, warning him that he must be of strong heart and be prepared to make some hard choices. Those choices unfold in the film in the tales of criminality, banality, lies, distortion, murder of one's closest family members, sorcery, and repeated visits to traditional oracles. In one scene, Andy goes out for dinner with his friends, including Paulo, who has four cars for his personal use—a Mercedes Benz, a Rolls-Royce, a Nissan Patrol, and a Lexus. Joining Andy and

---

[10] Jonathan Haynes, *Nollywood: The Creation of Nigerian Film Genres* (Chicago: University of Chicago Press, 2016), 18.

[11] *Living in Bondage*, directed by Chris Obi Rapu (Nigeria, 1992–93).

[12] See Emily Witt, *Nollywood: The Making of a Film Empire* (New York: Columbia Global Reports, 2017), 20.

[13] For a detailed analysis of this movie in the context of money and values, see chapter 2 of Haynes, *Nollywood*, 18–21.

Paulo was a rich businessman, who was expecting eight shipping containers of imported goods weekly. The rich friends enjoy a sumptuous meal and display their wealth in a lavish way. Andy is transfixed and cannot believe the immense wealth. They soon reveal to Andy the secret of their wealth: They all belong to a cult that requires that each of them sacrifices the person they love most to the same cult.

"I did it," says one man in the group. "I used my wife. Now I have three wives. I feed well; I ride whatever car I choose."

"I did it," says another. "I used my child. Now I ride V-Boot, ride Pathfinder."

"I used my dear mother. Today I'm money itself."

"I used my dear friend to do it. Today I have many friends. Courage!"

Andy's friend Paulo acquired all the cars and much other wealth by sacrificing his sister.[14]

The title of the film, *Living in Bondage*, is itself a commentary on the paradox of being rich while being chained in deception, greed, lies, and criminality through which Andy made money. The film critiques the prevailing values in modern African society about "making money," and the subvalues that mediate such quick wealth and quick-fixes to poverty. Unfortunately, religious narratives and claims are used to validate and legitimize such money-making and "success stories," even if indirectly. In most instances, such sudden wealth is seen as a blessing from God.

The way God is employed in the money-making business of some versions of religion in Africa is presented well in the movie, *Our Church Money*.[15] The vulnerability of poor people who often turn to God for help in the most destitute of times is increasingly being exploited by religious leaders who are viewed as custodians of hope for the underprivileged. Two prominent pastors in this movie, Jeremiah and Isaiah, present themselves as instruments of hope for people already ravaged by abject poverty and infertility. Pastor Isaiah, who genuinely desires to accompany the suffering people who came to him through masses, prayers of deliverance, and counseling, was envied by Pastor Jeremiah, who felt the former was using diabolic power to draw a huge crowd around himself to the detriment of his own ministry. Pastor Jeremiah consults a native doctor in

---

[14] See Witt, *Nollywood*, 21.

[15] *Our Church Money*, directed by Chigbo Onyemesili (Double Edge Productions, 2018).

order to secure extraordinary power, not only to attract members, but also to perform miracles. At a superficial level, he achieves his objective by sacrificing three virgins, and so causing the death of three innocent women. However, his fortune is short-lived, as the source of his ministerial power is exposed following a failed plot to malign Pastor Isaiah, who had remained famous despite losing most of his members to the fake pastor, Jeremiah. A striking feature of the story is the skepticism expressed by the believers regarding the authenticity of Pastor Jeremiah's miraculous powers, once the conditions of those he had purportedly cured worsened when they started worshipping at Pastor Jeremiah's church. The themes of this movie relate to the challenging and desperate conditions of people in our interviews—people who are searching for solutions to their problems. They are looking for solutions anywhere and from anyone, if there is even a faint possibility of escaping their terrible conditions of poverty, sickness, joblessness, persistent misfortune, and human betrayal and disappointments in life.

Another movie, *Heart Pains*,[16] contrasts a refusal to submit to the idols of money and false religion with seeking the face of the truth God through legitimate and faithful embrace of authentic religious practices. "Money answereth everything" is a common slogan in Nigeria, particularly among young people who believe that they could have or buy anything they desire (including love) as long as they are wealthy. In the movie, the character Alusiego has acquired wealth through cyber-money theft, an undertaking which has been baptized as "Yahoo" in Nigeria. Alusiego feels he could marry Ijendu, the girlfriend of Chimaobi, who is a poor village carpenter. Ijendu loves her boyfriend so much and always encourages him and trusts in a better future for them through the help of God. Vowing to snatch Ijendu from Chimaobi, Alusiego makes a life-changing promise to Ijendu's father, on the condition that he convinces his daughter to accept Alusiego's marriage proposal. All effort in this direction proved abortive, as Ijendu sticks with Chimaobi through all travails. Through God's interventions in their numerous trials, they attained a happy life. The reverse is the case for Alusiego, whose illicit source of wealth and attempts to discredit Chimaobi are uncovered, leading to Alusiego being sentenced to life imprisonment.

Art mirrors life in many ways. This is true of *Living in Bondage*. A much-neglected source of theology in Africa today is the world of the arts, including literature,

---

[16] *Heart Pains*, directed by Michael Jaja (Onyekachukwu Osy Okeke Jr. Production, 2018).

music, and social media. Cinema is the medium which is shaping the worldview of future generations of Africans.

African theology can also emerge from the lessons and interpretation of African movies. *Living in Bondage* is a commentary on contemporary African society, particularly regarding the challenging social conditions under which the majority of our people live today. Amid biting poverty and failing institutions, what kind of social ethics and missional praxis should be embraced for the reversal of the unacceptable trajectory of history in Africa? African societies today face fragmentation and competition in the shrinking social space that has been dominated by power blocs—ethnic, religious, political, social, class, and economic. The power differential in many African societies has created an ever-widening cycle of poverty and inexcusable suffering. Unfortunately, the continent's churches have sometimes been complicit in reinforcing these power differentials through the proclamation of good news of hope and consolation to the poor, without showing the people how their hope can be realized. Churches have sometimes also embraced a certain kind of counter-evangelical lifestyle and adopted forms of ecclesial life and structures that reinforce asymmetrical power relations and exploit the poor. This has hardened the foundations of structural violence in the continent.

The people I spoke with in the streets and the characters we find in *Living in Bondage* and *Heart Pains* are all crying out for a society that is built on a strong ethical foundation. They cry too for a solid religious foundation beyond a mere transactional relationship with God, or a profession of faith in the God-of-the-gaps whose job description is to fill in the gaps in our lives and paper over our individual and group failures.

A first obstacle is failure to understand the structural nature of poverty and the definition given to poverty in the Catholic Church. This is often applied in an unqualified way to Africa and to all those who are designated as poor. Without clarity about the terms being thrown around, and without paying attention to the experience and lived faith of the people, one runs the risk of turning African theology into a mere academic ethnographic exercise. When this happens, as is often the case, scholars simply accumulate ever more data, without translating the information into concrete solutions to people's daily problems.

The second obstacle follows from the first. Poverty has become a root metaphor or a hermeneutic for interpreting and assigning value or categories to people that we have designated as being at the existential peripheries. Theologians often do not pay attention to what James Scott calls "the everyday practices" or the "weapons of the weak" in their determination to resist the institutions that often neglect their agency or assign value or disvalue to them.[17] One of the greatest obstacles to hearing the cries of the poor is that we may be looking in the wrong places, or paying attention to the wrong practices. Theologians and commentators are often looking at the needs of the poor rather than the assets of the so-called poor—their personal resilience, relational resilience, resistance, collaborative effort, agency, and so on. In a theological and ecclesiastical sense, the poor have a *sensus fidei fidelium* to which the Church needs to pay attention.

We are confronted then with the challenge of developing a missional praxis of reversal which must subvert the present status quo in our continent. African theologians are called to be active in all efforts to counter the harmful and destructive effects of the present global order, which is clearly and consistently destroying the African continent. The churches of Africa should be poor churches, of the poor and for the poor. This requires a Gospel-driven social critique of the prevailing socioeconomic conditions in Africa, which are negatively determining life outcomes for millions of Africans. Churches are called to develop missional practices that arise from social critique, as well as diverse forms of witnessing and agency that can help reverse the present trajectory of history in Africa. This will also require the churches of Africa to untether themselves from unhealthy and unwieldy structures of power and authority, which do not represent the poor man of Galilee.

African people are searching for alternative ways of being and belonging that can help them courageously confront the underside of history in the continent resulting from institutional incoherence and instability. The churches of Africa must go ahead of them to help them discern the right choices to make. These positive and life-affirming choices will have enduring long-term benefits over unhealthy choices and vices, which are made in the heat of battle in the quest for survival. Such bad choices as one sees in *Living in Bondage* can only worsen people's situations, distort the values of Africa, and create permanent fissures in the social ecology, which may take generations to reverse. It is important to understand the structural nature of the social contagion in our continent, and the hope and promise buried in the hearts of our people and in the land of Africa. The necessary building blocks of

---

[17] James C. Scott, *Weapons of the Weak: Everyday Forms of Peasant Resistance* (New Haven, CT: Yale University Press, 1985).

an African theodicy must take into consideration the layers that shape the interpretative frames Africans deploy in understanding their history, and faith in God. Human freedom and agency are needed in cooperating with God in bringing that future about as individuals, churches, nations, and communities scattered throughout the continent.

Lessons from Doing *Matatu* Theology at the Peripheries

"We all know from experience how easy it is for some to ignore other people's suffering."[18] These words of Pope Francis are both an invitation and a vocation to me and indeed to all theologians, pastors, and people of faith to always place the suffering of others as the beginning and end of the church's work of evangelization. In entering the world of my brothers and sisters, I was transformed but also chastised on the conversion of my own theological framework. My experience of listening to the stories of my brothers and sisters on how they live with faith and hope amid suffering taught me the following lessons:

First is the importance of being an eyewitness to the life and reality of people. Theology must be an eyewitness account because the theologian is always with God's people as a travel companion, a participant in the drama of salvation. Second, is the culture of encounter that has been emphasized in many of the papal teachings of Pope Francis. Developing the methodology for the culture of encounter seems to me to be an essential task for theology today. The complex nature of society and the complexity of new forms and channels of communication, and new forms of idolatries and destructive and extreme ideologies of race, religions, free market, nation, tribe, and status make expedient the need to create spaces and sites for deep nontransactional intersubjective and intracommunal encounters capable of opening the spaces for God and the *other*. There is also within this dynamic the mutuality that is required in any genuine encounter, the loss of the self in the presence of another and the vulnerability that is mutually shared as an act of love, self-surrender and entry into the life of the other, and the common movement in this mutual exchange into a deeper experience of God.

Finally, there is the need for silence and humility. The desire to give answers to human problems and thematize and name what we see in the

---

[18] Visit to Refugees, 16 April 2016.

world are essential to the theological craft. Theologians need to give answers to what they see and what they have heard. However, in our encounters there are moments when the only thing that was audible to me and to my brothers and sisters at the existential peripheries was the gift of silence, sobs, and tears. We experienced some moments when words were not enough, and the only thing that made sense was nothing other than silence. Pastoral accompaniment and pastoral programs and designs often flounder before the complexity of human problems when the pastor loses the capacity to feel the pain of the other or to hear the voice of silence in the face of the human tragedy that often lies outside of the mainstream news and narratives of being and belonging. One is challenged again and again to return to something that has always been an essential dimension of theology, the mystical dimension, which invites the theologian to pause and ponder in silence, and the liberality of the spirit that is nourished by faith to seek wisdom in unfamiliar places and unseemly sites.

I relied on multiple sources for the stories of the people that I shared. It became clear to me gradually that theological and pastoral leadership will not succeed in our times when theologians are always on the front row, giving lectures, teaching and elucidating the truths of our faith or the rational foundation for our beliefs and practices. We also realize that pastoral accompaniment will not simply be developed through manuals that have to be followed by rote. There are some elements of surprise and metaxy that one experiences from the peripheries; in a very direct but honest way the people I encountered ministered to me about how to live in hope even when facing the worst of conditions. Whatever one may call it, the best way of leading as a theologian or a pastoral agent must begin and end with encounter, a deep encounter that becomes a moment of listening, silence, learning, and discerning what God is saying and doing in our midst. This moment is not a solipsistic moment; it is Trinitarian; it is a moment that we co-inhabit with others and when that *other* is someone on the peripheries, it can offer us truly a unique experience of touching the margins of heaven where God is incarnated in us by becoming more present to me in the *other* than I am to myself.

Conclusion

This chapter discusses different approaches to responding to suffering and smiling from the voices of everyday Africans on the streets. We emphasized theological accompaniment rather than a rush to a quick resolution of the complex conditions facing most Africans today. In his *Ad Theologiam Promovendam*, Pope Francis invites theologians to do theology as "a spiritual laboratory" grounded in the lived faith and contextual narratives of the people. The completion that people seek or the finite horizon they long for in the face of suffering and evil cannot happen through an accidental reversal of fortune, especially if they are caught in a trap of structural violence. Theology shows how the telos of these lives will conform to God's will through the worship of the true God, believing, talking, and acting correctly about God. This is a task that is challenging but not impossible in a world where the vices of *Living in Bondage* appear to dominate through all forms of idolatries, even in the sacred places, in the search for solutions to unacceptable social conditions in Africa.

In the "suffering and smiling" of Africans they are clinging to God. They may not fully explain why they cling to God, but theologians must constantly return to this experience of lived faith to give account of the hope of God's people (cf. 1 Peter 3:15–16). Theologians must also not give false hope to the people but must stimulate critical consciousness in the people so that they can courageously confront the dark forces that have turned the social, political, and economic life of many African countries into a nightmare because of the politics of the stomach. As Jean-François Bayart argues strongly, destroying the politics of the stomach in Africa is the key to Africa's future. According to him, the politics of the stomach is pervasive in Africa and creates the state of affairs in which being in any leadership position (secular or sacred) is like *a meal ticket*, and

> the idea of accumulation, opening up possibilities of social mobility and enabling the holder of power "to set himself." ... "Belly" also of course refers to corpulence—fashionable in men of power. It refers also to nepotism which is still very much a social reality with considerable political consequences. And, finally, in a rather more sinister way, it refers to the localization of forces of the invisible, control over which is essential for the conquest and exercise of power; manducation can perhaps be seen as a symbolic act of the dramatic, yet everyday, phenomenon of sorcery.[19]

---

[19] Jean-François Bayart, *The State in Africa: The Politics of the Belly*, 2nd ed. (Cambridge: Polity Press, 2009), lxxxv.

4

God in Africa

Modernity, Christianity, and Africa's Future

> The first thing to do, in rethinking how to think, is to move beyond simplification. Reality is complex; challenges are varied; history is full of beauty and at the same time marred by evil. When someone cannot or does not want to deal with its dramatic complexity, then he or she easily tends to simplify. Simplification, however, mutilates reality; it gives rise to empty and unilateral thinking and it generates polarization and fragmentation. That, for example, is precisely what ideologies do. Ideology is a simplification that kills: it kills reality, it kills thought, it kills community. Ideologies flatten reality to a single, shallow idea, which—like parrots—they then repeat obsessively and manipulate.
>
> —Pope Francis

African theology is Christian theology. It is not an isolationist theology that is concerned solely with African realities, but it is also a theology that speaks to the world because we live in an interconnected world. But more important, what God is revealing to African believers in their exuberant faith pilgrimage reflects what God is saying to God's people in every other part of the world, because as *Gaudium et Spes* teaches: "The joys and the hopes, the griefs and the anxieties of the men of this age, especially those who are poor or in any way afflicted, these are the joys and hopes, the griefs and anxieties of the followers of Christ. Indeed, nothing genuinely human fails to raise an echo in their hearts" (GS 1; see also GS 22).

African theology is also Catholic theology because it is the reflection of African believers on the universality of the Gospel message that speaks to all peoples in the search for intelligibility of what Christians believe and how to live as Christians in the world of today. However, African theology has a double loyalty: to the African Christian experience as Africans embrace the revealed truth of the Son of God in the Gospel message in Africa's social context; and to the Gospel message that speaks to all peoples in their lived faith, including African Christians who share with their siblings all over the world in the joy of the Gospel. In this double loyalty, African theology develops a deeper analysis of the philosophical foundations of the African worldview which is the religio-cultural vessel in which the Gospel is received, while also using these cultural frameworks to interpret, understand, and embrace the Christian revelation with an open-structured framework that characterizes the reception of religious truths among most African ethnic groups.

As we have shown in chapters 2 and 3, African people are living their faith amid suffering and smiling; belief in God is strong in Africa. In a survey conducted in 2017 in Uganda of sixty-seven Christians who were living on less than a dollar a day, Alex Ojacor and his team discovered that sixty-two of them had a strong hope in God. Thirty-five said that they faced some challenges of war, tribal conflicts, natural disasters, epidemics and poverty, and twelve admitted that these challenges worry them. However, the survey shows that all of them had a strong hope for a better future. None of the people surveyed despaired despite the challenges they faced. These respondents all affirmed their belief in the Lord Jesus Christ as the source of their hope. They too hoped that one day they would overcome and defeat the present challenges in their personal lives and in the country.

Many non-Africans and even some avant-garde African Christians might dismiss the answers that emerge from the belief and religious expressions of Africans; some others might shudder in suspicion at the many sites where people are finding God as we showed in chapter 3, regarding them often as illusions, enchantment, or superstition. Aylward Shorter argues that the legitimation of the belief of African Christians must be sought for the most part outside the traditional frames of baroque theology in the West. Rather, African theological sources emerge from a culturally fragmented Africa, but with possible comparisons and actual historical interactions with theological traditions outside Africa. Shorter admits that the emergence of African theologies are not threats to so-called mainstream theology and are not meant to destroy or alter the universal tradition of the Church (specifically Roman Catholicism). African theologies act as a corrective to that tradition in different ways:

> Firstly, it may awaken themes in universal Christianity which are dormant, or latent. Secondly, it may help to show that certain elements presented in Africa as essential in the universal tradition are in fact secondary elements, deriving from the particular Western cultural tradition.... The universality of Christian theology, therefore, turns out to be a developing universality keeping pace with a world in evolution. African theology will help the Church to open up new avenues for exploration, to develop a new awareness, in short, to cease to be a "White Church."[1]

Others have written about the experience and historical context of African Christianity in many ways and the specific ways in which African theology is helping to depolarize the theological spaces in world Christianity, and to recover the traditional teaching on marriage, family, gender, and sexuality, the embodied experience of Christianity, traditional Catholic popular devotions like the Sacred Heart of Jesus, different approaches to reconciliation, Marian movements, charismatic movements, and the cult of the saints.[2]

The African Christian experience, according to Tite Tienou, is closer to the biblical God than Western theologies in which the Trinity is construed in an ideational mode. In Western theology, Tienou argues, the central tasks

---

[1] Aylward Shorter, *African Christian Theology: Adaptation or Incarnation* (Maryknoll, NY: Orbis Books, 1977), 31.

[2] See the sources enumerated in Sas Conradie, *Towards Transformational Theology and Theological Education in Africa*, accessed July 17, 2024, https://acteaweb.org/wp-content/uploads/2022/02/Towards-Transformational-Theology-booklet.pdf. See also Emmanuel Katongole, "Africa," in *The Blackwell Companion to Catholicism*, vol. 69, ed. James J. Buckley, Frederick Bauerschmidt, and Trent Pomplun (New York: John Wiley & Sons, 2010), 133–37. See also David Costello, "Reconciliation and Prayer," in *Spirituality and Reconciliation*, ed. Tom Curran, Tangaza Occasional Paper, no. 4 (Nairobi: Paulines Publications Africa, 1997), 48–51.

are analysis of the Godhead, the nature of doctrines, the structure of the church, concepts, theological positions, the subject's consciousness, theoretical battles on what is immanent and what is transcendent. These latter conflicts have divided and weakened the churches in the West. Western theologies are increasingly removed, he adds, from the cultural imagination of their environments, as well as from the biblical world which it takes as source. However, the God of the Bible is the God whose attributes are not mere intellectual abstractions, because they arise out of specific contexts of faith and obedience. These are not attributes reached through theological or conciliar consensus but discovered as God reveals Godself to people in history.[3]

David Ngong underscores the importance of the contextual nature of issues facing contemporary Africa regarding the questions of who God is and where to find God. Ngong argues for a return to the roots, because the doctrine of God was developed in Africa in the theologies of Tertullian, Origen, Arius, Athanasius, and Augustine:

> When the Christian doctrine of God came to sub-Saharan Africa, it came through Western missionaries and the question that was raised was not so much how God was to be understood as Trinity but rather whether Africans were capable of conceptualizing the idea of God. This question was generally raised in a racist context that devalued much of African cultural ideas in order to justify colonialism and the conversion of Africans to the Christian faith.[4]

Ngong's proposal is that it is possible to own the heritage of ancient African Christian theological development of the Trinity as one of the many foundations to be explored in broadening the sources for conceptualizing God in African theology. How Africans conceptualize their religious faith in God will form the content of this chapter. The narratives of God in Africa must be placed side by side with the currents of modernity and the currents of secularization in the West and a strong cultural current in the West to move

---

[3] Tite Tienou, "Biblical Foundations for African Theology," *Missiology: An International Review* 10, no. 4 (October 1982): 444.

[4] David Tonghou Ngong, "Africa and the Christian Doctrine of God," in *A New History of African Christian Thought: From Cape to Cairo*, ed. David Tonghou Ngong (New York: Routledge, 2017), 54.

away from a moral order held in mainstream Christian tradition until recently on issues of theological anthropology, sexuality, gender, family, and worship. What we say of God will help us understand ourselves better; and what we say of ourselves as humans can help us understand God better. The theology of suffering and smiling in the context of Africa sheds a clear light on both who God is and who the human person is in African theology.

Why a Theological Inquiry about God in Africa?

Every theologian and every Christian community must give an account of God, and thus justify the central affirmation of the faith of the Christian community. As St. Peter counsels, "Always be prepared to give an account of the hope that is in you" (1 Peter 3:15). Contemporary theologies in the last two decades have not taken seriously the question of justifying belief in God. Rather, there is a greater emphasis on cultural battles and moral issues in current debates and divisions within and outside the churches and theological productions. We must not fail as theologians to demonstrate to the world the rationality of faith, and the intelligibility of the Church's doctrines, practices, morality, and spirituality. This is ever more important today because many people are abandoning the faith, and there is the threat of new forms of idols replacing the worship of the true God through what William T. Cavanaugh calls "misdirected worship," "a form of narcissism, an attempt at aggrandizing the self," "a type of entrapment or self-isolation from God and from other people" that results in "self-diminishment."[5] There is also the continuing gulf between ideologies of power and privilege in our churches and the cries of the weak and vulnerable who are victims of the demonic ideologies of state, religion, and neoliberal economic orthodoxies. These ideologies are often defended in some settings through religious narratives, Christian nationalism, and church teaching and practices. These ideologies also find their ways in the social hierarchies in our churches, the roles and ranks that many of us occupy as scholars and clerics, which by themselves validate and perpetuate aspects of these ideologies, misogyny, and social hierarchies in our religious institutions. In many instances, the Cross has become an instrument of oppression and validation of unequal power relations and exploitation, as well as a source for

---

[5] William T. Cavanaugh, *The Uses of Idolatry* (Oxford: Oxford University Press, 2024), 4.

legitimation of the suffering of the poor and people on the margins who are daily told to carry the consequences of the injustice in society as their Cross. Returning to the God question could help African theologians discover values and ideals capable of redirecting our people's gaze toward the image of God who is within us and beyond our human imagination. God's love is beyond measure, an absolute love which cannot be surpassed.

In Africa, such inquiry about God becomes necessary because of many competing, conflicting, and complementary notions of God. These require validation, rejection, or appropriation to justify the faith which is embraced by Africans. When one observes the Christian religion in Africa, it is obvious that the name of God has been co-opted or instrumentalized to prop up political systems and bad state actors who perpetuate misrule and extractive leadership in some African countries. The name of God has been manipulated by elites to "rouse the deepest feelings and emotions in individuals in Africa to cause violence, wars and destruction,"[6] thus posing a danger to human security and that of communities and nations. The name of God has been used in our continent to justify intolerance, gender violence, homophobia, sexism, and classism. In addition, the gullibility of the poor in Africa has been exploited to feed the insatiable materialistic appetite of some church leaders and hawkers of miracles. They claim to be the "big men," "big daddies," and "big mummies" of a Big, All-Conquering, and Prosperous God who makes people rich based on how much they can afford to contribute. The name of God has often been used in Africa to justify or rationalize preventable and treatable diseases, needless suffering, poverty, and the many destructive outcomes of failed governments, failed healthcare systems, failed social services, and fake and false religious practices. In combination, these have created a general sense of despair, restlessness, and frustration among poor people and young people.

However, the name of God has also been used to build schools, hospitals, refugee centers, and research institutes; to feed the hungry, defend human rights, fight dictatorship, advocate for human dignity and rights, and bring about constitutional order in some African countries. It has also been used to bring about peace, reconciliation, and healing in countries in Africa. What this book proposes is an approach to the worship of God and Christian theism not only in Africa but everywhere where God is embraced as a subject of

---

[6] Ezra Chitando and Joram Tarusarira, "Introduction," in Ezra Chitando and Joram Tarusarira, ed. *Religion and Human Security in Africa* (London: Routledge, 2019), 5.

relationship. This embrace is not to be presented or designed as an encounter with a divine functionary or a transactional Supreme Being whom we must constantly propitiate so that God can help unlock the complexities of our times and meet the human need for control, explanation, and prediction in the painful throes of life for many Africans, some of whom are still hanging on the cross of shame and suffering.

There is also a personal quest in this work. I am deeply troubled about the rising violence, terrorism, wars, civil unrests, and humanitarian disasters in Africa. Born after the civil war in my country, the compound where we lived in my early years, St. John's Primary School, Agbani, was a refugee camp. The Nigerian-Biafran war was the first modern genocide in Africa. My memory of the war is a collective one, passed on through those who experienced the war. Almost everything that I have learned about the Civil War in Nigeria was mediated through stories from my parents and teachers, and from history books and commentaries. I also learned about the war through the devastation I saw growing up in the brokenness that was postwar Eastern Nigeria. I remember the failed experiment on secession every time I visit home and see the wretched condition of the Biafran war veterans who beg along the highway in Oji River close to my ancestral home, Achi. How could I forget that day in 1977 as a little child when I saw my father crying profusely after a mass grave was found while a pit toilet was being dug at our elementary school?

About fifteen years ago, I came upon a study by the Canadian Society of Church History, which cited a report of Rev. E. H. Johnson, secretary for Overseas Missions and the Presbyterian Church in Canada. The report examined some of the ethical issues in the conduct of the Civil War by the federal side and their allies, especially the British government. The report urged a more thorough examination of the atrocities committed by the Nigerian government against the Biafrans, in light of the UN 1948 Genocide Convention.[7] Whereas the British government supplied 40 percent of Nigeria's arms and ammunition before the war, by the time the war began it had increased its supply of arms to the Federal Military Government by nearly 80 percent by 1968, and by 1969 it had risen to more than 97 percent. The matter of the conduct of the war by the Nigerian military junta using British arms was so serious that the Archbishop of Canterbury, the Archbishop of

---

[7] Edward Hewlitt Johnson Fonds, *The Presbyterian Church in Canada Archives* (1973); updated by Ruth Namisato and Bob Anger (Toronto, 2007, 2008).

York, and many British Lords and MPs called on the British government to ban exporting arms to Nigeria. The blockade of Biafra after the capture of Port Harcourt in May 1968 (air blockade, food blockade, weapons blockade, and information blockade) led to the deaths of hundreds of thousands of people, especially women, children, and other noncombatants. The outcome has never been fully independently investigated. Even though a British parliamentary observer team sent by the UK government concluded that no genocide was taking place, questions remained then as well as today about the objectivity of the report.[8]

What is of concern to me here regarding this discourse is that the first time I heard about God in the mouth of my dad was the cry of my father about this mass grave. It reminded him of so many friends and family members whom he lost in that terrible war, which cost close to three million Igbos their lives. I heard my father cry: *Where was God when this atrocity occurred?* After my father's death, I read some of his extant war diaries. Dad constantly wrote of God saving him as he hid from the battlefield, because so many family members and friends had perished and he needed to take care of the rest of the family. A look at the Biafran war cry reflects the image of an all-conquering God:

> We are Biafrans Fighting for our nation In the name of Jesus. We shall conquer. Biafra win! Biafra! We are Biafrans Fighting for our freedom In the name of Jesus. We shall conquer. Biafra win! Biafra! We are Biafrans Marching to the war front. In the Name of Jesus we shall vanquish. Biafra win! Biafra!

I grew up always wondering why God did not save our people. Who is this God whose name is invoked when people kill each other? However, as I started to immerse myself in the scientific study of the Christian scripture, I saw that some passages of Scripture, particularly in the Old Testament, have actually been invoked again and again in Christianity and other religions to justify violence

---

[8] See Mark Curtis, "How Britain's Labor Government Facilitated the Massacre of Biafrans in Nigeria—To Protect Its Oil Interest," https://www.declassifieduk.org/how-britains-labour-government-facilitated-the-massacre-of-biafrans-in-nigeria-to-protect-its-oil-interests/, accessed April 09, 2025. See also "Nigeria: Biafra International Observers," debated October 22, 1968, House of Lords, Hansard, vol. 296.

and atrocities of war in Africa, the Middle East, Europe, and elsewhere—Jihads, holy wars, and so on. Kenton Sparks rightly points out that the violent portrait of God, especially in the Old Testament, "strikes us as sinister and evil."[9] Jerome Creach (and many others) proposes that violent portraits of God constitute "one of the greatest challenges the church faces today."[10]

It is, therefore, obvious to me that if I must hold on to the Christian faith in the God whom we profess in the Creed, I must show that the God my people in Africa worship as the Christian God is not a God of war, of violence. Not a God who has prepared a lake of fire to incinerate the reprobate at the end of life. Not a God of destruction, or a God who takes sides with the mighty and the violent who wage wars and destroy creation in the name of God. This God is not a prosperity God who is proposed as the source of wealth for those blessed and a source of poverty for those who are damned. This God is not a God who calls young African babies and pregnant women to a heavenly home. This is not a God who wills that people should rest in peace with God in heaven through deaths from preventable and treatable diseases, through pandemics, accidents, poverty, starvation, and distress. It is not a God who saves some in accidents and permits others to die. I am challenged to help my people to embrace a God who is revealed to us as Love, and not "a God of the gaps," or a God who provides the grace and the grains for building the many sad pathological structures of power that reinforce structural violence, exploitation, and the modern idols of the marketplace of neoliberal capitalism in the world.

My second rationale for this work emerges from the changing demographics and diversity in world Christianity. We live now in a post-Christian West and a post-Western Christianity. Those who proclaimed that the twentieth century would be the Christian century with the West as the center, the moderator, and the mediator of this movement soon found out this was an illusion. Reality intruded by the middle of that century, particularly with the Depression, the World Wars, and the rising tide of postmodernism and secularism. The narratives and projects of Christendom led only to further

---

[9] *Sacred Word, Broken World: Biblical Authority and the Dark Side of Scripture* (Grand Rapids: Eerdmans, 2012), 37.

[10] Jerome F. D. Creach, *Violence in Scripture* (Louisville, KY: Westminster John Knox Press, 2013), 1, cited in Gregory A. Boyd, *Crucifixion of the Warrior God: Interpreting the Old Testament's Violent Portraits of God in light of the Cross*, vol. 1 (Minneapolis: Fortress Press, 2017), xxxix.

cultural alienation and spiritual bereavement for most people in the West, as they witnessed disaffiliation from the practice of the faith and from attachment to Christian religious symbols, rituals, and foundational narratives. The moral chaos of our times, and the destructive wars of the last centuries—partly nationalistic, partly economic, and partly religious—are all reminders of why the Christian century failed to materialize. As the late British scholar Andrew Walls predicted, if anyone wants to see the shape of the future of Christianity, the person has to look toward Africa. To use the words of Pliny the Elder, *ex Africa semper aliquid novi* (there is always something new coming out of Africa). The different notions of God and the arguments for God and the mechanistic theodicies which were developed in the West must be seen as models of theological inquiry that are open to dialogue and revision. They are not to be projected as the sole model of theodicy, or the sole theological structure for constructing a theodicy to be replicated and transmitted to non-Western contexts, root, stalk, and branch. There are issues and problems facing many Africans today that will require a different map of the universe and a different theological interpretation, understanding, response, and pastoral accompaniment. But African answers since they are Christian, in this regard, could also serve as a model for doing theology that can serve the world church and peoples outside Africa.

Peggy Levitt titled her work on how immigrants are helping to change the narratives of faith and life particularly in the United States, *God Needs No Passport*.[11] That is a metaphor, for me, of what is happening in world Christianity and in the wider world today. Transnational migration and transcultural and transreligious movements are now prevalent. God, unlike all of us, does not need a passport or customs control to enter a different culture. God does not have any passport. Thus, the transmission of religious faith cannot be controlled along our national, cultural, or even personal borders. The world must learn to live with religious pluralism; the West must learn in humility to embrace the new religious expressions and experiences from Africa and the non-Western world. The future of the world will be defined by how we embrace pluralism in a healthy manner and find the commonality of the *humanum* to collectively confront the challenges facing us today. We all need to learn with and in the presence of one another about how God is revealing the mystery of the inner divine life in itself and in history, as the Christian faith

---

[11] Peggy Levitt, *God Needs No Passport* (New York: New Press, 2007).

migrates across different cultural and spiritual frontiers. The Christian Gospels, as with other religious traditions, are like different tributaries of divine-human opportunities all canalizing into a common ocean of God's love and creative energy in the world.

The third and final motivation for this inquiry is more fundamental theologically and historically than the first two and relates to demonstrating the existence of God through an African ancestral grammar that challenges some of the current images of God in Africa and elsewhere. It is also a dialogue with some of the false claims developed in Western thought about African religions.[12] One challenge facing every historian is to maintain balance and objectivity. Another challenge is to tell the story from the side of the victims. Africa's history in general, and African Christian and religious histories in particular, have been told mainly by non-Africans. The story of Africa that persists in the minds of many Westerners even today depicts a land of desolation, misery, and crime. These were the very words of Thomas Fowell Buxton, writing about Africa in his *Memoir on the Backward Races* in the middle of the nineteenth century.[13] This negative framing of Africa as a lost continent and Africans as uncivilized, barbaric, and backward was common. The painful consequences of the tearing of Africans from their spiritual roots

---

[12] Even an account of God in Africa that claims to be respectful and humble in explaining theism in Africa to the West like Malcolm J. McVeigh in his scholarly engagement with Edward Smith's *The Secret of the African and African Beliefs and Christian Faith*, ends up actually distorting African religious beliefs and practices particularly with this much contested "deus otiosus"—the idea that God is remote in the African conception of reality. McVeigh writes, for instance, "African Traditional Religion generally pictures God as being far away and remote. This belief is seen clearly in the myths of God's departure which form part of the folklore of most tribes. In the beginning God and man lived together, but due to man's foolishness or perversity God retreated and is no longer in close contact with him. This withdrawal of God from the scene of daily life has had a profound effect upon the lives of men and results in a greater emphasis on the importance of lesser beings, fetishes and charms to carry on daily existence." He quotes Smith, who wrote, "When we come to speak of West Africa we shall find the tangled undergrowth of fetishism (so called) almost choking the religion associated with the Supreme Being." Malcolm J. McVeigh, *God in Africa: Conceptions of God in African Traditional Religion and Christianity* (Cape Cod, MA: Claude Stark, 1974), 22–23.

[13] Thomas Fowell Buxton, *Memoirs of Sir Thomas Fowell Buxton, Bart*, ed. Charles Buxton (London: John Murray, 1877).

through the projects of empire were very destructive because as Eboussi Boulaga argues, it uproots Africans

> out of their being-in-the-world, presenting them with the faith only at the price of depriving them of their capacity to generate the material and spiritual conditions of their existence. Henceforward these dominated persons will be able to find their truth only outside themselves, as the utterly-other-from-themselves-and-their-universe. The missionary discourse was a habit of propounding God, or the content of the faith, as the irruption into one's world of the purest strangeness, and conversion as the snatching of the candidate for Christianity from the jaws of perdition, which is confused with one's traditional mode of living and being human.[14]

Thus, the Christian God is presented as someone strange to Africa who has to be introduced through clear and distinct propositional statements and worshipped through rigid liturgical rituals and canonical forms that must be repeated without any additions or erasures for God to be made present in the most efficacious way, *ex opere operato!*

Today, one can still find these negative images of Africa as a dark continent where people shake hands with the devil, a heart of darkness, and a land of catastrophes; hopeless Africa, Africa's apocalypse, a land where all things must fight or die, and so on. These kinds of thoughts are based on racism, prejudice, and untested assumptions and stereotypes of Africa that go back to the time of transatlantic slave trade, colonialism, and the nineteenth-century missionary work in Africa. Some of the humanitarianism from the West to Africa is toxic charity and creates a dependency cycle and undermines the agency of Africa because it is often part of a continuing but failed quest to civilize Africa or humanize Africa or help Africa, based on a biased racialized reading of Africans and their cultures, religions, spiritualities, and worldviews. Patricia Daley's conclusion on what is wrong with the way Africans are construed in humanitarian work regarding refugees and migrants is a helpful insight:

> Despite their professed humanistic foundations, the actions of Western humanitarian agencies are often underpinned by social Darwinism ideology, especially at the point of aid between White

---

[14] Eboussi Boulaga, *Christianity without Fetishes* (Maryknoll, NY: Orbis Books, 1981).

Western and African humanitarian workers; the public prostitution of images of disaster victims; the infantilization of refugees, and the evacuation of Westerners during the Rwandan genocide and other conflict situations. Humanitarianism contributes maybe unwittingly to the reproduction of, and the persistence of, racial hierarchies and particularistic identities, be they ethnic, regional or gender based—a characteristic it shares with military institutions.[15]

The task of theology is foremost to follow the footprints of God in history, and to carefully discern and follow these footprints in their expressions in cultures, societies, and particularly in the actual faith of those who believe, especially in the context of the poor and the marginalized. The African theologian must be a good historian, who can enter deep into the layers of history, read the hidden transcript, and tell the stories of how God's people move from one level of meaning to another and what takes place in them and in their lives when they make this transition in view of the ultimate purpose of life. According to Miroslav Volf:

> The whole history of the world—including contemporary societies with their multiple and changing cultures, each with their partly overlapping, partly conflicting sets of beliefs and practices—is situated within the story of God's dealing with creation to redeem it and bring it to its final consummation. Christians should interpret the world and act in it in the light of that story.[16]

Telling the stories of God in Africa is a disruptive theological enterprise. It is a liberative theological historiography with a decolonizing intent. It is liberating and disruptive because it develops from retelling the African narrative of faith against the negative framing of peoples of African descent in world Christianity and politics, in Western theology and ecclesial history. This framing relates to theodicy, anthropology, and social life, among others. If African narratives of God and the self-identity of Africans are predominantly framed in negative terms of race, inferiority, paganism, animism, superstition, bizarreness, and so on, the challenge for the African theologian is to tell a different story. The

---

[15] Patricia O. Daley, *Gender and Genocide in Burundi: The Search for Spaces of Peace in the Great Lakes Region* (Kampala, Uganda: Fountain, 2008).

[16] Miroslav Volf, *A Public Faith: How Followers of Christ Should Serve the Common Good* (Grand Rapids: Brazos, 2011), 85.

task is to deconstruct these predominant ones, which are still as persistent and destructive today as they were in former times. I grew up believing that God was a white man and that all the saints were white. My Christian cultural models and spiritual *habitus* were white-coated and alienating. Later in life, they have become a form of spiritual and cultural violence that constantly troubles my soul while challenging my intellect to come up with something true about God in Africa. Most biblical narratives and morality were seen and mediated in the Christian academy in Africa through a Western lens and its negation of Blackness. Indeed, one of the greatest legacies of Pope John Paul II in Africa was the canonization of many Africans as saints. In no small way, this began to change the predominant images of our African ancestors as pagans who never "made it" to heaven, and that the models of holiness and goodness like the aesthetics of God were white.

God in Africa: Creator and Source of Human and Cosmic Flourishing

God was never an object of study in traditional African society. Africans celebrate religion. They live in a world where the existence and presence of God is so evident and assured that it would be, in this thinking, futile to attempt to justify the existence of God. How could one start proving to people what is so evident and present to them? How could one begin to tell traditional Africans about the existence and operation of God, in whom they live, move, and have their being? Traditional Africans do not debate about God. They live in what they perceive as a God-centered universe, in whose life and force all people can share without being impeded by others.

Traditional African societies had no heretics, and no doctrines, dogmas, or creeds that have to be recited every day in ritual celebration. They did not have a book of common prayer or a Roman missal. Every celebration was a new event in history, not a repetitive communal practice that is more of the same. Every religious event is a continuation of what has and continues to be central to the communal understanding of life and history—the vital principle or the bond of life which is to be upheld by all through a healthy and shared communal relationship. Traditional African religions were also tolerant and ecumenical. One could walk into any shrine or sacred grove in any town or village, even in places outside your own ethnic group, and be served a meal by worshippers. No one was denied a participation in the ritual meal if they were present at the celebration. No diviner would refuse to celebrate some divination rites for a visitor because he or she came from a different ethnic group or clan. Traditional African religionists practiced an open table, and there is no recorded evidence of religious persecution, religious discrimination, denominational differences, or people being martyred because of religious beliefs. No tribal religion professed to have an absolute or exclusionary claim to God and the things of God.

As Jacob Olupona argues, the fight over rightness or wrongness of belief has led to intolerance, fundamentalism, and radicalism in Africa today through some forms of Christianity and Islam. This is a modern malady, he admits, strange to faithful practitioners of traditional African ancestral religion.[17] Traditional Africans worried more about the rightness or wrongness of conduct relative to how it promoted human and cosmic flourishing. Laurenti Magesa agrees with Olupona on this, writing that spirituality and religion, for Africans, "does not primarily answer the question of what we should believe; it responds, rather to the question of how we should live."[18] It does not concern itself with what happens in the hereafter, but rather with what happens here and now, the conjunction of which when driven by life-affirming choices guarantees the future for the individual and the community in a holistic way.

My concern in this section is to outline how Africans talk about God. Through an ethnography carried out in Nigeria, Kenya, and Uganda, and with some Africans who live in the United States and Canada, I discovered overwhelming evidence of a strong cultural knowledge of the "job description" of God. This religio-cultural belief that God works for the good of creation has been retained in Christianity. According to Achille Mbembe, Christianity also makes a promise of some sort of exchange:

> The logic of Christianity is an imperial logic in the sense that it ties together in the same network the construction of organising concepts of the world here below and on high with an "imaginaire" of power, of authority, of society, of time, of justice and of dreams; in short, of history and its ultimate truth. The distinction between "temporal

---

[17] Jacob K. Olupona, *African Religions: A Very Short Introduction* (New York: Oxford University Press USA, 2014), 21.

[18] Laurenti Magesa, *What Is Not Sacred? African Spirituality* (Maryknoll, NY: Orbis Books, 2013), 32.

power" and "spiritual power" is therefore, in a sense, artificial.... Christianity is to a large extent a way of proclaiming "the truth," which is to say, a certain way of mentally and practically constructing earthly and celestial realities.[19]

There is a consistency to the transactional exchanges and practical construction of reality that is noticeable, for instance, in many Christian worship services in which the offering of "intentions" is encouraged. A random reading of these intentions in my pastoral work in Africa shows that most of them are requests for God to do certain things in the lives of people, for the dead, and for thanksgiving for favors received. Thanksgiving is itself a way of returning to God what God has given in anticipation that God will do more for the believer. This transactional and functional exchange in worship is common to most Africans I encountered in my research, whether they are Christians, Muslims, or believers in ancestral religion. Despite their religious differences, Africans agree broadly on what God does and worry less about who God is or whether God exists and where God dwells. A clear way of establishing this common belief on what God does is to examine the names given to God by various ethnic groups. They refer to any of these: Supreme Source of Life; the Origin and Destiny of all things; the All-powerful and All-provident God; the Source of Goodness and Life; the One who gives life and death; the one who provides wealth and family, and who guarantees the future.

Scholars generally agree that Africans in the past and African Christians and Muslims today have a functional notion of God as creator who is present in the lives of all things, rather than an ontological or metaphysical being. This perception could be gleaned from God's job description.[20] What God does includes providing health; safeguarding life and preventing sickness and untimely or accidental deaths; guaranteeing worldly salvation, wealth, offspring; and procuring for people otherworldly connections with ancestors, spirits, and lesser gods who are seen as having strong influence on the events in the here and now as mediators between humans and God. God is also the one who guarantees prosperity, fertility, vitality, and other ends. Indeed,

---

[19] Achille Mbembe, "Pouvoir, violence et accumulation," *Politique Africaine* 39 (1990): 27–28.

[20] Agbonkhianmeghe Orobator, *Theology Brewed in an African Pot* (Maryknoll, NY: Orbis Books, 2008), 2.

for Bolaji Idowu, God in Africa unifies everything because God gives life to all things, and for Africans God is "the real cohesive factor of religion," and without God every other thing in the African understanding and belief system will fall out of place.[21]

An Igbo proverb says that the chief priest who is always predicting destruction, suffering, doom, and misfortune will soon find that he or she will be abandoned by adherents. Elochukwu Uzukwu highlighted the instrumentalization of religion in African religion and how modern African authors like Chinua Achebe, Wole Soyinka, and Mongo Beti have critiqued this instrumentalization of religion not only in African religion but as it has been transmitted to African Christianity. Particularly in Achebe's *Arrow of God*, Uzukwu notes,

> Individuals and community are not a pawn in the hands of deities and experts. The community exercises liberty by withdrawing support from one deity (and its shrine guardian) and transferring it to another deity and shrine guardian. An Ikwerre proverb says it well: "The villagers may belong to a god, but the god also belongs to the villagers." The Yoruba have also the saying: "If humanity were not, the deities would not be."[22]

People thus will usually treat the diviner who is always predicting disaster as the servant of a false god, since people expect blessings and not curses from God. If God does not wish to bless people, then the chief priest's job is to find out what should be done to expiate the evil which is acting as an obstacle to divine blessing. When, for instance, one looks at the names of God in my native Igbo language we see that God is defined by what God does rather than who God is. Emefie Ikenga Metuh argues convincingly that in paying attention to the different names and attributes of God in Igbo language and the theophoric names Igbo people give to their children one can develop a good treatise on Igbo theodicy.[23]

---

[21] Bolaji Idowu, *African Traditional Religion: A Definition* (London: CMS Press, 1973), 104.

[22] Elochukwu Uzukwu, *God, Spirit, and Human Wholeness* (Eugene, OR: Pickwick Publications, 2012), 98.

[23] Emefie Ikenga Metuh, *God and Man in African Religion* (Enugu, Nigeria: SNAAP Press, 1999), 59.

Evaristus Ezeugwu and Gregory Chinweuba demonstrate that the name of God in Igbo traditional thought, Supreme Being, *Chukwu*, shows that God ranks highest in the spiritual realm.[24] Or to put it in Emefie Ikenga Metuh's account, the name Chukwu captures the belief that

> God is a creator. Creating is his prerogative; no other being can create. In fact, every other being is created. This is very clear to the Igbo mind. Igbo myths presume that God pre-existed the world and everything else that is known to exist. Making this assumption then, the myth then goes on to explain the existence of every other thing by means of special and direct interventions by Chukwu, who is an uncaused cause, an uncreated creator.[25]

The name Chukwu also shows how God functions in governing creation: God is mighty, God reigns above all, and has power over all other smaller gods (*chi*) in terms of what God does. The other names of God, *Chineke* and *Osebuluwa*, used for God, also relate to what God does. According to Ezeugwu and Chinweuba:

> The concept however is a combination of the Igbo words; "Chi"(spirit) and "ukwu" (great, big or high). When the Supreme Being is called "Chineke," it is a combination of Igbo words "Chi" (Spirit), "na" (that or who) and "eke" (create) designating the spirit that creates or causes everything into existence. When Igbos call him "Osebuluwa" or "Olisebuluwa," it is a combination of the words "olisa" (God), "bulu" (carry) and "Uwa" (world), meaning the Supreme Being who

---

[24] I do not intend to repeat what has been better presented in other writings on the evolution of scholarship on African theism. I recommend the work of Harvey J. Sindima. He has provided a very thorough summary of the important developments and scholars on African theism, including the name of God and the views of the pioneers of African theism like Jomo Kenyatta (*Facing Mount Kenya*), Joseph Danquah (*The Akan Doctrine of God*), Bolaji Idowu (*Olódùmarè: God in Yoruba Belief*), John Mbiti (*Concept of God in Africa*), and Alex Kagame (*La Philosophie bântu-rwandaise de l'Être*). See Harvey Sindima, *Classical Theories in African Religion* (Trenton, NJ: Africa World Press, 2019), 245–303.

[25] Metuh, *God and Man in African Religion*, 59–60.

carries and sustains the world. These names however manifest various functions of the Supreme Being and his place in human existence as perceived by indigenous Igbo people.[26]

However, when it comes to how God brings this abundant life about, there are diversities of practices and beliefs among Africans. This includes control of the outcomes of events, interpretation of misfortune and "bad deaths," and prediction of a better future. Religious affinity in Africa is permeable, with much movement in various directions, and borrowing and mixing of traditions, which are partly converging and partly diverging.[27] Religious affinity is not absolute, even in today's new religious movements in Christianity. This is true even against the push by African evangelicals for a purist notion of Christianity, through their negative characterization of African religions and excoriation of certain forms of traditional Christianity as contaminating and false. Viewed in this light, the unqualified charge of syncretism, superstitious belief, or "schizoid" faith by some African theologians or church leaders against African Christians who display this permeable loyalty seems simplistic. How God functions in the human world is not mechanistic but is dynamic because it involves the participation of humans in embracing life-affirming choices every day. This requires further elaboration, and here I will stand on the shoulders of Vincent Mulago.

As I have stated in several passages in this work, religious ideas permeate African thinking and provide an integrative frame for holding together the complexities and ambiguities of life. The questions of being and nonbeing, being rich or poor, suffering and smiling, war and peace, evil and good cannot be discussed outside a religious worldview. African traditions of thought tend to view reality not in terms of binary oppositions and mutually exclusive categories of either/or, but rather in an inclusive and coherent way of both/and. This duality, as against Western dualism, is a good plausibility structure which helps many Africans live with ambiguity and complexity, without giving up hope or falling into despair. An example is the relation between death and life; for instance, people might be dead but are seen as living-dead (ancestors), and the invisible world is perceived as having a real connection with humans

---

[26] Evaristus Chukwudi Ezeugwu and Gregory Emeka Chinweuba, "The Supreme Being in Igbo Thought: A Reappraisal," *Philosophia* 21 (2018): 27.

[27] Olupona, *African Religions*, 3.

in this material world.²⁸ This inclusive nature of reality and the primacy of life is what Vincent Mulago calls "vital participation."²⁹ Religions exist to promote vital participation, which is a sharing in the moral traditions of abundant life for the community and through sharing in the life of the ancestors. The ancestors of Africa are not worshipped, but revered and venerated, as Jomo Kenyatta writes of his Gikuyu ethnic group,

> I do not believe the Gikuyu worship their ancestors. They hold communion with them, but their attitude towards them is not at all to be compared with their attitude to the deity who is truly worshipped.... The words "prayer" and "worship," *gothaithaiya goikia-mokoigoro,* are never used in dealing with the ancestors' spirits. These words are reserved for solemn rituals and sacrifices directed to the power of the unseen.³⁰

It is a good starting point, looking at God's hand in the affairs of people to understand what it means to be human, the meaning of our existence here on earth, and the directions of history broadly conceived.

The theological articulation of vital participation by Mulago is an apt interpretation of this fundamental dimension of the African ancestral religious worldview. Mulago interprets *ntu* as life force instead of vital force.³¹ Mulago notes that African Traditional Religions (ATRs) are based on four essential elements: (1) unity of life and participation; (2) belief in the enhancement or diminution of beings, and the interaction of beings; (3) symbol as the principal means of contact and union; and (4) an ethic that flows from ontology.³² Two essential points—vital union/participation, and the enhancement and

---

[28] Gerrie ter Haar, *How God Became African: African Spirituality and Western Secular Thought* (Philadelphia: University of Pennsylvania Press, 2009), 19.

[29] Vincent Mulago, "Traditional African Religion and Christianity," in *African Traditional Religions in Contemporary Society*, ed. Jacob K. Olupona (New York: Paragon House, 1991), 120.

[30] Jomo Kenyatta, *Facing Mount Kenya* (New York: Vintage Books, 1965), 255, 256.

[31] Bénézet Bujo, "Vincent Mulago: An Enthusiast of African Theology," in *African Theology: The Contribution of the Pioneers*, ed. Bénézet Bujo and Juvénal Ilunga Muya (Nairobi, Kenya: Paulines Publications Africa, 2003), 18.

[32] Mulago, "Traditional African Religion and Christianity," 120.

diminution of life—will be considered in demonstrating the nature of African religions in the understanding of abundant life. This is particularly evident in African family tradition through which vital participation becomes concrete among the living, the dead, and the not yet born.

According to Mulago, vital union is the bond that joins the living and the dead in both a vertical and horizontal relationship. It is the life-giving principle in all beings. It is the result of communion, of participation in the one reality, and the one vital principle that unites various beings.[33] Life is seen not as mere physical existence, but an inseparable and interdependent mode of existence which draws from the ultimate source of all life, *Nyamuzinda* (the ultimate source of happiness, the *Imana*), and from the ancestors. Life involves participation with family, clan, community, ethnic group, ancestors, the land, earth, and God. To live is to be in the bosom of the community. It means to participate in the sacrality of life—all life is sacred—of God passed on through the ancestors. It means a prolongation of the deepest bonds that bring human and cosmic flourishing through descendants and the community. Life is understood in two ways: as community in blood (the principal and primordial element) and as community in possessions, a concomitant element making life possible.[34]

Mulago argues further that vital participation could be increased or decreased through the things that favor the growth of life in the community, or through the things that bring evil, like sorcery, witchcraft, spiritual or material injury, and evil spells. The choices people make in the film *Living in Bondage*, such as corruption, infidelity, and abuse of power, all arise from selfishness and greed. These choices, particularly those in contemporary African societies that create such much suffering for people, will be seen in this light as evil, because they diminish the life of the community and diminish human and cosmic flourishing. Suffering comes from bad choices made by people. This underlies the need for personal and communal conversion, which will involve the removal of sin and evil, as well as the rejection of selfishness and negative forces that destroy life and harmony among people. Conversion is needed to remove all things that destroy personal and communal lives, so that society encourages those virtues that promote life. People who act against the life of individuals or communities are invited to conversion and to perform rituals

---

[33] Mulago, "Traditional African Religion and Christianity," 120.
[34] Mulago, "Traditional African Religion and Christianity," 123.

of expiation, and restitution to avoid being starved of the vital life whose circuit flows through the life-affirming persons, families, and communities that promote abundant life.

This worldview underlies the intimate bond and interaction between every constituent member of society—the living and the dead, the human and the material, and all humans. Active participation by everyone in the common life is needed to preserve, promote, and protect the common good. This requires a just and equitable society where everyone counts, and where everyone's gifts are received and nurtured. Concerted efforts are needed to eliminate the vices and unjust structures that harm the full realization of the common good from which all should draw equally, as from a well or pool. The current situation in Africa—the politics of the stomach, extraction, extraversion, and violence; and some religious practices that are built on lies, deceptions, exploitation, and fake religious claims—are strange to this traditional African religio-spiritual worldview of abundant life. In traditional African religion such people who lie in the name of God or who destroy the common good through corruption will usually face severe consequences, including death, sanctions, or exile.

Three important features among many others in African theological development today can shed light on religion in Africa and the place of God.

The first is that African theologians are beginning to pay greater attention to the unique stories of Africa, and their richness, complexities, and ambiguities. Theologians are beginning to identify alternate sites in Africa where God is found especially because of the persistence today of poverty and its associated social contagions and suffering. As one respondent to my survey said to me, "We do God here and not talk about God." Given the challenging social context of life in Africa today, scholars often focus on the common religious experiences of people in Africa, and how they have developed because of these troubling social conditions.[35]

The second feature is that African theologians are highlighting the unique mediation of God-in-history in African religio-cultural groups, family, and self-understanding. These are presented as central to interpreting the past, understanding the present, and working toward a better future in Africa.

---

[35] Ebenezer Obadare, *Pentecostal Republic: Religion and the Struggle for State Power in Nigeria* (London: Bloomsbury, 2018); see also Marian Burchardt, "Salvation as Cultural Distinction: Religion and Neoliberalism in Urban Africa," *Cultural Sociology* 14, no. 2 (2020): 7.

African theologians are beginning to deepen the connection and continuity—as well as the limitations and discontinuity—between the traditional notions of God which they received from their ancestors and the received notions of God from Christianity and the revelation of God in Christ as testified by scriptural evidence and in the development of the creed from the first Christians to our times. Theologians who operate from this perspective focus on what Emmanuel Katongole calls the tension between the modern and premodern (and, one could add, the postmodern outlook in Africa) regarding Christology, religious symbols, rituals, divine power, and religious objects through which people get in contact with God (scapulars, grottos, perpetual adoration chapels, and rosaries, among others).[36]

Third is that God is the source and guarantor of abundant life. The ancestors are not God, but they have a mediatory role and serve as models of a good life. Indeed, the goal of worship of God and African spirituality is "to totally experience the 'good life' and to completely avoid the 'bad life.'"[37] Abundant life emerges as firm harmony in creation and in the human world, through right and respectful relationships. Such bonds enhance the realization of people's assets and the generous and other-affirming commitment to bringing one's gifts to enrich our common life. All manifestations of life and being display this element of participation. Community is thus conceived as a vital circuit in which everyone counts. This is the very hub whose proper functioning for traditional Africans is destroyed by the absence of reconciliation, justice, and peace in the community. Being poor or rich must be seen beyond individualistic claims or the runaway capitalistic tendencies in modern African societies, where, as in *Living in Bondage*, in many cases people in their desire to survive often make the wrong choice of seeking to acquire much wealth, and to think less of the common good and more about themselves. Being poor or rich is an invitation to a self-reflective and self-critical communal renewal to remove greed and selfishness in our societies. This can come through promoting Gospel-driven lifestyles that mirror authentic African communal social ethics and the priority of community. Gospel-driven lifestyles counter any promotion of self-fulfillment that is simply driven by a runaway desire for wealth at all costs, or the oppression, exploitation, and humiliation of the poor.

---

[36] Katongole, "Africa," 133.
[37] Magesa, *What Is Not Sacred?* 32.

This concept of life as participation could have various layers and differentiations among African peoples who are non-Bantu. Regardless, it underlies the apprehension of life and relationship at the deepest level of life-giving and other-affirming interactions among African peoples south of the Sahara. Community is intimately participatory and cosmic, but more important, community is ultimately directed to procuring the abundant life, which is human and cosmic flourishing.

Cyril Okorocha defines this abundant life regarding the Igbo people of West Africa:

> The goal of man's religious experience, salvation, is defined and sought in terms of *Ezi-Ndu*, the viable life: a life which goes far beyond merely being alive to include such desirabilities as health, prosperity, longevity, and offspring—the fertility of beast, land and mankind—as well as tranquility of order within society manifested in the reign of *ofo-na-ogu* in both public and private life. The whole religious philosophy is life-affirming.[38]

This view of life at the personal level means that a successful life is one that is lived in making significant contributions to the common good through service, hard work, family life, and other accomplishments. This is captured well in Chinua Achebe's *Things Fall Apart* in how the hero of the novel, Okonkwo, is contrasted with his father, Unoka, who was poor, "lazy and improvident and incapable of thinking about tomorrow." The narrative goes this way:

> When Unoka died he had taken no title at all and he was heavily in debt. Any wonder then that his son Okonkwo was ashamed of him? Fortunately, among these people a man was judged according to his worth and not according to the worth of his father. Okonkwo was clearly cut out for great things. He was still young but he had won fame as the greatest wrestler in the nine villages. He was a wealthy farmer and had two barns full of yams and had just married his third

---

[38] Cyril C. Okorocha, *The Meaning of Religious Conversion in Africa: The Case of the Igbo of Nigeria* (Aldershot: Avebury, 1987), 204.

wife. To crown it all, he had taken two titles and had shown incredible prowess in two inter-tribal wars. Age was respected among his people, but achievement was revered.[39]

Laurenti Magesa, after a survey of the different aspects of abundant life as the goal of ATRs, concludes that the basis for the procurement of abundant life is ancestral communion: "The imperative of community and harmony that determines the ethical agenda of life in African Religion deeply concerns the ancestors. By their character and attributes, they link the individuals in a clan and the visible and invisible world."[40] These ancestors ensured order, security, and prosperity. Loyalty to ethnic norms which preserved the moral universe and thus secured the common good was important. Ancestral communion, therefore, reflects a desire on the part of the living to sustain the common good through observance of moral and spiritual requirements, which are all based on a religious vision. This was essential for the good of everyone—the living, the dead, and the not yet born:

> From the perspective of African Religion, then, illness, poverty, and other calamities point to a moral disorder in relationships, from the most elementary in the family to the most complex in the society. If the family, lineage, and clan enjoy good health and relative prosperity, particularly when the birth rate is good and the children survive to adulthood, it is believed that there is a good rapport in the network of relationships. The ancestors are happy, the vital force is strong, and there is harmony in the land and in creation. Such abundance of life is a clear indication that the population is upright with regard to the ancestors.[41]

God is omnipresent in every aspect of life in Africa. The basis for theodicy in Africa is not texts but lived lives and human experiences in their variations and complexities. African Christians are finding God in their suffering and smiling as we demonstrated in chapter 3, but who this God is whom they find in their suffering and smiling remains the object of theological inquiry today.

---

[39] Chinua Achebe, *Things Fall Apart* (New York: Anchor, 1994), 8.
[40] Laurenti Magesa, *African Religion: The Moral Traditions of Abundant Life* (Maryknoll, NY: Orbis Books, 2002), 77.
[41] Magesa, *African Religion*, 77.

Thinking right about God and acting right toward God in the face of suffering and pain in Africa and the structural violence that diminish the quality of life in Africa are of concern to theology. This is because in giving account of hope amid suffering in Africa, God is often under judgment. In addition, knowing the God revealed in Jesus Christ, and modeling one's actions on his Words and deeds, are consequential for the solutions and praxis of hope that are offered to Africans today. However, to know God as revealed in God's Son in Africa does not require spending time only in libraries or poring over tomes on the theology of suffering. Rather, one should go to healing homes, visit churches, attend religious crusades and revivals, visit hospitals and jails, go to the slums, go to marketplaces, attend parliament or social functions, and travel by road to hear the *matatu* theologians' live sermons in buses, and to hear hawkers of different herbs and medications who sell their wares and talk about God to travelers in tandem. One should listen to the ringtones of phones, to religious programs on television, to radio and social media, and to the blaring proclamations coming from the megaphones of towers of churches and the minarets of mosques in Africa. In these voices, the cries that Africans lift unto God and the problems and testimonies believers share in the altar calls in public worship services in many churches show even in imperfect ways the intimations and light of God.

It is not surprising that accounts of God and the sacred in Africa, of healing and deliverance, of breaking of the yoke of poverty or the cycle of misfortune relate to everything and follow people everywhere. These accounts show the complexity of the African religio-cultural world, which might appear irrelevant and even irreverent to other cultural contexts outside Africa. Many African Christian scholars are not experts in just one area of theology, because their theology is a "rolling theology" that is concerned with the quotidian issues that emerge in their societies. This approach picks up themes and issues based on what are seen to be the problems confronting God's people in Africa. Many of us African theologians no longer have the luxury of specializing in any exclusive disciplinary silo. Rather, we are constantly being challenged to immerse ourselves in our people's lives and histories, suffering and smiles, and accompany them to find the footprints of God, which can lead them in small ways every day to human and cosmic flourishing.

Such matters that theologians and pastors are dealing with in Africa as have been shown in chapter 3 include interfaith dialogue, ancestral traditions and curses, funeral rites, terminal illness, tragic deaths and misfortunes, the meaning of family life, social and political issues, equity and diversity, tribal affinities, cultural and spiritual identities, poverty eradication, gender rights, and the rights of minorities. Each of these can help characterize theodicy in Africa, because each of these in contemporary theological discourse is suffused with narratives of God's work, God's presence, and the unseen forces and powers either working with or against God or with or against people's interests and wellbeing.

What I am writing here about belief in God in Africa relates to the Christianity that emerged in Africa after the missionary work of Western Christians in the continent beginning from the 1960s and what it has retained or forgotten from Africa's past. As Thomas Oden notes, one must be conscious of a narrow reading of modern Christian history when it comes to Africa, where often people think that Christianity in Africa was strictly imported from the North or the West. He proposes that whereas many modern African scholars of religion and theology have fought to give voice to the narratives of faith in God in Africa, "in African traditional religious patterns, motifs, rituals and memories," he asserts the best weapon for African theologians is the ancient texts of African Christianity.[42] As much as I am sympathetic to this position, I see today's African Christians as not having an unmediated connection to ancient African Christianity. The connection is more emotive than conceptual, and it is worth deepening that historical connection both theologically and spiritually for African theology and churches in Africa. However, an uninterrupted diffusionist account of African Christianity from the first five hundred years of the early church's presence in Alexandria, Carthage, Numudia, Nubia, and Ancient Kush (Ethiopia) that does not take into account cultural mediation, variation, rejections, and appropriations that have lasted for over two thousand years on the continent of Africa seems simplistic and ahistorical.

I locate my discourse within the school of thought that argues that the birth of modernity in Africa, and the disruptions caused by modernity in Africa, began with the introduction of Western Christianity, slavery, colonialism, and the emergence of the nation-states in Africa. This created what has been called the African predicament.[43] In this, African peoples are suspended between channels of history and cultural forces with which

---

[42] Thomas Oden, *How Africa Shaped the Christian Mind: Rediscovering the African Seedbed of Western Christianity* (Downers Grove, IL: IVP Academic, 2010), 25–26.

[43] Peter P. Ekeh, "Development Theory and the African Predicament," *Africa Development/Afrique et Développement* 11, no. 4 (1986): 1–40.

they are grappling rather unsuccessfully to understand and manage. The convergence theory of history and global economy is proving to be a will-o'-the-wisp for Africa, while creating greater stress than ever on all fronts. This leaves Africa in a crushing tension of contending modernities and contending narratives of God. (Whether these are birth pangs or deathtraps are beyond the range of my concern here.) This view is shared by most African scholars, especially those who embrace postcolonial critical social theories of history and the decolonization of theology and Christianity in Africa. Ogbu Kalu puts it this way: "Of all these bearers of the African burden, the missionary was also paradoxically, the best symbol of the colonial enterprise. He devoted himself sincerely to the ideals of colonialism: the expansion of civilization, the dissemination of Christianity, and the advance of progress."[44]

Missionaries to Africa had no single motive. Neither can an aspect of modernity introduced by the missionaries be identified that has persisted in every part of Africa with the same cultural tempo or tenor. History is fluid, including that of missionary work in Africa and of Western modernity. The factors that unleashed modernity in global history produced differing consequences in Africa that the West could not control. One consequence is that Christianity assumed a life of its own in Africa and continues to expand today with churches of the West seemingly helpless as the church in Africa spread with the people's chosen beliefs, practices, behavior, and sense of community. The missionaries saw the colonial presence and pacification of Indigenous peoples as part of divine providence. They opened the Gospel to the natives and cleared the way for a network of evangelization to link Africa and the home country, while missionaries were provided the security and support needed for their work.[45]

In some instances, the missionaries saw the colonialists as impeding the cause of the Gospel. For example, Charles Lavigerie (1825–1892), in his fight for abolition, aligned with European powers, but he sometimes

> promoted independent actions by his missionaries, who were supported by coalitions with European civil society. Although Lavigerie lobbied the colonial governments, his missionaries

---

[44] Ogbu Kalu, quoted in Olúfémi Táíwò, *How Colonialism Preempted Modernity in Africa* (Bloomington: Indiana University Press, 2010), 52.

[45] Adrian Hastings, *The Church in Africa 1450–1950* (Oxford: Clarendon, 1994), 408.

demonstrated a tendency toward autonomous action and even establishing alternative sovereignties, contributing to the *sans frontières* character of missionary abolitionism.[46]

In his efforts to convert the people, Lavigerie worried that the French governor of Algeria would not allow his seminarians to study Arabic to enable evangelizing the Muslims. He appealed to Napoleon III and Pope Pius IX. Lavigerie resisted all attempts to stop the evangelizing mission of the White Fathers in Algeria and the rest of today's Francophone Africa. In the end he prevailed and sent his missionaries to present-day Zanzibar, Uganda, Tanganyika, Mali, and Burkina Faso.[47]

A consensus among historians is that the colonialists and missionaries shared a common commitment to "civilizing" Africa. A transition began in Western missionary activities in Africa, with the positive consequences of the use of vernacular literature, hymnody, and liturgy. In the West, the so-called barbarians abandoned their old pantheons and embraced the God of the Lord Jesus Christ, which thus merged with the highest expression of the Good in the Greek philosophical tradition. In Africa, the God of the Lord Jesus Christ was also conceived in African names among the Yoruba, Igbo, and Akan peoples of West Africa, among others. These names include *Olurun*, *Chukwu*, and *Nyame*.[48]

Lamin Sanneh calls attention to the phenomenological effects of missionary activities in terms of the Christian experience of Africans, which went beyond any Westernizing ideology. The living reality of the missionaries and the historical setting of their unreflective translation of the Gospel into African cultural idioms through the conveyor belt of Indigenous languages sometimes undermined the constructed theories of the cultural project of the missionaries.[49] The Bible and the catechism were

---

[46] David M. Gordon, "Slavery and Redemption in the Catholic Missions of the Upper Congo, 1878–1909," *Slavery & Abolition* 38, no. 3 (2017): 584.

[47] Robert Calderisi, *Earthly Mission: The Catholic Church and World Development* (New Haven, CT: Yale University Press, 2013), 105.

[48] See Andrew Walls, *The Cross-Cultural Process in Christian History* (Maryknoll, NY: Orbis Books, 2005), 42.

[49] Vincent Donovan's book *Christianity Rediscovered* (Maryknoll, NY: Orbis Books, 1978) demonstrates this self-reflective conversion of many Western missionaries that promoted a change in the way they became open to African cultures. See also

presented in over one thousand African languages within a period of less than fifty years. The cross-cultural impetus is evident that the missionaries gave not only to African Christian religion, but also to the critical and constructive reformulation of African cultures, languages, and societies in general. Also evident is the interior capacity of African languages and cultures for cultural experimentation and adaptation to meet changing needs and circumstances.

The translation of the Gospel and Christianity into African languages led to African agency in the work of spreading the Good News. According to Lamin Sanneh, "By implication, the mother-tongue speakers themselves became the indispensable partners of the historical transplanting of Christianity, and, at a deeper level, the unrecognized pace-setters for the enterprise of mission."[50] Adrian Hastings makes the same conclusion using examples from Igboland, the Xhosa, Sotho, and Shonaland:

> The Christian advance was a black advance or it was nothing.... Whether in time a missionary did actually arrive might make rather little difference to the work of preaching, teaching, conversion, the brunt of which was almost always borne at the primary level by black teachers. The missionary negotiated with chiefs and colonial authorities, arranged the building of houses, the translation and printing of texts, taught the teachers, punished irregularities, supervised the overall advance of the mission—all important functions but ones which by themselves do not at all explain the actual process of conversion.[51]

The most successful mission enterprises in Africa during the missionary period were those carried out by Africans, whether it was the pioneering efforts of African liberated slaves in Sierra Leone beginning in 1792, or that of William Wade Harris, or of Bishop Ajayi Crowther. The continued expansion of the

---

Sanneh's account of the cultural momentum set in motion in Africa by the translation of Christianity into African languages, and how this led to Christian expansion in Africa as African Christians saw a narrative of continuity in cultural categories between ATRs and Christianity; Lamin Sanneh, *Encountering the West: Christianity and the Global Cultural Process* (Maryknoll, NY: Orbis Book, 1993), 73–116.

[50] Lamin Sanneh, "Christian Mission in the Pluralist Milieu: The African Experience," *Missiology: An International Review* 12, no. 4 (October 1984): 431.

[51] Hastings, *The Church in Africa*, 437–38.

Christian faith came from Africans becoming missionaries to their brothers and sisters. This was difficult for Western missionaries to fully embrace, but was an inevitable process inherent in Christianity.[52]

Three cultural currents in missionary enterprise affect the shape of contemporary Christianity in Africa: (1) The tension between those who still seek a synchronizing Westernized church, especially within the Catholic tradition, where there is an overarching influence of the Roman Church in the nature and shape of local initiatives. (2) The indigenizing principle is robust in its claims and aspirations toward making Christianity an African project, and seeking to find God in the community rather than in the heavens. (3) A strong current of rejection exists in Africa of even the most positive heritage of Christianity. This is often found in some reactionary theologies in many African churches, especially in the face of secularization and the culture wars that have dealt possibly mortal blows to Western Christianity. A post-Western Christianity has been ushered in and a post-Christian Western society in which Africa is now the main player. However, in considering these factors there is a persistent question that has stayed in my consciousness: What could have happened if Christianity developed first in Africa and from Africa to Europe? This question was posed by Robert Rattray with regard to the religious belief of the Ashanti people of Ghana:

> I sometimes like to think, had these people been left alone to work out their own salvation, perhaps someday an African Messiah would have arisen and swept their pantheons clean of the fetish.... West Africa might then have become the cradle of a new creed which acknowledged One Great Spirit, who, being One, nevertheless

---

[52] On how the translation of Christianity valorized the agency of Africans, see, for instance, Stephen Gray, "Missionary Researchers and Researching Missions: A South African View of Cultural Colonisation at the Millennium," *Journal of Theology for Southern Africa* 105 (November 1999): 17–25. See also David A. Shank, "Mission Relations with the Independent Churches in Africa," *Missiology: An International Review* 13, no. 1 (January 1985): 23–44. On the validation of the active African element and the effect of Black missionaries in the shaping of African Christian Religion, see Jehu Hanciles, "Back to Africa: Abolitionists and Black Missionaries," in *African Christian Religion: An African Story*, ed. Ogbu U. Kalu (Trenton, NJ: Africa World Press, 2007), 167–89.

manifested himself in everything around him and taught men to hear his voice in the flow of the waters and in the sound of the winds in the trees.[53]

The God of Our Ancestors

The ethnography I carried out between 2007 and 2011 on ancestral traditions among ethnic groups in Kenya, Uganda, and Nigeria shows that most Africans interviewed had an ancestral worldview. This strong association of God with ancestral traditions suggests that every account of God in African Christianity must show the relationship of the ancestors to God, and how their lives testify to the belief in the existence of God in the concrete history of Africans who hold to this belief. Bénézet Bujo argues forcefully:

> The Black African must rediscover his roots so that the ancestral tradition may enrich postcolonial people and make them adopt a critical attitude towards modern society. Then Africa will be able to breathe with a new life which neither idealizes the past, simply because one is black, nor treats the past as an idol. What is needed is a new synthesis. It is not a question of replacing the God of the Africans but rather of enthroning the God of Jesus Christ, not as the rival of the God of the ancestors, but as identical with God.[54]

This the heart of the matter in African theology today on the question: "Where is God?" Olupona cautions African theologians to search for God in the performative symbols of God in God's creation in Africa. This is especially so for African cultures, worldviews, spiritualities, and religions. According to Olupona, the images of God systematized in African theology are alienating to Africans because they are similar to the images of the white God, which Africans learned of from Western missionaries and colonialists.[55] Olupona argues that

---

[53] Robert S. Rattray, *Religion and Art in Ashanti* (London: Oxford University Press, 1969), vi, cited in Sindima, *Classical Theories in African Religion*, 261.

[54] Bénézet Bujo, *African Theology in Its Social Context*, trans. John O'Donohue (Maryknoll, NY: Orbis Books, 1992), 15–16.

[55] Jacob Olupona, "Major Issues in the Study of African Traditional Religion," in *African Traditional Religions in Contemporary Society*, ed. Jacob Olupona (New York: Paragon House, 1991), 28–29.

a basic question for any meaningful theological study of African religion is: How did Africans themselves experience their world in a fashion we can still call religious? This question is similar, he argues, to one by the anthropologist Benjamin Ray: "The debate about African 'monotheism' might have ended long ago if both sides had recognized that African Supreme Beings are like but unlike Western concepts of God."[56] The missing link here is how to insert the person of Jesus Christ in this narrative of God in a way to show some continuities and discontinuities. The African God, Olupona argues, is one in which the sacred and the profane tend to be symmetrical. The ordinary human experience is mimetic of the transcendence of the sacred. Olupona calls for a phenomenological-hermeneutical investigation and interpretation of the mythological thought of Africans.

This complex layering of God narratives is seen in some of the results from my ethnography. In my field study of thirty-seven religious groups in Kenya, Uganda, and Nigeria, three discoveries about God stand out.

First is a persistence of ancestral worldviews, beliefs, and traditions among African Christians and practitioners of ATRs. God is understood in ancestral traditions as present in history through family and communal bonds. Ancestors are seen as god-like figures who influence the destiny of the living; ancestral traditions help secure for Africans—Christians and non-Christians—a belief in the Supreme God and the continuation of communal life after death. To the question about proof of life after death, most people consulted in this research pointed to the continued influence and presence of their ancestors who work for their good.

Many African theologians have employed the ancestral image as a symbol for representing Christ, because they see in Christ the new Adam who recapitulates the past, heals the present, and assures the glorious future for all creation.[57] In African religious traditions, among most African ethnic

---

[56] Benjamin Ray, cited in Olupona, "Major Issues," 28–29.

[57] See, for instance, Hans Schwarz's summary of this evolution of African Christology through the writings of John Mbiti, Desmond Tutu, and Kwesi Dickson in *Theology in Global Context* (Grand Rapids, MI: William B. Eerdmans, 2005), 500–516. A similar study is presented by Diane Stinton; see her "Africa, East and West," in *An Introduction to Third World Theologies*, ed. John Parratt (Cambridge: Cambridge University Press, 2004). Some significant Christological works in Africa include: Enyi Ben Udoh, *Guest Christology: An Interpretative View of the Christological Problem in Africa* (Frankfurt: Peter Lang, 1988); John Samuel Pobee, ed., *Exploring*

groups ancestral veneration is at the heart of African religion and morality. The image of the ancestor is seen as capable of revealing the continuing presence of Christ in history and links the past to the present in a concrete way. It is also capable of both unlocking the spiritual and ethical moorings of Africans in their search for God, while shedding light on the person of Christ and his universal offer of salvation for Africans in a new way.

The African ancestor is the "living dead," whose memory lives on and whose life continues to influence the destiny of his or her progeny. The ancestor is not an imperfect man or woman who needs to be purified in purgatory after death to make a perfect satisfaction for sin. He or she is not a damned soul whose sinfulness led to eternal punishment or hell, unless one may consider the *damnatio memoriae* of a community against an evil man or woman who passes on as a form of hell. The evil person suffers not simply because his or her soul is languishing in hell, but because it is forgotten. His or her story remains with the community as a bold reprimand or rejection of any life which is lived in selfishness, through acts that harmed the community.

The ancestral image is powerful because every division in a family, clan, or community is interpreted as wounding the ancestral spirit and diminishing vital participation. Even in contemporary African societies, when dealing with intractable conflicts and division many families will retire into the ancestral grove for dialogue and sober reflection guided by the spirit of the ancestor. The same happens when divisions and wars lead to bloodshed and destruction. The healing rituals are meant not to bring about retributive justice, but to bring about restorative justice and satisfy the troubled spirits of the ancestors and purify the memory of the living—a kind of theological social autopsy. The continuing reflection on the words and deeds of the ancestors helps the community to bond and to increase participation in vital union. This has an analogical relation to the anamnetic contemplation on the words and deeds of Christ.

Afro-Christology (Frankfurt: Peter Lang, 1992); Department of Systematic Theology, *Incarnating Christ Today* (Nairobi: Paulines Publications Africa, 2001); Aylward Shorter, *Jesus and the Witchdoctor: An Approach to Healing and Wholeness* (Maryknoll, NY: Orbis Books, 1985). John V. Taylor quoted in Kwame Bediako, *Jesus and the Gospel in Africa, History and Experience,* with an introduction by Hans Visser and Gillian Bediako (Maryknoll, NY: Orbis Books, 2004), xi. Victor I. Ezigbo, *Re-imagining African Christologies: Conversing with the Interpretations and Appropriations of Jesus in Contemporary African Christianity* (Eugene, OR: Wipf and Stock, 2010).

The second discovery is that while all my informants and focus groups accept ancestral worldviews, ancestral rituals are diverse and are accepted or rejected by some Christians in the interaction of Gospel and culture.

The third discovery is that the nature of ancestral rituals overlaps in ATRs and African Christian religion. In some worldviews, African Christians and practitioners of African religions share a strong belief in the bond that the ancestors help establish between the living and the spiritual world. Hence burial rites must be done according to required customs by both groups. However, differences occur at the level of symbols and practice.[58]

Regarding how the ancestors influence the living, one of my respondents, a Catholic nun who traces her ancestry to the Kaonde and Luvale ethnic groups of Zambia, acknowledged that she is influenced by her ancestors. She said:

> My relatives, especially my grandparents who are dead, influence my life. I believe that they are watching over me. All those connected to me by ancestry are watching over me. I remember that whenever I go home, my father, who is a practicing Catholic, will always blow into my ears and call on our ancestors to take care of me. I always feel protected wherever I go with the invisible presence of the spirits of my ancestors, whose power my father always invoked.[59]

Another nun, from Kondoa in the Dodoma region of Tanzania, agreed that ancestral beliefs affect the Christian faith because many Christians do not believe strongly in the power of Christ. According to her, many people in her ethnic group attribute evil and good to the ancestors. She pointed out that when people are sick, instead of first going to the doctor they sometimes go to the cemetery or the burial place of their living dead to ask them why they are allowing such sickness into the family.[60]

---

[58] My respondents come from different ethnic groups: Luo, Kikuyu, Meru, Igbo, Kaonde, Luvale, Yao, Dinka, and Yoruba.

[59] From a June 16, 2007, interview with a Roman Catholic nun from Zambia, conducted at the Tangaza Female Hostel, Lang'ata, Nairobi, Kenya, on how her ancestral worldview influences her Christian faith and cultural imagination.

[60] From a June 17, 2007, interview with a Tanzanian Roman Catholic nun on how her ancestral worldview influences her Christian faith, conducted at the Tangaza Female Hostel, Lang'ata, Nairobi, Kenya.

Ancestral beliefs and traditions influence the worldview of Africans. From the pattern of convergence of meaning and symbols established in my field research, ancestral tradition is a hermeneutical key for interpreting the movement of history among many Africans in Christianity and ATRs in the various ethnic groups I covered. A Roman Catholic young man who works at the Catholic University of Eastern Africa, Nairobi, told me:

> Ancestors are there because even though you do not see them physically, they are there. I feel they are talking to me, but I do not think I should feed them, but I know they influence my life for good and not for evil because they love their living progenies and are everywhere.[61]

Respondents whom I spoke to in a focus group interview at my ancestral home, Adu Achi in Eastern Nigeria, acknowledged that Christians and even some Christian pastors come to them to seek answers to the challenges and tragedies in the family line. These Christians believe in ancestral myths and ancestral curses, which could come upon them if they do not "feed" their ancestors, or if they do not perform the right ancestral rituals like slaughtering a traditional African cow for one's father at death. The *Ezemuo* (chief priest of the *Ajalla* deity of Adu Achi) told me in a focus group conversation that three types of clients come to his shrine:[62] (1) Members of his ATR group who come to perform ritual sacrifices, and who also join him in the weekly and seasonal feasts in the traditional reading and celebrations of the yearly cycle. (2) Practitioners of ATRs from other villages who come to him for divination with regard to ancestral rites and traditions that relate to ancestors of Adu Achi village. This normally includes the village *ada* (women from Adu Achi married to men in other villages and towns). (3) Christians who come to seek answers from their ancestors when they are visited with some inexplicable tragedies in the family line, as well as Christians who come to him to request that he slaughter the traditional

---

[61] From a June 5, 2007, group interview with theology students and workers of the Catholic University of Eastern Africa Press, on how the ancestors influence their vision of the future.

[62] From an August 8, 2006, interview with the *Ezemuo* (chief priest) of the Ajalla deity of Adu Achi in Eastern Nigeria, along with six other priests of ATRs, to find out the creed, code, and customs of the Igbo ancestral beliefs, traditions, and practices. The interview was conducted at the sacred shrine of the Ajalla deity.

cow as the final ritual of funeral for one who meets the requirements of being an ancestor at death.

When I asked him whether he thinks these acts of Christians are syncretic, he answered:

> The ancestors are the same for Christians and for non-Christians. The Church and ATRs do not conflict at all. Our role here as *Ezemuo* is to help people find answers to the problems of life. The ancestors want us as their children to live an abundant life. We do not kill people or harm people. If anyone comes to my shrine asking me to kill another or to proclaim an oracle against another, I will send the person away with a warning. It is not wrong for Christians to come here to find ways in which they must make the ancestors happy so that the ancestors can bless them. Many of them who came found answers to their problems and often greet me with gratitude when I meet them along the road.[63]

An ethnographic study carried out by the Pew Forum on Religion and Public Life, published in 2010, surveyed nineteen countries in Africa. It corroborates my findings that large numbers of Africans who are deeply committed to Christianity or Islam believe in witchcraft, evil spirits, sacrifices to ancestors, traditional religious healers, reincarnation, and other elements of African religions.[64] The African religio-cultural ancestral worldview continues to occupy the interests of many scholars today because it is central to Africa's appropriation of Christianity. In my home diocese of Awgu in Eastern Nigeria, a main source of conflict in the Catholic Church is about burial rites and ancestral funerary rituals, which can be observed at certain times, on certain days, and with the slaughter of an African-bred cow.

The notion of God in Africa is being mediated through these religio-cultural ancestral frameworks in a functional and performative way. According to Ogbu Kalu, missionary historiography and accounts by Western colonial administrators, travelers, and anthropologists give the impression that African gods were in retreat, that is, that ATRs were

---

[63] From an August 8, 2006, interview with the *Ezemuo* (chief priest) of the Ajalla deity.
[64] See Pew Research Center, "Tolerance and Tension: Islam and Christianity in Sub-Saharan Africa," April 15, 2010, section titled "Executive Summary."

in decline.⁶⁵ Relying on external data, their conclusion was that Western modernity—with its rationality, science, and Western-type Christian faith—had displaced the traditional religious systems and cultures of Africans. Such displacement was perceived as a sign of the ethical, scientific, and spiritual superiority of Western Christianity over ATRs. The speed with which Africans converted to Christianity was also seen as proof that Africans freely gave up their "fetishes" and other aspects of their religious practices. Anthropologists like James Frazer conclude that religious changes in Africa validate the evolutionary unilinear theory of the abandonment of religious traditions by primitive societies for a "higher" religious tradition.⁶⁶ Thus, religious change or African conversion from ATR to Christianity is interpreted as a social evolution and an inevitable progressive movement.⁶⁷ Although the question of religious conversion is one that would take me too far afield, African theologians like the late Kwame Bediako argue that African Christianity is a new stage in the evolution of African religio-cultural traditions. Thus, one cannot speak of conversion in terms of a cultural break,⁶⁸ but those like Byang Kato argue that African Christianity should be a clean break from the ancestral past.⁶⁹

To conclude this section, I now summarize what I have gained from the narratives of God in Africa from the ancestral model.

First, Africans do not see God as a divine threatener, the vengeful one who has prepared separate spheres in the afterlife for the good and the bad—the good who will enjoy eternal life in heaven, and the bad who will suffer eternal damnation in hell. The notions of hell, heaven, and purgatory were accepted by African Christians as one of the items in the "total package"

---

⁶⁵ Ogbu U. Kalu, "The Gods in Retreat: Models for Interpreting Religious Change in Africa," in *The Gods in Retreat: Continuity and Change in African Religions*, ed. Emefie Ikenga Metuh (Enugu, Nigeria: Fourth Dimension, 1986), 1.

⁶⁶ Ulrich Berner, "Africa and the Origin of the Science of Religion: Max Müller (1823–1900) and James George Frazer (1854–1941) on African Religions," in *European Traditions in the Study of Religion in Africa*, ed. Frieder Ludwig and Afe Adogame (Wiesbaden: Harrassowitz Verlag, 2004), 141–49.

⁶⁷ Berner, "Africa and the Origin," 4.

⁶⁸ Kwame Bediako, "Understanding African Theology in the 20th Century," *Themelios: An International Bulletin for Theological and Religious Studies Students* 20, no. 1 (1994): 16–18.

⁶⁹ Byang Kato, *Theological Pitfalls in Africa* (Kisumu, Kenya: Evangel, 1975), 169.

of Western-type Christianity and worldview which they embraced. Most African Christians whom I interviewed did not see life after death in the binaries of hell and heaven. They believe in ancestral communion, a shared life between the living and the living-dead, as well as the not-yet-born and the entire cosmos.

This unbroken bond of life is never destroyed by death except for those people who are considered evil and harmful, who destroyed lives, and lived a bad life. There is a divine punishment for such people; they belong to the realm of evil spirits whose spirits are often appeased and, in some cases ritually exterminated, to prevent them from harming the living. However, most people I interviewed did not think anyone can determine what happens to the evil ones, and whether God has prepared a special place of punishment for them. They are simply forgotten, their memories damned, and their spirits chained and so unable to harm the living. Most Africans are too preoccupied with navigating the challenges of life today. They are more concerned about surviving the tempests in the here and now than what happens in the hereafter. They worry about eternity, but it is not a present quest, and not as important as taking care of their children and passing on the family tradition to them so that the progeny can continue.

Second conclusion is at the level of actual faith, the plausibility structure, and religio-cultural experience. Most Africans whom I interviewed for this research were more interested in how to procure God's blessing for this present life, how to get their daily bread through God's grace, and what they can do to procreate, and preserve and promote their family line. They were also concerned more with issues of health and well-being, communal life, poverty, and ecology than being preoccupied about where to spend their next life. They expressed concern about the life after this one and pray that God will be merciful or reward them in the next life, but this is not the primary driver of their religious life or moral conduct.

One of the most radical differences between African worldviews regarding religion, spirituality, life after death, and the future and what Western Christianity teaches is that most of my African conversation partners do not accept the existence of two worlds, the world here and the hereafter. Africans embrace "duality," finding it difficult to understand the "dualism" and divisiveness which characterize most themes in Christian theology in the West. These themes of dualism include nature and grace, nature and the supernatural, God the Father and God the Mother, God and the world, God and the devil, saints and sinners, humans and nonhumans, and faith and works. Gerrie ter Haar writes:

African traditions of thought tend to view reality not in terms of binary oppositions and mutually exclusive categories—in other words, in terms of either/or. Rather, they tend to view reality in categories that are inclusive—in terms of and/and. Hence, in African discourses, a person can be considered as being dead while physically alive, like a zombie, a living person who is spiritually dead. Vice versa, a person can be physically dead, but considered to be spiritually alive, like an ancestor. Thus, people may be invisible, yet "really" present, in the form of spirits, which so many Africans believe to exist. The same logic applies in African Christianity, in which the invisible world is perceived to have a real existence and to interact with humans in the visible, material world.[70]

In this worldview, everything belongs. As Magesa puts it, everything is sacred in this universe of meaning, where the bond of life is sustained by the participation of all and right relationships between people.[71] This worldview makes it natural for African Christians to easily embrace the idea of the Trinity as a community of persons and relations. Mutuality, shared gifts, friendship, love, relationship, cooperation, and participative living are qualities that they can grasp as an ideal African ancestral bond of human and divine opportunities. Thus, developing an African Trinitarian theology seems to me a better possibility for building African Christianity, and African ethics and social life.

This way of thinking is also needed in the world today, with its increasing failures to find common ground in our doctrinal battles and politics. This does not mean that Africans do not accept the principle of noncontradiction, but rather that there is an openness to exploring the relationships between seemingly contradictory realities, and an admission that life is a shared relationship in which all things count. This stance leads to the acceptance in the African worldview of complementary duality rather than contradictory dualism.

God in Africa: A Western God in an African Robe?

Some Africans reject ancestral God-talk in African Christianity. Charles Nyamiti argues, for instance, that the African notions of God are at the level of common sense and lack a theoretical foundation, and so should be

---

[70] Ter Haar, *How God Became African*, 19.
[71] Magesa, *What Is Not Sacred?* 40.

supplemented through Western concepts of God. However, he admits that such integration of Western theologies should not be appropriated to distort African cultural identity and values, but to enrich them.[72] Regarding the doctrine of God, Nyamiti writes:

> It goes without saying that the African has much to learn from the Christian faith about how to purify and complete his beliefs about God. But it is also true that the Christian has something to learn from the traditional Africans; not in the sense of new doctrines, but in the sense of new insights and new ways of understanding God. It is not only from the positive aspects of African theism that Christians can learn, but also from its very shortcomings and errors.[73]

Nyamiti argues strongly that the ancestral notion of God in Africa is inadequate. Most African theologians will agree with him. What is disputed is how he and many other theologians in Africa have tried to translate the image of God in Africa through Western concepts and categories.

Some African scholars reject the translation that Nyamiti employs in his theological writings on God and the ancestors in Africa. Whereas Nyamiti frames the relations between African theology and Western theologies in complementary terms,[74] other writers use dialectical terms to capture this relationship.[75] Influential African voices on this matter include Okot

---

[72] Charles Nyamiti, *Studies in African Christian Theology*, ed. Charles Nyamiti, vol. 1, *Jesus Christ, the Ancestor of Humankind: Methodological and Trinitarian Foundations* (Nairobi: CUEA, 2005), 15–16.

[73] Charles Nyamiti, "The Doctrine of God," in *A Reader in African Christian Theology*, ed. John Parratt (London: SPCK, 1997), 57.

[74] See, for instance, Charles Nyamiti's criticism of Shorter's review of his work and his characterization of Nyamiti as a theologian who uses African categories and worldviews scientifically and philosophically in an inherited theological system, in Charles Nyamiti, "Reply to Aylward Shorter's Review," *African Ecclesial Review* 20, no. 3 (June 1978): 169–75.

[75] Some of these views are informed by the experience of slavery, colonialism, racism, and the present underdevelopment of Africa. The reading of African history and literature from the viewpoint of the West has greatly distorted African reality in many ways. See, for instance, J. N. K. Mugambi, *Critiques of Christianity in African Literature* (Nairobi: East African Educational, 1992); see also Chinweizu Onwuchekwa

P'Bitek[76] and Ikenga-Metuh,[77] Eugene Uzukwu,[78] Eboussi Boulaga,[79] and Bénézet Bujo,[80] among others. Western theologians Gerrie ter Haar[81] and Frans Wijsen[82] call attention to how the imposition of Western theologies on Africa destroys creativity and autonomy in African Christianity.

P'Bitek is one of the strongest critics of the application of Western philosophies and theologies to African God-talk, including: (1) Western distortion of African history and religion through misinterpreting African cultures and religions (such as in the work of E. E. Evans-Pritchard, Godfrey Lienhardt, and Geoffrey Parrinder); and (2) African distortion of African history and cultures through the hellenization of African religions (including

---

Jemie and Ihechukwu Madubuike, *Toward the Decolonisation of African Literature: Library of African Diasporic Literature and Criticism* (Washington, DC: Howard University Press, 1983); on the negative effects of racism, colonialism, and slavery on the interpretation of African identity, see Frantz Fanon, *Black Skin, White Masks*, trans. Charles Lam Markmann (New York: Grove, 1967); on the positive and negative effects of Western philosophy and theology on African Christianity and theology, see Luke Nnamdi Mbefo, *Christian Theology and African Heritage* (Onitsha, Nigeria: Spiritan, 1996); see also the influential work by Chancellor Williams, *The Destruction of Black Civilization* (Chicago: Third World Press, 1987); the influential work of Innocent Onyewuenyi continues the recovery of African philosophy and theology which the Egyptologist Cheikh Anta Diop started; see Innocent Chilaka Onyewuenyi, *The African Origin of Greek Philosophy: An Exercise in Afrocentrism* (Nsukka, Nigeria: University of Nigeria Press, 2005).

[76] Okot P'Bitek, *African Religions in Western Scholarship* (Nairobi: Kenya Literary Bureau, 1970).

[77] Emefie Ikenga Metuh, *African Religions in Western Conceptual Schemes: The Problems of Interpretations* (Ibadan, Nigeria: Pastoral Institute, 1987).

[78] Elochukwu E. Uzukwu, *A Listening Church: Autonomy and Communion in African Churches* (Maryknoll, NY: Orbis Books, 1996).

[79] Eboussi Boulaga, *Christianity without Fetishes* (Maryknoll, NY: Orbis Books, 1981).

[80] Bénézet Bujo, *Foundations of an African Ethic: Beyond the Universal Claims of Western Morality*, trans. Brian McNeil (New York: Crossroad, 2001); Bénézet Bujo, *The Ethical Dimension of Community: The African Model and the Dialogue Between North and South*, trans. Cecelia Namulondo Nganda (Nairobi: Paulines Publications Africa, 1998).

[81] Ter Haar, *How God Became African*.

[82] Frans Wijsen, *Seeds of Conflict in a Haven of Peace: From Religious Studies to Inter-Religious Studies in Africa* (Amsterdam: Rodopi, 2007).

works of Bolaji Idowu, John Mbiti, K. A. Busia, J. B. Danquah) by Africans "who dress up African deities with Hellenic robes and parade them before the Western world."[83] According to Jesse Mugambi, P'Bitek worries that:

> Instead of carrying out systematic studies of the beliefs of their peoples, and presenting them as the African peoples actually know them, the African scholars, smarting under the insults from the West, claimed that African peoples knew the Christian God long before the missionaries told them about it. African deities were selected and robed with awkward Hellenic garments.[84]

P'Bitek argues that although the oldest Christian church in Africa, the Ethiopian Orthodox Church, was established in the fourth century before the Fall of Rome in 410, it has not exerted any influence in the extension of the Christian faith in Africa.

P'Bitek's views belong to the "invention of African religion" school of thought and claims that not only Westerners but also African scholars of religion have tended to Westernize African religions.[85] As P'Bitek puts it: "The interpretation of African deities in terms of the Christian God does not help us to understand the nature of the African deities as African peoples conceive them."[86] P'Bitek proposes that rather than being preoccupied with repetitive Christian rituals and proving to the West that African deities can also be presented and understood in Western robes for the sake of the West, he invites Africans to deepen their own religious and cultural heritage. He exhorts Africans to seek hermeneutical keys to understand the African predicament and the challenges that face the people. Solutions to the crisis of modernity in Africa should be sought through this commitment to the cultural and social realities facing the people, rather than upholding the narratives, institutions, and structures of theism in the West, with its alienating features that rob

---

[83] P'Bitek, *African Religions in Western Scholarship*, 41.

[84] Mugambi, *Critiques of Christianity*, 93.

[85] For a good history of Western African religions and the argument that the pre-Christian Africans were more God-fearing and had a better existential saving knowledge of God than present African Christians, see David Westerlund, *African Religion in African Scholarship: A Preliminary Study of the Religious and Political Background* (Stockholm: Almqvist and Wiksell, 1985), 52–56.

[86] P'Bitek, *African Religions in Western Scholarship*, 50.

Africans of a path to self and group understanding.

Theologians in this "invention of African religion" group argue that African religion has unique ethics grounded in African ancestral religion. This grounding needs to be outside of Western theistic formulations as a kind of specific *ius gentium*. One example is the appeal to natural law. African thought is not propositional but symbolic; African thinking found in most ethnic groups of Africa as I indicated earlier is not based on the order of *ratio*, but is linked in a causal chain of vital principles and intrinsic and organic connections in which everything counts. Vital principles, or vital forces, as indicated in the work of Mulago and Magesa are key to understanding African ontology: What is mediated in any relationship is vital force, and this relationship is universal, embracing all things—human and nonhuman—in an unbreakable chain of relationship and participation. The organizing wisdom that holds all things together is God and the mediatory roles of the ancestors and the spiritual world. Reason is not simply logical organization of thoughts and ideas, but the collective memory of the community. Transcending and transforming this memory enriches or diminishes the participation of all in vital force, which is the collective energy that pulsates in the heart of the community.

African theologies are rejecting the theistic abstractions and generalizations of the defunct missionary faith, with its excessive objectivism, transcendental abstractions, and discursive rationalization. In its place, African Christians are finding hope and strength in the God of their ancestors, whom they identify as the God of the Lord Jesus, as well as the God of Abraham, Moses, and Elijah. This is a God who is Trinity as a community of persons and inclusion and participation and the model and source of the community of all things created. This God has power to change everything, to restore that which is broken, and break every yoke, whether it is political, economic, social, cultural, or spiritual. This God cannot be separated from the daily joys and pains of life, the suffering and smiles of people or from the pathos and vicissitudes of ordinary human experience. This God is not simply a heavenly creature waiting to punish and reward people, but rather a God who is present concretely, relationally, and lovingly in the history of people—the living, the dead, and the not-yet born. Humans, and the entire cosmos as well.

This God is Supreme but is not removed from human history and can be encountered in the bonds of love and relationship that work together for human and cosmic flourishing. The African God participates in every breath I take, in the connections and pathways that converge around the bond of life. This God is the source of all things that enhance human and cosmic life, and this God is opposed to everything that diminishes life. This God is the source of human and cosmic flourishing and abundant life. Every being, and all reality, and all humans and spirits, whose existence and action promote human flourishing, are all sharing in the being and actions of God. This God invites all humanity to embrace one another and the whole of creation as one family sharing a common home.

This is the image of God many African theologians are developing in their Christological discourse, a God who is always unfolding as we enter deeper relationships. This is a God revealed to us in Christ, who fills our hearts, our lives, and our world with divine energy and momentum, which continues to stretch, enrich, and divinize us in the movement of the divine spirit as the thread of love that potentiates and infuses all things with energy. This God, revealed and mediated in Christ, always expands beyond our human horizon in beauty, goodness, and truth. In this experience and divine embrace, life is sacred, and humanity and all creation are on a sacred walk with God, surrounded by the presence and communion of our ancestors and all creation.[87] Everyone is invited to this sacred dance of life. All have a place, and all are called to enact here and now practices that promote human and cosmic flourishing and eco-ethical spirituality and ethics. Suffering and evil diminish this life, but they are also to be seen as a sign of the incompleteness of life that invites patience and greater cooperation with others and solidarity with life-affirming persons and religions, and with all created things to strengthen relationships of love and friendship to support those who suffer.

Fighting with Witches and Wizards in Africa: The Politics of God and the Crisis of Religion in Africa

Two crises characterize Africa's embrace of modernity. They not only have defined Africa's social context, but they underlie contestations in Africa today about God. The crises are the postcolonial state and post-Western missionary

---

[87] As Luis Alonso Schokel points out: "Christ did not only speak words; He is a Word, an expression, in His very being and in his acts and speech. Therefore, since Christ is the ultimate revelation of God, any new knowledge of God must consist in penetration ever deeper into the fullness which dwells in Him, all of the New Testament is one, since it derives from and speaks of this mystery." Luis Alonso Schokel, *The Inspired Word: Scripture in the Light of Language and Literature*, trans. Francis Martin (Montreal: Palm Publishers, 1965), 104.

Christianity in Africa. Understanding these dual crises and the God factor in both spheres largely explains the persistent social issues facing Africa, creating so much suffering and making it impossible for Africa to escape the poverty trap.

The postcolonial state refers to the failure of African nations to build strong national institutions and structures that promote, protect, and preserve the common good, and equally and fairly guarantee social mobility for all citizens. Elias Bongmba demonstrates that the human predicament in Africa is directly correlated with the crisis of the postcolonial state. He characterizes this crisis using four "Ps" common in the abuse and misuse of power in Africa: "the privatization of power, the pauperization of the state, the prodigalization of the state, and the proliferation of violence."[88]

The state in Africa today is the theater of deadly struggles for power—kill or be killed in most cases—and of different claims to the power of God in gaining, retaining, and transmitting power. Many African heads of state publicly profess their faith, and many of them have their own residential priests and prophets who propitiate for them before God and ward off from them the attacks of witches and wizards. Archbishop Milingo of Lusaka in his heyday while still in the Catholic Church was known for having extraordinary powers to cast out demons. He wrote in his book *Face to Face with the Devil* that many politicians sought his help to break the yoke in their lives, which they had brought upon themselves by consorting with witches and wizards and making pacts with Satan in their search for security, political power, wealth, and protection.[89] Some of these African leaders consort with witch doctors (*sangoma*), diviners, and priests because they believe that whereas they may control the physical world that they see, the spiritual leaders provide spiritual victory, war chest, and divine backup through the invisible powers that are more powerful than what is seen in the realm of the natural. Instances of witchcraft and sorceries abound in the political field in Africa. In Kenya, for instance, President Moi established a presidential commission on Demon Worship and Witchcraft. Even though the report was never publicly released, President Moi was quick to point at the opposition as the ones who were consorting with witch doctors while attacking those he referred to as satanists

---

[88] Elias K. Bongmba, *The Dialectics of Transformation in Africa* (New York: Palgrave Macmillan, 2006), 9–37.

[89] See Emmanuel Milingo, *Face to Face with the Devil* (Victoria, Australia, 1991), cited in Stephen Ellis and Gerrie ter Haar, "Religion and Politics in Sub-Saharan Africa," *Journal of Modern African Societies* 36, no. 2 (June 1998): 198.

in Kenya "implying that they were to be found in the ranks of the opposition parties."[90] But a critical look at Kenya in the 1990s when belief in witchcraft and accusations of politicians practicing witchcraft and sorcery were growing shows that the dictatorial and strongman tactics of President Moi had destroyed the social fabric and economic lives of the people and brought unmitigated suffering and poverty upon the people in the throes of the HIV/AIDs crisis. As Aylward Shorter and Joseph Njiru noted with regard to the commission on demon worship in Kenya, this commission

> may serve to distract the popular mind from dwelling on the real causes of economic inequality and hardship in the country; but on the other hand, among thinking people, it may serve to underline the enormity of the injustice that has been perpetrated by the affluent, ruling class against the poor and destitute. In a situation in which more than a quarter of the population does not have enough to live on, and a tiny elite is rich beyond the dreams of avarice, it may well appear that affluence is diabolical.[91]

Shorter and Njiru strongly suggest that the social paranoia created by this Devil Worship Commission is only a reflection of the moral bankruptcy and social insecurity created by the government's failings in the country. The suffering of the people is, therefore, not to be attributed to any devil. Rather, what the government of the day should address and what the people should mobilize against are corruption, extortion, bad governance, and the oppression of the poor, which, they propose, could never have been addressed "through exotic rituals involving nakedness and the drinking of human blood or through submerging the personalities of hysterical people."[92]

President Mathieu Kérékou of Benin retained the services of Mohamed Amadou Cisse, nicknamed "djine" or "the devil," a Malian marabout who was known to publicly espouse devil worship. He also is reputed to have worked for President Bongo of Gabon and Mobutu of Zaire.[93] Kérékou was defeated in the 1991 elections after ruling Benin for seventeen years, but later came

---

[90] Ellis and Ter Haar, "Religion and Politics in Sub-Saharan Africa," 189.
[91] Aylward Shorter and Joseph N. Njiru, *New Religious Movements in Africa* (Nairobi: Paulines Publications Africa, 2001), 52.
[92] Shorter and Njiru, *New Religious Movements in Africa*, 53.
[93] Ellis and Ter Haar, "Religion and Politics in Sub-Saharan Africa," 189.

back to politics in 1996 and swept to victory as a born-again Christian. He publicly repented of his sins and asked the people for forgiveness and then employed a Pentecostal worldview of the kingdom of good and evil, and his mysterious encounters with God while he was out of power, to win over the people of Benin. As Camilla Strandsbjerg puts it, Kérékou used his spiritual encounters with God, and his newfound faith in the true God, to reinforce his image as a true democrat and to denounce his past and reject the traditional religion of vodun and occult forces, which he practiced in his first stint as a Marxist president.[94] Kérékou, in his second time in power (1996–2006) clothed himself in religious language and imagery. In May 1997, to give one example out of many, he claimed to have received a prophecy from Latin America that God had predicted economic and social prosperity in Benin. The words of this prophecy, which were proclaimed to the nation by the Minister for Interior, read as follows:

> There is wealth in the soil of Benin.... I see Benin becoming an important pole of commerce.... It will happen to Benin but only with the help of the President and the authorities of Benin.... Your force will be in the image of these days, said the Everlasting One.... God will give you intelligence and power. He is ready to start the second phase. In 1998, the third phase will begin, and he will see the fruits appear.[95]

This prophecy was sold to the politicians and translated into political promise and practice that could be fulfilled if all the politicians "converted to the religion of Kérékou and thereby to his political program."[96]

Former Gambian president, Yaya Jammeh, one of the most brutal dictators in West Africa, had a coterie of palace marabouts and Islamic diviners. He was often seen clutching Islamic prayer beads, the Misbahah, conjuring up the Holy names of God. The best friend of the late Robert Mugabe of Zimbabwe, even in the worst of times for the people, was a Jesuit priest who had unlimited access to him, and who prayed for him

---

[94] Camilla Strandsbjerg, "Kérékou, God and the Ancestors: Religion and the Conception of Political Power in Benin," *African Affairs* 99, no. 396 (July 2000): 401.

[95] Strandsbjerg, "Kérékou, God and the Ancestors," 408.

[96] Strandsbjerg, "Kérékou, God and the Ancestors," 405.

and was his constant counselor. Mugabe, a former altar server, would famously say that only God could remove him from the seat of power. The long wars between the RENAMO rebels and the FRELIMO ruling party in Mozambique were not only legitimated and sustained through the ideological pacts each had with either the Soviet Union or the West, but also through the fight between Catholics and Protestants. Many African dictators are either pastors or have spouses who are ministers in church. The late President Pierre Nkurunziza of Burundi, whose country came to the brink of war in 2015 over his attempt to change the constitution to remove the fixed term limit, had a charismatic prophetess as wife, who would often sing spiritual songs on national radio.

President Yoweri Museveni of Uganda as of 2024 has ruled the country for more than thirty years, and is entrenched in power. Beyond being blessed by God with a wife who is a minister in a Pentecostal church, he has the backing of many religious leaders. Indeed, the worst form of atrocities ever committed in modern-day Africa in the name of the Christian God were done by the Lord's Resistance Army and (as well as the Movement for the Restoration of the Ten Commandments of God) in Uganda. The LRA was started by Alice Lakwena and continued by Joseph Kony, who has been indicted by the International Criminal Court at The Hague. I have seen the terrible effects of these atrocities in Northern Uganda, South Sudan, and in the Central African Republic. Some religious leaders whom I consulted in Uganda (Gulu, Soroti, Adjoumani, Kampala, and Mbarara) told me that the year before a national election is usually a blessed year from God, because the president and his acolytes will normally make visits to launch one project or another for the church. My home country of Nigeria was once rated by the BBC many years ago as the most religious country in the world,[97] but it is unfortunately still among the most corrupt countries in Africa and is the second most unsafe country in Africa after South Africa. It is also a country where over half a million people are displaced today because of radical Islamic fundamentalism, all in the name of God.

In Zambia there is a National Day of Prayer, which is usually preceded by all kinds of religious rituals nationally and locally propitiating God. There is also a national voodoo day in Benin Republic, a holiday to celebrate voodoo and the power of God. Before the 2010 football World Cup in South Africa,

---

[97] BBC News, "Nigeria Leads in Religious Belief," *BBC One-Minute World News*, February 26, 2004, http://news.bbc.co.uk/2/hi/programmes/wtwtgod/3490490.stm.

sangomas were invited to perform rituals at the opening ceremony, to secure victory for the national team and safety for all the visitors.

Many examples can be given demonstrating the effects of this fragmentation of societies in Africa, and the crisis of the nation-state and the pathological ways in which God is inserted into the equation because politicians like most of their constituents in Africa "believe that real power has its roots in the invisible world and that therefore the cultivation of spiritual power is vital for their continued political existence."[98] What is evident from the foregoing is that enabling structures and institutions are absent in African nation-states that could secure the foundations of constitutional democracies, rule of law, checks and balances, and promote and preserve the common good. This is partly a reflection of the failure of the God narrative on the continent, which is often deployed to rationalize the glaring failings of government and corrupt and extractive leadership. This narrative is also used to mollify the restive populace, and guard against their revolting against these idols of power. The same God narrative is used to justify senseless deaths in Africa, and the suffering and unfulfillment of the majority of African young people, elders, women, and children. No strong liberation theology or political theology of resistance and protest has percolated into the vast religious structures of the land, as a potential source of a counternarrative of reversal.

A similar process is seen in the second crisis of modern Africa, the post-Western missionary phase of African Christianity. The postcolonial gift of states to Africa was a cargo-product made abroad and delivered to Africa without respect for Africa's own narratives or social arrangements. Likewise, the missionary churches in Africa—particularly Roman Catholics, the Anglican Communion, Methodists, Baptists, Presbyterians, Lutherans, and the Reformed Tradition—were also established without paying serious attention to local processes or cultural and religious traditions. What the soldiers did with their armored tanks, bullets, and cannons in bringing down the state, and what the dictators did in expropriating the wealth of the state for themselves and their own groups, also happened in mainline Christianity. This was a related but parallel context, done through preachers, prophets, priests, the big men/daddies and thick madams/mamas of these burgeoning churches.

The Pentecostals have no guns or bullets, but they have the Bible, social media, and the megaphone, and unique ability to harvest the riches of

---

[98] Ellis and Ter Haar, "Religion and Politics in Sub-Saharan Africa," 190.

God and the powers of the Holy Spirit.[99] With these tools, what were once considered fringe movements led by "uninformed and false" pastors, preachers, and prophets are fast becoming the new faces of Christianity in Africa. These groups are now African religious subalterns, offering strong alternatives to the Western-mission-founded churches with whom they now compete for space, and for access to money, corridors of power, and membership.[100]

Peter Berger's marketplace theory of religious affinity fits well this narrative of the dizzying array of choices available to adherents of the Christian religion concerning where to access the powers of God and the defeat of the forces of evil through a theodicy which serves as "the indispensable substratum on which later legitimating edifices can be constructed."[101]

The Pentecostal revival in Africa shows that fragmentation in the churches of Africa is only a religious version of what is happening in African states. Ethnic groups, rebel leaders, and factions of political parties (among others) are breaking away from the state. Communities are forming social capitals to provide for themselves outside the formal apparatus of failed social agencies and institutions of the state. Unlike the postmodern fragmentation in the West, the African fragmentations do not seem to be grounded on any theory of social progress or resistance to change. Neither have African theologies succeeded in addressing this crisis of belief, beyond the dismissive stance often proposed by many theologians in the mainline churches of Africa that Pentecostalism and new religious movements in Africa are emerging from the negative cultural forces from outside Africa, or the failure of Christian conversion in Africa. Hence the constant effort to default to responding to the inevitable mushrooming of religious groups (which many priests from the Catholic Church in Africa and other mainline churches imitate) by introducing more spiritual formation, and more rigorous enforcement of religious codes, and traditional liturgical norms

---

[99] David Maxwell, "Christianity and the African Imagination," in *Christianity and the African Imagination: Essays in Honor of Adrian Hastings*, ed. David Maxwell and Ingrid Lawrie (Leiden: Brill, 2002), 19–20.

[100] On the Pentecostalization of African Christianity as African reformation, see Allan Anderson, *An Introduction to Pentecostalism* (Cambridge: Cambridge University Press, 2008), 104.

[101] Peter L. Berger, *The Sacred Canopy: Elements of a Sociological Theory of Religion* (New York: Anchor, 1990), 54.

and practices in churches and society in the Catholic Church and other mainline churches.

The arguments of Paul Gifford offer us concluding thoughts on the travails of Africa, God, and Christianity. Gifford criticizes mainline African Catholic theologians for neglecting the actual faith of Africans, and doing what Pope Francis calls "desktop theology" without paying serious attention to the hidden cultural grammar driving the momentum of religious expansion in Africa. This kind of theology, according to him, fails to address questions about healing of diseases, sorcery, witchcraft, and ancestral curses and blessings, what he calls an "enchanted Christianity." He argues that in Africa problems such as joblessness, homelessness, sickness, childlessness, business failure, failure to find a spouse are always seen through a religious enchantment. It is:

> the worldview that sees spirits, demons, spiritual powers at play in all areas of life, and responsible for every illness. Spirits and witchcraft were said to be responsible for illness, misery, poverty, hunger and misfortune. One particular spirit was said to cause AIDS, and "to have put HIV blood in the veins" of one sufferer called up to be cured.[102]

Gifford contends that rather than seeking solutions to these problems through structural analysis, functional rationality, and political and economic reform, Africans are seeking diagnosis of diseases and social problems, as well as remedies for the suffering and pain of Africans, through religious claims and counterclaims. This search for religious solutions can be seen, for example, through diagnosing which spirit was responsible for the diseases or the problem, and then exorcism and deliverance.[103] Disenchantment, Gifford contends, has taken place in the West with the movement away from a spirit-filled cosmos by way of a secularizing process. This comes through a purely rational and predictable notion of progressive history, dictated by human rationality and governed by scientific principles. Gifford holds to the Weberian thesis of a decline in religion through a secularization process, occurring with a loosening of affinity to a world inhabited by spirits, as well as the marginalization of religion, and the rejection of enchanted religion. He argues that the Catholic Church is coming to the realization that religion

---

[102] Paul Gifford, *Christianity, Development and Modernity in Africa* (London: Hurst, 2015), 3–4.

[103] Gifford, *Christianity, Development and Modernity in Africa*, 4.

is inescapably shaped by forces beyond authoritative statements about the essentials of the faith.[104] In this view, religion is being defined and influenced by other factors, such as social and cultural forces that are intimately connected with but not exclusively validated by religious narratives.

Gifford asserts that African theologians have been more concerned with defending an essentialist notion of Christianity that is beautiful and externally glorious in its authority structure, hierarchy, and sacramental system. Also defended is a notion of a pristine African culture untouched by the forces of history. The appeal to African cultural traditions and the defense of such cultural claims on the part of theologians, according to Gifford, is defeatist, and does more harm than good to Africa and Christianity. Such an appeal does not help to find workable solutions to the suffering and uncertainties of life that define the African predicament. The notion of enchanted African Christianity and the neglect of this world of meaning by African theology, Gifford argues, ignore the reality and thus glories in a transcendental notion of Catholicism and African traditions, and a constant turn to African cultures as a solution. Agreeing with Paul Bowers, Gifford attests:

> The most traumatic event in African history was its encounter with the West, which led not only to a loss of political control, but also to a damaged self-understanding. Thus, Independent Africa's preoccupations have been to resist continued Western economic domination and assert African identity vis-à-vis the West, especially by affirming its identity with Africa's traditional heritage and resisting Western intellectual hegemony.[105]

Africa is caught in a double jeopardy, both of which, according to Gifford, need to be addressed. African theologians must do a serious internal cultural critique of the actual faith of the people and of why it continues to grow in its enchantment through African Pentecostalism and African Catholic Charismatic groups. But he insists that African theologians, rather than facing the "enchanted worldview of spiritual forces and spiritual causality" as the beginning of inculturation, are more concerned with defending African culture against the West, even if this promotes further enchantment. In wanting to be faithful to an

---

[104] Gifford, *Christianity, Development and Modernity in Africa*, 84.
[105] Gifford, *Christianity, Development and Modernity in Africa*, 125.

enchanted Catholicism, African Catholic theologians are unable to address issues that are hampering Africa's progress, and which Africans find challenging—marriage, authority structures, Africa's approach to fighting diseases and healing, African Pentecostalism, and African Charismatic groups.[106]

Gifford's points are worth considering against Africa's unsuccessful romance with Western modernity in both the rise of Pentecostalism and the prosperity Gospel and healing churches, and the stuttering experiment of Africa with Western-type democratization. Both realities are the structural beams on which the African predicament with the suffering and pains, unfulfillment and instability, poverty amid wealth, which have afflicted Africa, are built. There are some merits to Gifford's critique of religion in Africa, particularly the instrumentalization and weaponization of God and the mentality of blaming God or the devil for everything wrong in Africa; and the constant flights with devils, witches, wizards, and water spirits and exorcisms to remove evil and suffering in Africa, while propitiating God to bring blessing. This mind-set of "doing religion" (Atalia Omer) is not a good way of thinking rightly of God and acting rightly as believers.

Bénézet Bujo proposes that addressing the suffering and evil in Africa will require "a steady spiritual effort" that goes beyond prayers and devotions to self-denial and training in the virtues and the habits of love and solidarity. Rather than simply praying that people be lifted out of the situation of suffering and "delivered from all evil," as Christians say in the Lord's Prayer, African Christians should stand up to oppressive structures and evil and selfish people who are corrupting the African traditions of abundant life. God, he proposes, cannot save Africa when African Christians are passively standing by, praying and fasting without taking concrete steps to receive God's grace that will enable them to exercise the power and agency that God has given them. Ultimately, Bujo insists that a fundamental question that African believers must constantly pose to themselves is: "What should we do to hasten our liberation by God and to contribute to the coming of his kingdom as expressed in the *Our Father*?"[107]

However, Gifford's perspective of enchantment needs to be more complexified and nuanced. As William Cavanaugh rightly argues, even though

---

[106] Gifford, *Christianity, Development and Modernity in Africa*, 127.

[107] Bénézet Bujo, *The Impact of the Our Father on Everyday Life: Meditations of an African Theologian*, trans. Sippala Humphrey and Silvano Borruso (Nairobi: Paulines Publications, Africa, 2002), 99.

the West describes itself as disenchanted and governed by the kind of scientific and functional rationality that Gifford writes about, the West is also caught in a different kind of enchantment to a different god or rather myriads of idols because of what people worship in the West that holds the loyalty and affinity of many. So, what has diminished in the West, according to Cavanaugh,

> is explicit worship of the Jewish and Christian God; what has not diminished is worship. The idea of a disenchanted, secular, and this-worldly West is complicated by among many other things, some positive, some not—the prevalence of commodity fetishism, ritualized nationalism, and faith in the "invisible hand" of the market to lead us to the promised land.[108]

A similar point on the substitution of God by something else people worship in a post-Christian Europe was made by Karen Armstrong:

> If the God of classical Western theism is dead for a large proportion of the population, this simply means that, once again, we are undergoing a period of religious transition. Even in post-Christian Europe, the quest for ecstasy continues, with or without God. We are so constituted that when one source of transcendent experience dries up, we simply seek it elsewhere.[109]

At any rate, it is important that African theologians immerse themselves in the daily struggles of the people of God in Africa and critically interrogate the claims about God. Most important, the gaze of the African theologians must be fixed on how the name of God is used in politics in Africa today in an irrational way to manipulate the people and reinforce elite privileges and power and fuel ethnic politics and cover up the corruption and failings of successive governments in many African states. The instrumentalization of religion in Africa and the weaponization of witchcraft and religious institutions (Christian, ATR, and Islam) to exploit and impoverish the poor, and sustain illiberal democracies

---

[108] William T. Cavanaugh, *The Uses of Idolatry* (Oxford: Oxford University Press, 2024), 3.

[109] Karen Armstrong, *A History of God*, quoted in Agbonkhianmeghe E. Orobator, *Theology Brewed in an African Pot* (Maryknoll, NY: Orbis Books, 2008), 14.

and state capture by a greedy elite in Africa is one of the greatest sources of the suffering of the innocent in Africa.[110] Sadly, the convergence of the interests of few elites in religion and politics in Africa continues unabated because theologians and scholars who clearly grasp these new forms of colonialism of the soul and society of Africa have not made unraveling this complex knot a focus of their research, publication, and counter-hegemonic and anti-demonic advocacy and pastoral accompaniment of God's people in Africa.

Conclusion: God in Africa, God in the World

Belief in God, and religious faith, should bring about conversion and transformation of people's lives and the societies in which they live. Conversion is the interior transformation of people's minds and cultures toward human and cosmic fulfillment, and daily fashioning of a new people for God whose daily choices reflect the religious values and ethics of the Gospel. Conversion of lives and societies is the very heart of the Gospel and central to the mission and message of Jesus Christ. Any notion of God is false if it does not make people at home with themselves and with their world, and with other people and the cosmos. Any notion of God that does not make people better in mind, heart, and soul—that is, that does not make them loving and lovable and equipped to become agents and protagonists in their own lives and guardians of the lives of others and the world of nature—is false. Also false is any notion of God that alienates people from themselves and their cultures, imprisoning them in false religious narratives and social pathologies that are opposed to the reign of God in both Christianity and ATRs.

How then can we talk about God in our suffering and smiling in a way that sets the sights of African peoples beyond the imprisoning walls of this present social context in Africa, which is far from the dream of our ancestors and the will of the God of our ancestors?

Bernhard Udelhoven, a German missionary in Zambia, offers an important concluding point for this chapter.[111] He proposes that fractures in relationships have led to many fissures and many cycles of decay in Africa and the world. It is this breakdown of relationships in Africa today that African

---

[110] See Patrick Chabal and Jean-Pascal Daloz, *Africa Works: Disorder as Political Instrument* (Oxford: International African Institute, 1999), 64–76.

[111] Bernhard Udelhoven, *Unseen Worlds: Dealing with Spirits, Witchcraft, and Satanism* (Lusaka, Zambia: Fenza, 2015).

theology must courageously seek to reweave by speaking rightly of God, of the self, culture, society, nature, the world around us, and all things so that right conduct, authentic subjectivity, pragmatic agency of reversal of unacceptable history can be triggered through right thinking. Udelhoven helps us to get to the roots of the crisis of modernity in Africa, especially the crumbling of the bonds of love and unity at all levels of the social ecology in Africa. But the crisis of modernity is not only happening in Africa; it is happening in the entire world. There is a collapse in the world of meaning and an invention of false sources and distortions of erstwhile symbols of meaning and integration which sadly have left many people empty and unhappy. Modernity has rightly rejected the premodern God that was presumed to be the source of order for the cycle of history and time; the God who gave rhythm to nature and governed all things well and who is blamed for any disorder in the world. Suffering was explained in premodern times through appeals to God either to rescue those who suffer or to be merciful to those who brought suffering upon themselves or on others through their sins. But as people moved from these premodern commonsensical images of God to the modern era, the search for a replacement of the premodern God or for meaning in the God of modernity continues to be an ongoing quest. Repairing the broken bonds of love and relationships and strengthening the bond of love and solidarity in the world at all levels, and in energizing the spiritual springs that enrich the lives of all is the path to the praxis of hope for humans today. How God is inserted into this dynamic as origin, source, and end is the ceaseless quest that will always remain an open-ended pilgrimage. This was the import of Karen Kilby's wisdom at the end of her study on suffering and the Christian life, when she answers the question how humans can allow themselves not to be seduced into claims about kenosis, vulnerability, and fragility in these words:

> First, we have to cultivate a certain ascesis, a certain restraint, the capacity not to find meaning where it does not exist or where we have no right to it.... Secondly, we have to cultivate a certain incompleteness; we have to remember to keep a place in our theological system, or our theological reflections, for hope in that which goes absolutely beyond anything these systems can offer or grasp, hope in the eventual triumph of love over suffering, joy over loss.[112]

---

[112] Karen Kilby, "The Seduction of Kenosis," in *Suffering and the Christian Life*, ed. Karen Kilby and Rachel Davies (London: T&T Clark, 2021), 174.

In traditional African thinking, God is the source, destiny, and pattern of relationship. God is relationship. The transformational bond of life that God makes possible in creation takes us to our ancestral roots as Africans. It reminds us of our history and of the blessings that course through our human and cosmic history as God's gracious gifts. It reminds us that the God of our silent tears and the God of our weary years, as our ancestors sang during the Slave Trade, has sustained us despite suffering, racism, prejudice, and global injustice.

God is the source and destiny of all things and spins the web of relationships that keeps everything in right order and connections. This is what in many African cultures is often represented by the Nguni word, *Ubuntu*—I exist through others; I am related therefore I exist; I participate fully in the web of life; therefore, I am complete. *Ubuntu* is thus Africa's moral tradition of cosmic *koinonia*, the ethics that affirms the sacredness and sublime dignity of the earth and all things in it. This could be seen as a form of cosmic liturgy, a celebration of the peace and harmony in creation wherein all things relate in a healthy and wholesome manner.

This sublimity of the human in the web of creation is also seen in the Eastern Orthodox tradition, as a form of liturgy following the tradition of Gregory of Nyssa from his *The Life of Moses*. Gregory invites us to listen to the voice of nature; in gazing at our lives and the book of nature, we can see the face of God and the beauty that God has endowed the earth and all things in it. Ecumenical Patriarch Bartholomew describes Gregory's view: "Each plant, each animal, and each micro-organism tells a story, unfolds a mystery, relates an extraordinary harmony and balance, which are interdependent and complementary. Everything points to the same encounter and mystery."[113]

Ubuntu as cosmic indwelling of God—and our summons to dwell together with others, humans, animals, and the entire cosmos—is the only way we can be at home with ourselves. Sin leads to broken relationships and the absence of God or exile from God. *Ubuntu* affirms God as the source, being, and goal of our relationships, as mediated through our African ancestors and all those who live and model this pattern of life.

Jesus the Christ healed this rupture in our human and cosmic world. He showed us it is possible for us to become a point of contact and relationship

---

[113] See Ecumenical Patriarch Bartholomew, *On Earth as in Heaven: Ecological Vision and Initiatives of Ecumenical Patriarch Bartholomew* (New York: Fordham University Press, 2012), 129.

through those virtues and values we admire in the saints and our African ancestors. He bandaged the wounds of those who were wounded like the Good Samaritan, and by taking our place, brought us home to our true selves by standing in solidarity with us to the point of death. The Spirit of God gives us the strength to build this kind of relationship. This basic Christian understanding fulfills all that Africans in their religious traditions seek for in God and hope to bring about in ethical choices that are life-affirming and life-giving. It promotes the prophetic witnessing to seed hope in the African soil and in our world in an organic and integral manner.

African theologians must follow God's footprints in the history of our continent and the world. We must develop intellectual and performative habits to see the signs that lead to God and to prophetic performance and reject those religious pathologies that lead our people further away from the light, the truth, the way, and the life. The source of this truth, life, and way is Jesus our African Ancestor and our human Ancestor who has wrought Salvation for us in this greatest act of Cosmic *Ubuntu*. He gave away everything so that we can have everything, a sharing in the ancestral divine life that is without limit in its beauty, and without measure in its fullness and fruitfulness.

5

Freedom, Suffering, and Predestination

Lessons from a Slave Narrative

> The feeling of the nation must be quickened; the conscience of the nation must be roused; the propriety of the nation must be startled; the hypocrisy of the nation must be exposed; and its crimes against God and man must be proclaimed and denounced.
>
> —Frederick Douglass

How can sense be made of a good God when the people who worship the same God think that same God has made them superior to you? How can you continue to believe in the God of the Lord Jesus Christ, and participate in Christian communities, when some Christian communities continue to promote, defend, and legitimize white supremacy, discrimination against Black people, and social and economic policies that degrade, destroy, and insult the dignity of your race?

Many of us who were born and raised in Africa often do not understand the destructive effects of racism and its pervasive grip on our African American brothers and sisters in the United States until one experiences racism firsthand in North America and Europe. African theologies such as African Christianity cannot be done without deep and ongoing conversation with our siblings in the West and in the Diaspora in our collective struggle for freedom. In this chapter, I introduce such a dialogue between the African theology of suffering and smiling and African American liberation theology vis-à-vis the destructive impact of racism on people of African descent.

The history of racism against people of African descent, and its different ways of manifesting itself in the Church, nations, and globally, leaves in every Black person traces of a collective memory—social, historical, religious, and cultural—as they try to define and understand their present through objects, persons, and events in the past. As Frederick Ware argues, "From a heuristic point of view, collective memory is extremely valuable: it makes the past intelligible and accessible for present thought and action. Collective memory is a reconstruction of the past, whatever of it is yet available for present reflection."[1] African theologies are siblings of African American theologies, and both draw from this collective memory and common lamentation through diverse experiences of being caught in this battle for freedom and agency. Bryan Massingale asserts that theologians must take on the question of "privilege, institutional violence, racialization of the other, dehumanization of entire groups, and the essentialization of the white or European as paradigmatically human."[2] At the gathering of theologians where Massingale made this statement, participants recognized these dehumanizing tendencies: "We cannot, then, give an adequate account of present controversies and moral responsibilities—much less develop a Catholic theological ethics for a world church—if we fail to attend to the voices of the dark bodies that hover over and haunt our histories despite our embarrassed silence and studied neglect."[3]

African theologies have so far failed to develop an antiracist theology of reversal, or a theology of solidarity and fraternity with our Black siblings in the Diaspora. If this continues, so too will a white-washed theology, and a narrow and fragmented account of Black history and experience. This approach sugarcoats the pain, pathos, and cycle of decay that have marked world history since 1619, when the first Black slaves landed in the United States.

This chapter seeks a dialogue between African theology and African American experience, especially on the questions of freedom, suffering, and predestination. I reflect on the questions of enslaved Black persons who asked

---

[1] Frederick L. Ware, *African American Theology: An Introduction* (Louisville, KY: Westminster John Knox, 2016), 31.

[2] James Keenan, *Catholic Theological Ethics Past, Present, and Future: The Trento Conference*, ed. James F. Keenan (Maryknoll, NY: Orbis Books, 2011), 1–7, cited in Bryan Massingale, "Has the Silence Been Broken? Catholic Theological Ethics and Racial Justice," *Theological Studies* 75, no. 1 (2014): 136.

[3] Massingale, "Has the Silence Been Broken?" 136.

"Where is God?" as they were forced from their native African land in chains. A slave narrative written by Olaudah Equiano will form the textual content of my analysis. The question of where God is in Africa could also be illuminated through listening to the lamentations of our Black brothers and sisters in North America, Europe, Latin America, and the Caribbean (the African Diaspora). These stories do not settle the questions of where and who God is, nor do they offer definitive answers to the contradictions and ambiguities of history. However, rich narratives can help theologians and pastors engage the people at their level of religious consciousness and meaning, and in their lived faith so as to accompany them and lift them up from their sites of pain.

Whatever judgment is made about such stories of lived faith and experiences are open to further conversations and revisions. However, it is worth noting that Equiano, an eighteenth-century African enslaved person, interprets his condition of servitude in similar language of those of modern-day African Christians; he also uses a framework of predestination. Comparing his views with contemporary views can show what is changing in the worldview of people of African descent, what has remained constant, and why.

My Aunt Cried All Night on Her Knees

My auntie, Virginia, is a deeply religious woman. She belongs to a small religious sect in Nigeria, the Sabbatarians. Some of this group believe in the Jewish religious ancestry of Blacks and look forward to the liberation of Blacks all over the world, just as God delivered Israel from slavery and bondage and restored them to the Promised Land. My aunt has a degree in secretarial studies and good knowledge of biblical narratives. Following the tradition of this sect, she does not have sophisticated knowledge of the larger historical context of the biblical texts. She and I do not often agree on the interpretation of the biblical texts. Unlike her, I study and do biblical exegesis, but unlike me, she seems to have a more direct and unmediated connection with the biblical word, and easily finds resonance between those texts and historical events.

My aunt and my mum visited me in Chicago in 2018. (As is typical with me since I left my home country, Nigeria, I welcome family and friends from Africa to visit and spend time in a Black neighborhood with me. This has continued whether I was living in Rome or Toronto or now in Chicago.) I took my aunt and mum to the South Side, and we visited St. Sabina, one of the largest Black Catholic parishes in Chicago. We passed the house of the Obamas, continued to Oak Forest, then through Cicero, and back to my home. I tried as much as possible not to comment as we took our tour, and to allow them to observe, interpret, and judge for themselves what they were seeing. However, my aunt started to ask questions. "Why is this Black neighborhood so run-down? Why are so many young Black men roaming the streets? Don't they have a job? Why are they so poor? Why are there no shopping malls here? This does not look like America." Her questions reminded me of the same questions I asked between 2002 and 2004, when I visited Black neighborhoods in Rome, Milan, Paris, Toronto, Berlin, and London, and saw the same ghettoized existence that shook the very fiber of my being then, as it does even today.

I tried as much as I could to answer her questions by sharing with her my own pains in trying to understand the struggle of African Americans to function in this historically oppressive condition. I shared with her what I have seen every day in my own daily interactions with people where I have lived—the United States, Canada, and Italy. I recounted recently standing in front of an elevator. When the door opened, a white female emerged and, terrified by my presence, immediately turned red and descended into a panic. I said nothing, but wondered how the sight of me could produce such torrents of anxiety in this lady. I told my aunt that sometimes I have observed white women awkwardly step aside when they see me walking toward them on a sidewalk. I told her I was once asked to find another rectory in Chicago because I was Black, even as a white priest was welcomed into the same rectory while I was asked to leave. I realized that the white pastor in the rectory had an implicit bias against me.

I told her of being invited to consult on the pastoral plan for a diocese in North America, only to be uninvited because the coordinating priest was not comfortable with a Black priest with a mind of his own. He wanted me to be a token member who felt happy to be in the group, but without expressing any opinions. I also shared with her my stories of being in a parish where some white parishioners would not receive communion from me or shake my hand. When I confronted one of them one day, she had no reasonable answer to give. I told my aunt of instances where I had prepared couples for marriage in Canada and in the United States, only to be told eventually by them for reasons unbeknown to me that they have decided that a white priest will do the wedding instead. I told my aunt that amid interactions with white Christians and theologians I have often wondered what is wrong with our world. Or, self-deprecatingly, whether something is wrong with me as a Black person. I am sad to report that the clear majority of Black males have similar experiences.

That evening, I showed my aunt the USCCB publication, *Open Wide Our Hearts*, which says:

> To understand how racism works today, we must recognize that generations of African Americans were disadvantaged by slavery, wage theft, "Jim Crow" laws, and by the systematic denial of access to numerous wealth-building opportunities reserved for others. This has left many African Americans without hope, discouraged, disheartened, and feeling unloved. While it is true that some individuals and families have thrived, significant numbers of African Americans are born into economic and social disparity. The poverty experienced by many of these communities has its roots in racist policies.[4]

I shared with her the devastating generational effects of slavery, segregation, and the widespread use of violence, including the lynching of more than 4,000 Black men, women, and children across 800 counties throughout the United States between 1877 and 1950. I spoke too of the racist policies of the Donald Trump government, and about white Christian nationalism in Europe. I recounted my anger at the killing of Laquan McDonald in Chicago in 2014 by a white police officer, and how reading of the dastardly police shooting of Walter Scott in South Carolina in 2015 (and the horrible killing of George Floyd in Minnesota in 2020) sent cold chills down my spine. It could have been me! I am filled with a deep sense of anger and outrage at what has become a pattern of white police officers hunting down Black men and killing them in cold blood, as if to say that their lives are expendable and disposable.

When we finished dinner that night, and after my mum, who was recovering from a stroke, had gone to bed, I told my aunt that if she was strong I would like her to watch a documentary. I wanted to help her receive a fuller picture of what I was trying to share with her, especially what Mike

---

[4] United States Conference of Catholic Bishops, *Open Wide Our Hearts: The Enduring Call to Love—A Pastoral Letter Against Racism*, https://www.usccb.org/issues-and-action/human-life-and-dignity/racism/upload/open-wide-our-hearts.pdf, 14.

Davis calls the "prison-industrial complex"[5] of California. So, I played the documentary film *13th* for her while I went to my study. She could not finish watching it. She went to her room and cried aloud so much that I wanted to take her to the hospital. Amid her weeping, she beseeched: "God, where are you? God, what have we Black people done against you that you have allowed these horrors to happen? God, did our ancestors offend you so much that you will let this genocide and destruction of your people to continue! God, rise up and break this yoke on our neck because this is not the Promised Land which your covenant guaranteed for us your people!"

Her questions reminded me of the question Katie Cannon asked at a young age when she realized she could not go to the library because she was Black, and she could not play in the park with white kids because she was Black. Cannon asked: "What did we do as Black people that was so bad? A good God would not do this."[6] This is the same question that James Cone posed as a child in the face of the social suffering of Blacks: "If God loves Black people, why then do we suffer so much?"[7] This is a central question which has occupied my own mind. It is also one of the motivations for this book.

My aunt needed the help of a pill to sleep that night. Since then, she has struggled with nightmares and bouts of depression because of what she saw on the South Side of Chicago and in the documentary. These shook the very foundation of her life, faith, and belief in both American exceptionalism and the justice and mercy of God. Her reaction and tears touched me profoundly, making me question myself. Why do I not cry anymore seeing these signs of racism against Blacks in America, in the Church, and in many parts of the world? Have I become so desensitized that these atrocities have become routine and normalized in my perception of reality and white supremacy? Have I shown enough anger in my writings

---

[5] Cited in Keeanga-Yamahtta Taylor, "The Emerging Movement for Police and Prison Abolition," *New Yorker*, May 7, 2021, https://www.newyorker.com/news/our-columnists/the-emerging-movement-for-police-and-prison-abolition.

[6] Neil Genzlinger, "Katie Cannon 68, Dies; Lifted Black Women's Perspective in Theology," *New York Times*, August 14, 2018, https://www.nytimes.com/2018/08/14/obituaries/katie-cannon-68-dies-lifted-black-womens-perspective-in-theology.html.

[7] James Cone, *The Cross and the Lynching Tree* (Maryknoll, NY: Orbis Books, 2011), 154.

and advocacy? What forms of disruptive agency am I generating in my thoughts and in my action against the institutional, systemic, and ecclesial racism that is ravaging America, the worldwide church, and the globe? What does freedom mean for African Americans after the passing of the Civil Rights Acts, and what does freedom mean for Africans with independence and the end of apartheid?

The Journey of Freedom for People of African Descent

The story of freedom for Africa and for all peoples of African descent begins for me with the widely read slave autobiography, *The Interesting Narrative of the Life of Olaudah Equiano*, published in 1789.

M. Shawn Copeland proposes we read African American spirituals as revealing something hidden from human view or apophatic wisdom cast in paradoxes that defies and counters conventional wisdom.[8] I propose that reading the narrative of an enslaved Black person such as Olaudah Equiano lifts the veil on the hidden wounds of slavery. It presents powerful apocalyptic imagery that can bring to consciousness in many ways the painful, long walk for freedom of people of African descent. The images and words I reverence through this account may also help us all think of the many people who look like Equiano, and who are facing the same painful realities that he faced in the ongoing struggle for life today, more than two hundred years after his death in 1797. Using Equiano's painful narrative of freedom's journey as the main text for my own account of freedom, I argue that like his, the stories of most people of African descent have been characterized for over five hundred years by the same persistent painful realities. These are captivity to the contradictions of history; the fight for survival; promise, providence and peril, dominion and damnation; and their strong faith in God.

Every Christmas when I sing "O Holy Night," translated into English from the French by the Unitarian minister and music critic John Sullivan Dwight, I wonder: When will this suffering, existential homelessness, racism, poverty, and pain end for people of African descent? When shall my people truly be free? The lyrics of Dwight, which ring hollow to many Blacks, go like this:

---

[8] M. Shawn Copeland, *Knowing Christ Crucified: The Witness of African American Religious Experience* (Maryknoll, NY: Orbis Books, 2018), 32.

> Truly he taught us to love one another;
> His law is love, and His Gospel is peace;
> Chains shall he break, for the slave is our brother,
> And in his name all oppression shall cease.[9]

Many people of African descent in the United States, Brazil, Haiti, South Africa, Sudan, Ethiopia, United Kingdom, France, and Nigeria (to mention but a few) do not enjoy abundant life and are not flourishing. Most of them are denied the possibility of living in peaceful and prosperous societies and nations. It is therefore the task of an accountable theology to dig into the reasons for this sad situation, through a wider historical analysis. Many Africans today—and African Americans in the United States, Canada, and anywhere in the world—who are members of our churches need answers. What difference does it make, belonging to the church? What do the birth and the death of the Son of God mean? What does theology offer in repairing their world, redressing historical wrongs, and transforming the structures of oppression and injustice that have persisted since the time of the slave trade?

The sad realities faced by many people of African descent have nothing to do with Blackness, genes, culture, geography, or space. They have everything to do with the many social, commercial, religious, and political determinants of poverty, health, social hierarchy, and exclusion in the course of history.

These realities are firmly embedded in the construction of history in different versions of Christianity. Some of these versions have been appropriated in our theologies, spirituality, morality, and teachings on divine providence, suffering, theodicy, and eschatology. It is important to critically examine religious and theological claims as to the meaning of freedom and eschatology, and the theological account of how history unfolds among all peoples and through human agency. This examination should extend to interpretation of the forces driving the trajectory of history that constantly produce different outcomes for people because of their place of birth, race, sex, location, and other socially constructed identities and hierarchies.

---

[9] J. S. Dwight, "Christmas Song: Cantique pour Noel," *Musical World* 19, cited in Christopher J. Kellerman, *All Oppression Shall Cease: A History of Slavery, Abolitionism, and the Catholic Church* (Maryknoll, NY: Orbis Books, 2022), 116.

This critical examination is particularly important since some of the claims of Christendom—with its projects, ideas, and ideals of church and state, grace and freedom, human nature, and sin and redemption—are built on a narrow epistemology, and narrow notions of God, divine providence, and eschatology. These projects were implemented in non-Western societies by Western imperialists and missionaries, with consequences including slavery, racism, and white supremacy. These are among other sad images that we see in Equiano's narrative. It is important then to critically analyze such notions as freedom, liberal and illiberal democracies, international development, and humanitarianism. Some of the contentious issues of our times merit investigation, such as immigration, poverty, terrorism, health inequity, and the false notion of the convergence of history through modernity and the construction of the global order.

I cannot fully unpack these complicated converging forces, but I wish to at least show the outline of their destructive reach and the way they function today by taking us back to their initial beginnings in the slave trade. Much can be learned from the narratives of African enslaved persons.

In telling the story of freedom through the narrative of an enslaved African person who managed to reclaim his own voice and agency, I am also recounting the story of a people, the people of African descent. Equiano's slave narrative is a communal narrative, a prosopography told in the most suffocating and destructive of circumstances. But his notion of community is not simply limited to his own Black people and race, but includes all of humanity. Enslaved persons, like the millions of poor and suffering people throughout the world, understand the meaning of our common humanity more than those who enslaved them. However, as Equiano points out, there is no limit to the extent to which human greed and thirst for capital can take humans who will stop at nothing to acquire capital. Angela Davis writes with clarity about this abuse, showing how people are pushed into small prisons: "Neoliberalism attempts to force people to think of themselves only in individual terms and not in collective terms."[10]

---

[10] Angela Y. Davis, *Freedom Is a Constant Struggle: Ferguson, Palestine, and the Foundations of a Movement* (Chicago: Haymarket, 2016), 29.

Equiano gives his motive for writing as the good of our common humanity:

> I am not so foolishly vain as to expect from it either immortality or literary reputation. If it affords any satisfaction to my numerous friends, at whose request it has been written, or in the smallest degree promotes the interest of humanity, the ends for which it was undertaken will be fully attained, and every wish of my heart gratified.[11]

Many enslaved persons never live to tell their own stories, like the many poor people today who are dying needlessly because of preventable wars, diseases, poverty, and violence. May this, my imperfect offering, be an ancestral tribute to all people who are dying in our world today because of our destructive economies and violent nation-states. May this short account honor the millions of Black people and oppressed peoples throughout the world. These are our siblings, whose stories as victims of captive historical forces remain buried in the rising rubble of lies, deception, exploitative assaults on their personhood and autonomy. These have come through an unjust global order, false democracies, and manipulations that characterize neoliberal capitalism and its associated projects that began in the last five hundred years with the trans-Atlantic slave trade. The body bags that are produced by our systems and economies—the economies that kill, as Pope Francis calls them[12]—among the poor and oppressed people throughout the world should remind us all that freedom is more than a word.

I am standing boldly on Olaudah Equiano's shoulders as I tell my people's stories of freedom, in cyclical movements: captivity, condemnation, and Crucifixion. My people are fighting for life. Until Black people throughout the world enjoy human flourishing and abundant life wherever they wish to live, the words "redemption" and "salvation" will continue to ring hollow to us. I invite you into this struggle against the idols of power, money, race, nationalism, and exclusion in our nations, churches, and religious groups.

---

[11] Olaudah Equiano, *The Interesting Narrative of the Life of Olaudah Equiano, or Gustavus Vassa, the African* (New York: Simon and Brown, 2012), 12.

[12] Francis, *Evangelii Gaudium*, apostolic exhortation, November 24, 2013, https://www.vatican.va/content/francesco/en/apost_exhortations/documents/papa-francesco_esortazione-ap_20131124_evangelii-gaudium.html, sec. 53.

I invite you to become participants rather than spectators, because the freedom and liberation of our common humanity is tied to the freedom and liberation of billions of people the world over. They are condemned to die by the convergence of adverse historical factors legitimated through structures and systems created by states, religious institutions, and international organizations, both local and global.

Freedom: A Short Conceptualization

Before fully engaging Equiano, I want to say how I understand freedom. I can only be descriptive. Freedom for me as an African is more than a word that can be defined. Freedom is a condition that can be described within contexts in which people are born, grow up, live, work, and have their being. Freedom should be told as a story; it is a story of journeys—mine, yours; your people, my people; my humanity, your humanity; my world, your world. Where are we going, and how can we get there together?

I use an African communal philosophy, so the conceptualization of freedom, in my thinking, can be framed through three fundamental and related questions. What can I do? (capability). Where and how can I do what I desire to do? (opportunities). What moves me to act, and why do I do what I do? (motivation). The answers to these three questions offer the possibility of seeing in the stories of people's daily lives the favorable and adverse conditions and factors for everyone's ultimate fulfillment and happiness through participation in the web of life. I am free when I can participate fully in the life of the community and contribute to creating the possibilities in the community for human and cosmic flourishing for all. In the words of a woman leader in Soroti, Uganda, I met in the course of my work for the Canadian Samaritans for Africa, "We are not asking for money, but that the obstacles be removed on our path to the future that God willed for us."

I will expand on the third question, that of motivation. Susan Michie and her coauthors define motivation as "all those brain processes that energize and direct behavior, not just goals. It includes habitual processes, emotional responses, as well as analytical decision-making."[13] African social theorist

---

[13] Susan Michie et al., "The Behavior Change Wheel: A New Method for Characterizing and Designing Behavior Change Interventions," *Implementation Science* 6, no. 42 (April 23, 2011): 4.

Achille Mbembe offers a framework for entering this realm of reasoning: What moves people to act must first be based on their location not in terms of spatial setting, place, or space, but within the stream of history.[14] For people of African descent, this location is what Frantz Fanon writes about at the end of his book *Black Skin, White Masks* when he says, "I am my own foundation."[15] The Black person, he argues, is motivated to claim this foundation not in a solipsistic manner, but as an act of resistance to being voided by external factors and circumstances. He or she must recover his or her agency through a reconstitution of "this capacity to be oneself and to act for oneself" as an inner fire surging forth "from the depths of an extraordinary arid and sterile zone" of nonbeing in the eyes of non-Blacks.

Mbembe argues one cannot conceptualize freedom and the future of people of African descent without confronting the question of "actuality," that is, who we are today because of our journeys. It is easy to speak about freedom and perhaps the theologies of freedom, or to blame the victims for their poverty and suffering.[16]

However, for most people of African descent, to use the words of James Weldon Johnson's "Lift Every Voice and Sing," we wish to become the protagonists of our own history. This is because, as our ancestors did in the past, we still sing the "harmonies of liberty" embodying the lesson that our "dark past has taught us," as we confront the realities we face today when "Hope unborn had died." We contemplate with our ancestors the many roads that "our tears have watered" on "the blood of the slaughtered" in our "gloomy past" filled with our "weary years" and "silent tears."

Mbembe locates the motivation of peoples of African descent in acting or not acting to change the arc of history in "the will to live and the future of affirmation especially where the reign of negation dominates" the long road of tears and blood that we have traversed. It is a struggle to live again; to re-exist; to develop thought processes that can potentiate actions for the reversal of history for people of African descent. These actions are our struggles to

---

[14] Achille Mbembe, "Thinking about the World from the Vantage Point of Africa," in *To Write the Africa World*, ed. Achille Mbembe and Felwine Sarr (Cambridge, UK: Polity, 2023), 270.

[15] Frantz Fanon, quoted in David Macey, "I Am My Own Foundation," *Theory, Culture & Society* 27, no. 7–8 (2010): 33–51, https://doi.org/10.1177/0263276410383707.

[16] Mbembe, "Thinking about the World," 270.

breathe again, because "I can't breathe!" It is a struggle to wrestle for ourselves a historical agency denied us through the systems, so that we can "move beyond the cruel alternatives: Kill or be killed."[17]

In the words of James Cone: "What is the meaning of this unspeakable Black suffering—suffering that is so deep, so painful and enduring that words cannot even begin to describe it?" His answer to the question he poses offers an answer to my search for the meaning of freedom for people of African descent, as to what moves us to act and the obstacles on our way:

> Only the song, dance, and the shout—the voices raised to high heavens and bodies swaying from side to side—can express both the wretchedness and the transcendent spirit of empowerment that kept Blacks from going under, as they struggled, against great odds, to acknowledge humanity and freedom denied.[18]

Olaudah Equiano:
The African Enslaved Person Who Told His Own Story

Arna Bontemps credits Olaudah Equiano for pioneering the literary genre that came to be known as slave narratives.[19] The narratives are personal and intimate, and open up the world of persons who were held in the bondage of slavery. Other narratives were available before and concurrent with Equiano's, including the moving autobiographies of Briton Hammon (1760), James Albert Ukawsaw Gronniosaw (1774), John Marrant (1785 and 1789), and Venture Smith (1798). As with Equiano's, all were spiritual biographies of captivity, condemnation, contaminating narratives, and death. *The Interesting Narrative of the Life of Olaudah Equiano, or Gustavus Vassa, the African* (1789 and 1791), has been described as "probably the most artful and influential Black narrative in English before Frederick Douglass's *Narrative* appeared in 1845."[20]

The abolitionists who encouraged enslaved persons to tell their stories as a form of spiritual autobiography found in the narratives of Olaudah something

---

[17] Mbembe, "Thinking about the World," 270.

[18] Cone, *The Cross and the Lynching Tree*, 124.

[19] Arna Bontemps, "The Slave Narrative: An American Genre," in *Great Slave Narratives*, ed. Arna Bontemps (Boston: Beacon, 1969), xiv.

[20] See Theodore Dwight Weld, Angelina Grimke, and Sarah Grimke, eds., *American Slavery as It Is: Testimony of a Thousand Witnesses* (New York: American Anti-Slavery Society, 1839), 7.

that goes beyond spiritual biography. His work is a critical account of the evil of slavery, and the loss of human freedom and dignity suffered by him and Black persons held in the captivity of slavery. It is also an expression of a hope for freedom—if not for him, at least for those Blacks who will come after him, and the entirety of humanity. Many Black persons who were enslaved sought different ways to "reorient their worldviews," and tell the stories of their ordeal or sing their pains into dance, and pray their sorrows into tears—all were part of their way of finding freedom.[21] In the words of Alice Sewell, a former enslaved person, "We prayed for dis day of freedom. We come four and five miles to pray together to God dat if we don't live to see it, to please let our chillen live to see a better day and be free, so dat dey can give honest and fair service to de Lord and all mankind everywhere."[22]

There are generally three important moments described in these slave narratives, and Olaudah's follows the same pattern. First is the capture, and subjection into bondage and enslavement. Second is the condemnation to nonexistence, natal alienation, deracination, and social death[23] in the journey through the Middle Passage from Africa to North America, Europe, the Caribbean, or Latin America. Olaudah was enslaved in all these places as he was moved from one master to another, and from one country to another. The third is the crucifixion: the strife of an enslaved person between life and death in the fight for freedom. To stay alive, to survive, and to be human when people around you want to neuter you and reduce you to nothing.

This third phase is usually filled with scenes of suffering and humiliation that worsen all the marks identified by Orlando Patterson as characteristic of slaves: natal alienation, social death, deracination, loss of dignity and respect, and treatment as personal property because the enslaved person does not belong. He or she is a nonperson.[24]

As well, gaining freedom meant remaining permanently under bondage and facing racism. It was slavery by other means, with incarceration, lynching, and other forms of barriers that made the life of a freed Olaudah worse than enslavement.

---

[21] Copeland, *Knowing Christ Crucified*, 158.

[22] Norman R. Yetman, ed., *Voices from Slavery* (New York: Holt, Rinehart and Winston, 1970), 263.

[23] Orlando Patterson, *Slavery and Social Death: A Comparative Study, with a New Preface*, 2nd ed. (Cambridge, MA: Harvard University Press, 1982).

[24] Patterson, *Slavery and Social Death*, 1–6.

Reading Equiano's narrative offers a model for reading the conditions of African Americans and peoples of African descent in the world today. We as Black people are living a new form of slavery through other means, and it is our vocation to fight for the liberation of our people.

I will give some examples of these three moments, as I ask you to think of what freedom means for you today, and for people who look like Equiano.

Captivity, Condemnation, Suffering, and Divine Providence[25]

Olaudah was kidnapped when he was eleven. He was kidnapped with his sister and taken to the coast: "The only comfort we had was being in each other's arms all that night and bathing each other with our tears" (chapter 2). A recurrent theme in Equiano's narrative is the hand of Providence. He seems to have found God at every stage in his treacherous journey into slavery. For example, he reasons that the loss of freedom left him in the merciful hand of divine providence: "I regard myself as a particular favorite of heaven" (p. 3). He thanks God when he is under servitude to Mr. King, and is treated better than with his previous master: "I blessed God for the hands into which I had fallen" (p. 81). Even his name, Olaudah, signifies for him that he bore the seal of fate—"Olaudah" means "vicissitude or fortune; one favored and having a loud voice and well spoken."

In chapter 5, he writes strongly about his regular prayer to God to help him obtain his liberty, while he also works hard (using every honest means) to obtain his freedom (p. 96). Being a predestinarian, he thinks that "whatever fate had determined must ever come to pass; and therefore, if ever it were my lot to be freed nothing could prevent me, although I should at present see no means or hope to obtain my freedom" (p. 96).

In chapter 1 he writes of divine providence: "I might say my sufferings were great: but when I compare my lot with that of most of my countrymen, I regard myself as a particular favorite of Heaven, and acknowledge the mercies of Providence in every occurrence of my life" (p. 8).

Paul Edwards and Rosalind Shaw note the constant deployment by Equiano of expressions like "I must look up to God Mighty in the top for right," and "Providence was more favorable to us than we could have

---

[25] Equiano, *The Interesting Narrative*; citations in this section are given in the text as chapter or page number in parentheses.

expected." This is important since it has been said that Africans are incurably religious, but what this incurable religious attachment has brought to Africans or upon them has not been deeply explored. However, one of the saddest contradictions Olaudah recounts in his *Narrative* is the violence he suffers at the hands of those he calls "Christian depredators," even after he received baptism and became a Christian.[26] He is mortified by the discrimination he suffers and sees, including the refusal of white Christian pastors to bury a Black woman's little baby (chapter 8). He draws a contrast between his own exercise of limited freedom in avoiding sin and doing harm to no one, and the abuse of freedom of his white oppressors: "O ye nominal Christians! Might not an African ask you, learned this from your God, who says unto you, Do unto all men as you would men should do unto you?" (p. 87).

The same outrage is expressed by Frederick Douglass with his description of "Christianity and its collusion with southern sociopolitical structures":[27]

> The dealers in bodies and souls of men erect their stand in the presence of the pulpit, and they mutually help each other. The dealer gives his blood-stained gold to support the pulpit, and the pulpit, in return, covers his infernal business with the garb of Christianity. Here we have religion and robbery the allies of each other—devils dressed in angels' robes, and hell presenting the semblance of paradise.[28]

There is an internal critique of a certain kind of Christian religious faith in Olaudah's account, showing he does not embrace Christianity in an uncritical way. However, his critical stance against the scandalous choices of white Christians and the discrimination and social hierarchies they created and sustained to keep Blacks in chains do not extend to the way he presents God as the one who saves him from death amid an oppressive slaving society. The

---

[26] Paul Edwards and Rosalind Shaw. "The Invisible Chi in Equiano's Interesting Narrative," *Journal of Religion in Africa* 19, no. 2 (1989): 146–56.

[27] Alexis S. Wells-Oghoghomeh, "Re-evaluating Roots: Slavery as Source and Challenge for African American Theology," in *T&T Clark Handbook of African American Theology*, ed. Antonia Michelle Daymond, Frederick Ware, and Eric Williams (London: T&T Clark, 2019), 19.

[28] Frederick Douglass, *Narrative of the Life of Frederick Douglass, An American Slave, Written by Himself* (Boston: Bedford, 1993), 105–6.

question is, Would God have troubled to save him if there were no slavery? Why did God not save the millions of other Black people who perished during the Middle Passage, or on the slave farms and under the whips and wickedness of their white oppressors? One could excuse Olaudah, because his narrative was the first of many. Along with the spirituals, these grew into important sources for Black and liberation theologies. Over time, these provided "an alternative and oppositional form of Christianity that foregrounds the issues of social justice and social change."[29]

Equiano oscillates between describing his free and beautiful home in Africa and the chaos and suffering of his enslavement. He writes of his motherland, Africa, as a land that is "uncommonly rich and fruitful," a land that produces all kinds of food and vegetables. A land where everyone works together—men and women—in tilling the earth, where everyone enjoys freedom to participate in the common good. "Everyone contributes something to the common stock; and as we are unacquainted with idleness, we have no beggars" (p. 18). He speaks of Africa as beautiful, and African women as "uncommonly graceful, alert and modest . . . cheerful and affable—two of the leading characteristics of our nation" (p. 18). He sees his birth as a promise, and his land of birth, the African motherland, as a promise. Through the iron hand of fate, he is taken into slavery, and lives the rest of his life precariously, on the verge of death, despair, and pain.

During his journey through the Middle Passage, Olaudah writes that he watched the beatings, the poor treatment, and the insufferable sights beneath the ship's deck. Some of his mates cry, "Give me freedom or give me death," as they jump to their death into the Atlantic. He recounts, "I now wished for the last friend, death, to relieve me." He reflects on the many sad nights during the voyage he was often woken by "the shrieks of the women, and the groans of the dying that rendered the whole scene of horror almost inconceivable" (p. x). However, the "scenes of horror" (p. 98) that characterize his life from captivity to the end of his *Narrative* demonstrate that for Olaudah and the millions of his siblings caught in this iniquitous and perilous slave trade the three questions about freedom arise. What do you want to or desire to do?

---

[29] Cheryl Townsend Gilkes, "'Go and Tell Mary and Martha': The Spirituals, Biblical Options for Women, and Cultural Tensions in the African American Religious Experience," in *Womanist Theological Ethics: A Reader*, ed. Katie Geneva Cannon, Emilie M. Townes, and Angela D. Sims (Louisville, KY: WJK, 2011), 219.

Where and how can you do it? What moves you to act? Why do you do what you do? For those enslaved, these can be answered only in the negative. The very act of seeking to answer these questions opens a world of tears, pain, betrayal, suffering, and death. It is in a word, a world that said "NO" to Equiano. Today's world continues to say "NO" to most people of African descent through destructive economic policies that kill the poor, immigration, employment, and health systems and structures that objectify, thing-ify, instrumentalize, erase, exclude, dehumanize, patronize, belittle, and even exterminate the Black other, and sundry other subjects considered expendable and disposable in our neoliberal capitalist societies.

As Equiano writes with clarity, "I would rather die than allow myself to be treated so badly because to me life has lost its relish when freedom is gone" (p. 96). The social conditions of Blacks who were liberated in parts of America in the early nineteenth century were as bad as those still held in captivity at the time Equiano was writing. Equiano sees this as a product of racialized thinking driven by godlessness, greed, and violence. He writes that no Black person should accept the simulacra of freedom by also accepting to be insulted, plundered, and mistreated, without any possibility of redress. Likewise, he decries accepting "a mockery of freedom" by continuing to accept "the misery of slavery" (p. 98).

Three Lessons

In a moving passage in his narrative, Equiano writes that what gave him calm was his belief in Providence: "I soon perceived what fate had decreed no mortal on earth could prevent" (p. 76). With no friend to bring him comfort, and no hope to bring cheer, and no help from heaven above to put an end to his misery, he bore his bruised and battered body with dignity. His relief is that the night that comes upon him puts an end to his miserable and toilsome day, and sees God alone in heaven as the only one who can give him succor.

Equiano's narrative raises three concerns for me. First is the role of churches and theologies in undermining the journey of freedom in America and the world. Each in its role often papers over the deep contradictions and trajectory of history that continue to unfold in the rivers of blood and tears of people of African descent, as well as minoritized individuals and marginalized peoples. This is done often with the "God of the gaps" concept of God's will—God has a purpose in all things. Or the constant message one receives in moments of tragedy and suffering—"Carry it like your Cross." We often talk about freedom, God's will, hope, and suffering as abstract terms.

As Christopher Kellerman writes, the history of slavery is too horrible, too tragic to be put in words. The sad thing is that the Christian faith, to which most of us theologians are committed, has "been so wrong, so callous, so caught up in the ways of the world as the cause of so much harm, century after century after century."[30] A discussion of freedom must begin with truth-telling, and listening to the hidden stories of pain, and narratives of people of African descent throughout the world. Their history is made of many capillaries going back to their forebears' slavery. Churches and theologies should provide moral clarity and prophetic and pragmatic solidarity, without sugarcoating this shameful history or the ongoing racism in the Church and society against people of African descent.[31] Churches must create room for lamentation, and so must our politics, classrooms, and public spaces. It is only by hearing narratives such as Equiano's and those who are condemned to die by the prevailing systems, structures, and institutions that society can begin to atone for the sins against freedom, of which many theologians and Church leaders are still beneficiaries or perpetrators.

My second concern is that theologians must move away from disembodied or spiritualized notions of freedom and grace. These include free choice of the will (St. Augustine), divine judgment, and predestination. An embodied and socialized narrative of freedom asks the three questions regarding freedom I proposed. When applied to individuals and groups, these can help us locate the barriers and roadblocks to the march to freedom. We can learn what freedom means for people who are too injured from hearing "NO" to their agency and being, rather than worrying about theological or philosophical concepts of freedom.

Finally, my third concern is the myth that democracies guarantee freedom and that the presence of freedom in neoliberal democracy brings prosperity. These are advanced, for instance, by the Atlantic Council's *Freedom and Prosperity Initiative*, and Amartya Sen's *Development as Freedom*. Critical reappraisal of this myth is needed. The mission of theologians today must be to develop the compass for a liberation historiography. I have in mind

---

[30] Kellerman, *All Oppression Shall Cease*, 214.

[31] Olga Segura, *Birth of a Movement: Black Lives Matter and the Catholic Church* (Maryknoll, NY: Orbis Books, 2021), 75.

the kind that can free our minds from imprisonment to worn-out categories and terms like freedom, liberal democracy, and Christian nationalism. These grew from the Western construction of an unjust global order, and the false promise of convergence of global history through modernity. We now speak of illiberal democracy, and we see the wreckage of democratic experiments, from Hiroshima to Kiev, from Kigali to Aleppo, and from Gaza to El Paso.

As an African, I have watched convulsion in the African continent in the five decades since my birth after the first modern genocide in Africa, the Biafran war. I watch sadly the new geopolitical battles between the United States, China, Russia, France, and the United Kingdom playing out again in Africa and in the Middle East. Some of the same forces that conspired to enslave our ancestors like Equiano are now gathering like vultures over the African Motherland as modern saviors of Africa.

The stories of many African young people have become like Equiano's. This time they are not being forced or kidnapped from a beautiful Africa. Rather, they are leaving the wreckage of the failed promises of modernity in Africa, and looking for escape routes to the countries of their oppressors. Like Equiano, some of them ask their pastors and imams for prayer so that God may guide them safely across the perilous uncharted sandy terrain of the Sahara or across the Mediterranean. They come back to their houses of prayer to give thanks to God if they arrive safely in North America or western Europe. Their African countries gained independence from the erstwhile colonialists, and they received the promise of better days, but all is dissipating before their very eyes. Some of them are so desperate they volunteer on the Russian side or answer the Kiev government's call for volunteer fighters for Ukraine.

In 2020, young Sudanese flooded the streets and asked for their freedom from oppression, tyranny, and death at the hands of a dictator. Hundreds of these young people paid with their lives. Today (2025) these young people have fled their war-ravaged country. Many are wandering on the lonely paths of forests and valleys, trying to escape from Sudan, or hiding from bombs and bullets flying over their land from Khartoum to Darfur. Like Naima whom we met in the introduction, some of them are being violated, maimed, and killed, and many of them are victims of human trafficking and modern-day slavery.

In South Africa during June of 1955, the African National Congress (ANC), the South African Indian Congress, the South African Colored People's Organization, and the Congress of Democrats signed the famous *Freedom Charter*. This offered the most articulate and widely circulated understanding and interpretation of freedom for Africans and peoples of African descent. Today South Africa's most popular party is no longer the scandal-ridden ANC, but the Economic Freedom Fighters led by Julius Malema. Today South Africans, like the South Sudanese, are asking questions. What is freedom? Where lies the future for us? Where is God?

Conclusion

According to Emily Esfahani Smith, those who can contribute to creating a better situation for future generations are those who "tell redemptive stories about their lives, or stories that transition from bad to good. In these stories, the tellers move from suffering to salvation—they experience a negative event followed by a positive event that resulted from the negative event and therefore gives their suffering some meaning."[32]

Jonathan Adler et al. identify four themes common in narrative identity, especially of individuals and groups: agency, communion, redemption, and contamination. I am concerned here with the last two, redemption and contamination, regarding the way stories of Black people have been told. Redemption, Jonathan Adler and co-authors argue, is about how people move from what is bad news or bad reality—for example, having a personal tragedy, or experiencing discrimination and rejection—to finding one's way to a positive and good outcome, and reclaiming one's voice and one's future:

> Like canonical American stories of upward social mobility, rags to riches, and liberation from oppression, the narrative of recovery is an especially common redemptive story wherein the protagonist regains an early goodness, innocence, or health. Personal stories of recovery from illness may lead to personal growth, a reconceptualization of one's priorities, richer connections with others, or a deepening of one's spirituality. In each instance, the negative health experience is narrated as having led to a valued outcome.[33]

---

[32] Emily Esfahani Smith, *The Power of Meaning: Finding Fulfillment in a World Obsessed with Happiness* (New York: Broadway, 2017), 108–9.

[33] Jonathan M. Adler et al., "Variation in Narrative Identity Is Associated with Trajectories of Mental Health over Several Years," *Journal of Personality and Social Psychology* 108, no. 3 (2015): 476.

The positive outcome may not fully drown out the negative precursor, but Adler and his colleagues propose that the ability to "glean some positivity amidst the struggle" has the potential for perceiving redemptive in-breaking that could lead to a positive outcome.

The other common theme of interest of narrative identity is contamination of one's stories. This can come in the face of adverse situations, which pollute the potential positivity. Or, as they found in their longitudinal studies, such pollution can affect individuals who are seeking health and well-being. According to Adler and his colleagues, "Contamination sequences follow the trajectory from good to bad. In these stories, scenes that start out positive are narrated as ending negatively. Whereas redemption sequences find a positive seed amid negative experiences, the negativity in contamination sequences is described as overwhelming or polluting the preexisting positivity."[34] This dynamism is employed in James Cone's account of the Cross and the fate of Black people in the face of racism and discrimination.

James Cone rereads the history of salvation through the corresponding history of slavery, lynching, and racism in America. The Cross is a sign of punishment and contamination, just like the lynching tree. The Cross, as a sign also of rejection and hatred, was transformed into a sign of liberation and redemption. White supremacy, Cone writes, "tears faith to pieces and turns the heart away from God; personal and communal suffering which comes from the human hate for black people pushes every black person to struggle on how to make sense between being black and being Christian."[35] This is particularly so because white supremacy was a Christian invention. It is sustained today in America and in the West through Christian narratives of God, suffering, whiteness, and the perception of Blackness as a disease. The way Cone rereads the suffering of Blacks is critical for four ways people of African descent can write theology as Black people.

The first way is being-with the people. Our theologies cannot be meaningful if we are not with our people, if we do not have "the smell of the sheep."[36] If we are elitist and comfortable with and untouched by the chaos

---

[34] Adler et al., "Variation in Narrative Identity," 478.

[35] Cone, *The Cross and the Lynching Tree*, 153.

[36] Francis, "Chrism Mass Homily of Pope Francis," March 28, 2013, https://www.vatican.va/content/francesco/en/homilies/2013/documents/papa-francesco_20130328_messa-crismale.html.

in our people's lives, we will not be credible, nor can we make any effect through our writings. A convenient theology of privilege and power from Black theologians would be a betrayal of the work and lives of our ancestors.

Second, Cone writes that he was "consumed by a passion to express myself about the liberating power of the black religious experience." He transgresses traditional manualistic Eurocentric theologies, with their abstractions and obtuse rationality. He rejects the claim that God was white and that the images of God and the saints, as well as biblical narratives and morality, must be seen and mediated through Western eyes with negation of Blackness. He writes: "All of my work since that first book (*Black Theology & Black Power*) has involved an effort to relate the Gospel to the black experience—the experience of oppression as well as the struggle to find liberation and meaning."[37] Black theology cannot be relevant to meeting the questions of the times if it is a consumerist theology. We must be adept not simply with papal documents and theological interpretations of other cultures and races. We must also be about the task of producing knowledge and practice that can stir the hearts of our people with hope. We are to steer them upward to the mountain top, beyond the stultifying and destructive social conditions that ravage Blacks' souls.[38]

Third, Cone finds liberating joy in the Cross and in the person of the Lord Jesus Christ, but not by spiritualizing the Cross and suffering. Rather, for Cone, "God's loving solidarity can transform ugliness—whether Jesus on the Cross or a lynched black victim—into beauty, into God's liberating presence. Through the powerful imagination of faith, we can discover the 'terrible beauty' of the cross and the 'tragic beauty' of the lynching tree."[39] Black theologies must show how the reign of justice and liberation can dawn for the oppressed. As Black civil rights lawyer Bryan Stevenson notes, what many Black people in the world today need is not mercy, pity, or handouts, but justice. Black and African theologies must show how the justice of God is being enacted in our present history through the agency of the Christian Gospel, and particularly counter to the continued state murder of thousands of African Americans through oppressive penal systems.

---

[37] Cone, *The Cross and the Lynching Tree*, 154.

[38] See Bryan Stevenson, *Just Mercy: A Story of Justice and Redemption* (New York: One World, 2015).

[39] Cone, *The Cross and the Lynching Tree*, 162.

The final of these four ways is the question of liberation historiography and agency in Black theology. As John Ernest insists,

> Blackness is understood not simply in terms of skin color but in relation to the historical structures of social order that have been informed over time by various applications of the ideology of race and by the social technologies of control that have been both inspired and justified by these shifting ideologies.[40]

Cone seeks what Katherine Clay Bassard calls a theology that emerges from the experience of the African American community and serves as "a cultural production in the very act of performing community."[41] The sources of Cone's theology are diverse—biblical narratives as retold by African American communities, poems, songs, blues, Black spirituals, and Black preaching. In doing this, Cone shows it is possible to find more than only redemptive emergence from the pain and suffering of Black people. A liberating historiography can also be seen within the resistance and courage of Black people, born of their faith in God.

Ernest sees in Cone's liberation theology "an approach to history shaped, on one hand, by black Christian belief and, on the other, by the pressures of a developing white American historiography that threatened to alienate African Americans from a historically informed understanding of individual and collective identity."[42] Consider Ernest's description of liberation historiography as

> the attempt to liberate African Americans from an other-defined history so as to provide them with agency in a self-determined understanding of history—and since the ultimate determination of historical authority and agency was God's, these writers—James Cone, Dwight Hopkins, Robert Young, David Walker before them—read the dual texts of human oppression and biblical destiny to

---

[40] John Ernest, *Liberation Historiography: African American Writers and the Challenge of History, 1794–1861* (Chapel Hill: University of North Carolina Press, 2004), 14.

[41] Katherine Clay Bassard, "The Daughters' Arrival: The Earliest Black Women's Writing Community," *Callaloo* 19, no. 2 (1996): 513.

[42] Ernest, *Liberation Historiography*, 15.

determine their position in a larger and largely unknowable narrative of providential history.[43]

By way of conclusion, I wish to return to my aunt, Virginia. I was home in Nigeria for Christmas in 2023, and she took me aside and asked me a serious question with tears in her eyes. "When are you coming home?" I said that I do not know and asked her when she would be visiting me again in the United States. Like my mum, she has decided that she does not want to visit this country (the United States) again, and actually wants me to return to Nigeria. They have concluded that I can never attain the best possible for me as a Black man in America. But I was touched that my aunt could see herself in the suffering of African Americans which gnawed at her liver and ripped her heart asunder.

Sometimes, I sense a huge gulf between Africans and African Americans; sometimes we fight each other and become our worst enemies. The hope of W. E. B. Du Bois, Marcus Garvey, and Bob Marley for greater convergence among Blacks throughout the world seems to be a remote possibility. This occupies my mind often as I reflect on my own experiences, and how my theology could be constructed in solidarity with the suffering and pain of my Black brothers and sisters in any part of the world.

Another thought emerged from my conversation with my aunt about returning home. I asked myself, "Where is home for you?" This is a question most of us Africans who have lived abroad particularly know will arise when we encounter any new person. But it is also a question that I hear from my own African American brothers and sisters who often long for a place that they would call home; hence their enthusiastic response to the Year of Return launched by the Ghanaian government in 2019 celebrating the 400th anniversary of the first Black slave arriving in Virginia. Homelessness is the Black condition in the contradiction of history, and its forced migratory patterns, which began with the slave trade. These continue today in human trafficking, modern-day slavery, and the forced exodus of Blacks throughout the world. Bob Marley popularized this in his song, "Exodus": "Movement of Jah people."

A similar question I am accustomed to hearing is, "Where do you come from?" When I am asked that, I am reminded of my roots and origins in the

---

[43] Ernest, *Liberation Historiography*, 18.

African Motherland, and it takes me back to the memory of my ancestry. This brings together for me many ideas: slavery, racism, apartheid, colonialism, nationality, white supremacy, Christian white nationalism and its variants in conservative African attachment to the vestiges of dying Western Christian forms of worship and belief; it takes me back to the tragedies of tribalism and xenophobia in Africa, wars, and my own exilic life, all of which have been part of my own stories. But how do we answer questions of our identity and our origin through our faith as Christians and as theologians of African descent? How does the African American answer, and what forms of alienation can answering bring up for many people of African descent? When I think of the genocides in Africa, the oppression of Blacks in America by whites, and the oppression of Africans by fellow Africans on the African continent, I wonder how we can begin to reshape our understanding of our shared history and the ineluctability of our shared destiny. How can we continue through our theologies to fight against a false consciousness and false sense of history and a false God and a false social hierarchy of humans?

We must make the journey of people like Olaudah our own, and run farther and faster than they did if we are to overcome a second slavery for this generation of Africans and Africans in Diaspora, and the next.

Conclusion

Hope in God

> Jesus is a specialist at turning our deaths into life, our mourning into dancing (cf. Psalm 30:11).... Let us not keep our faces bowed to the ground in fear, but raise our eyes to the risen Jesus. His gaze fills us with hope, for it tells us that we are loved unfailingly and that however much we make a mess of things, his love remains unchanged. This is the one, non-negotiable certitude we have in life: his love does not change. Let us ask ourselves: *In my life, where am I looking? Am I gazing at graveyards, or looking for the Living One?*
>
> —Pope Francis[1]

This book argues that the persistent suffering and pain in Africa and among people of African descent are not part of God's will for them. Thus, rather than offer quick solutions and hope, theologians and churches must enter deeper into the pains of many people in the injustice and tragedies of modern global history and its destructive economies, politics, and some misleading and false religious teachings and claims about God. African theologians are invited to pay closer attention today to the lived faith and experience of African Christians. African Christians are holding on to God as the one and only certainty that will not fail them when other things around them show signs of weakness and instability. But it is important that they be led to think correctly

---

[1] Francis, "Homily of His Holiness Pope Francis, Easter Vigil in the Holy Night of Easter," April 20, 2019, https://www.vatican.va/content/francesco/en/homilies/2019/documents/papa-francesco_20190420_omelia-vegliapasquale.html, sec. 2.

of God, so that they can understand themselves better, and courageously confront the social evils and systems that have conspired to turn the world into a valley of tears for billions of people all over the world. I have shown different approaches by African theologians, scholars of religious studies, and church leaders to interpreting, judging, and responding to the lived faith of God's people in Africa. What becomes obvious is that the received theologies and methods for pastoral care, as well as the structures, institutions, and systems in churches in Africa, have not kept pace with the lived faith and experiences of the people. This is also true of African theologies, which have not been able to capture the cultural and spiritual imagination of everyday Christians. Nor have they been able to influence pastoral practice or spiritual development in the continent. This is why the politics and ethics of Africa have not been transformed by either the growth in religiosity in the continent, the strong growth in the Christian population, or the growing theological publications from Africa.[2]

The question today is no longer whether there is an African theology or African ecclesiology or African political theology, to mention but a few. The question is no longer about whether Africans believe in God or not, but rather what kind of God they worship and whether this God is the true God revealed by Jesus Christ. The fundamental question is about the relevance and impact of Africana and Black theologies for addressing the deepest desires of Africans for abundant life on the continent and why these theologies have not made significant inroad in changing the ethics and direction of history for the communities for which they were written.

Five Claims of This Book

I have made and defended five claims for African theology in this book, and I wish to highlight them to bring this work to conclusion. The first claim *concerns accountability* for what is going on in the lives of the people by paying attention to the *suffering and smiling* that is the daily reality of most Africans. The second is *about accompaniment*, through following the stories of the lives

---

[2] Serious efforts are being made to develop a political theology in Africa. Recent scholarship appears in a collection of essays: Dion A. Forster and H. Jurgens Hendriks, *African Public Theology* (Cumbria, UK: Langham, 2020). See also Emmanuel Katongole, *The Sacrifice of Africa* (Grand Rapids, MI: Eerdmans, 2011).

of the people and showing the presence or absence of God in their journey. The third claim *is the question of God and how theologians can help Africans think and act correctly* about God revealed in the person of Jesus Christ. The fourth *focuses on action*, showing how people can act together to respond in solidarity and prophetically to overcome the social evils and structural sins that ravage the lives of God's people in Africa. The fifth claim relates to how as *God's people we can embody hope in our collective grief and lamentation* for what is not working in our history and our social context and in our churches. How can hope be fused in the concrete history of the people through the agency of individuals, communities, churches, and other entities?

First, the growth in Christian population in Africa demands corresponding growth in theological production in Africa. This accompaniment of theological accountability can show the presence or absence of God in the movement of the Spirit in the current history of Africa. In this book's introduction and chapter 4, I demonstrate that there is a crisis of modernity, and that this is felt strongly in Africa, with devastating consequences. For Africa, the promise of convergence brought through Christianity, Islam, and the modern state has created greater divergence in Africa, and between Africa and the rest of the world. This is unleashing a destructive force that has undermined the cultural practices, moral traditions, institutions, and social bonds that held people together. What we see in the continent is greater fragmentation as people fight for social space and small zones of dominance to maintain some control over others and/or of a small reference group—in religious institutions or the political arena—to protect parochial interests.

The fissures in Africa are deep and expanding, and the appeal to religious claims and counterclaims that suffuse the social space has not offered an exit route from this accelerating crisis of history. Religious and political leaders in most of Africa do not seem to grasp the enormity of this fragmentation. Neither do they see the loss of traditional claims to authority and validation of truth, which is pulling the rungs of power from under their feet. Those who hold power and those who are powerless are caught in this contradiction. The answers being offered in theology and through preaching feature the prosperity gospel, healing ministry, and charitable and humanitarian outreach mainly from outside Africa, but sometimes within the continent. These are simply Band-Aid solutions that continue to perpetuate the weak institutions of the state and of religion. They also replicate the condescending and paternalistic patron-client exchanges that Africa inherited from the white enslavers, colonialists, and missionaries. To address this complexity that threatens the future of Africa and the Christian enterprise in Africa, new theological approaches are needed for the cultural and social experience of Christianity and for deepening the understanding of who God is and where God is to be found.

Such approaches must be "made-in-Africa," and not a patchwork woven around theoretical, conceptual, and theological frameworks borrowed from outside Africa or developed through proof-texting to reinforce one entrenched theological or doctrinal position or another. Restlessness abounds among young people in Africa, accompanied by the cry for a new Africa and a more accountable, credible, and active Church that accompanies God's people. Theologians of Africa can no longer be content with theologizing to themselves, and seeking an "impact factor" for papers written or books published with Western agencies. The impact factor needed is how our theologies can really help God's people and the Church to move in the direction of transformative faith that leads to the realization (even in small measures) of the fruits of the eschatological reign of God.

Jean-Marc Ela underlines this point of transformation of Africa regarding two SECAM (Symposium of Episcopal Conferences of Africa and Madagascar) documents, *Justice and Evangelization in Africa* from 1981, and *The Church and Human Promotion in Africa Today* from 1984. Ela cautions that theologians in Africa should not see their task as that of being a mouthpiece of the Roman curia or the praise-singer of the powerful in Africa. Rather, African theologians must commit themselves fully to doing thorough research to help find practical solutions to the problems facing the continent. African theologians, Ela insists, must risk plunging into the theological task by fixing their gaze on how God can assume flesh in the drama of daily lives of African men and women. The concerns and questions of African Christians in their suffering and social conditions revolve around how the memory of the Gospel and the living of the message can be a source of liberation for them as they embrace the true God as revealed through the Son of God.[3]

The second claim of this book is that to accompany God's people, theologians in Africa need to pay attention to where God is by focusing on where God's people are. Chapters 2 and 3 examined the lives of African Christians who have died and the conditions of those who are alive in view of the centrality of scripture in the formation of a Christian consciousness. Chapter 3 particularly

---

[3] Jean-Marc Ela, *Repenser la théologie africaine* (Paris: Karthala, 2003), 10–11.

examined the different approaches to suffering through *matatu* theology. I drew inspiration for doing theology through this approach from the peripheries of the bus stops by paying attention to the teachings of Pope Francis on theology as spiritual biography, and the formation of the Luke-Acts literary canon. The preface to the Gospel of Luke (1:1–4) begins this way:

> Seeing that others have undertaken to draw up an account of the events that have taken place among us, exactly as these were handed down to us by those who from the outset were eyewitnesses and ministers of the word, I in my turn, after carefully going over the whole story from the beginning, have decided to write an ordered account for you.

The writer speaks of the account or narrative (*diegesis*) in the preface of "events that have taken place among us"—*pragmata peplerophoremena*. Luke concentrates his narrative on the efficacy of Christ's actions and presence as witnessed in the community. Furthermore, Luke's use of "account" or "narrative" refers to all that has taken place—great and small, good and bad, life and death, sin and righteousness. Nothing is left out. To tell the story of "all that has taken place," the narrator must be present in the story and pay attention to every detail. Not only the spoken words, but the unspoken words, symbols, signs, songs, stories, artistic works, and cultural and spiritual artifacts. Everything reveals the presence of God. Luke's preface notes he "examined everything carefully" to make sure that no aspect of "what happens" or "what happened" or "what is happening" in the community is excluded from his story, and nothing is minimized or distorted by lack of attention.

In Luke-Acts, the author wants to put forward an ordered account. This is not a matter of the Gospel's logical or chronological coherence, but rather of the whole story coming together because the Lord is present in the story. The shattered lives of people and the complex challenges facing the early Christian community are presented as moving in a certain direction. That direction goes beyond death and destruction because Christ is present to bring all things together. The story is complete, with a beginning, a complex middle, and an ordered and happy salvific ending. It is a continuum that is integrated by the participation of all in the life of all, and by the presence of Christ through the presence of the church in bringing order amid the disorder. This extant chaos is inflicted on wounded hearts and a wounded world by sin, poverty, suffering, and pain. The summons to Theophilus from the writer in Luke and Acts of the Apostles, indicating the account is being put together for him to believe, is an assurance that God is present in history through Our Lord Jesus Christ. God is particularly present in the broken history in the closeness of the Son to those who are outside the gate—the voiceless, persecuted, forgotten, wounded, lost, and alienated of this world and all those who are *suffering and smiling*.

As in Luke-Acts, those in Africa at the peripheries and on the streets and bush paths, in the healing homes, and dying in the Sahara or drowning in the Mediterranean are the brothers and sisters of the homeless Jesus Christ. In going to encounter them, we are connecting with those we have made to feel disposable and outsiders in the drama of history and our ecclesial life. Following the tradition of Luke-Acts, I have proposed in chapters 3 and 4 that it is possible to tell the stories of what God is up to in Africa by exploring some of the most painful but hopeful dramas playing out before our eyes. The best account we can give as theologians in Africa, or elsewhere, must be a first-person account. It is not to be something we received as second-hand information without creative and critical appropriation, producing merely regurgitated formulae, or citations of Western theologians or proof-text magisterial sources.

African theologians should be eyewitnesses (*autoptes*, Acts 1:2) to what they write about. Presence with the people enables the theologian to do what the writer of the First Letter of Peter calls an *apologia* (confession or an answer, 3:15–16) of the hope and light the theologian experiences *in situ* amid the people. The eyewitness must follow closely (*parakoloutheo*, Acts 1:3) and participate fully in the life of individuals and the community of faith. He or she must be present and hear and see what the people who live that experience live and see every day. The resulting account is not something that is to be told from a distance. One must tell the story as an insider, and as one who accompanies. It must be a grounded account, where the writer is in touch with the very flesh of the phenomena being described. It is to be an account that one tells from a first-person perspective as a witness to what one is describing. This approach gives the prospect of producing a hermeneutical integration[4] of the narrative of the footprints of God in the lived faith and daily experience of God's people.

---

[4] Francis, *Veritatis Gaudium*, apostolic constitution, December 17, 2017, https://www.vatican.va/content/francesco/en/apost_constitutions/documents/papa-francesco_costituzione-ap_20171208_veritatis-gaudium.html, sec. 5.

The third claim is that in doing theology in Africa—and particularly in responding to the question "Where is God?"—African theologians must pay attention to and be familiar with all the resources in the intellectual tradition of the Church and the current teaching of the Magisterium. This is why I have spent a greater time on Pope Francis's attempt to renew Catholic theology through *Veritatis Gaudium* and *Ad Theologiam Promovendam*. This teaching has strong roots in the Catholic intellectual tradition pioneered in the writings of St. Augustine and St. Thomas Aquinas. The theological writings of Augustine and Aquinas have remained as legible markers in the vast pages of Catholic intellectual tradition on how to do contextual theology. This includes paying attention to tradition, assimilating cultural and intellectual contexts within one's writing, and developing a theology and pastoral teaching that are relevant to the people. That their works and thoughts are still relevant today is a testament to the depth and richness of what these two great minds accomplished. They challenge African theologians to do more than simply restate doctrines and theologies, do patchwork scholarship, or parrot existing theologies.

The fourth claim of this book is that in responding to the question of where God is in Africa, theologians must take into consideration all the traditions of theology that have enabled believers to deepen an understanding of the revelation of God in the person of the Lord Jesus Christ—scripture, writings of theologians from all cultures, and the *sensus fidei* of African Christian voices from the peripheries. What Africans believe about God is of importance in how they understand, interpret, and respond to the daily challenges and struggles that face them and how to see fellow Africans and the differences of tribes, races, creed, and denominations. The argument made here is that the question of God is still an object of ongoing theological inquiry because the images of God in Africa today have proven inadequate in the construction of a better Africa—in church and other religious groupings or in the state. African theologians must thus reexamine their theological writings, and Christian pastors and preachers must examine their consciences about the Gospel they are proclaiming to see whether it is still the liberating, saving, and healing good news that Jesus proclaimed with so much authority and with great fruitfulness in terms of conversion and transformation. It seems to me that the images of God in Africa today have proven inadequate for constructing African social ethics, building an inclusive nation-state, and bringing about faith communities that truly reflect the central ecclesial image chosen by African bishops at the First African Synod (1994) that the Church is a family of God. What has been done with and in the name of God in Africa in the post–Vatican II African churches and the post-independent African nations cannot sustain abundant life in Africa. The God-talk in Africa today is proving shockingly incapable of convincing many people that the African notions of God and the celebration of God's presence in the liturgical assembly or the exuberant faith expressions of African Christians transcend the idolatries of the past in Africa or elsewhere, and modern idolatries in current history.[5]

God as an Existential Crisis for People of African Descent in Their Search for Hope

The fifth and final claim of this book concerns hope. All theodicies, like every theology, must end in hope. Ka Mana proposes that the central mission of African theologies is to embody a ministry of hope, through

> the creation of a visionary, creative and resourceful society for the struggle against all the negative forces that Africa is suffering from, the debilitating powers of sorcery, witchcraft and witch beliefs, and the social-political and economic powers that are embodied in the harmful and sterile institutions and social structures, whether local or international.[6]

This is the central concern of chapter 5, where I used the narrative of an enslaved African person, Olaudah Equiano, to show the elusiveness of hope. It also shows the contradictions of the claims of hope and predestination in the lives of Africans and people of African descent outside Africa. Christian belief is that God touches everything that happens to us. William Barclay points this out clearly when he discusses the possibility of conversion, that is, our turning back to God: "If God is no more than indifferent, there is no

---

[5] A similar argument has been made by Paulinus Odozor in "One and the Same? The Debate over God-Language in African Christianity," in *Joseph Ratzinger and the Future of African Theology*, ed. Maurice Ashley Agbaw-Ebai and Matthew Levering (Eugene, OR: Pickwick, 2021).

[6] Ka Mana, *Christians and Churches of Africa Envisioning the Future: Salvation in Jesus Christ and the Building of a New African Society* (Akropong-Akuapen, Ghana: Regnum Africa, 2002), 102–3.

point in turning to one who in any event does not care."⁷ Barclay contrasts the Christian God with notions of God among the Greeks and Romans. The Stoics insisted that God must be insulated from all feelings to be God. God must "know no grief, have no emotions, show no grief and express no love." The Epicureans "insisted that if the serenity of God is to be maintained, then God cannot have any interest in the world, for God to have any concern with the world would bring dispeace to His unbroken peace, for concern and serenity are mutually contradictory."⁸

Barclay wonders how we can turn to this kind of God who is "inexorable law, avenging justice, unapproachable holiness." This kind of God does not offer any welcome, and is only waiting for our obliteration and condemnation. Humans will flee in terror from this kind of God. We will become hopeless and despair if we do not have faith in a God who is touched by our human condition, and is actively at work in us to bring us to the fulfillment that God longs for. God made us beautiful from all eternity.⁹

We return to the question, "Where is God in our silent tears as Africans?" Ilia Delio writes with clarity and insight about contemporary culture and the tendency to escape from human pains and troubles rather than embrace them with faith and courage:

> Human tears are so abundant in every part of the world that sadness is the face of daily life. We often shut down in the face of human misery because we feel our helplessness, our weakness, our inability to act. It is easier sometimes not to show emotion than to join in the human valley of tears. It is easier to live privately than to be involved in the pain of others. As one television commercial reminds us "who has time for pain?" The answer in the Western world is, "no one." We do not have time for pain or suffering or any type of disorder in the human condition and, because we have no time, pains and suffering abound.¹⁰

---

⁷ William Barclay, *Turning to God: Conversion in the New Testament* (London: Epworth, 1963), 29.

⁸ Barclay, *Turning to God*, 30.

⁹ Barclay, *Turning to God*, 30.

¹⁰ Ilia Delio, *The Humility of God: A Franciscan Perspective* (Cincinnati, OH: Franciscan Media, 2005), 89.

The disorder in the human condition, and how our human tears capture this disorder, was depicted well in Picasso's *The Weeping Woman*. This painting offers us roads for contemplation into the world of human suffering, and especially as personified in women, whom Picasso said are "suffering machines."[11]

I have not resolved here in this book the ambiguity of "suffering and smiling." It is not my intention to do so. There is a sense of incompleteness in everything that we do as humans, and it is liberating to embrace human finitude. But people caught in this crisis of history and this cycle of suffering and pain must be given a reason to hope. In other words, why and how can we Africans continue to believe in a good God amid our tears and pains? Charles H. Long helps me pose this question even more poignantly in his description of the encounter of Africans with God as a sort of existential crisis:

> To whom does one pray from the bowels of a slave ship? To the gods of Africa? To the gods of the masters of the slave vessels? To the gods of the unknown and foreign land of enslavement? To whom does one pray? From the perspective of religious experience, this was the beginning of African American religion and culture. In the forced silence of oppression, in the half-articulate moans of desperation, in the rebellions against enslavement—from this cataclysm another world emerged.[12]

This is an ambiguity that we find in the Old Testament, as well in the journey of Israelites to the Promised Land. When we search Scripture, especially the Old Testament, we are faced with ambiguities about God, human finality, and evil.

The story of the golden calf in the Book of Exodus could be read as an account of a people's search in their exilic state for military, political, economic, and social solutions. It is the story of the people's search for hope. Instances are many of the people's rejection of Moses or rebellion against God, despising God, disloyalty or misplaced trust, or sinning against God. Examples include

---

[11] André Malraux, *Picasso's Mask*, trans. June Guicharnaud with Jacques Guicharnaud (New York: Holt, Rinehart and Winston, 1976), 138.

[12] Charles H. Long, cited in Frederick L. Ware, "Methodologies in African American Theology," in *The Oxford Handbook of African American Theology*, ed. Katie G. Cannon and Anthony B. Pinn (Oxford: Oxford University Press, 2014), 127.

the case of the spies (Numbers 13), the cry of the people before crossing the Red Sea (Exodus 14), the near uprising at the waters of Massah and Meribah (Exodus 17), and the tale of Dathan and Abiram despising the Lord (Numbers 16:30). These had nothing exclusively religious about them. All reflect the people's concerns for quotidian issues—water, food, health, safe passage in dangerous territories, labor, lodging, land, and security with their neighbors.

This search for hope and safety is manifested in the people's response to and reaction against God. At Massah, the people are said to have tested God "because the Israelites quarreled and tested the Lord, saying, is the Lord among us or not?" (Exodus 17:2, 7). Another example is the spies sent to spy on the Promised Land, and reporting that the land was flowing with milk and honey, but that the inhabitants were huge people before whom the spies appeared like grasshoppers. For the spies, save for Caleb and Joshua, the people of Israel are incapable of occupying the land of their neighbors. This negative report is seen by God as mistrust in God's divine power to bring about God's purposes. In response to the report, the people mobilize in opposition to Moses, saying, "Let us choose a captain, and go back to Egypt" (Numbers 14:4). According to Gili Kugler:

> Their guilt is presented as unacceptable behavior exclusively toward God; disbelief in God's signs ([Numbers] 14: 11b, 22a) and testing and disobeying God ([Numbers] 14: 22b). However, all these examples reflect the people's behavior and not really what they believe because they too are like the surrounding nations because they fail to trust God despite numerous divine actions and signs that God gave for verification.[13]

In my reading of these texts, the relationship between God and Israel can be interpreted purely as the search by the people who are fleeing from oppression for hope, constructed for secular ends rather than their search for God as an end. Instances of God's mercy, promises, liberation, and covenant abound in the Pentateuch. In the examples here, the distinction between secular and religious ends is blurred. The charge of idolatry hangs on the elusive search

---

[13] Gili Kugler, "The Threat of Annihilation of Israel in the Desert: An Independent Tradition within Two Stories," *Catholic Biblical Quarterly* 78, no. 4 (2016): 637.

for who God is, where God can be found, where the solutions to the people's problems could be found, who the human person is, and his or her ultimate destiny. What is false and true in the objective of this search is of concern. However, we do not have any definite answer as to why the people should be faithful and loyal to the God of Moses, and not to the golden calf. In their desire for worship and for a complete horizon of meaning and safety, they are constantly oscillating between fear and fulfillment, between the presence of God and the absence of God, and between blessings and curse. Life and death all come apace from the same source—the God of Moses.

Kugler notes that "stories about the ways in which God executes threats to destroy communities and nations are not unusual in the Hebrew Bible."[14] The God of the Pentateuch across its four main traditions (Yahwist, Elohist, Deuteronomic, and Priestly) display in equal measure a capacity and determination to bring about adverse consequences on the chosen. We have examples of God killing humankind in its entirety a few generations after creating them (Genesis 6–8) and demolishing the sinful inhabitants of cities soon after the rehabilitation of humanity (Genesis 19). In the crossing of the Red Sea, as the hymn Christians sing on Easter Vigil goes, "Pharaoh and his chariots he cast into the sea" (cf. Exodus 14:10–21). The Book of Joshua describes God's assistance in defeating and destroying former nations of Canaan (chapters 6–11) and taking their lands. The First Book of Samuel presents the killing of virtually all the people of Amalek in compliance with divine instruction (chapter 15). As Gregory Boyd posits, for many Christian believers it takes different levels of spiritual transformation and transition to come to terms with the images of God in the Old Testament. The God who commands people to mercilessly slaughter "anything that breathes" (Deuteronomy 20:16), the God who prompts parents to kill their children (Genesis 22:1–27), and the God of many other violent behaviors, is exactly represented in the incarnate Jesus, as the Letter to the Hebrews indicates (Hebrews 1:3).[15]

The people of Israel are exposed to the same level of punishment from God as those of other nations. They face constant divine wrath and threats of annihilation. In the worship of the golden calf, there are dire consequences. In Numbers 13–14, God kills the spies who bring the negative report and

---

[14] Kugler, "The Threat of Annihilation of Israel in the Desert," 632.

[15] See Gregory A. Boyd, *The Crucifixion of the Warrior God: Interpreting the Old Testament's Violent Portraits of God in Light of the Cross* (Minneapolis: Fortress, 2017).

punishes the people who complained and doubted God's power to bring about what God promised the people of Israel.

What is not of God and what is of God, and what are true and false gods, are often complicated in theology and in politics and social ethics. God brings about good and bad fortunes for God's chosen people as well as for those who worship other gods. When we read these narratives from the view of the underclass of this world, it might be that creating the golden calf is an act of resistance against an all-conquering God and an all-powerful male leader, Moses. It might be that the ten spies who warn the people not to take the land of other people are the voices of reason rather than of disbelief in the march to Canaan to conquer people in the name of God. After all, it is reasonable to expect that an attacked people will fight back and be strong enough to defend their land. Could it be the God of Moses is the problem, rather than the people who worship other gods? By the same token, rather than dismiss the prayers and hopes of Africans while suffering and smiling, one can see them as an act of resistance. Indeed, most Africans believe that there is hope for the future and that God is taking them through the desert to the promised land, like God did for the biblical Israelites. How can this resistance be turned into a means of reversal of their lot?

God-talk must be placed side by side with idolatry critique. Indeed, no valid idolatry critique can occur that does not begin from and lead back to a God-critique—the kind of God that people worship and the kind of God that people hold onto in places like Africa as the answer to all their problems and how this actually plays out in the daily lives of the people and in their political and religious institutions, spirituality, and moral life. The notion of God naturally leads to a theological anthropology based on human finality, fulfillment, and the ultimate purpose of the moral demand, so that God's will may be done on earth as it is in heaven. This is important everywhere, but more important for people who look like me. African theologians must pay attention to what the Western construction of God has become for many non-Western societies. Non-Western people came under the influence of Christendom ideas and the Western construction of God and idols. These people are subjected to a cultural agenda of the West mediated through this kind of God-talk, where hope is only wishful thinking and a heavy existential burden amid cultural and spiritual chaos.

Indeed, the God presented in Western Christian accounts as the true God that Africans embraced is the God who sends people to hell or purgatory and those who are faithful to heaven. This God takes sides with warring parties, takes people's land, sanctions slavery and cultural genocide, and kills people. It is a God in whose name the West has triumphed over the rest, as Rodney Stark sings of.[16] This is the God who takes sides with males and the cisgender to the exclusion and even damnation of the rest, the God in whom we trust as the guarantor of American exceptionalism. This God is also the God who rewards followers with prosperity, and some others with poverty, who saves some from accidents and allows others to perish.

This God is an idol that has been promoted for so long in our churches and in many forms of Christianity, not only in Africa, but elsewhere. Africans embraced that God in large numbers, either through Christianity or Islam. The current crisis of religion and the state in Africa and the painful tragedy of the African predicament that we see in the daily lives of Africans today are the collateral damage of worship of this kind of God. The pathological and transactional religious dramas we see around us in the African Motherland have not helped my people answer their questions: Where is God? Who is God? Who does it mean to be human surrounded by so much suffering and pain? How can human and cosmic flourishing emerge in our present history as the fruits of the eschatological fulfillment of God's reign?

Where Is Hope?

Jürgen Moltmann writes:

> The God of hope is the God of freedom. In him no boundaries are set, nor does he set any. He breaks through defenses of anxiety and the walls of care. He breaks through boundaries which we ourselves have set in order to distinguish ourselves from other men and to affirm ourselves. He breaks into the boundary of our solitude in which we have hidden so that no one will come near us. He steps over the boundary of race, in which man loathes man, and the boundaries of class and strata in society. He despises the difference between black

---

[16] See Rodney Stark, *How the West Won: The Neglected Story of the Triumph of Modernity* (Washington, DC: Regnery Gateway, 2014); see also Rodney Stark, *America's Blessings: How Religion Benefits Everyone, Including Atheists* (West Conshohocken, PA: Templeton, 2013).

and white, poor and rich, educated and uneducated; for he seeks men—poor, suffering, hating and ugly, cramped and stunted men—and accepts them as they are. That knowledge makes us free and is a source of support. We can hope in him—the God of freedom.[17]

Hope is an invitation to freedom exercised by God and offered to human beings. This boundary-shattering God wishes to free humans from enslavement to the idols of the self, nations, cultures, races, religions, ideologies, and greed and many other things that enchain humanity in a cycle of decay. When humans are freed from these deceptive and destructive attachments and barriers to the realization of the fruits of the eschatological reign of God in history, they experience the exhilarating irruption of a new creation and embrace the courage to live in hope with and in the presence of one another and the whole of creation on this earth our common home.

In *Spes non Confundit*, Pope Francis prays that the Jubilee Year of 2025 may be "a moment of genuine, personal encounter with the Lord Jesus, the 'door' (cf. John 10:7, 9) of our salvation, whom the Church is charged to proclaim always, everywhere and to all as 'our hope' (1 Timothy 1:1)."[18] How can this encounter, demonstrated in this book as a daily spiritual staple for Africans, become real in the context of Africans? As Emmanuel Katongole observes, many Africans are asking not for descriptions, prescriptions, projections, or predictions of hope, but rather they want to see hope, feel hope, and live hope through an account of hope in lived faith and human experience.[19] For Katongole, the question "What does hope look like?" can be answered by pointing to stories of hope and redemption in the lived faith and activities in many sites of hope in Africa where people are saying to the darkness, "We beg to differ." Katongole sees the Church in Africa as "a rich laboratory of hope" because it is providing witnesses "of what hope looks like in the context of violence and war," and showing how the "the theological

---

[17] Jürgen Moltmann, *The Gospel of Liberation*, trans. H. Wayne Pipkin (Waco, TX: Word Books, 1973), 27.

[18] Francis, *Spes non Confundit*, Bull of Indiction of the Ordinary Jubilee of the Year 2025, May 9, 2024, https://www.vatican.va/content/francesco/en/bulls/documents/20240509_spes-non-confundit_bolla-giubileo2025.html, sec. 1.

[19] Emmanuel Katongole, *Born from Lament: The Theology and Politics of Hope in Africa* (Grand Rapids, MI: Eerdmans, 2017), 26.

grammar of hope" can be applied to the social brokenness through "ongoing works of social repairs."[20]

Daring to imagine a different way of thinking and acting in the world today is a good way to re-found the theological virtue of hope on solid principles and practices of solidarity from the daily experiences of God's people. This would be better than mouthing moral platitudes, empty talks, echo chambers through synods, and pleasant writings on hope that are not mediated through the narratives of God's people. While hanging on the Cross, God's people are demonstrating how to engage God in their sufferings by cooperating with grace in bringing about a new event through their narrative of reversal.

Hope is a firm conviction that God is in control of all things, and an assurance of God's will and power to realize in history God's creative and saving will through the Son of God, and the divine promise of blessing and goodness for creation. Hope is born from faith in God (Hebrews 11:1), who makes all things possible. Hope is also the gift received in faith that moves the human heart to hold onto God's promises of better outcomes in history through human agents who courageously align themselves with God's will. Hope emerges from concrete virtuous choices by human beings out of love for God, one another, and the world that has been given to us as our home by God. Hope, love, and faith are intimately connected. They are not successive moments, for example, faith first, then love, then hope. They are rather perichoretic, like the relationship of the Trinity: faith, hope, and love abide, and they are immersed in each other.

Hope moves the human person to embrace human finality. This is not as a threat to diminishment, extinction, or annihilation, but rather as liberty. The one who has hope is freed from being perpetually entangled in the contingent movement of history or things beyond us. I have hope; I am no longer caught up in successive traps of anxiety, or cycles of despair and desolation. This can occur, for instance, when I think of my own end, or the end of all things, the threats from the evil that surrounds me, or even my lack of control over the vicissitudes of history. Why is this freedom possible? Because in the logic of grace, the person who has hope falls not into an abyss, but into the hands of God, and is upheld by the experience of God's love flooding the heart.

Through hope, I am anchored in the life of God through God's Son. Not in a magical way, but through the union of my will and that of God's Son.

---

[20] Katongole, *Born from Lament*, 264–65.

Through this union, there emerges in me spontaneously positive values and life-affirming virtues like courage, character, and endurance, especially at the deepest level of my human vulnerability. Hope is thus my ceaseless movement, born of faith, to grab the hand of God, and be open to grace by allowing my human vulnerability and the precarity of human contingency to meet the infinity of divine transcendence. This is the dynamic at work in the text of St. Paul: "Hope does not disappoint, because God's love has been poured into our hearts through the Holy Spirit that has been given to us" (Romans 5:5). Horizontal and vertical dynamics are at work in the human through the love and grace of God that the Christian believes in and receives in faith. It is at this horizontal and vertical juncture where the Cross of the Son of God stands that I realize my own limits, and my own finitude and precarity, which are often as all-encompassing and overpowering as freedom. At this juncture I find myself always taking hold of God, whose grace radically turns me toward this God of love and freedom with trust, rather than being afraid of my human finality and temporality, and what is to come.

Every day I see my own weaknesses, my lack of ability to meet the ends of my purposes. It is at that moment of realizing this existential boundary that one either flies from human limitations, or fights the flight in a Sisyphean battle that will never end. However, rather than a perpetual fight to the finish that certainly does not offer anything other than more misery and pain, the person of faith moves from fighting the inevitability of our human finality by coming to the foot of the Cross. Once there, one is moved to see that whatever is considered a threat, whatever is feared that can harm, whatever worries about the future, are all shattered by the boundlessness of the Cross. Limits are placed beyond which my human finality and the evils and pains associated with them cannot go. But it is only human finality that is defeated here, for the limit of the Cross is not a destruction of life or of the beauty of the earth. It is an opening to life by the radical transformation of our human finality and the defeat of human pride and selfishness, which limit creation from realizing the fullness of the gift God has given to us.

The Cross opens a new horizon beyond my limits because the Lord God, as a song goes, will "shepherd me beyond my fears and from death will set me free." The Cross is what hope looks like—a triumph over human finality that is not simply projected as an emerging Elysium or an illusory eruption, but a gift that I receive every day as I embrace the revelation of Love through the Lord Jesus Christ as the Truth, the Life, and the Way. The Cross reenacts the human cycle of pain and solace, of despair and hope, of fear and freedom. By embracing the Cross, I reenact with all my human weaknesses the priorities and practices of the Lord through a self-giving and non-transactional love for God and my neighbors, especially those who cannot pay me back, or praise me, or honor me. Indeed, Calvary is reenacted every day when I say to the darkness, "I beg to differ." This is not simply a speech, but a way of being that is saturated with divine grace. This way is capable of opening human eyes to see glimmers of hope, and to co-create with God new sites of hope every day when I live beyond myself. I thus can see more of God and less of me in my daily effort to do good. The more I open myself to this boundless, unconditional, and unconditioned love, and live beyond my limit in this love, the freer I become and the more I cooperate with God and others in bringing hope about in history.

Hope is also to be understood through the memory of the Church. The Church is born out of this memory: the contemplation in the Eucharist of how the self-giving love of one man's life becomes the treasure of all humans and the entirety of creation. The Church celebrates in faith the memory of what God has done to teach, save, heal, and liberate us from falling into the abyss of hopelessness and death. The Church is the capacious space where the stories of the great deeds of God are celebrated in the stories or narratives of the acts of the saints. This is what I think of when I read Hebrews 12:1, that we are surrounded by a cloud of witnesses. The mystery of being surrounded by God, the saints, the angels, family, friends, and the earth our home is perpetually like God's burning bush, which emits every moment the effulgence of God's love, grace, and power. When one truly enters this mystery, we cannot be afraid of what is to come. This memory of being surrounded should elicit an inner strength and character in the storms of life, because one sees oneself as belonging to a network of relationships and equipped with a relational resilience to fight evil in the world that is both horizontal (with all things in the created order), and vertical (with all the spiritual gifts and beings in the heavenly places). This history of being surrounded takes us back to our roots—we are heirs of this beautiful heritage that goes back to the Trinity.

We are not abandoned to battle the challenges of life alone. I am a part of this stream of God's love, and of grace, overflowing with power that is beyond me. Our daily efforts to bring this present world with all its ambiguities to conform to God's will are potentiated by this realization, that the work that we do and the life that we lead are filled with the mystery of divine presence and love. So, I can say that my life is not my own. This gives one the freedom to live fully without fear, and offers the willing soul a rationale to embrace the path of humility and open one up to being used by God to realize in history God's will for creation. This is the openness we see in Mary, who is not afraid to believe that what was promised her by God will be fulfilled (Luke 1:45). She is filled with grace, because she is empty of herself, and of pride, self-assurance, attachments to idols, and any narcissistic tendencies. She makes herself available to love. She hopes against hope. She carries hope in her because she freely conceives God in her womb and freely contemplates hope in her heart. As the Scripture says, "She carried all these things" (the promises of God) in her heart (Luke 2:19). Mary also exercises a similar dynamic faith and active and courageous disposition of trust and hope when at the foot of the Cross she ponders the contradictions of life and suffering. She stands strong and tall in hope at the foot of the Cross, and is not bowed down in grief and despair, because she believes the boundary of her human pain and loss at the death of her Son will be shattered by the boundless power of God on the Day of Resurrection. God will manifest to the whole world the triumph of love and the way of the Lord.

The Praxis of Hope

How can the Church today develop and embrace the hope that meets the needs of this present moment? Theological ethicists are expected to provide the Church today with the tools to do this. However, they cannot themselves contribute to this important task if they are caught in the intellectual logjam that often imprisons us. We can have a rigid attachment to our perspectives, in schismatic binary thinking that limits people's ability to listen to new insights and points of view that challenge time-worn certainties. This enslavement to one's viewpoint is not simply an intellectual staple at the dinner table of conservatives. It is also found aplenty on the intellectual menu of progressives—all of us have sinned and fallen short of the truth of God (cf. Romans 3:23). As theologians and pastors, we need ongoing conversion as an intellectual and spiritual pilgrimage that can flood our souls and our minds with new truths, new springs of love, and new moments of hope. Only hopeful and humble theological ethicists can offer the Church and the world ethics of hope. Angry, divisive, self-assured, and dour theological ethicists prolong the sadness and anger in the Church and in the world. Such theologians provide, sometimes without intending it, the chains to hold all of us in a fearful and painful cycle of intellectual, doctrinal, and ethical warfare. This has seized the Church even at this kairotic moment.

The Church exists as a space of belonging where all God's people can find a home. The Church serves as a site of learning, where people unlearn false realities and embrace the truth of God. This can help one, for example, to discover the beauty of diversity through the trinitarian model. In this kind of space, people are inspired to embrace ethical choices that are inspired by the Gospel, and which help to bring about in history the fruits of the reign of God. The hope that the Church gives to the world can offer a reversal of history, through practices and daily choices that provide an alternative history from the current cycle of decay. This comes through a reenacting of what happened at Calvary—the selfless and non-transactional love of God. The Cross is a sign of the refusal to act in a selfish or prideful way. It is a sign of refusing to objectify or abuse others, and it is the boundary beyond which human evil and injustice cannot go. The Cross offers a logic for an ethics of hope that is grounded on the use of power to do good in an unrestricted, unconditional, and inclusive manner. "When I am lifted upon the Cross, I will draw ALL people to myself" (John 12:32).

The Church is a space for reimagining a better possible world through cruciform faith, love, and hope. The Church is an inclusive space where people are moved to embrace life-giving ethics of hope, which makes concrete in people's lives and cultures the saving and transforming grace of the Risen Lord. This saving hope is particularly needed in those places where people feel deep wounds and suffer injustice and the painful consequences of oppression and suffering. Hope is a movement that shows people in their lived realities that their history is not contaminated, but that there is a reversal which is real in an experience of redemptive history today. Christian hope is not an idea or an ideal, it is a real practice of reversal of history, a concrete emergence of a new agency. It is a new experience of triumph and release from the chokehold of history for those who have been battered by poverty, oppression, war, discrimination, racism, injustice, manipulation, and other social evils driven by greed, selfishness, and cultural and nationalistic hubris, built on the smelly foundation of neoliberal capitalism.

For this hope to come upon the earth, there is need for the Church and God's people to move away from what I call the pleasant poetics of hope, to a prophetic ethics of hope. The pleasant poetics of hope is the all-too-familiar reaction to social problems where church leaders and ministers use moral suasion and spiritual platitudes to drown the historical injustice and deep human pain borne by those who suffer. It is also found in the pleasant and feel-good prayers and wishes to the poor and the victims of history that God will take care of them, and things will be well someday without telling them the "how." These preachings are appealing to the ears, but end up being only empty rhetoric. People's hope for change might temporarily be raised, but will ultimately fail to show how change could come about. It is like the preaching which many of our African ancestors heard in the slave plantations, which spoke to them of a God who is pacified by their suffering and who accepts their death as an offering like that of God's crucified Son, all while keeping them enslaved!

The pleasant poetics of hope also blames the victims of history as violent, terrorizing, lazy, and criminal—inviting them to change their lives so that their conditions would change. However, those who mouth these bromides fail to speak of conversion of hearts for those who benefit from white privilege, and the long exploitation of people in the Global South by Western nations, churches, and peoples. It does not show how the Church could begin a process of reform of our institutional culture and hierarchy of power and privilege, which are often coupled to political ideologies and systems of racism, oppression, and neoliberal capitalism. The pleasant poetics of hope is a false hope, because it fails to address how to change the factors that have conspired to bring the sad circumstances under which many people in the world have suffered for centuries. The pleasant poetics of hope is an empty religious noise that often ends up emptying the Gospel of its force, saving truth, and power.

The prophetic ethics of hope, in contrast, is the commitment by the Church and all her members (theologians, pastors, leaders, and all) to become architects of a new future, by embracing the practices and priorities of the Lord Jesus, especially at the foot of the Cross. It is born from an ecclesial practice that by its very character and manifestations is a reimagination of a new future and of a possible new world and a possible new Church. It challenges all in the Church to a change in attitude and behaviors through the conversion of hearts. This change could begin simply by asking whether what we see in our world today represents to any discerning mind God's will for creation. One can also focus more attention on how one is benefiting from the existing social and ecclesial hierarchies, and the need for all of us to exit the path of privilege and power built on and sustained by injustice, falsehood, oppression, and manipulation of the truth and the poor, even in our religious institutions. The prophetic ethics of hope leads to a change in mind-sets, a change in our ecclesial priorities and practices, and a change in the Church's teaching, institutional culture, and hierarchy of power and privilege. The Church can become truly a poor and merciful church. This can lead to a firm resolve and commitment to turn our anger and outrage at the senseless and sinful suffering in the world today into daily acts of reversal of history, by working for the realization of a just and peaceful world for all of God's people, and especially the marginalized.

An essential part of this kind of hope is that it is prophetic and oriented to practice. It is prophetic because it requires listening to the cries of the victims of history, and correctly reading the signs of our present times through the pathos and cries of those who live at the existential peripheries of life. By embodying the pathos of the poor and the broken throughout its systems and structures, the Church becomes a credible site for reimagining a different world, while amplifying the voices of the poor in a noisy world. As prophets of hope, theological ethicists of the Church and all Christians must become architects of a different future. This means that our Church's central mission should be informed by the cries and anguish of the long-suffering victims of history, and that our liturgies celebrate the diversity in our traditions. Our Church needs to provide a space to lament for those who have been held down by the injustice partly started and legitimated through some of the teachings and practices of churches, and the dysfunctional ethics of some theological traditions and theodicies.

Hope is practice. Hope is a story of a new event emerging from an unacceptable one. Hope is a person, Jesus Christ, the boundary beyond which evil cannot go. Those who come to him and embrace his priorities and practices become also borders between good and evil. This is so because hope is concerned with constructing a new pathway of reversal, through a conscious counter-witnessing which can change the status quo. It is liberating and humbling to know that we can develop the ethics of hope for our times. This ethics can strengthen the agency of the oppressed to become architects in their own history. Theological ethicists must commit themselves to a new way of life, to a new ethics, and a new moral and spiritual journey. This can transform the inner life of the Church and the hearts of all men and women, and guide history in the direction of love, justice, and peace for all.

African theologians must become the finger of John, pointing to signs of the saving, liberating, and healing hope in the Church and in the world.

We must pay attention to the narratives of God's people, and how we can landscape the ethics of hope from the rough ground and the stony pathways where people of love and faith are refusing to allow God's seeds of promise to die for the poor, betrayed, and forsaken in Africa and anywhere in the world. Hope is what history becomes when faith is translated into daily praxis through courageous commitments to resist evil and to bring about good through self-sacrificing love for another, especially those who suffer the ravages of history.

Bibliography

Achebe, Chinua. *Home and Exile*. Edinburgh: Canongate, 2003.
Achebe, Chinua. *Hopes and Impediments: Selected Essays*. New York: Anchor, 1990.
Achebe, Chinua. *Things Fall Apart*. New York: Anchor, 1994.
Adichie, Chimamanda Ngozi. "The Danger of a Single Story." TED talk, July, 2009. https://www.ted.com/talks/chimamanda_ngozi_adichie_the_danger_of_a_single_story.
Adler, Jonathan M., Ariana F. Turner, Kathryn M. Brookshier, et al. "Variation in Narrative Identity Is Associated with Trajectories of Mental Health over Several Years." *Journal of Personality and Social Psychology* 108, no. 3 (2015): 476.
Akinwale, Anthony. "Religion as a Moral Virtue: Thomas Aquinas and a Recent Poll." CATHAN Presidential Address, 2004.
Anderson, Allan. *African Reformation: African Initiated Christianity in the 20th Century*. Trenton, NJ: Africa World Press, 2001.
Anderson, Allan. *An Introduction to Pentecostalism*. Cambridge: Cambridge University Press, 2008.
Asti, Francesco. *Per una theologica del popolo di Dio: Principio unitario, forme, paradigme e prospettive*. Rome: Libreria Editrice Vaticana, 2022.
Barclay, William. *Turning to God: Conversion in the New Testament*. London: Epworth, 1963.
Barrett, David. *Schism and Renewal in Africa: An Analysis of Six Thousand Contemporary Movements*. Nairobi: Oxford University Press, 1968.
Bassard, Katherine Clay. "The Daughters' Arrival: The Earliest Black Women's Writing Community." *Callaloo* 19, no. 2 (1996): 513.
Bayart, Jean-François. *The State in Africa: The Politics of the Belly*, 2nd ed. Cambridge: Polity Press, 2009.

BBC News. "Nigeria Leads in Religious Belief." *BBC One-Minute World News*, February 26, 2004. http://news.bbc.co.uk/2/hi/programmes/wtwtgod/3490490.stm.

Bediako, Kwame. *Jesus and the Gospel in Africa, History and Experience*. With an introduction by Hans Visser and Gillian Bediako. Maryknoll, NY: Orbis Books, 2004.

Bediako, Kwame. "Understanding African Theology in the 20th Century." *Themelios: An International Bulletin for Theological and Religious Studies Students* 20, no. 1 (1994): 16–18.

Benedict XVI. "Address to Members of the Special Council for Africa of the Synod of Bishops." Yaoundé, March 18, 2009. *Acta Apostolicae Sedis* (AAS) 101 (2009): 310.

Benedict XVI and Robert Cardinal Sarah. *From the Depths of Our Hearts: Priesthood, Celibacy, and the Crisis of the Catholic Church*. Translated by Michael J. Miller. San Francisco: Ignatius, 2020.

Benjamin, Walter. "Excavation and Memory." In *Selected Writings*, vol. 2: *1927–1934*, translated by Rodney Livingstone et al., edited by Michael W. Jennings, Howard Eiland, and Gary Smith. Cambridge, MA: Belknap Press of Harvard University Press, 1999.

Berger, Peter L. *The Sacred Canopy: Elements of a Sociological Theory of Religion*. New York: Anchor, 1990.

Berner, Ulrich. "Africa and the Origin of the Science of Religion: Max Müller (1823–1900) and James George Frazer (1854–1941) on African Religions." In *European Traditions in the Study of Religion in Africa*, edited by Frieder Ludwig and Afe Adogame. Wiesbaden: Harrassowitz Verlag, 2004.

Bevans, Stephen. *Community of Missionary Disciples: The Continuing Creation of the Church*. Maryknoll, NY: Orbis Books, 2024.

Bevans, Stephen. *Models of Contextual Theology*. Maryknoll, NY: Orbis Books, 2001.

Bongmba, Elias K. *The Dialectics of Transformation in Africa*. New York: Palgrave Macmillan, 2006.

Bongmba, Elias Kifon, ed. *The Routledge Handbook of African Theology*. London: Routledge, 2020.

Bontemps, Arna. "The Slave Narrative: An American Genre." In *Great Slave Narratives*, edited by Arna Bontemps. Boston: Beacon, 1969.

Bortoli, Ferruccio de. "Benedetto XVI non è una statua Partecipa alla vita della Chiesa." *Corriere della Sera*, March 5, 2014. https://www.corriere.it/cronache/14_marzo_04/vi-racconto-mio-primo-anno-papa-90f8a1c4-a3eb-11e3-b352-9ec6f8a34ecc.shtml.

Boulaga, Eboussi. *Christianity without Fetishes*. Maryknoll, NY: Orbis Books, 1981.

Boyd, Gregory A. *The Crucifixion of the Warrior God: Interpreting the Old Testament's Violent Portraits of God in Light of the Cross*. Minneapolis: Fortress, 2017.

Bujo, Bénézet. *African Theology in Its Social Context*. Translated by John O'Donohue. Maryknoll, NY: Orbis Books, 1992.

Bujo, Bénézet. *The Ethical Dimension of Community: The African Model and the Dialogue between North and South*. Translated by Cecelia Namulondo Nganda. Nairobi: Paulines Publications Africa, 1998.

Bujo, Bénézet. *Foundations of an African Ethic: Beyond the Universal Claims of Western Morality*. Translated by Brian McNeil. New York: Crossroad, 2001.

Bujo, Bénézet. *The Impact of the Our Father on Everyday Life: Meditations of an African Theologian*. Translated by Sippala Humphrey and Silvano Borruso. Nairobi: Paulines Publications, Africa, 2002.

Bujo, Bénézet. "Introduction to the Tshibangu-Vanneste Debate." In vol. 1 of *African Theology: The Contribution of the Pioneers*, edited by Bénézet Bujo and Juvenal Ilunga. Nairobi: Paulines Publications Africa, 2003.

Bujo, Bénézet. "Vincent Mulago: An Enthusiast of African Theology." In *African Theology: The Contribution of the Pioneers*, edited by Bénézet Bujo and Juvénal Ilunga Muya. Nairobi, Kenya: Paulines Publications Africa, 2003.

Burchardt, Marian. "Salvation as Cultural Distinction: Religion and Neoliberalism in Urban Africa." *Cultural Sociology* 14, no. 2 (2020): 7.

Busch, David. "Missionary Theology in Africa." *Journal of Theology for Southern Africa*, no. 49 D (1984): 19.

Butler, Judith. *Frames of War: When Is Life Grievable?* London: Verso, 2016.

Buxton, Thomas Fowell. *Memoirs of Sir Thomas Fowell Buxton, Bart*. Edited by Charles Buxton. London: John Murray, 1877.

Calderisi, Robert. *Earthly Mission: The Catholic Church and World Development*. New Haven, CT: Yale University Press, 2013.

Catholic Information Service for Africa. "Ghana: Speak with One Voice, Cardinal Sarah Tells African Bishops." *Cisa News Africa*, June 12, 2015. http://cisanewsafrica.com/ghana-speak-with-one-voice-cardinal-sarah-tells-african-bishops-on-synod/.

Cavanaugh, William T. *The Uses of Idolatry*. Oxford: Oxford University Press, 2024.

Certeau, Michel de. "Railway Navigation and Incarceration." Translated by Steven Rendall. In *The City Cultures Reader*, 2nd ed., edited by Malcolm Miles, Tim Hall, and Iain Borden. London, Routledge, 2004.

Chabal, Patrick. *Africa: The Politics of Suffering and Smiling*. Pietermaritzburg, South Africa: University of Kwazulu-Natal Press, 2009.

Chabal, Patrick, and Jean-Pascal Daloz, *Africa Works: Disorder as Political Instrument*. Oxford: International African Institute, 1999.

Chinweizu, Onwuchekwa Jemie, and Ihechukwu Madubuike. *Toward the Decolonization of African Literature: Library of African Diasporic Literature and Criticism*. Washington, DC: Howard University Press, 1983.

Chitando, Ezra, and Joram Tarusarira. Introduction to *Religion and Human Security in Africa*, edited by Ezra Chitando and Joram Tarusarira. London: Routledge, 2019.

Clark, Carroll D. "The Contribution of William Fielding Ogburn." *Midwest Sociologist* 16, no. 2 (Spring 1954): 6.

Clements, Fiona, and Fiona Tasker. "Living through the Paschal Mystery: Surviving Cancer Narratives Told by Older Roman Catholic Women." *Journal of Religion, Spirituality & Aging* 27, no. 1 (2015): 48–66.

Cocks, Joan. "The Violence of Structures and the Violence of Foundings." *New Political Science* 34, no. 2 (2012): 221–27.

Cone, James. *The Cross and the Lynching Tree*. Maryknoll, NY: Orbis Books, 2011.

Congar, Yves. *True and False Reform in the Church*. Translated by Paul Philibert. Collegeville, MN: Liturgical Press, 2011.

Conradie, Sas. *Towards Transformational Theology and Theological Education in Africa*. Accessed July 17, 2024. https://acteaweb.org/wp-content/uploads/2022/02/Towards-Transformational-Theology-booklet.pdf.

Copeland, M. Shawn. *Knowing Christ Crucified: The Witness of African American Religious Experience*. Maryknoll, NY: Orbis Books, 2018.

Copeland, M. Shawn. "Wading through Many Sorrows: Toward a Theology of Suffering in a Womanist Perspective." In *Womanist Theological Ethics: A*

Reader, edited by Katie Geneva Cannon, Emilie M. Townes and Angela D. Sims. Louisville, KY: WJK, 2011.

Costello, David. "Reconciliation and Prayer." In *Spirituality and Reconciliation*, edited by Tom Curran, 48–51. Tangaza Occasional Paper, no. 4. Nairobi: Paulines Publications Africa, 1997.

Creach, Jerome F. D. *Violence in Scripture*. Louisville, KY: Westminster John Knox Press, 2013.

Culley, Robert C. "An Approach to the Problem of Oral Tradition." *Vetus Testamentum* 13, no. 2 (April 2, 1963): 113–25.

Daley, Patricia O. *Gender and Genocide in Burundi: The Search for Spaces of Peace in the Great Lakes Region*. Kampala, Uganda: Fountain, 2008.

Davis, Angela Y. *Freedom Is a Constant Struggle: Ferguson, Palestine, and the Foundations of a Movement*. Chicago: Haymarket, 2016.

Delio, Ilia. *The Humility of God: A Franciscan Perspective*. Cincinnati, OH: Franciscan Media, 2005.

Department of Systematic Theology. *Incarnating Christ Today*. Nairobi: Paulines Publications Africa, 2001.

Dhavamony, Mariasusai. "Religion II: Phenomenology." In *Dictionary of Fundamental Theology*, edited by René Latourelle and Rino Fisichella. New York: Crossroad, 1994.

Diamond, Jared. *Guns, Germs, and Steel: The Fate of Human Societies*. New York: W. W. Norton, 1999.

Dillard, Angela. *Guess Who's Coming to Dinner Now? Multicultural Conservatism in America*. New York: New York University Press, 2001.

Donovan, Vincent J. *Christianity Rediscovered*. Maryknoll, NY: Orbis Books, 1978.

Douglass, Frederick. *Narrative of the Life of Frederick Douglass, An American Slave, Written by Himself*. Boston: Bedford, 1993.

Douthat, Ross. *To Change the Church: Pope Francis and the Future of Catholicism*. New York: Simon & Schuster, 2018.

Downing, Bridget Agnes. "Karl Rahner's Pastoral Theology: A Study of Its Implications for the Christian in the Modern World." PhD diss., Fordham University, 1986. *ETD Collection for Fordham University*, AAI862854, https://research.library.fordham.edu/dissertations/AAI8628541.

Dube, Musa W. "'God Never Opened the Bible to Me': Women Church Leaders in Botswana." *Studies in World Christianity and Interreligious Relations* 48 (2014): 317–40.

Dwight, J. S. "Christmas Song: Cantique Pour Noel." *Musical World* 19.

Dzubinski, Leanne, and Anneke Stasson. *Women in the Mission of the Church: Their Opportunities and Obstacles throughout Christian History*. Grand Rapids, MI: Baker, 2021.

Easterly, William. *The White Man's Burden: Why the West's Efforts to Aid the Rest Have Done So Much Ill and So Little Good*. New York: Penguin, 2006.

Ecumenical Patriarch Bartholomew. *On Earth as in Heaven: Ecological Vision and Initiatives of Ecumenical Patriarch Bartholomew*. New York: Fordham University Press, 2012.

Edwards, Paul, and Rosalind Shaw. "The Invisible Chi in Equiano's Interesting Narrative." *Journal of Religion in Africa* 19, no. 2 (1989): 146–56.

Ekeh, Peter P. "Development Theory and the African Predicament." *Africa Development/Afrique et Développement* 11, no. 4 (1986): 1–40.

Ela, Jean-Marc. *Afrique: L'Irruption des pauvres: Société contre ingérence, pouvoir et argent*. Paris: L'Harmattan, 1994.

Ela, Jean-Marc. *My Faith as an African*. Translated by John Pairman Brown and Susan Perry. Maryknoll, NY: Orbis Books, 1990.

Ela, Jean-Marc. *Repenser la théologie africaine*. Paris: Karthala, 2003.

Ellis, Stephen. "Tuning in to Pavement Radio." *African Affairs* 88, no. 352 (1989): 321–30.

Ellis, Stephen, and Gerrie ter Haar, "Religion and Politics in Sub-Saharan Africa." *Journal of Modern African Societies* 36, no. 2 (June 1998): 175–201.

Enang, Kenneth. *The Nigerian Catholics and the Independent Churches: A Call to Authentic Faith*, Nairobi: Paulines Publications Africa, 2013.

Equiano, Olaudah. *The Interesting Narrative of the Life of Olaudah Equiano, or Gustavus Vassa, the African*. New York: Simon and Brown, 2012.

Ernest, John. *Liberation Historiography: African American Writers and the Challenge of History, 1794–1861*. Chapel Hill: University of North Carolina Press, 2004.

Ezeugwu, Evaristus Chukwudi, and Gregory Emeka Chinweuba. "The Supreme Being in Igbo Thought: A Reappraisal." *Philosophia* 21 (2018): 26–47.

Ezigbo, Victor I. *Re-imagining African Christologies: Conversing with the Interpretations and Appropriations of Jesus in Contemporary African Christianity*. Eugene, OR: Wipf and Stock, 2010.

Fanon, Frantz. *Black Skin, White Masks*. Translated by Charles Lam Markmann. New York: Grove, 1967.

Forster, Dion A., and H. Jurgens Hendriks. *African Public Theology*. Cumbria, UK: Langham, 2020.
Francis. *Ad Theologiam Promovendam*. Apostolic letter. November 1, 2023. https://www.vatican.va/content/francesco/it/motu_proprio/documents/20231101-motu-proprio-ad-theologiam-promovendam.html.
Francis. "Address of His Holiness Pope Francis to the Italian Theological Association." December 29, 2017. https://www.vatican.va/content/francesco/en/speeches/2017/december/documents/papa-francesco_20171229_associazione-teologica-italiana.html.
Francis. "Chrism Mass Homily of Pope Francis." March 28, 2013. https://www.vatican.va/content/francesco/en/homilies/2013/documents/papa-francesco_20130328_messa-crismale.html.
Francis. *Evangelii Gaudium*. Apostolic exhortation. November 24, 2013. https://www.vatican.va/content/francesco/en/apost_exhortations/documents/papa-francesco_esortazione-ap_20131124_evangelii-gaudium.html.
Francis. *Fratelli Tutti*. Encyclical letter. October 3, 2020. https://www.vatican.va/content/francesco/en/encyclicals/documents/papa-francesco_20201003_enciclica-fratelli-tutti.html.
Francis. *Gaudete et Exsultate*. Apostolic exhortation. March 19, 2018. https://www.vatican.va/content/francesco/en/apost_exhortations/documents/papa-francesco_esortazione-ap_20180319_gaudete-et-exsultate.html.
Francis. "Greeting of Pope Francis to the Synod Fathers during the First General Congregation of the Third Extraordinary General Assembly of the Synod Of Bishops." October 6, 2014. https://www.vatican.va/content/francesco/en/speeches/2014/october/documents/papa-francesco_20141006_padri-sinodali.html.
Francis. "Homily of His Holiness Pope Francis, Easter Vigil in the Holy Night of Easter." April 20, 2019. https://www.vatican.va/content/francesco/en/homilies/2019/documents/papa-francesco_20190420_omelia-vegliapasquale.html.
Francis. "Homily of Pope Francis." Mass, imposition of the pallium and bestowal of the fisherman's ring for the beginning of the Petrine Ministry of the Bishop of Rome. March 19, 2013. https://www.vatican.va/content/francesco/en/homilies/2013/documents/papa-francesco_20130319_omelia-inizio-pontificato.html.
Francis. "Homily of Pope Francis." XXVIII World Youth Day. July 27, 2013. https://www.vatican.va/content/francesco/en/homilies/2013/documents/papa-francesco_20130727_gmg-omelia-rio-clero.html.

Francis. *Laudato Si'*. Encyclical letter. May 24, 2015. https://www.vatican.va/content/francesco/en/encyclicals/documents/papa-francesco_20150524_enciclica-laudato-si.html.

Francis. "Letter of His Holiness Pope Francis to the Grand Chancellor of the 'Pontificia Universidad Católica Argentina' for the 100th Anniversary of the Founding of the Faculty of Theology." https://www.vatican.va/content/francesco/en/letters/2015/documents/papa-francesco_20150303_lettera-universita-cattolica-argentina.html.

Francis. *Spes non Confundit*. Bull of Indiction of the Ordinary Jubilee of the Year 2025. May 9, 2024. https://www.vatican.va/content/francesco/en/bulls/documents/20240509_spes-non-confundit_bolla-giubileo2025.html.

Francis. *Veritatis Gaudium*. Apostolic constitution. December 17, 2017. https://www.vatican.va/content/francesco/en/apost_constitutions/documents/papa-francesco_costituzione-ap_20171208_veritatis-gaudium.html.

Gaitskell, Deborah. "Hot Meetings and Hard Kraals: African Bible Women in Transvaal Methodism, 1924–1960." *Journal of Religion in Africa* 30, no. 3 (2000): 277–309.

Geertz, Clifford. *Local Knowledge: Further Essays in Interpretative Anthropology*, 3rd ed. New York: Basic Books, 2003.

Genzlinger, Neil. "Katie Cannon, 68, Dies; Lifted Black Women's Perspective in Theology." *New York Times*, August 14, 2018. https://www.nytimes.com/2018/08/14/obituaries/katie-cannon-68-dies-lifted-black-womens-perspective-in-theology.html.

Gerhardsson, Birger. *Memory and Manuscript: Oral Tradition and Written Transmission in Rabbinic Judaism and Early Christianity*. Grand Rapids, MI: Eerdmans, 1998.

Gerstenberger, Erhard, and Wolfgang Schrage, *Suffering: Biblical Encounters Series*. Translated by John Steely. Nashville, TN: Parthenon Press, 1980.

Gifford, Paul. *Christianity, Development and Modernity in Africa*. London: Hurst, 2015.

Gilkes, Cheryl Townsend. "'Go and Tell Mary and Martha': The Spirituals, Biblical Options for Women, and Cultural Tensions in the African American Religious Experience." In *Womanist Theological Ethics: A Reader*, edited by Katie Geneva Cannon, Emilie M. Townes, and Angela D. Sims. Louisville, KY: WJK, 2011.

Girard, Jocelyn. "Quels intérêts sert le cardinal Sarah?" *Présence-Information Religieuse*, January 21, 2020. http://presence-info.ca/article/opinion/quels-interets-sert-le-cardinal-sarah/.

Goldenberg, David. *The Curse of Ham: Race and Slavery in Early Judaism, Christianity, and Islam*. Princeton, NJ: Princeton University Press, 2003.

Gordon, David M. "Slavery and Redemption in the Catholic Missions of the Upper Congo, 1878–1909." *Slavery & Abolition* 38, no. 3 (2017): 577–600.

Gray, Stephen. "Missionary Researchers and Researching Missions: A South African View of Cultural Colonisation at the Millennium." *Journal of Theology for Southern Africa* 105 (November 1999): 17–25.

Gutiérrez, Gustavo. *The God of Life*. Maryknoll, NY: Orbis Books, 1991.

Gutiérrez, Gustavo. *On Job: God-Talk and the Suffering of the Innocent*. Translated by Matthew J. O'Connell. Maryknoll, NY: Orbis Books, 1987.

Gutiérrez, Gustavo. "Theological Language: Fullness in Silence." In *The Density of the Present: Selected Writings*. Maryknoll, NY: Orbis Books, 1999.

Hanciles, Jehu. "Back to Africa: Abolitionists and Black Missionaries." In *African Christian Religion: An African Story*, edited by Ogbu U. Kalu. Trenton, NJ: Africa World Press, 2007.

Hastings, Adrian. *African Christianity: An Essay in Interpretation*. London: Geoffrey Chapman, 1976.

Hastings, Adrian. *The Church in Africa, 1450–1950*. Oxford: Clarendon, 1994.

Haynes, Jonathan. *Nollywood: The Creation of Nigerian Film Genres*. Chicago: University of Chicago Press, 2016.

Healey, Joseph G. *African Stories for Preachers and Teachers*. Nairobi, Kenya: Paulines Publications, 2014.

Heidegger, Martin. *Basic Writings*. Edited by David Farrell Krell and Martin Heidegger. New York: HarperCollins, 1993.

Hundu, Jacob T., and Joseph Azembeh. "Pastorpreneurship: A Critical Analysis of Proliferation of Churches in Nigeria." *SBS Jos J Religious Studies Humanities* 1 (2018): 43.

Idowu, Bolaji. *African Traditional Religion: A Definition*. London: CMS Press, 1973.

Ilo, Stan Chu. "Ebola and the Ravages of History in Paul Farmer: A Catholic Theological Ethical Response to Global Health Inequity in Africa." *Journal of Moral Theology* 4, CTEWC Book Series 4 (February 19, 2023): 271–98.

Ilo, Stan Chu. *The Face of Africa*. Eugene, OR: Wipf & Stock, 2012.

Ilo, Stan Chu, ed. *Handbook of African Catholicism*. Maryknoll, NY: Orbis Books, 2022.

Ilo, Stan Chu. *A Poor and Merciful Church: The Illuminative Ecclesiology of Pope Francis*. Maryknoll, NY: Orbis Books, 2018.

Ilo, Stan Chu. "Reform from the Margins: Pope Francis and the Renewal of Catholic Theology." In *All the Ends of the Earth: Challenge and Celebration of Global Catholicism*, edited by Jane E. Linahan and Cyril Orji. Maryknoll, NY: Orbis Books, 2020.

Ilo, Stan Chu, ed. *Wealth, Health, and Hope in African Christian Religion: The Search for Abundant Life*. Lanham, MD: Lexington Books, 2018.

Ilo, Stan Chu, and Idara Otu. "Theology of Development." In *The Routledge Handbook of African Theology*, edited by Elias Bongmba. New York: Routledge, 2020.

Ilo, Stan Chu, and Gabriel T. Wankar. "Church and Development in African Catholicism." In *Handbook of African Catholicism*, edited by Stan Chu Ilo. Maryknoll, NY: Orbis Books, 2022.

Ilo, Stan Chu, and Gunda Werner. "Identity within Identities: Communicative Theology through Biography." In *Anders Gemeinsam—Gemeinsam Anders? In Ambivalenzen Lebendig Kommunizieren*, edited by Maria Juen. Hergestellt, Germany: Matthias Grunewald, 2015.

Irele, Abiola. "Orality, Literacy, and African Literature." In *African Literature: An Anthology of Criticism and Theory*, edited by Tejumola Olaniyan and Ato Quayson. Malden, MA: Blackwell, 2013.

Jenkins, Philip. *The New Faces of Christianity: Believing the Bible in the Global South*. Oxford: Oxford University Press, 2006.

Jennings, Mark Alan Charles. "Great Risk for the Kingdom: Pentecostal-Charismatic Growth Churches, Pastorpreneurs, and Neoliberalism." In *Religion and Theology: Breakthroughs in Research and Practice*. Hershey, PA: IGI Global, 2020.

John Paul II. *Fides et Ratio*. Encyclical letter. September 14, 1998. https://www.vatican.va/content/john-paul-ii/en/encyclicals/documents/hf_jp-ii_enc_14091998_fides-et-ratio.html.

John Paul II. *Tertio Millennio Adveniente*. Apostolic letter. November 10, 1994. https://www.vatican.va/content/john-paul-ii/en/apost_letters/1994/documents/hf_jp-ii_apl_19941110_tertio-millennio-adveniente.html.

Kalu, Ogbu U. "The Gods in Retreat: Models for Interpreting Religious Change in Africa." In *The Gods in Retreat: Continuity and Change in African Religions*, edited by Emefie Ikenga Metuh. Enugu, Nigeria: Fourth Dimension, 1986.

Kalu, Ogbu U. "Introduction: The Shape and Flow of African Church Historiography." In *African Christianity: An African Story*, edited by Ogbu Kalu. Trenton, NJ: African World Press, 2007.

Kalu, Ogbu U. *Power, Poverty and Prayer: The Challenges of Poverty and Pluralism in African Christianity, 1960–1996*. Trenton, NJ: Africa World Press, 2006.

Kasper, Walter. *That They May All Be One: The Call to Unity Today*. New York: Burns and Oates, 2004.

Kato, Byang. *Theological Pitfalls in Africa*. Kisumu, Kenya: Evangel, 1975.

Katongole, Emmanuel. "Africa." In *The Blackwell Companion to Catholicism*, vol. 69, edited by James J. Buckley, Frederick C. Bauerschmidt, and Trent Pomplun. New York: John Wiley & Sons, 2010.

Katongole, Emmanuel. *Born from Lament: The Theology and Politics of Hope in Africa*. Grand Rapids, MI: Eerdmans, 2017.

Katongole, Emmanuel. *The Sacrifice of Africa: A Political Theology for Africa*. Grand Rapids, MI: Eerdmans, 2011.

Katongole, Emmanuel. *Who Are My People? Love, Violence, and Christianity in Sub-Saharan Africa*. South Bend, IN: University of Notre Dame Press, 2022.

Keenan, James F., ed. *Catholic Theological Ethics Past, Present, and Future: The Trento Conference*. Maryknoll, NY: Orbis Books, 2011.

Kelber, Werner H. *The Oral and the Written Gospel: The Hermeneutics of Speaking and Writing in the Synoptic Tradition, Mark, Paul, and Q*. Philadelphia: Fortress, 1983.

Kellerman, Christopher J. *All Oppression Shall Cease: A History of Slavery, Abolitionism, and the Catholic Church*. Maryknoll, NY: Orbis Books, 2022.

Kenyatta, Jomo. *Facing Mount Kenya*. New York: Vintage Books, 1965.

Kenzo, Mabiala Justin-Robert. "Thinking Otherwise about Africa: Postcolonialism, Postmodernism, and the Future of African Theology." *Exchange* 31 (2002): 323–41.

Kerr, David A., and Kenneth R. Ross, eds. *Edinburgh 2010: Mission Then and Now*. Oxford: Regnum, 2009.

Kilby, Karen. *God, Evil and the Limits of Theology*. London: T&T Clark, 2021.

Kilby, Karen. "The Seduction of Kenosis." In *Suffering and the Christian Life*, edited by Karen Kilby and Rachel Davies. London: T&T Clark, 2021.

Kilby, Karen, and Rachel Davies, eds. *Suffering and the Christian Life*. London: T&T Clark, 2021.

Kinkupu, Léonard Santedi, Gérard Bissainthe, and Meinrad Hebga. *Des prêtres noirs s'interrogent: Cinquante ans après*. Paris: Karthala, 2006.

Kolawole, Mary E. Modupe. "Women's Oral Genres." In *African Literature: An Anthology of Criticism and Theory*, edited by Tejumola Olaniyan and Ato Quayson. Malden, MA: Blackwell, 2007.

Kristof, Nicholas. "In Sudan, Evil Is Resilient—and So Is Heroism." *New York Times*, September 29, 2024. Accessed October 11, 2024.

Kugler, Gili. "The Threat of Annihilation of Israel in the Desert: An Independent Tradition within Two Stories." *Catholic Biblical Quarterly* 78, no. 4 (2016): 632–47.

Latourelle, René, and Rino Fisichella, eds. *Dictionary of Fundamental Theology*. New York: Crossroad, 2000.

Levitt, Peggy. *God Needs No Passport*. New York: New Press, 2007.

Lonergan, Bernard. *Method in Theology*. Toronto: University of Toronto Press, 1999.

Macey, David. "I Am My Own Foundation." *Theory, Culture & Society* 27, no. 7–8 (2010): 33–51. https://doi.org/10.1177/0263276410383707.

Macquarrie, John. *The Humility of God*. London: SCM, 1978.

Magesa, Laurenti. *African Religion: The Moral Traditions of Abundant Life*. Maryknoll, NY: Orbis Books, 2002.

Magesa, Laurenti. "Epilogue: Dreaming about the Future of the Church in Africa." In *Handbook of African Catholicism*, ed. Stan Chu Ilo. Maryknoll, NY: Orbis Books, 2022.

Magesa, Laurenti. *What Is Not Sacred?: African Spirituality*. Maryknoll, NY: Orbis Books, 2013.

Malraux, André. *Picasso's Mask*. Translated by June Guicharnaud with Jacques Guicharnaud. New York: Holt, Rinehart and Winston, 1976.

Maluleke, Tinyinko. "The Rediscovery of the Agency of Africans: An Emerging Paradigm of Post–Cold War and Post-Apartheid Black and African Theology." *Journal of Theology for Southern Africa* 108 (November 2000): 411–12.

Maluleke, Tinyiko. "Why I Am Not a Public Theologian." *Ecumenical Review* 73, no. 2 (April 2021): 307–8.

Mana, Ka. *Christians and Churches of Africa Envisioning the Future: Salvation in Jesus Christ and the Building of a New African Society*. Akropong-Akuapen, Ghana: Regnum Africa, 2002.

Marcel, Gabriel. *Being and Having*. New York: Harper Torchbooks, 1965.

Marsh, Charles. "Introduction: Lived Theology: Method, Style, and Pedagogy." In *Lived Theology: New Perspectives on Method, Style, and Pedagogy*, edited by Charles Marsh, Peter Slade, and Sarah Azaransky. Oxford: Oxford University Press, 2017.

Marsh, Charles, Peter Slade, and Sarah Azaransky, eds. *Lived Theology: New Perspectives on Method, Style, and Pedagogy*. Oxford: Oxford University Press, 2017.

Martin, Dale B. *Sex and the Single Savior: Gender and Sexuality in Biblical Interpretation*. Louisville, KY: Westminster John Knox Press, 2006.

Massingale, Bryan. "Has the Silence Been Broken? Catholic Theological Ethics and Racial Justice." *Theological Studies* 75, no. 1 (2014): 133–55.

Maxwell, David. "Christianity and the African Imagination." In *Christianity and the African Imagination: Essays in Honor of Adrian Hastings*, edited by David Maxwell and Ingrid Lawrie. Leiden: Brill, 2002.

Mbefo, Luke Nnamdi. *Christian Theology and African Heritage*. Onitsha, Nigeria: Spiritan, 1996.

Mbembe, Achille. "Pouvoir, violence et accumulation." *Politique Africaine* 39 (1990): 7–24.

Mbembe, Achille. "Thinking about the World from the Vantage Point of Africa." In *To Write the Africa World*, edited by Achille Mbembe and Felwine Sarr. Cambridge, UK: Polity, 2023.

McDermott, John. "Suffering." In *Dictionary of Fundamental Theology*, edited by René Latourelle and Rino Fisichella. New York: Crossroad, 2000,

McElwee, Joshua J. "Bishops Deliberate Whether One Rule Applies to All Divorced People after 'Amoris Laetitia.'" *National Catholic Reporter*, October 6, 2017. https://www.ncronline.org/news/bishops-deliberate-whether-one-rule-applies-all-divorced-people-after-amoris-laetitia.

McKenzie, John L. *Dictionary of the Bible*. New York: Macmillan, 1965.

McVeigh, Malcolm J. *God in Africa: Conceptions of God in African Traditional Religion and Christianity*. Cape Cod, MA: Claude Stark, 1974.

Mejia, Rodrigo. "'*Matatu* Theology': My Experience as a Hekima Pioneer Living in St. Joseph the Worker Parish, Kangemi." *Hekima Review*, no. 68 (May 2024).

Metuh, Emefie Ikenga. *African Religions in Western Conceptual Schemes: The Problems of Interpretations.* Ibadan, Nigeria: Pastoral Institute, 1987.

Metuh, Emefie Ikenga. *Comparative Studies in African Traditional Religions.* Onitsha, Nigeria: Imico, 1987.

Metuh, Emifie Ikenga. *God and Man in African Religion.* Enugu, Nigeria: SNAAP Press, 1999.

Michie, Susan, Maartje M. Van Stralen, and Robert West. "The Behavior Change Wheel: A New Method for Characterizing and Designing Behavior Change Interventions." *Implementation Science* 6, no. 42 (April 23, 2011): 1–12.

Milingo, Emmanuel. *Face to Face with the Devil.* Victoria, Australia, 1991.

Moltmann, Jürgen. *The Gospel of Liberation.* Translated by H. Wayne Pipkin. Waco, TX: Word Books, 1973.

Moltmann, Jürgen. *The Spirit of Life: A Universal Affirmation.* Translated by Margaret Kohl. Minneapolis, MN: Fortress, 2001.

Mudimbe, V. Y. *The Invention of Africa: Gnosis, Philosophy, and the Order of Knowledge.* Bloomington: Indiana University Press, 1988.

Mugambi, Jesse N. K. *The Church in Africa: Towards a Theology of Reconstruction.* Nairobi, Kenya: AACC, 1991.

Mugambi, Jesse N. K. *Critiques of Christianity in African Literature.* Nairobi: East African Educational, 1992.

Mulago, Vincent. "Traditional African Religion and Christianity." In *African Traditional Religions in Contemporary Society*, edited by Jacob K. Olupona. New York: Paragon House, 1991.

Ngong, David Tonghou. "Africa and the Christian Doctrine of God." In *A New History of African Christian Thought: From Cape to Cairo*, edited by David Tonghou Ngong. New York: Routledge, 2017.

Nolan, Albert. *Hope in an Age of Despair.* Edited by Stan Muyebe. Maryknoll, NY: Orbis Books, 2010.

Nyamiti, Charles. "The Doctrine of God." In *A Reader in African Christian Theology*, edited by John Parratt. London: SPCK, 1997.

Nyamiti, Charles. "Reply to Aylward Shorter's Review." *African Ecclesial Review* 20, no. 3 (June 1978): 169–75.

Nyamiti, Charles. *Studies in African Christian Theology*. Vol. 1 of *Jesus Christ, the Ancestor of Humankind: Methodological and Trinitarian Foundations*. Nairobi: CUEA, 2005.

Obadare, Ebenezer. *Pentecostal Republic: Religion and the Struggle for State Power in Nigeria*. London: Bloomsbury, 2018.

Obiechina, Emmanuel N. *Language and Theme: Essays on African Literature*. Washington, DC: Howard University Press, 1990.

Obiechina, Emmanuel N. *Nchetaka: The Story, Memory and Continuity in Igbo Culture*. Ahajioku Lecture 1994. Owerri, Nigeria: Ministry of Information and Social Development, 1994.

Oden, Thomas. *How Africa Shaped the Christian Mind: Rediscovering the African Seedbed of Western Christianity*. Downers Grove, IL: IVP Academic, 2010.

Odozor, Paulinus. "One and the Same? The Debate over God-Language in African Christianity." In *Joseph Ratzinger and the Future of African Theology*, ed. Maurice Ashley Agbaw-Ebai and Matthew Levering. Eugene, OR: Pickwick Publishers, 2021.

Oduyoye, Mercy Amba. *Hearing and Knowing: Theological Reflections on Christianity in Africa*. Maryknoll, NY: Orbis Books, 1993.

Oduyoye, Mercy Amba, and Musimbi Kanyaro, eds. *The Will to Arise: Women, Tradition, and the Church in Africa*. Maryknoll, NY: Orbis Books, 1997.

Ogburn, William Fielding. *Social Change With Respect to Culture and Original Nature (1922)*. Lavergne, TN: Kessinger, 2009.

Okorocha, Cyril C. *The Meaning of Religious Conversion in Africa: The Case of the Igbo of Nigeria*. Aldershot: Avebury, 1987.

Olupona, Jacob K. *African Religions: A Very Short Introduction*. New York: Oxford University Press USA, 2014.

Olupona, Jacob K. "Major Issues in the Study of African Traditional Religion." In *African Traditional Religions in Contemporary Society*, edited by Jacob Olupona. New York: Paragon House, 1991.

Omer, Atalia. *Decolonizing Religion and Peacebuilding*. Oxford: Oxford University Press, 2023.

Onyewuenyi, Innocent Chilaka. *The African Origin of Greek Philosophy: An Exercise in Afrocentrism*. Nsukka, Nigeria: University of Nigeria Press, 2005.

Orobator, Agbonkhianmeghe. *Theology Brewed in an African Pot*. Maryknoll, NY: Orbis Books, 2008.

P'Bitek, Okot. *African Religions in Western Scholarship*. Nairobi: Kenya Literary Bureau, 1970.
Parratt, John, ed. *An Introduction to Third World Theologies*. Cambridge: Cambridge University Press, 2004.
Patterson, Orlando. *Slavery and Social Death: A Comparative Study, with a New Preface*. 2nd ed. Cambridge, MA: Harvard University Press, 1982.
Pew Research Center. "Tolerance and Tension: Islam and Christianity in Sub-Saharan Africa." April 15, 2010.
Phan, Peter. "Doing Theology in World Christianities: Old Tasks, New Ways." In *Relocating World Christianity: Interdisciplinary Studies in Universal and Local Expressions of the Christian Faith*, ed. Joel Cabrita, David Maxwell, and Emma Wild-Wood (Leiden: Brill, 2017).
Pius X. *Il Fermo Proposito*. Encyclical. June 11, 1905. https://www.vatican.va/content/pius-x/en/encyclicals/documents/hf_p-x_enc_11061905_il-fermo-proposito.html.
Pobee, John Samuel, ed. *Exploring Afro-Christology*. Frankfurt: Peter Lang, 1992.
Pontifical Academy for Life. *Rescuing Fraternity Together*. Rome: Librería Editrice Vaticana, 2021.
Putti, Joseph. *Theology as Hermeneutics: Paul Ricoeur's Theory of Text Interpretation and Method in Theology*. San Francisco: International Scholars, 1994.
Rahner, Karl. "Karl Rahner: What the Church Officially Teaches and What the People Actually Believe—1981." In *Readings in Church Authority: Gifts and Challenges for Contemporary Catholicism*, edited by Gerard Manion, Richard Gaillardetz, Jan Kerkhofs, and Kenneth Wilson. Aldershot, England: Ashgate, 2003.
Rapu, Chris Obi, dir. *Living in Bondage*. Nigeria, 1992–93.
Rattray, Robert S. *Religion and Art in Ashanti*. London: Oxford University Press, 1969.
Ratzinger, Joseph. "Christ, Faith and the Challenge of Cultures." Address to the Presidents of the Asian Bishops' Conference, Hong Kong, March 2–5 1993. https://www.vatican.va/roman_curia/congregations/cfaith/incontri/rc_con_cfaith_19930303_hong-kong-ratzinger_en.html sec. 2.
Ratzinger, Joseph. *Introduction to Christianity*. Translated by J. R. Foster. New York: Herder and Herder, 1970.
Ricoeur, Paul. *From Text to Action: Essays in Hermeneutics*. London: Continuum International, 2008.

Ricoeur, Paul. *Hermeneutics and the Human Sciences*. Edited and translated by John B. Thompson. Cambridge: Cambridge University Press, 1981.

Ricoeur, Paul. *Time and Narrative*. Vol. 3. Translated by Kathleen Blamey and David Pellauer. Chicago: University of Chicago Press, 1990.

Robert, Dana L. *Christian Mission: How Christianity Become a World Religion*. Chichester, UK: Wiley-Blackwell, 2009.

Robert, Dana. "World Christianity as a Women's Movement." *International Bulletin of Missionary Research* 30, no. 4 (October 2006): 180–88.

Ryan, Robin. *God and the Mystery of Human Suffering: A Theological Conversation across the Ages*. New York: Paulist Press, 2011.

Sanneh, Lamin. "Christian Mission in the Pluralist Milieu: The African Experience." *Missiology: An International Review* 12, no. 4 (October 1984).

Sanneh, Lamin. *Disciples of All Nations: Pillars of World Christianity*. Oxford: Oxford University Press, 2008.

Sanneh, Lamin. *Encountering the West: Christianity and the Global Cultural Process*. Maryknoll, NY: Orbis Books, 1993.

Sanneh, Lamin. *Whose Religion is Christianity: The Gospel beyond the West*. Grand Rapids, MI: Eerdmans, 2003.

Sarr, Lucie. "The Image Cardinal Robert Sarah Cuts in Africa." *La Croix International*, February 1, 2020. https://international.la-croix.com/fr/afrique/the-image-cardinal-robert-sarah-cuts-in-africa.

Schneider, Joseph. "Cultural Lag: What Is It?" *American Sociological Review* 10, no. 6 (December 1945): 786–91.

Schokel, Luis Alonso. *The Inspired Word: Scripture in the Light of Language and Literature*. Translated by Francis Martin. Montreal: Palm Publishers, 1965.

Schwarz, Hans. *Theology in Global Context*. Grand Rapids, MI: William B. Eerdmans, 2005.

Scott, James C. *Weapons of the Weak: Everyday Forms of Peasant Resistance*. New Haven, CT: Yale University Press, 1985.

Segundo, Juan Luis. *Our Idea of God*. Translated by John Drury. Maryknoll, NY: Orbis Books, 1974.

Segura, Olga. *Birth of a Movement: Black Lives Matter and the Catholic Church*. Maryknoll, NY: Orbis Books, 2021.

Shank, David A. "Mission Relations with the Independent Churches in Africa." *Missiology: An International Review* 13, no. 1 (January 1985): 23–44.

Shaw, R. Daniel. "Beyond Contextualization: Toward a Twenty-First Century Model for Enabling Mission." *International Bulletin of Missionary Research* 34, no. 4 (October 2010): 208–15.

Shaw, Rosalind. "The Invention of 'African Traditional Religion.'" *Religion* 20, no. 4 (October 1990): 339–53.

Shea, William M. "The Subjectivity of the Theologian." *The Thomist* 45, no. 2 (1981): 194–218.

Sigg, Michele Miller. "*The Dictionary of African Christian Biography* and the Story of Ethiopian Christianity," *International Bulletin of Missionary Research* 39, no. 4 (October 1, 2004): 206.

Shorter, Aylward. *African Christian Theology: Adaptation or Incarnation.* Maryknoll, NY: Orbis Books, 1977.

Shorter, Aylward. *Jesus and the Witchdoctor: An Approach to Healing and Wholeness.* Maryknoll, NY: Orbis Books, 1985.

Shorter, Aylward, and Joseph N. Njiru. *New Religious Movements in Africa.* Nairobi: Paulines Publications Africa, 2001.

Sindima, Harvey. *Classical Theories in African Religion.* Trenton, NJ: Africa World Press, 2019.

Smith, Emily Esfahani. *The Power of Meaning: Finding Fulfillment in a World Obsessed with Happiness.* New York: Broadway, 2017.

Smith, Linda Tuhiwai. *Decolonizing Methodologies: Research and Indigenous Peoples.* 2nd ed. London: Zed, 2012.

Sobrino, Jon. *Where Is God? Earthquake, Terrorism, Barbarity, and Hope.* Translated by Margaret Wilde. Maryknoll, NY: Orbis Books, 2004.

Sparks, Kenton L. *Gods Word in Human Words: An Evangelical Appropriation of Critical Biblical Scholarship* (Grand Rapids: Baker Academic, 2008).

Spradley, James P. *Participant Observation.* Fort Worth, TX: Holt, Rinehart and Winston, 1980.

Stanley, Brian. "Africa Through European Christian Eyes: the World Missionary Conference, Edinburgh 1910." In *African Identities and World Christianity in the Twentieth Century*, edited by Klaus Koschorke in cooperation with Jens Holger Schjørring. Wiesbaden, Germany: Harrassowitz Verlag, 2005.

Stanley, Brian. "Discerning the Future of World Christianity: Vision and Blindness at the World Missionary Conference, Edinburgh 1910." In *2010Boston: The Changing Contours of World Mission and Christianity*, edited by Todd M. Johnson, Rodney L. Petersen, Gina Bellofatto, and Travis Myers. Eugene, OR: Pickwick, 2012.

Stanley, Brian. *A World History: Christianity in the Twentieth Century.* Princeton, NJ: Princeton University Press, 2018,

Stark, Rodney. *America's Blessings: How Religion Benefits Everyone, Including Atheists*. West Conshohocken, PA: Templeton, 2013.

Stark, Rodney. *How the West Won: The Neglected Story of the Triumph of Modernity*. Washington, DC: Regnery Gateway, 2014.

Stinton, Diane. "Africa, East and West." In *An Introduction to Third World Theologies*, edited by John Parratt. Cambridge: Cambridge University Press, 2004.

Strandsbjerg, Camilla. "Kérékou, God and the Ancestors: Religion and the Conception of Political Power in Benin." *African Affairs* 99, no. 396 (July 2000): 395–414.

Táíwò, Olúfémi. *How Colonialism Preempted Modernity in Africa*. Bloomington: Indiana University Press, 2010.

Taylor, Keeanga-Yamahtta. "The Emerging Movement for Police and Prison Abolition." *New Yorker*, May 7, 2021. https://www.newyorker.com/news/our-columnists/the-emerging-movement-for-police-and-prison-abolition.

Ter Haar, Gerrie. *How God Became African: African Spirituality and Western Secular Thought*. Philadelphia: University of Pennsylvania Press, 2009.

Tienou, Tite. "Biblical Foundations for African Theology." *Missiology: An International Review* 10, no. 4 (October 1982): 435–48.

Tonstad, Linn. "On Vulnerability." In *Suffering and the Christian Life*, ed. Karen Kilby and Rachel Davies. London: Bloomsbury, 2019.

Tutu, Desmond. "Whither African Theology?" In *Christianity in Independent Africa*, edited by E. Fashole-Luke. London: Rex Collings, 1978.

Tveitereid, Knut. "Lived Theology and Theology in the Lived." In *The Wiley Blackwell Companion to Theology and Qualitative Research*, 1st ed., ed. Peter Ward and Knut Tveitereid. New York: John Wiley & Sons, 2022.

Udelhoven, Bernhard. *Unseen Worlds: Dealing with Spirits, Witchcraft, and Satanism*. Lusaka, Zambia: Fenza, 2015.

Udoh, Enyi Ben. *Guest Christology: An Interpretative View of the Christological Problem in Africa*. Frankfurt: Peter Lang, 1988.

Ukpong, Justin S. "Popular Readings of the Bible in Africa and Implications for Academic Readings: Report on the Field Research Carried Out on Oral Interpretation of the Bible in Port Harcourt Metropolis, Nigeria, under the Auspices of the Bible in Africa Project, 1991–1994." In *The Bible in Africa: Transactions, Trajectories and Trends*, edited by Gerald O. West and Musa Dube. Boston: Brill, 2001.

United States Conference of Catholic Bishops. 2018. "Open Wide Our Hearts: The Enduring Call to Love—A Pastoral Letter Against Racism." https://www.usccb.org/issues-and-action/human-life-and-dignity/racism/upload/open-wide-our-hearts.pdf.

Uzoigwe, G. N. "A Half Century of Historical Writing in Africa, 1950–2000." In *Emergent Themes and Methods in African Studies: Essays in Honor of Adiele E. Afigbo*, edited by Toyin Falola and Adam Paddock. Trenton, NJ: African World Press, 2009.

Uzukwu, Elochukwu. *God, Spirit, and Human Wholeness*. Eugene, OR: Pickwick, 2012.

Uzukwu, Elochukwu E. *A Listening Church: Autonomy and Communion in African Churches*. Maryknoll, NY: Orbis Books, 1996.

Venema, Henry Isaac. *Identifying Selfhood: Imagination, Narrative, and Hermeneutics in the Thought of Paul Ricoeur*. Albany: State University of New York Press, 2000.

Volf, Miroslav. *A Public Faith: How Followers of Christ Should Serve the Common Good*. Grand Rapids, MI: Brazos, 2011.

Walls, Andrew F. *The Cross-Cultural Process in Christian History*. Maryknoll, NY: Orbis Books, 2005.

Walls, Andrew F. "Eusebius Tries Again." In *Enlarging the Story: Perspectives on Writing World Christian History*, edited by Wilbert Shenk. Maryknoll, NY: Orbis Books, 2002,

Walls, Andrew. "Kwame Bediako and Christian Scholarship in Africa." *International Bulletin of Missionary Research* 32, no. 4 (2008): 188–93.

Walls, Andrew F. "Towards Understanding Africa's Place in Christian History." In *Religion in a Pluralistic Society: Essays Presented to Professor C. Baëta*, edited by John S. Pobee, 180–89. Leiden: Brill, 1976.

Ward, Peter, and Knut Tveitereid, eds. *The Wiley Blackwell Companion to Theology and Qualitative Research*, 1st ed. New York: John Wiley & Sons, 2022.

Ware, Frederick L. *African American Theology: An Introduction*. Louisville, KY: Westminster John Knox, 2016.

Ware, Frederick L. "Methodologies in African American Theology." In *The Oxford Handbook of African American Theology*, edited by Katie G. Cannon and Anthony B. Pinn. Oxford: Oxford University Press, 2014.

Weld, Theodore Dwight, Angelina Grimke, and Sarah Grimke, eds. *American Slavery as It Is: Testimony of a Thousand Witnesses*. New York: American Anti-Slavery Society, 1839.

Wells-Oghoghomeh, Alexis S. "Re-evaluating Roots: Slavery as Source and Challenge for African American Theology." In *T&T Clark Handbook of African American Theology*, edited by Antonia Michelle Daymond, Frederick Ware, and Eric Williams. London: T&T Clark, 2019.

Westerlund, David. *African Religion in African Scholarship: A Preliminary Study of the Religious and Political Background*. Stockholm: Almqvist and Wiksell, 1985.

Wijsen, Frans. *Seeds of Conflict in a Haven of Peace: From Religious Studies to Inter-Religious Studies in Africa*. Amsterdam: Rodopi, 2007.

Williams, Chancellor. *The Destruction of Black Civilization*. Chicago: Third World Press, 1987.

Witt, Emily. *Nollywood: The Making of a Film Empire*. New York: Columbia Global Reports, 2017.

Wrogemann, Henning. *Intercultural Theology*. Translated by Karl E. Böhmer. Vol. 1 of *Intercultural Hermeneutics*. Downers Grove, IL: IVP Academic, 2016.

Yetman, Norman R., ed. *Voices from Slavery*. New York: Holt, Rinehart and Winston, 1970.

Index

13th, 221

Academic Staff Union of Universities (ASUU), 147
accountability, theological, 31, 76, 243–44
Achebe, Chinua, 173, 180
Achi, 13, 163
Acholi, 19
ada, 47, 192
Adam, Naima, 5
Adams, Marilyn McCord, 6
Adler, Jonathan, 236–37
Ad Theologiam Promovendam, 55, 57–58, 156, 248
Adu Achi, 192
African Americans
  civil rights, 222, 238
  liberation theology, 216
  oppression, 219–20
  and slave narratives, 230
  and spirituals, 222
  and suffering, 129n5, 240
  theology, 114–16, 217, 239–40

African Catholicism, 27, 35, 70, 79–80, 210
African Charismatic movements, 32, 209–10
African Christianity
  and ancestral tradition, 43, 188, 194, 196
  importance of diversity, 20–21, 32
  and missional theology, 73, 75–76, 206
  vs. Western theologies, 159, 183
African Diaspora, 218
African independent churches (AICs), 85
African National Congress (ANC), 235
African Reformation, 32
African religions
  characteristics, 48, 193
  and ethics, 200
  hellenization of, 198
  homogenization, 18–19
  importance of ancestors, 181, 190–91

African religion *(continued)*
  instrumentalization, 173
  monotheism, 189
  syncretism, 175
  and Western thought, 167
  See also African Traditional Religions
African theologians
  and African society, 17, 42, 60, 64, 69, 71, 80, 85–86, 178–79
  challenges, 21, 58, 62, 87–88, 135, 153
  ecumenical work, 81–82
  education, 67–70
  and missionaries, 20
  and politics, 211
  and scripture, 31–32
  and Western thought, 65, 96–97, 183, 209, 247–48
African theologies
  and African-American theologies, 216–17
  characteristics, 78–79
  cultural context, 30, 86–89, 160–61, 188, 200, 243
  defining, 72–74
  and film, 152
  hermeneutics, 21, 68
  and liberation theology, 116
  origins, 82–83
  and Pentecostal movements, 207
  and synodality, 42
  universality, 37, 157–59
  vs. Western thought, 64, 69
African Traditional Religions (ATRs)
  and ancestral rites, 191–92
  characteristics, 176, 181
  and Christianity, 186–87, 189, 193–94, 212
  depictions of God, 167*n*12
  myth and narrative, 33, 43
  theism, 18–19
Afro-pessimism, 34–35
afterlife, 46, 194
Age of Extremes, The, 64
AIDS crisis. *See* HIV/AIDS crisis
Ajalla, 192
Akan Doctrine, The, 174*n*24
Akinsowan, Abiodun, 91
alayes, 129
Algeria, 185
anawim, 113
ANC (African National Congress), 235–36
ancestors
  and Christianity, 48, 188–90, 200–201
  as living-dead, 175, 190
  reverence toward, 14–15, 43, 114, 172, 176–77, 181, 190–93
ancestral rites, 192
Anderson, Allan, 29, 32
apartheid, 222, 241
apologia, 247
Aquinas, Thomas, 56, 62, 248
Arab Africans, 20*n*36
area boys. *See* alayes
Arius, 160
Armstrong, Karen, 211
Arrow of God, 173
Ashanti, 187
Asti, Francesco, 86

ASUU. *See* Academic Staff Union of Universities
Athanasius, 160
Atlantic Council, 234
ATRs. *See* African Traditional Religions
Atyam, Angelina, 110
Augustine of Hippo, 56, 62, 160, 234, 248
Auschwitz, 8–9

Balokole movement, 91
baptism, 86, 231
Barankitse, Maggy, 110
Barclay, William, 249–50
Barrett, David, 142
Barth, Karl, 65
Bartholomew I, 214
Bassard, Katherine Clay, 239
Bayart, Jean-François, 156
Bediako, Kwame, 83, 194
Benedict XVI, 21, 27. *See also* Joseph Ratzinger
Benin, 203–5
Benjamin, Walter, 129
Berger, Peter, 207
Beti, Mongo, 173
Bevans, Stephen, 73
Biafra, 146, 163–64, 235
Bible
   importance for African Christians, 142–44
   translations into African languages, 85
Birmingham (Alabama), 8
Black Skin, White Masks, 227

Black Theology & Black Power, 238
Blondel, Maurice, 65
Bongmba, Elias, 202
Bongo, Ali, 203
Bonhoeffer, Dietrich, 117
Bontemps, Arna, 228
Born from Lament, 99, 110–11
Boulaga, Eboussi, 168
Bowers, Paul, 209
Boyd, Gregory, 253
British government, 163–64
Bujo, Bénézet, 64n43, 68, 188, 210
Burundi, 205
Busia, K.A., 199
Butler, Judith, 107
Buxton, Thomas Fowell, 167

Calvary, 259, 261
Canaan, 253–54
Canadian Samaritans for Africa, 17, 226
Canadian Society of Church History, 163
Cannon, Katie, 221
cantus firmus, 117
Catholicism
   and Africa, 26–27, 30, 79–80, 89, 134, 152, 208–9
   conflicts with traditional religions, 193, 202
   criticisms of, 59
   and missionary work, 42, 49
Cavanaugh, William T., 161, 210–11
Centenary Bank, 134
Chad, 6, 20n36
Chicago, 34, 218–21

child labor, 133
chiliastic movements, 32
Chineke, 174
Chinweuba, Gregory, 174
Christology, 32, 179, 201
Chukwu, 174, 185
Church and Human Promotion in Africa Today, The, 245
cinema, 125, 149–52, 177
Cisse, Mohamed Amadou, 203
Civil Rights Acts, 222
Clements, Fiona, 123
climate change, 42, 87, 94
Collins, Addie Mae, 8
colonialism, 183–85
Cone, James, 100, 113–14, 221, 228, 237–39
Congar, Yves, 89
Congress of Democrats (South Africa), 235
contamination, narratives of, 35, 109, 236–37
conversion, 84, 160, 186, 194, 212, 248–49
Copeland, M. Shawn, 100, 115, 129n5, 222
corruption, 87, 132, 135, 203, 211
Council of Trent, 70
COVID-19 pandemic, 33, 35, 58, 145, 148
Creach, Jerome, 165
Cross and the Lynching Tree, The, 100
Crowther, Ajayi, 186
curses, 74, 76, 113, 173, 182, 192, 208, 253

Daley, Patricia, 168
Danquah, Joseph, 174n24, 199
Darfur, 5, 235
Davis, Angela, 224
Davis, Mike, 220–21
decolonization, 67, 71, 169, 184
Delio, Ilia, 250
demons, 4, 202, 208
denominationalism, 80–81
Des prêtres noirs s'interrogent, 64, 83
Destiny Changers Enterprise, 143
Development as Freedom, 234
Devil Worship Commission, 203
Diamond, Jared, 20n36
diasporas, 23, 68, 83, 216–17, 241
diegesis, 246
Dinka, 19
diversity, 20n36, 28–30, 32, 68, 263
divination, 171
divine intervention, 36, 118, 134, 137
divine providence, 4, 13, 38, 146, 184, 223–24, 230
Dlamini, Paolina, 91
dogma, 22, 60, 97, 170
Douglass, Frederick, 228, 231
Dube, Musa W., 91
Du Bois. W.E.B., 4, 240
Dupuis, Jacques, 65
Dwight, John Sullivan, 222

East Africa, 19, 64n43, 85, 91, 130–31
Eastern Nigeria, 13, 24, 138, 140, 146, 163, 192–93
Ebola, 35, 131

ecclesial practices, 54, 106, 262
ecclesiastical studies, 49, 59, 66, 68
Economic Freedom Fighters, 236
economies
   destructive, 51, 105, 225, 242
   global, 92, 184
eco-theology, 95
Ecumenical Association of African Theologians, 21
ecumenism, 29, 81, 170
Edwards, Paul, 230
Egypt, 30
ekklesia, 53
Ela, Jean-Marc, 22, 88n81, 245
Ellacuría, Ignacio, 119
Ellis, Stephen, 9
Enang, Kenneth, 142
"end SARS" movement, 135
Enlightenment, 121
Epicureanism, 250
epidemics, 35, 102, 104, 131, 158
Equiano, Olaudah, 38, 218, 222, 224–26, 228–35, 241, 249
Ernest, John, 239
eschatology, 30, 38, 115, 223–24, 255
ethics, 50, 87, 94, 176, 212, 214, 243, 263–64. *See also* Ubuntu
Ethiopian Orthodox Church, 199
ethnic groups, 5, 170–72, 176–77, 191–92, 200, 207
ethnography, 16, 27, 38, 48, 55, 91, 171, 188–89, 193
"Eulogies to the Martyred Children," 8
Evangelii Gaudium, 49, 92

evangelization, 63, 85, 154, 184–85, 245
Evans-Pritchard, E.E., 19, 198
Exodus, 251–53
exorcisms, 46, 79, 114, 208, 210
Ezemuo, 192–93
Ezeugwu, Evaristus Chukwudi, 174
Ezi-Ndu, 180

Facing Mount Kenya, 174n24
Fanon, Frantz, 227
Federal Military Government (Nigeria), 163
fetishism, 19, 80, 167n12, 187, 194
Fiducia Supplicans, 63
film. *See* cinema
First African Synod (1994), 248
First Vatican Council. *See* Vatican I
Floyd, George, 220
folktales, 90–91. *See also* oral tradition
Foster, Peter, 91
Francis (Pope), 49–60, 94, 99, 101, 105–7, 110, 125, 130, 154, 156, 248, 256
Fratelli Tutti, 11, 50, 101, 105
Frazer, James, 194
Freedom and Prosperity Initiative, 234
Freedom Charter, 235
From the Depths of Our Hearts, 27
fundamentalism, 171, 205

Gabon, 203
Garvey, Marcus, 240
Gates, Henry Louis, 90
Gaudium et Spes, 157
Geertz, Clifford, 26, 65

genocide, 6, 124, 163–64, 221, 235, 241
Gerstenberger, Erhard S., 102
Ghana, 187, 240
Gifford, Paul, 208–11
Gikuyu, 176
Global North, 126
global order, 224–25, 235
Global South, 29–30, 82, 84, 126, 262
God, Evil and the Limits of Theology, 100
"God Never Opened the Bible to Me," 91
golden calf, 251, 253–54
Good Samaritan, 11, 15, 37, 99, 101, 105–8, 112, 126, 215
grace, 3, 9, 100, 124–25, 257–60
Greco-Latin thought, 70n47
Greek thought, 65, 83, 185, 250
Gregory of Nyssa, 214
Gronniosaw, James Albert Ukawsaw, 228
Gullah, 129n5
Guns, Germs, and Steel, 20n36
Gutiérrez, Gustavo, 100, 116–20

Hall, M. Elizabeth Lewis, 12–13
Hammon, Briton, 228
Harris, William Wade, 186
Hastings, Adrian, 64, 186
Hauerwas, Stanley, 65
Haynes, Jonathan, 148
Heart Pains, 151–52
Hellenism, 84, 198
Hendriks, H. Jurgens, 243n2

hermeneutics, 42, 68–69, 75, 99, 105, 152
Hinze, Bradford, 115
HIV/AIDS crisis, 16, 131, 203, 208
Hobsbawm, Eric, 64
homelessness, 131–33, 208, 240
homogeneity, 20, 69, 71
Hopkins, Dwight, 239
humanitarianism, 168–69, 224
human trafficking, 17, 118, 235, 240
Husserl, Edmund, 65

idolatry, 114, 118, 154, 156, 249, 252, 254
Idowu, Bolaji, 18–19, 173–74, 199
Igbo, 13, 24, 44, 129, 148, 164, 173–74, 180, 185
"I Have a Dream," 8
Ikwerre, 173
Imana, 177
inculturation, 70, 83, 209
Independent Africa, 209
infant mortality, 14
"In Sudan, Evil Is Resilient—and So Is Heroism.," 4
intercultural hermeneutics, 76, 80–81
Interesting Narrative of the Life of Olaudah Equiano, The, 222, 228
interfaith dialogue, 28, 74, 182
International Criminal Court, 205
intersubjectivity, 52
inwu chu, 13–14, 47
Islam, 10, 48, 171, 193, 204, 211, 244, 255

Israel, 46, 252–54
Israelites, 251–52

Jammeh, Yaya, 204
Janjaweed, 5. *See also* Rapid Support Forces
Jim Crow laws, 220
John Paul II, 99, 101–5, 170
Johnson, E.H., 163
Johnson, James Weldon, 227
John XXIII, 107
Justice and Evangelization in Africa, 245

Kagame, Alex, 174*n*24
Kalu, Ogbu, 64, 90, 184, 193
Kaonde, 191
Kasper, Walter, 82*n*65
Kato, Byang, 194
Katongole, Emmanuel, 4, 68, 99, 108–13, 115–16, 124, 179, 256
Kellerman, Christopher, 234
kenosis, 108, 213
Kenya, 135, 202–3
Kenyatta, Jomo, 174*n*24, 176
Kérékou, Mathieu, 203–4
Kilby, Karen, 100, 116, 121–25, 213
King, Martin Luther Jr., 8
Knowing Christ Crucified, 100, 115
koinonia, 214
Kolawole, Mary Modupe, 91
Kony, Joseph, 205
Kristof, Nicholas, 4–7
Kugler, Gili, 252–53
Kuti, Fela Aníkúlápó, 1–3, 11, 117
kwashiorkor, 146

Lakwena, Alice, 205
La Philosophie bântu-rwandaise de l'Être, 174*n*24
Latin America, 41, 81, 93, 118, 204, 218, 229
Laudato si', 53, 94
Lavigerie, Charles, 184–85
Letter to the Hebrews, 101, 253, 257, 259
Levitt, Peggy, 166
liberation theology, 100, 116, 206, 216, 232
Liberia, 35
Lienhardt, Godfrey, 198
Life of Moses, The, 214
Living in Bondage, 136, 148–53, 156, 177, 179
logocentrism, 24
Lonergan, Bernard, 65, 71
Long, Charles H., 251
Lord's Resistance Army (LRA), 205
Luke, 31, 106, 246–47
Luo, 19
Luvale, 191
lynching, 4, 113, 115, 220, 229, 237–38

Macquarrie, John, 126
Magesa, Laurenti, 17, 43, 84, 171, 181, 196, 200
Magisterium, 58–60, 78, 248
Malema, Julius, 236
Maluleke, Tinyiko, 88
Mana, Ka, 249
manducation, 156
marabout, 203

Marcel, Gabriel, 123
Marley, Bob, 240
Marrant, John, 228
Marsh, Charles, 77
Massingale, Bryan, 217
matatu, 38, 127, 130, 145, 182, 246
Mater et Magistra, 107
maternal mortality, 14
Mbembe, Achille, 171, 227
Mbiti, John, 68, 82, 174n24, 199
McDonald, Laquan, 220
McMartin, Jason, 12–13
McNair, Denise, 8
McVeigh, Malcolm J., 167n12
Meeting African Religions, 19
Mejia, Rodrigo, 127
Memoir on the Backward Races, 167
metaxy, 68, 155
Metuh, Emefie Ikenga, 173–74
Michie, Susan, 226
micro-credit unions, 35
Middle Passage, 229, 232. *See also* slavery
Midrash, 8
Milingo, Emmanuel, 202
millennials, 96
Misbahah, 204
missional theologies, 73, 75–76, 206
missionaries, 71, 73, 78, 85, 90–91, 183–87, 206, 224
Mobutu Sese Seko, 203
Moloch, 118
Moltmann, Jürgen, 9, 77, 255
monotheism, 19, 189
Moses, 251–54

Movement for the Restoration of the Ten Commandments of God, 205
movies. *See* cinema
Mozambique, 205
Mugabe, Robert, 204–5
Mugambi, Jesse, 199
Mulago, Vincent, 175–77, 200
multidisciplinarity, 56
Museveni, Yoweri, 205
mythological thought, 43, 189

Napoleon III, 185
narratives of contamination, 35, 109, 236–37
National Day of Prayer (Zambia), 205
National Youth Service Corps (NYSC), 143
Negritude movement, 84
neocolonialism, 84
neoliberalism, 10, 36–37, 92, 165, 224–25, 233–34, 261–62
neo-Scholasticism, 65
Newman, John Henry, 65
Ngong, David, 160
Nguni, 214
Nigeria
    Civil War, 163–64
    Eastern, 13, 24, 138, 140, 146, 163, 192–93
    economy, 92, 144–45
    film industry, 136, 149
    government, 46, 163
    hardship in, 46–47, 140–42, 144–45, 147–48, 205

"suffering and smiling," 1–3, 129, 134–35
    theodicy in, 136–37
Nigeria-Biafra war, 146, 163
Night, 7–8
Njiru, Joseph, 203
Nku, Christina, 91
Nkurunziza, Pierre, 205
Nollywood, 38, 148–49
ntu, 176
Nuer, 19
Nyame, 185
Nyamiti, Charles, 68, 196–97
Nyamuzinda, 177
Nyirumbe, Rosemary, 110
NYSC. *See* National Youth Service Corps

Obiechina, Emmanuel, 24, 90–91
Oden, Thomas, 183
Odozor, Paulinus, 68
Oduyoye, Mercy Amba, 68, 80, 91
ofia ajuju, 15
ofo-na-ogu, 180
Ojacor, Alex, 158
Okorocha, Cyril, 180
Okullu, Henry, 79
Okure, Teresa, 68
Old Testament, 164–65, 251, 253
Olisebuluwa, 174
Olódùmarè, 174n24
Olupona, Jacob, 171, 188–89
Olurun, 185
Omer, Atalia, 36, 210
On the Christian Meaning of Human Suffering. See *Salvifici Doloris*
ontology, 24, 200
onwu chi, 13
Open Wide Our Hearts, 220
oracles, 14, 47–48, 149, 193
oral traditions, 24, 90
Origen of Alexandria, 160
Osebuluwa, 174

PACTPAN (Pan-African Catholic Theology and Pastoral Network), 17
pandemics, 61, 104, 107, 165
Pannenberg, Wolfhart, 65
Parrinder, Geoffrey, 198
Paschal Mystery, 3, 103, 123–24
Pastor Aeternus, 57
pastoral work, 54–55, 86, 172, 243
Patrick Chabal, 3
Patterson, Orlando, 229
Paul, 258
P'Bitek, Okot, 197–99
Pentecostal movements, 29–30, 32, 82n65, 142, 204–7, 209–10
Phan, Peter, 84
Phiri, Isabel, 91
Picasso, Pablo, 251
Pius IX, 185
Plato, 65
Pliny the Elder, 166
pluralism, 54, 69–70, 166
pneumatology, 32
political theology, 83, 206, 243
polytheism, 19
Pontifical Academy for Life, 105
Port Harcourt, 164
post-Christian societies, 165, 187

postcolonialism, 20, 35, 67, 85, 92, 184, 201–2, 206
post-independence Africa, 11, 38n62, 96
poverty, 93–94, 106, 131, 134, 150–52
prayer, 2, 30, 43–44, 47, 111, 139, 144–47, 150, 210, 235, 254
predestination, 217–18, 234, 249
premature death, 13–14, 47
Presbyterian Church, 163
Primal Vision, The, 18
prophetic ethics, 261–63
prophetic theology, 33, 111–13, 120, 234, 263
protest atheism, 115
protest theism, 112, 115
Providence, 60, 222, 230, 233

racism
  Africa, 34–35, 37
  and Afro-pessimism, 35
  and providence, 4
  scientific, 91
  and theology, 64, 234
  United States, 115, 216–17, 220–22, 229, 237
radio trottoir, 38
Rahner, Karl, 65, 77–78
Rapid Support Forces, 5–7. *See also* Janjaweed
Rattray, Robert, 187
Ratzinger, Joseph, 21, 103. *See also* Benedict XVI
Ray, Benjamin, 189
Rescuing Fraternity Together, 105

restorative justice, 190
retributive justice, 190
revelation, 23, 45, 60, 62, 76, 98–99, 103, 106, 248
Ricoeur, Paul, 128
rites
  ancestral, 14, 47, 176, 192–93
  Christian, 37, 168, 199
  funerary, 14, 47, 193
Rwanda, 124, 169
Ryan, Robin, 101

Sabbatarians, 218
sacrifices, 148, 150, 176, 192–93
Sahara, 108, 180, 235, 247
salvation
  among Igbo, 180
  and evil, 122
  and suffering, 103, 236–37
  and theology, 154
  and Ubuntu, 215
Salvifici Doloris, 101, 104–5
Samuel, 253
sangoma, 202, 206. *See also* witch doctors
Sankofa, 128
Sanneh, Lamin, 29–30, 85, 185–86
Sarah, Robert, 26
saviorism, 105
Schokel, Luis Alonso, 201n87
Scholasticism, 57
Scott, James, 153
Scott, Walter, 220
Second Vatican Council. *See* Vatican II

Secret of the African and African Beliefs and Christian Faith, The, 167n12
secularization, 160, 187, 208
Sen, Amartya, 234
sensus fidei, 26, 37, 59, 61, 136, 153, 248
Sewell, Alice, 229
Shaw, Daniel, 22n39
Shaw, Rosalind, 20, 230
Shea, William, 22n38
Shonaland, 186
Shorter, Aylward, 158, 197n74, 203
Sierra Leone, 186
Sindima, Harvey J., 174n24
Sixteenth Street Baptist Church bombing, 8
slave narratives, 38, 218, 223–25, 228–29, 232–33, 249
slavery
  and African Christianity, 37
  and African Christians, 241
  historical repercussions, 220, 222, 230, 251
  modern-day, 17, 118, 235, 240
  and providence, 4
  and theology, 234
slave trade, 92, 168, 214, 223–25, 232, 240, 251
Smith, Edward, 167n12
Smith, Emily Esfahani, 236
Smith
  Linda, 67
  Venture, 228
Sobrino, Jon, 100, 116, 118–20
social mobility, 156, 202

sorcery, 43, 149, 156, 177, 202–3, 208, 249
Sotho, 186
South Africa, 93–94, 205, 235–36
South African Colored People's Organization, 235
South African Indian Congress, 235
South Sudan, 6, 17, 92, 133, 205, 236
Soviet Union, 93, 205
Soyinka, Wole, 173
Sparks, Kenton, 165
Spes non Confundit, 256
spirituals, 114, 232
Stark, Rodney, 255
state capture, 93
Stoics, 250
Strandsbjerg, Camilla, 204
structural violence, 4, 11, 15, 33, 51, 105, 119, 152, 156, 165, 182
Sub-Saharan Africa, 18, 160
Sudan, 4–7, 10, 19, 91–92, 133, 223, 235
suffering and smiling, 1–2, 73, 129, 143, 146, 149, 156, 251
Sufism, 10
Symposium of Episcopal Conferences of Africa and Madagascar (SECAM), 26, 245
syncretism, 48, 80, 175
Synod on Synodality (2024), 35, 42
Synod on the Family (2014), 56
Synod on the Family (2015), 26

Taban, Paride, 110
Tasker, Fiona, 123

Taylor, J.V., 18
Ter Haar, Gerrie, 9, 19n32, 195, 198
Tertullian, 160
theism, 167n12, 174n24, 197, 199
theodicy
  African, 38, 110, 136–37, 154, 181, 183, 207
  and hope, 249
  as justification, 118, 121
  popular, 38
  and suffering, 3, 9, 26, 33–34, 100, 121, 129, 137
  Western, 65, 166, 169
theology
  and accountability, 31, 76, 243–44
  and Afro-pessimism, 34
  decolonizing, 182–84
  and faith, 61–62, 97
  and hermeneutics, 80–81, 99
  and hope, 39, 41
  liberation, 100, 116, 206, 216, 232
  matatu, 127, 130, 145
  Pope Francis on, 50, 53–60, 110, 156–57
  popular, 38
  praxic, 119
  prophetic, 33, 111–13, 120, 234, 263
  and protest, 126
  and salvation, 154–55
  and suffering, 4, 9, 38, 45–46, 73–74, 87–88, 101, 116, 120, 156, 182

systematic, 21, 77
and Ubuntu, 88n81, 94
Western, 63–68
theotokos, 78
Things Fall Apart, 180
Thomas, Douglas E., 18
Thomism, 65, 69
Tienou, Tite, 159
Tillich, Paul, 65
Tonstad, Linn, 112
tribalism, 110, 132, 241
Trinity, 51, 76, 78, 159–60, 196, 200, 257, 259
Tutu, Desmond, 3
Tveitereid, Knut, 78
Twi, 128

Ubuntu, 39, 50, 52, 88, 94, 214–15
Udelhoven, Bernhard, 212–13
Uganda, 16–17, 38, 45, 49, 113, 130, 132–34, 158, 188–89, 205, 226
UN Genocide Convention (1948), 163
United States, 38, 84, 126, 166, 171, 216–17, 219–20, 223, 235, 240
Uzukwu, Elochukwu, 68, 173

Vanneste, Alfred, 64n43
Vatican I, 57
Vatican II, 69–70, 84, 92, 96, 249
Veritatis Gaudium, 49–50, 54, 56, 130, 248
violence of love, 112–13
Volf, Miroslav, 169
voodoo, 205

Walker, David, 239
Walls, Andrew, 28, 83, 166
Ware, Frederick, 217
"We Are Climbing Jacob's Ladder," 114
Weeping Woman, The, 251
Wesley, Cynthia Diane, 8
West Africa, 85, 167*n*12, 180, 185, 187, 204
West African Examination Council (WAEC), 144
Western Christianity, 65, 183, 187, 194–95
Where Is God?, 118
Where Is God, 100
white supremacy, 34–35, 85, 115, 216, 221, 224, 237, 241
Wiesel, Elie, 7–8
Wijsen, Frans, 198

witchcraft, 17, 38, 43–44, 48, 76, 177, 193, 202–3, 208, 210–11, 249
witch doctors, 32, 202
World Bank, 93
World Council of Churches, 81
World Cup (2010), 205
"Wrestling Jacob," 114
Wrogemann, Henning, 81

Xhosa, 186

Yoruba, 173, 185
Young, Robert, 239

Zaire, 203
Zambia, 191, 205, 212
Zimbabwe, 204